D1084167

THE TESTS OF LIFE

A STUDY OF
THE FIRST EPISTLE OF ST. JOHN

BY THE

Rev. ROBERT LAW, B.D., D.D.

PROFESSOR OF NEW TESTAMENT LITERATURE AND EXEGESIS
KNOX COLLEGE, TORONTO

THIRD EDITION

BAKER BOOK HOUSE

Grand Rapids, Michigan

Reprinted 1968 by Baker Book House
Paperback edition issued January 1979

ISBN: 0-8010-5501-6

Originally published by
T. & T. Clark, Edinburgh

First Edition . . *March 1909*
Second Edition . . *October 1909*
Third Edition . . *March 1914*

Standard Book Number: 8010-5501-6

PHOTOLITHOPRINTED BY CUSHING - MALLOY, INC.
ANN ARBOR, MICHIGAN, UNITED STATES OF AMERICA
1979

PREFACE

As only a portion of the contents of this volume could be orally delivered, I have not thought it necessary to adhere to either the form or the title of "Lecture," but have assigned a separate "Chapter" to each principal topic dealt with. The method adopted in this exposition of the Epistle—that, namely, of grouping together the passages bearing upon a common theme—will be found, I trust, to have advantages which compensate in some measure for its disadvantages. That it has disadvantages, as compared with a continuous exposition, I am well aware. These, however, I have endeavoured to minimise, by supplying in the first chapter a specially full analysis of the Epistle, by careful indexing, and by making liberal use of cross-references. For the convenience of the reader, I have set down in the footnotes such exegetical details as seemed most necessary to explain or to establish the interpretation adopted; but where these involved lengthy or intricate discussion, they, along with all minuter points of exegesis, have been relegated to the Notes at the end of the volume. In these Notes the text of the Epistle is continuously followed.

The points of textual difference between the various critical editions of the Epistle are comparatively unimportant, and I have seldom found it necessary to refer to them. The text used is that of Tischendorf's Eighth Edition; but in one passage (5^{18}) I have preferred the reading indicated in our Authorised Version and in the Revisers' margin.

Among the commentators to whom I have, of course, been indebted, I mention Westcott first of all. Owing, perhaps, to natural pugnacity, one more readily quotes a writer to express dissent than to indicate agreement; but, though I find that the majority of my references to "Westcott" are in the nature of criticism, I would not be thought guilty of depreciating that great commentary. With all its often provoking characteristics, it is still, as a magazine of materials for the student of the Epistle, without a rival. Huther's and Plummer's commentaries I have found specially serviceable; but the most original, beautiful, and profound is Rothe's, of which, it is somewhat surprising to find, no full translation has yet appeared. I desire, besides, to acknowledge obligation to J. M. Gibbon's *Eternal Life*, a remarkably fine popular exposition of the Epistle; and to Professor E. F. Scott's *Fourth Gospel*, for the clear light which that able work throws upon not a few important points — as well as for much provocative stimulus. But there is no book (except Brüder's *Concordance*) to which I have been more indebted than to Moulton's *Grammar of New Testament Greek*, the next volume of which is impatiently awaited.

Professor H. R. Mackintosh, D.D., of New College, and the Rev. Thomas S. Dickson, M.A., Edinburgh, have placed me under deep obligation by exceptionally generous and valuable help in proof-reading. Mr. David Duff, B.D., not only has rendered equal service in this respect, but has subjected the book, even in its preparatory stages, to a rigorous but always helpful criticism—a labour of friendship for which I find it difficult to express in adequate terms the gratitude that I owe and feel. Finally, I am grateful, by anticipation, to every reader who will make generous allowance for the fact, that the preparation of this volume has been carried through amid the incessant demands of a busy city pastorate, and who will attribute to this cause some of the defects which he will, no doubt, discover in it.

EDINBURGH, *January* 1909.

THE Second Edition having been exhausted, I am informed that the publishers are willing to undertake the issue of a Third, and the testimonies I have received to the practical helpfulness of the book, especially from ministers and missionaries in various parts of the world, encourage me to hope that other readers may still find it acceptable for the same best of all reasons. Repeated and careful study of the Epistle, since these Lectures were written, has not led to change or material modification in any of the exegetical interpretations or theological deductions advanced in them. One paragraph, in which I ventured to express myself as to the 'kernel' of the Johannine problem, has been deleted in the present edition; not because I now regard the opinions there stated as untrue, but because I recognise the unwisdom of attempting to deal in any summary fashion with a problem so complex. In several passages I have modified the form of expression, where it seemed unduly dogmatic; but there are others, which, in point of arrangement and expression, I could have wished to rewrite to an extent which neither the time presently at my disposal, nor the conditions of publication permit.   An endeavour has been made to take account of recent additions to the literature of the Epistle, especially Mr. Brooke's commentary in the "International Critical" series.   It is a genuine satisfaction to find that the view which I have offered of the historical setting of the Epistle, and also of its peculiar structure, is endorsed by Mr. Brooke—a satisfaction which is scarcely lessened by the fact that he prefers Haring's particular scheme of analysis to mine (p. 24 *inf.*).

TORONTO, *December* 1913.

CONTENTS

ABBREVIATIONS

The following works are referred to as follows, other titles being cited in full :—

ABBOTT . . . *Johannine Vocabulary* (A. & C. Black, 1905), and *Johannine Grammar* (A. & C. Black, 1906).

BEYSCHLAG . . *Neutestamentliche Theologie.* Zweite Auflage. Halle, 1896.

CANDLISH. . . *The First Epistle of St. John.* A. & C. Black, 1877.

DB . . . . *A Dictionary of the Bible.* Ed. by Dr. Hastings. T. & T. Clark, 1898–1904.

EBRARD . . . *Biblical Commentary on the Epistles of St. John.* T. & T. Clark, 1860.

GIBBON . . . *Eternal Life.* By the Rev. J. M. Gibbon. Dickinson, 1890.

GRILL . . . . *Untersuchungen über die Entstehung des vierten Evangeliums.* J. C. B. Mohr, 1902.

HAUPT . . . *The First Epistle of St. John.* Clark's Foreign Theological Library, 1879.

HOLTZMANN . . *Hand-Commentr. zum Neuen Testament.* Vierter Band. Freiburg i. B. 1891.

HÄRING . . . *Theologische Abhandlungen zum Carl von Weizsäcker gewidmet.* Freiburg i. B. 1892.

HUTHER . . . *Critical and Exegetical Handbook to the General Epistles of James and John.* T. & T. Clark, 1882.

JPT. . . . . *Jahrbücher für protestantische Theologie.*

LÜCKE. . . . *Commentary on the Epistles of St. John.* Thomas Clark, 1837.

MAURICE . . . *The Epistles of St. John.* Macmillan & Co., 1857.

MOULTON . . . *Grammar of New Testament Greek.* Vol. i. T. & T. Clark, 1906.

PFLEIDERER . . *Das Urchristentum.* Zweite Auflage. Berlin, 1902.

PLUMMER . . . *The Epistles of S. John.* In the Cambridge Greek Testament for Schools and Colleges.

ROTHE . . . . *Der erste Brief Johannis.* Wittenberg, 1878.

SCOTT . . . . *The Fourth Gospel, its Purpose and Theology.* T. & T. Clark, 1906.

STEVENS . . . *The Johannine Theology.* Scribner's Sons, 1904.

WEISS . . . . *Die drei Briefe des Apostel Johannis.* Von Dr. Bernhard Weiss. Göttingen, 1900.

WEIZSÄCKER . . *The Apostolic Age of the Christian Church.* Second edition. Williams & Norgate, 1897.

WESTCOTT . . *The Epistles of St. John.* Third edition. Macmillan & Co., 1892.

THE FIRST EPISTLE OF ST. JOHN

CHAPTER I.

STYLE AND STRUCTURE.

ON a first perusal of the Epistle, the effect of which one can at least try to imagine, the appreciative reader could not fail to receive a deep impression of the strength and directness of the writer's spiritual intuition, and to be charmed by the clear-cut gnomic terseness of many of his sayings; but not less, perhaps, would he be impressed by what might seem to him the marks of mental limitation and literary resourcelessness,—the paucity of ideas, the poverty of vocabulary, the reiteration, excessive for so brief a composition, of the same thoughts in nearly the same language, the absence of logical concatenation or of order in the progress of thought. The impression might be, indeed, that there is no such progress, but that the thought, after sundry gyrations, returns always to the same point. As one reads the Epistle to the Romans, it seems as if to change the position of a single paragraph would be as impossible as to lift a stone out of a piece of solid masonry and build it in elsewhere; here it seems as if, while the things said are of supreme importance, the order in which they are said matters nothing. This estimate of the Epistle has been

endorsed by those who are presumed to speak with
authority. Its method has been deemed purely aphoristic;
as if the aged apostle, pen in hand, had merely rambled on
along an undefined path, bestrewing it at every step with
priceless gems, the crystallizations of a whole lifetime of
deep and loving meditation. The "infirmity of old age"
(S. G. Lange) is detected in it; a certain "indefiniteness,"
a lack of "logical force," a "tone of childlike feebleness"
(Baur); an "absolute indifference to a strictly logical and
harmoniously ascending development of ideas" (Jülicher).
It is perhaps venturesome, therefore, to express the opinion
that the more closely one studies the Epistle the more one
discovers it to be, in its own unique way, one of the most
closely articulated pieces of writing in the New Testament;
and that the style, simple and unpremeditated as it is, is
singularly artistic.

The almost unvarying simplicity [1] of syntactical structure, the absence of connecting, notably of illative, particles,[2]
and, in short, the generally Hebraic type of composition
have been frequently remarked upon; yet I am not sure
that the closeness with which the style has been moulded
upon the Hebraic model, especially upon the parallelistic
forms of the Wisdom Literature, has been sufficiently
recognised. One has only to read the Epistle with an
attentive *ear* to perceive that, though using another language, the writer had in his own ear, all the time, the
swing and the cadences of Old Testament verse. With
the exception of the Prologue and a few other periodic
passages, the majority of sentences divide naturally into
two or three or four στίχοι.

Two-membered sentences are common, both synthetic
and antithetic, which are strongly reminiscent of the

---

[1] The writer's efforts in more complex constructions are not felicitous. Cf.
e.g. 2²⁷ 5⁹.

[2] δέ occurs with only one-third of its usual frequency; μέν, τε, οὖν, do not
occur at all; γάρ, only thrice.

Hebrew distich. Examples of the synthetic variety
are :

> " He that loveth his brother abideth in the light,
> And there is none occasion of stumbling in him " (2^{10}) ;

or,

> " Hereby know we love, because He laid down His life for us :
> And we ought to lay down our lives for the brethren " (3^{16}).

Of the antithetic, one may quote :

> " And the world passeth away, and the lust thereof :
> But he that doeth the will of God abideth for ever" (2^{17}) ;

or,

> "Whosoever abideth in Him sinneth not :
> Whosoever sinneth hath not seen Him, neither known Him " (3^{6}).

Commoner still are sentences of three members, which,
in the same way, may be called tristichs ; as :

> " That which we have seen and heard declare we unto you also,
> That ye also may have fellowship with us :
> Yea, and our fellowship is with the Father, and with His Son Jesus
> Christ " (1^{3}) ;

or,

> " Beloved, no new commandment write I unto you,
> But an old commandment which ye had from the beginning :
> The old commandment is the word which ye heard " (2^{7}).

Resemblances to the tetrastich also are found :

> " For whatsoever is begotten of God overcometh the world :
> And this is the victory that overcometh the world, even our faith.
> Who is he that overcometh the world,
> But he that believeth that Jesus is the Son of God " ($5^{4, 5}$) ;

or,

> "Little children, it is the last hour :
> And as ye heard that Antichrist cometh,
> Even now have arisen many Antichrists ;
> Whereby we know that it is the last hour " (2^{18}).[1]

The Epistle presents examples, also, of more elaborate
combinations : as in 1^{6}–2^{2}, where the alternating verses

---

[1] An instance of "introverted" parallelism, in which the first and fourth
lines, and the second and third, answer to each other.

^{6. 8. 10} and ^{7. 9} 2¹ are exquisitely balanced both in thought and expression[1]; and in 2^{12-14}, where we have a double parallel tristich:

> " I write . . . I write . . . I write :
> I have written . . . I have written . . . I have written."

The author's literary art achieves its finest effects in such passages as 2^{7-11} and 2^{15-17} (where one could fancy that he has unconsciously dropped into a strophic arrangement of lines), and in the closing verses of the Epistle (5^{18-21}), consisting of alternating tristichs and distichs:

> " We know that every one that is begotten of God sinneth not ;
> But he that was begotten of God keepeth himself,
> And the Wicked One toucheth him not.
>
> We know that we are of God,
> And the whole world lieth in the Wicked One.
>
> We know that the Son of God is come,
> And hath given us an understanding to know the True One,
> And we are in the True One, in His Son Jesus Christ.
>
> This is the True God, and Life Eternal ;
> Little children, guard yourselves from idols." [2]

It is not suggested that there is in the Epistle a conscious imitation of Hebraic forms; but it is evident, I think, that no one could have written as our author does whose whole style of thought and expression had not been unconsciously formed upon Old Testament models.

---

[1] The structure is broken by the interjected address, " My little children, these things write I unto you that ye sin not." This being removed, the continuation of the parallelism is clear.

[2] In the *Expository Times* (June–November 1897) there is an interesting series of articles by Professor Briggs on the presence of Hebrew poetical forms in the N.T. He does not touch on the Johannine writings; but his method, if applied to the Epistle, would yield results beyond what I have ventured to suggest.

But we pass to the more important topic, the structure of the Epistle. As has been already said, the impression left upon some, who cannot be supposed to have been cursory readers, is that the Epistle has no logical structure and exhibits no ordered progression of thought. This estimate has a measure of support in the fact that there is no portion of Scripture regarding the plan of which there has been greater diversity of opinion. It is nevertheless erroneous.

The word that, to my mind, might best describe St. John's mode of thinking and writing in this Epistle is "spiral." The course of thought does not move from point to point in a straight line. It is like a winding staircase— always revolving around the same centre, always recurring to the same topics, but at a higher level. Or, to borrow a term from music, one might describe the method as contrapuntal. The Epistle works with a comparatively small number[1] of themes, which are introduced many times, and are brought into every possible relation to one another As some master-builder of music takes two or three melodious phrases and, introducing them in due order, repeating them, inverting them, skilfully interlacing them in diverse modes and keys, rears up from them an edifice of stately harmonies; so the Apostle weaves together a few leading ideas into a majestic fugue in which unity of material and variety of tone and effect are wonderfully blended. And the clue to the structure of the Epistle will be found by tracing the introduction and reappearances of these leading themes.

These[1] are Righteousness, Love, and Belief. For here let me say at once that, in my view, the key to the interpretation of the Epistle is the fact that it is an

---

[1] The following list includes most, if not all, of the leading ideas found in the Epistle—God, True One, idols—Father, begotten of God, children of God,—Son of God, Word of Life, Christ come in the flesh, Jesus—Spirit, spirits— anointing, teaching, witnessing—word, message, announcing—truth, lie, error—beholding,

apparatus of *tests*; that its definite object is to furnish its readers with an adequate set of criteria by which they may satisfy themselves of their being " begotten of God." " These things write I unto you, that ye may know that ye have eternal life " (5^{13}). And throughout the Epistle these tests are definitely, inevitably, and inseparably—doing righteousness; loving one another; and believing that Jesus is the Christ, come in the flesh, sent by the Father to be the Saviour of the world. These are the connecting themes that bind together the whole structure of the Epistle. After the prologue, in fact, it consists of a threefold repetition and application of these three fundamental tests of the Christian life. In proof of this statement let us, in the first instance, examine those sections of the Epistle in which the sequence of thought is most clearly exhibited. The first of these is 2^{3-28}, which divides itself naturally into three paragraphs, (A) 2^{3-6}, (B) 2^{7-17}, (C) 2^{18-28}.

Here A (2^{3-6}) obviously consists of a threefold statement, with significant variations, of the single idea, that righteousness (" keeping His commandments," " keeping His word," " walking, even as He walked ") is the indispensable test of " knowing God " and " abiding in Him." In B (2^{7-17}) the current of thought is interrupted by the parenthetical passage, 2^{12-14}; but, this being omitted, it is apparent that here, also, we have a paragraph formed upon one principal idea—Love the test of the Christian Life, the test being applied positively in 2^{7-11} (the " new commandment "), and negatively in 2^{15-17} (" Love not the world "). In C (2^{18-28}), again, the unity is obvious.

believing, knowing, confessing, denying—brotherhood, fellowship—righteousness, commandment, word of God, will of God, things that are pleasing in His sight—sin, lawlessness, unrighteousness—world, flesh, Antichrist, Devil—blood, water, propitiation, Paraclete, forgiveness, cleansing—abiding, passing away—Beginning, Last Hour—Parousia, Day of Judgment, manifestation, hope—boldness, fear—asking, receiving—overcoming.

The theme of the paragraph is—the Christian life tested by Belief of the truth, of which the Anointing Spirit is the supreme Witness and Teacher, that Jesus is the Christ and the Son of God.

If, next, we examine the part of the Epistle that extends from 2^{29}–4^6, we find precisely the same topics recurring *in precisely the same order.* We have again three paragraphs (A) 2^{29}–3^{10a}, (B) $3^{10b-24a}$, and (C) 3^{24b}–4^6. And, again, it is evident that in A we have the test of Righteousness, in B the test of Love, and in C the test of Belief.

In the third great section of the Epistle (4^7–5^{21}), though the sequence of thought is somewhat different, the thought-material is identical; and for the present it is sufficient to point out that the leading themes, the tests of Love (4^{7-12} and 4^{16b-21}), Belief (4^{13-16a} and 5^{5-12}), and Righteousness ($5^{18,\ 19}$) are all present, and that they alone are present.

We seem, then, to have found a natural division of the Epistle into three main sections, or, as they might be most descriptively called, " cycles," in each of which the same fundamental thoughts appear, in each of which the reader is summoned to bring his Christian life to the test of Righteousness, of Love, and of Belief. With this as a working hypothesis, I shall now endeavour to give an analysis of the contents of the Epistle.

Passing by the Prologue (1^{1-4}), we have the

FIRST CYCLE, 1^5–2^{28}.

Walking in the Light tested by Righteousness, Love, and Belief.

It begins with the announcement, which is the basis of the whole section, that " God is Light, and in Him is no darkness at all " (1^5). And, since what God is determines the condition of fellowship with Him, this is set forth : first, negatively (1^6)—" If we say that we have fellowship with Him and walk in darkness " ; then positively (1^7)—" If we walk in the Light as He is in the Light." What, then, is it to walk in the Light, and what to walk in darkness ? The answer to these questions is given in all that follows, down to 2^{28}.

PARAGRAPH A, 1^8–2^6.*

Walking in the Light tested by Righteousness : first, in confession of sin (1^8–2^2) ; secondly, in actual obedience (2^{3-6}).

(*a*) The first fact upon which the Light of God impinges in human life is Sin ; and the first test of walking in the Light is sincere recognition of the true nature, the guiltiness, of Sin ($1^{8, 9}$). This test is applied both negatively—" If we say that we have no sin," and positively—" If we confess our sins."

But, in the Light of God, not only is Sin, wherever present, recognised in its true character as guilt ; it is revealed as universally present. Whence arises a second test of walking in the Light—" If we say that we have not sinned, we make Him a liar," etc.

What follows is very significant. Obviously the writer had intended to continue—" If we confess that we have sinned, we have a Paraclete with the Father, Jesus Christ the Righteous " (thus carrying forward the parallel series of antitheses : $1^{6, 8, 10}$ = walking in darkness, $1^{7, 9}$

---

* In order to avoid complexities in our preliminary survey (p. 6), 2^3 was taken as the starting-point, the structure being more clearly marked from that point onward. But this first Cycle really includes the whole from 1^5. The verses (1^8–2^2) which deal with the confession and removal of sin and those (2^{3-6}) which deal with conduct, are both included in the ethical guarantee of the Christian Life. That recognition of sin in the Light of God and that renunciation of it which are involved in its sincere confession are inseparable in experience from the "keeping of God's commandments" and "walking as Christ walked,"—are the back and the front, so to say, of the same moral attitude toward life.

and what would have been 1^{11} = walking in the light). But before he writes this, his pen is arrested by the sudden fear that some might be so infatuated as to wrest these broad evangelical statements into a pretext for moral laxity. He therefore interposes the earnest *caveat*, " My little children, these things write I unto you, that ye sin not"; then carries forward the train of thought in slightly different forms, " And if any man sin," etc. ($2^{1.\ 2}$).

But if confession of sin is the test of walking in the Light, confession itself is to be tested by its fruits in new obedience. If impenitence, the " lie " of the conscience (1^8), renders fellowship with God impossible, no less does disobedience, the " lie " of the life (2^4). This is the purport of the verses that follow (2^{3-6}). Christian profession is to be submitted to the test of Christian conduct; of which a threefold description is given—" keeping God's commandments " (2^3) ; " keeping His word " (2^5) ; and " walking even as He (Christ) walked " (2^6). With this the first application of the test of Righteousness is completed.

PARAGRAPH B, 2^{7-17}.

Walking in the Light tested by Love.

(A) Positively—the old-new commandment (2^{7-11}).

This is linked on to the immediately preceding verses by the word " commandment." Love is the commandment which is " old," familiar to the Apostle's readers from their first acquaintance with the rudiments of Christianity (2^7) ; but also " new," a commandment which is ever fresh and living to those who have fellowship with Christ in the True Light, which is now shining forth (2^8). But from this follows necessarily, that " He that saith he is in the light, and hateth his brother, is in darkness." The antithesis of $2^{8.\ 9}$ is then repeated, with variation and enrichment of thought, in $2^{10, 11}$. (Then follow the parenthetical verses $^{12-14}$, the motive for the insertion of which will be discussed elsewhere.[1] These being treated as a parenthesis, the unity of the paragraph at once becomes apparent.)

(*b*) Negatively. The commandment to love is completed by the great "Love not" (2^{15-17}). If walking in the light has its guarantee in loving one's "brother," it is tested no less by not loving the "world." One cannot at the same time participate in the life of God and in a moral life which is dominated by the lust of the flesh, the lust of the eyes, and the vainglory of the world.

PARAGRAPH C, 2^{18-28}.

Walking in the Light tested by Belief.

The Light of God not only reveals Sin and Righteousness, the children of God (our "brother") and the "world" in their true character, so that, walking in that Light, men must confess Sin and follow after Righteousness, love their "brother" and not love the "world"; it also reveals Jesus in His true character as the Christ, the Incarnate Son of God. And all that calls itself Christianity is to be tested by its reception or its rejection of that truth. In this paragraph, it is true, the Light and the Darkness are not expressly referred to. But the continuity of thought with the preceding paragraphs is unmistakable. Throughout the whole of this first division of the Epistle the point of view is that of Fellowship with God, through receiving and walking in the Light which His self-revelation sheds upon all things in the spiritual realm. Unreal Christianity in every form is comprehensively a "lie." It may be the Antinomian lie of him who says "he has no sin" (1^8), and, on the other hand, is indifferent to keeping God's commandments (2^4); the lie of lovelessness (2^9); or the lie of the Antichrist who,

---

[1] See Chapter XV.

claiming spiritual enlightenment, denies that Jesus is the Christ (2^{22}). Every one who does this walks in darkness, and asserts what is untrue and impossible, if he say or suppose that he has fellowship with God, Who is Light. Minuter analysis of this paragraph is, for our present purpose, unnecessary.

SECOND CYCLE, 2^{29}–4^6.

Divine Sonship tested by Righteousness, Love, and Belief.

The first main division of the Epistle began with the assertion of what God is relatively to us—Light; and from this it deduced the condition of our fellowship with Him. The light of God's self-revelation in Christ becomes to us the light in which we behold ourselves, our sin, our duty, our brother, the world, the reality of the Incarnation; and only in acknowledging the " truth " thus revealed and loyally acting it out can we have fellowship with God. The point of view is ethical and psychological. This second division, on the other hand, begins with the assertion of what the Divine nature is in itself, and thence deduces the essential characteristics of those who are " begotten of God." Righteousness, Love, Confession of Christ are the proofs, because the results, of participation in the Divine nature ; Sin, Hate, Denial of Christ, the proofs of non-participation. The point of view is, predominantly, biological. The key-word is " begotten of God."

PARAGRAPH A, 2^{29}–3^{10a}.

Divine Sonship tested by Righteousness.

Here (2^{29}) the idea of the Divine Begetting is introduced for the first time. And, as the first test applied to Fellowship in the Light was the attitude toward Sin and

Righteousness, so, likewise, it is the first applied to the life of Divine sonship. As the Light convicts of sin and at the same time reveals both the content and the absolute imperative of Righteousness, so the Divine Life begotten in man has a twofold action.[1]   The harmony of the human will with the Divine, which is the necessary result of the community of nature, reveals itself both in "doing righteousness" and in entire antagonism to sin.   " If ye know that He is righteous, know that every one also that doeth righteousness is begotten of Him."   But here the writer is immediately arrested by the wonder and thanksgiving that fill and overflow his soul at the thought that sinful men should be brought into such a relation as this to God. "Behold what manner of love!" (3^{1a}). This leads him further to contemplate, first, the present concealment of the glory of the children of God (3^{1b}); then, the splendour of its future manifestation (3^2); and, finally, the thought that the fulfilment of this hope is necessarily conditioned by present endeavour after moral likeness to Christ leads back to the main theme of the paragraph, that the life of Divine sonship is, by necessity of nature, one of absolute Righteousness, of truceless opposition to sin (3^{4-10a}). This is now exhibited in a fourfold light: (1) in the light of what sin is, lawlessness (3^4); (2) in the light of Christ—the purpose of all that is revealed in Christ is the removal and abolition of sin (3^{5-7}); (3) in the light of the Divine origin of the Christian life—only that which is sinless can derive from God ($3^{9,\ 10a}$); (4) intertwined with these cardinal arguments there is a fourth, that all that is of the nature of sin comes from a source which is the antithesis of the Divine, and which is in active hostility to the work of Christ—the Devil (3^{8-10a}). The last clause of the paragraph reverts to and logically completes the proposition with which it began. To the positive, "Every one that

[1] The parallelism is strikingly close. Cf. 3^3 with 2^6, 3^{6a} with 2^{5b}, 3^{6b} with 2^4.

doeth righteousness is begotten of God" (2^{29}), is added the negative, "Whosoever doeth not righteousness is not of God" (3^{10b}). The circle is completely drawn. The "begotten of God" include all who "do righteousness"; all who do not are excluded.

PARAGRAPH B, 3^{10b}–24^{a}.

Divine Sonship tested by Love.

In structure, this paragraph is less regular; its contents are not so closely knit to the leading thought. But what the leading thought is, is clearly fixed at the beginning: "He that loveth not his brother is not begotten of God" (3^{10b}). That brotherly love is the test of Divine sonship is the truth that dominates the whole. Instead, however, of developing this thought dialectically, the Apostle does so, in the first instance, pictorially; setting before us two figures, Cain and Christ, as the prototypes of Hate and Love. The contemplation of Cain and of the disposition out of which the first murder sprang (3^{12}), suggests parenthetically an explanation of the World's hatred of the children of God (3^{13}); but, chiefly, the truth that in loving our brethren we have a reliable guarantee that we have passed from death unto life (3^{14}); while, on the other hand, whosoever hateth his brother is potentially a murderer and assuredly cannot have the Life of God abiding in him (3^{15}). Next, in glorious contrast to the sinister figure of Cain, who sacrificed his brother's life to his morbid self-love, the Apostle sets before us the figure of Christ who sacrificed His own life in love to us, His brethren (3^{16a}); and draws the inevitable inference that our life, if one with His, must obey the same spiritual law (3^{16b}). In 3^{17} this test is brought within the scope of everyday opportunity; and is followed (3^{18}) by a fervent exhortation to love "not in word, neither with the tongue, but in deed and in truth." This introduces a restatement of the purport of the whole paragraph—that such Love is the test of all Divine sonship, and affords a valid and accessible ground of assurance before God, even should our own hearts condemn us ($3^{19, 20}$). In the remainder of the paragraph the subject of assurance and its relation to prayer is further dwelt upon ($3^{21, 22}$). And, finally, in setting forth the grounds upon which such assurance rests, the Apostle combines all the three cardinal tests—Righteousness (" keeping His commandments," 3^{22}), Belief (" in the name of His Son Jesus Christ," 3^{23a}), and Love (3^{23b}). All these are, in fact, " commandments," and he that keepeth them abideth in God, and God in him (3^{24a}).

PARAGRAPH C, 3^{24b}–4^6.

Divine Sonship tested by Belief.

Here, again, the test to be applied is broadly and clearly indicated at the outset. " Hereby know we that He abideth in us, by the Spirit [1] which He hath given us." As in the corresponding paragraph 2^{18-28}, so here also the argument is conducted in view of the concrete historical situation, upon the consideration of which we do not now enter. The essence of the paragraph lies in $4^{2, 3b}$ and ^{6b}: " Hereby know ye the Spirit of God. Every spirit that confesseth that Jesus is the Christ come in the flesh is of God ; and every spirit that confesseth not Jesus is not of

---

[1] It is necessary to say here, although a fuller discussion will be given later, that, in the Epistle, the Spirit is regarded solely as the Spirit of Truth, whose function is to testify of Christ, to reveal the Divine glory of His Person, to inspire belief in Him, and to prompt confession of Him as the Incarnate Son of God. The "knowing" by "the Spirit which God hath given us" is not immediate but inferential. It does not proceed from any direct subjective testimony that " God abideth in us," but is an inference from the *fact* that God hath given us that Spirit without whom no man calleth Jesus Lord.

God." "By this we know the Spirit of truth and the spirit of error."

To recur to the general structure of the Epistle, it may be noted that we have found the first and second "cycles" corresponding exactly in subject-matter and in order of development. In 1^5-2^6 and in $2^{29}-3^{10a}$ the Christian life has been tested by its attitude to Sin and Righteousness, in 2^{7-17} and in $3^{10b-24a}$ by Love, and in 2^{18-28} and $3^{24b}-4^6$ by Belief.

THIRD CYCLE, 4^7-5^{21}.

Inter-relations of Love, Belief, and Righteousness.

In this closing section the Epistle rises to its loftiest heights; but the logical analysis of it is the hardest part of our task. The subject-matter is identical with that which has been already twice used, not a single new idea being introduced except that of the "sin unto death." But the order and proportion of treatment are different; the test of Righteousness takes here a subordinate place ($5^{2, 3}$ 5^{18}); and the whole "Cycle" may be broadly divided into two sections, the first, 4^7-5^{3a}, in which the dominant theme is Love (with, however, the Christological passage 4^{13-15} embedded in it); the second, 5^{3b-21}, in which it is Belief. The same practical purpose is still steadfastly adhered to as in the preceding "Cycles"—the application of the three great tests to everything that calls itself Christian. But here an additional aim is, I think, partly discernible, namely, to bring out the necessary connections and inter-relations of Righteousness, Love, and Belief. Hitherto the writer has been content to exhibit these simply as collateral elements in the Christian life, each and all indispensable to its genuineness. He has made no serious effort to show why these three elements must coalesce in the unity of life,—why the Life of which one manifestation is Belief in the Incarnation must also manifest itself in keeping God's commandments and loving one another. Here, however, as he traverses the same ground for the third time, he does seem to be feeling after a closer articulation. Thus in 4^{9-16} the inner connection between Belief and Love is strongly suggested; in $5^{2\cdot 3a}$ we find the synthesis of Love and Righteousness; and in 5^{3b-5}, the synthesis of Righteousness and Belief. Without asserting that the writer's conscious purpose in this third handling of his material was to exhibit these interdependencies, it may be said that in this consists its distinctive feature.

SECTION I. 4^{7}–5^{5a}.

LOVE.

PARAGRAPH A, 4^{7-12}.

The genesis of Love.

Christian Love is deduced from its Divine source. Regarding Love, the same declaration, precisely and verbally, is now made as was formerly made regarding Righteousness (2^{29}). "God is Love"; and every one that loveth is begotten of God (4^{7} and, negatively, 4^{8}). But here, feeling his way to a correlation of Love and Belief, St. John advances to the further statement, that the mission of Christ alone is the perfect revelation of the fact that the nature of God is Love (4^{9}); nay, that it furnishes the one absolute revelation of the nature of Love itself (4^{10}). From this follows the inevitable consequence, "If God so loved us, we ought also to love one another" (4^{11}); and the assurance that, if we love one another, the invisible God abideth in us; His nature is incorporate with ours; His Love is fulfilled in us (4^{12}).

Paragraph B, 4¹³⁻¹⁶.

The synthesis of Love and Belief.

As in 2^{20-28} and $3^{24b}-4^{6}$, the gift of the Spirit, by whom confession is made of Jesus as the Son of God, is cited as proof that God abideth in us and we in Him (4^{13-15}), and seems to be merely collateral with the proof already adduced from "loving one another" (4^{12}). But it becomes evident, on closer examination, that the two paragraphs (4^{7-12} and 4^{13-16}) stand in some more intimate relation than this. We observe the parallel statements, "If we love one another, God abideth in us" (4^{12}); then, "Whosoever shall confess that Jesus is the Son of God, God abideth in him and he in God" (4^{15}); then a second time, "He that abideth in love abideth in God, and God in him" (4^{16}). We observe, further, that the confession of Jesus as the Son of God (4^{16}) is paralleled by the statement that "the Father sent the Son to be the Saviour of the world" (4^{14}), which points back to that revelation of God as Love ($4^{9. \ 10}$) in which the moral obligation and spiritual necessity of loving one another have been already disclosed (4^{11}). And we observe, finally, that the confession of Jesus as the Son of God, sent by the Father to be the Saviour of the world ($4^{14. \ 15}$), is personally appropriated in this, "We know and have believed the Love which God hath toward us," followed by the reiterated "God is Love; and he that abideth in Love abideth in God, and God in him" (4^{16}). Thus closely observing the structure of the passage, we cannot doubt that the writer is labouring to express the truth that Christian Belief and Christian Love are not merely concomitant, but vitally one. Yet, what the inter-relation of the two is in the Apostle's mind; which, if either, is anterior and instrumental to the other; whether we are begotten through the medium of spiritual perception into love, or through the medium of love into spiritual perception, it would be hazardous to say.

PARAGRAPH C, 4^{17}–5^{3a}.

The effects, motives, and manifestations of Love.

1. The effect of Love is assurance toward God ($4^{17.\ 18}$). It is a notable example of the symmetry with which the Epistle is constructed that the sequence of thought here is minutely the same as in $3^{19.\ 20.}$ Here, as there, Love has, as its immediate result, confidence toward God; and with precisely the same condition, that Love be in "deed and in truth" (cf. $3^{18.\ 19}$ with 4^{20}).

2. The motives to brotherly Love: These are God's love to us (4^{19}), the only possible response to which is to love one's brother (4^{20}); the express commandment of Christ (4^{21}); and the instincts of spiritual kinship (5^1).[1]

3. The synthesis of Love and Righteousness.

This is exhibited in a two-fold light. True love to man is righteous, and is possible only to those who love God and keep His commandments (5^2). True love to God consists in keeping His commandments (5^{3a}).

SECTION II. 5^{3b-21}.

BELIEF.

PARAGRAPH A, 5^{3b-12}.

The power, contents, basis, and issue of Christian Belief.

It may seem sufficiently arbitrary to make the clause "And His commandments are not grievous" the point of

---

[1] Throughout this portion of the Epistle, each thought is so closely inter-locked, as well with what precedes as with what follows, that it is impossible to divide it at any point which shall not seem more or less arbitrary. I have made 5^2 the beginning of a subsection; but obviously it is also the requisite complement to 5^1. There, loving "him that is begotten" is the sign and test of loving "Him that begat"; here, conversely, loving God and "keeping His commandments" is the sign and test of "loving the children of God."

departure for a new paragraph. But so closely is the texture of thought woven in these verses, that the same objection would apply equally to any other line of division. There is, however, an obvious transition in 5^{3-5} from the topic of Love to that of Belief; and it seems most suitable to regard the transition as effected at this point. "This is the Love of God, that we keep His commandments," is St. John's last word concerning Love. All that is now to be said has as its subject, more or less directly, Belief. And, while the clause "and His commandments are not grievous" is intimately linked on to the first half of the verse by the common topic "commandments," it introduces an entirely new train of thought.

1. The synthesis of Belief and Righteousness ($5^{3b.\ 4}$). God's commandments are not burdensome to the believer. That which would make them burdensome, the power of the World, is overcome by the victorious divine power given to every one who is "begotten of God"; and the medium through which the victorious power is imparted is our Christian Belief.

2. The substance of Christian Belief is that "Jesus is the Son of God, even He that came by water and by blood" ($5^{5.\ 6}$).

3. Next, the basis on which it rests is: the witness of the Spirit (5^7); the coincident witness of the Spirit, the water and the blood (5^8); which is the witness of God Himself (5^9); and which, when received, becomes an inward and immediate assurance, a self-evidencing certitude (5^{10a}). On the other hand, to reject this witness is to make God a liar (5^{10b}).

4. The issue of Christian Belief. The witness of God to His Son Jesus Christ is fundamentally this, that He is the source of Eternal Life to men (5^{11}). This Life is the present possession of all who spiritually possess Him; and to be without Him is to be destitute of it (5^{12}).

The end of the paragraph thus answers sublimely to its beginning. That which has eternal life in it (5^{12}) must conquer, and alone can conquer, the World, whose life is bound up with transitory aims and objects. Because it makes the truth that " he that doeth the will of God abideth for ever " a living power, faith wins its everlasting victory over the world which " passeth away with the lust thereof."

PARAGRAPH B, 5^{13-21}.

The conscious certainties of Christian Belief.

1. Its certainty of Eternal Life. To promote this in all who believe in the name of the Son of God is the Apostle's purpose in writing this Epistle (5^{13}).

2. Its certainty regarding Prayer (5^{14-17}). " If we ask anything according to God's Will, He heareth us " (5^{14}); and, consequently, we have these things for which we have made petition (5^{15}). An example of the things which we may ask with assurance is " life " for a brother who sins " a sin not unto death " (5^{16a}); and an example of the things regarding which we may not pray with such confidence is the restoration of a brother who has committed sin unto death (5^{16b}). To this is appended a statement regarding the nature and effect of sin (5^{17}).

3. The certainty regarding the regenerate Life, that Righteousness is its indefeasible characteristic, that it is a life of uncompromising antagonism to all sin (5^{18}).

4. The certainty as to the profound moral contrast between the Christian life and the life of the world (5^{19}).

5. The certainty of Christian Belief as to the facts upon which it rests, and the supernatural power which has quickened it to perception of those facts (5^{20a}).

Then with a final reiteration of the whole purport of the Epistle, " This is the true God and Eternal Life " (5^{20b}), and an abrupt and sternly affectionate call to all believers

to beware of yielding the homage of their trust and dependence to the vain shadows which are ever apt to usurp the
place of the True God, the Epistle ends, " Little children,
keep yourselves from idols " (5^{21}).

SYNOPSIS.

THE PROLOGUE, 1^{1-4}.

FIRST CYCLE, 1^5-2^{28}.

THE CHRISTIAN LIFE, AS FELLOWSHIP WITH GOD, CONDITIONED
AND TESTED BY WALKING IN THE LIGHT.

1^5. The fundamental announcement, " God is Light."

PARAGRAPH A, 1^6-2^6.

$1^{6. 7}$. General statement of the condition of fellowship with God, Who
is Light.

1^8-2^6. *Walking in the Light tested by the attitude to Sin and Righteousness.*

To walk in the Darkness.	*To walk in the Light.*
a. To deny sin as guilt, 1^8.	a. To confess sin as guilt, 1^9.
β. To deny sin as fact, 1^{10}.	β. To confess sin as fact, $2^{1. 2}$.
γ. To say that we know God and not keep His commandments, 2^4.	γ. To keep His commandments, 2^3.
δ. Not to walk as Christ walked, 2^6.	δ. To keep His word, 2^5.
	ε. To walk as Christ walked, 2^6.

PARAGRAPH B, 2^{7-17}.

Walking in the Light tested by Love.

(*a*) By love of one's brother (vv.$^{7-11}$).
 [Parenthetic address to the readers (vv.$^{12-14}$).]
(*b*) By not loving the World (vv.$^{15-17}$).

PARAGRAPH C, 2^{18-28}.

Walking in the Light tested by Belief.

2^{18}. Rise of the antichrists.
2^{19}. Their relation to the Church.
$2^{20. 21}$. The source and guarantee of the true Belief.
$2^{22. 23}$. The crucial test of Truth and Error.
$2^{24. 25}$. Exhortation to steadfastness.
$2^{26. 27}$. Reiterated statement of the source and guarantee of the true
Belief.
2^{28}. Repeated exhortation to steadfastness.

SECOND CYCLE, 2^{29}-4^6.

THE CHRISTIAN LIFE, AS THAT OF DIVINE SONSHIP, APPROVED BY THE SAME TESTS.

PARAGRAPH A, 2^{29}-3^{10a}.

Divine Sonship tested by Righteousness.

2^{29}. This test inevitable.

3^{1-3}. The present status and the future manifestation of the children of God : the possession of this hope conditioned by assimilation to the purity of Christ.

3^{4-10a}. The absolute contrariety of the life of Divine Sonship to all sin.

a. In the light of the moral authority of God (v.^{4}).

β. In the light of Christ's character and of the purpose of His mission (vv.$^{5-7}$).

γ. In the light of the origin of Sin (v.^{8}).

δ. In the light of its own Divine source (v.^{9}).

ϵ. In the light of fundamental moral contrasts (v.^{10a}).

PARAGRAPH B, $3^{10b-24a}$.

Divine Sonship tested by Love.

$3^{10b.\ 11}$. This test inevitable.

3^{12}. Cain the prototype of Hate.

3^{13}. Cain's spirit reproduced in the World.

3^{14a}. Love, the sign of having passed from Death unto Life.

$3^{14b.\ 15}$. The absence of it, the sign of abiding in Death.

3^{16}. Christ the prototype of Love ; the obligation thus laid upon us.

$3^{17.\ 18}$. Genuine Love consists not in words but in deeds.

3^{19-22}. The confidence toward God resulting from such Love, especially in Prayer.

$3^{23.\ 24b}$. Recapitulatory ; combining, under the category of His "commandment," Love and also Belief on His Son Jesus Christ. Thus a transition is effected to Paragraph C.

PARAGRAPH C, 3^{24b}-4^6.

Divine Sonship tested by Belief.

3^{24b}. This test inevitable.

4^1. Exhortation in view of the actual situation.

$4^{2.\ 3}$. The true Confession of Faith.

4^{4-6}. The relation thereto of the Church and the World.

THIRD CYCLE, 4[7]–5[21].

CLOSER CORRELATION OF RIGHTEOUSNESS, LOVE AND BELIEF.

SECTION I. 4[7]–5[3a].

LOVE.

PARAGRAPH A, 4[7-12].

The genesis of Love.

4[7. 8]. Love indispensable, because God is Love.
4[9]. The mission of Christ the proof that God is Love.
4[10]. The mission of Christ the absolute revelation of what Love is.
4[11]. The obligation thus imposed upon us.
4[12]. The assurance given in its fulfilment.

PARAGRAPH B, 4[13-16].

The synthesis of Belief and Love.

4[13]. The True Belief indispensable as a guarantee of Christian Life, because the Spirit of God is its author.
4[14. 15]. The content of the true Belief, " Jesus is the Son of God."
4[16]. In this is found the vital ground of Christian Love.

PARAGRAPH C, 4[17]–5[3a].

The effect, motives, and manifestations of Love.

4[17. 18]. The effect, confidence toward God.
4[19]–5[1]. The motives to Love : (1) God's love to us ; (2) the only possible response to which is to love our brother ; (3) Christ's commandment ; (4) the instincts of spiritual kinship.
5[2- 3a]. The synthesis of Love and Righteousness.

SECTION II. 5[3b-21].

BELIEF.

PARAGRAPH A, 5[3b-12].

The power, contents, basis, and issue of Christian Belief.

5[3b. 4]. The synthesis of Belief and Righteousness. In Belief lies the power of obedience.
5[5. 6]. The contents of Christian Belief.
5[7-10]. The evidence upon which it rests.
5[11. 12]. Its issue, the possession of Eternal Life.

PARAGRAPH B, 5¹³⁻²¹.

The certainties of Christian Belief.

5¹³. Its certainty of Eternal Life.

5¹⁴·¹⁵. Of prevailing in Prayer.

[5¹⁶. Instance in which such certainty fails.]
[5¹⁷. Appended statement regarding Sin.   ]

5¹⁸. Of Righteousness, as the essential characteristic of the Christian Life.

5¹⁹. Of the moral gulf between the Christian Life and the life of the World.

5²⁰. Of itself, the facts on which it rests, and the supernatural power which has given perception of these facts.

5²¹. Final exhortation.

Note.—After this chapter was completely written, there came into my hands an article by Theodor Häring in the *Theologische Abhandlungen Carl von Weizsäcker gewidmet* (Freiburg, 1892). I am gratified to find that in this article, which is of great value, the analysis of the Epistle is on precisely the same lines as that which I have submitted. The only difference worth noting is that Häring, by combining Righteousness and Love, finds in each "cycle" only two leading tests, which he calls the "ethical" and the "Christological." This gives a more logical division ; but I am still of opinion that my own is more faithful to the thought of the Epistle, in which the comprehension of Righteousness and Love under any such general conception as "ethical" is not achieved.

CHAPTER II.

The Polemical Aim of the Epistle.

ALTHOUGH explicit controversial allusions in the Epistle are few, — are limited, indeed, to two passages ($2^{18.\ 19}$ 4^{1-6}) in which certain false teachers, designated as "antichrists," are unsparingly denounced, — there is no New Testament writing which is more vigorously polemical in its whole tone and aim. The truth, which in the same writer's Gospel shines as the dayspring from on high, becomes here a searchlight, flashed into a background of darkness.

But, though the polemical intention of the Epistle has been universally recognised, there has been wide diversity of opinion as to its actual object. By the older commentators generally, it was found in the perilous state of the Church, or Churches, addressed. They had left their "first love"; they had lapsed into Laodicean lukewarmness and worldliness, so that their sense of the absolute distinction between the Christian and the unchristian in life and belief had become blurred and feeble. And it was to arouse them from this lethargy—to sharpen the dulness of their spiritual perceptions — that the Epistle was written. But not only does the Epistle nowhere give any sign of such an intention; it contains many passages which are inconsistent with it ($2^{13.\ 14.\ 20.\ 21.\ 27}$ $4^4\ 5^{18-20}$).

Unmistakably its polemic is directed not against such evils as may at any time, and more or less always do,

beset the life of the Church from within, but against a
definite danger threatening it from without.   There is a
" spirit of error " (4^6) abroad in the world.   From the Church
itself (2^{19}) many false prophets (4^1) have gone forth, cor-
rupters of the gospel, " antichrists " who would deceive the
very elect.   And, not to spend time in statement and
refutation of other views, it may be asserted as beyond
question that the peril against which the Epistle was
intended to arm the Church was the spreading influence
of Gnosticism, and, specifically, of a form of Gnosticism
that was Docetic in doctrine and Antinomian in practice.
A very brief sketch of the essential features of Gnosticism
will suffice to show not only that these are clearly reflected
in the more explicitly controversial utterances of the Epistle,
but that the influence of an anti-Gnostic polemic is traceable
in almost every sentence.

Of the forces with which Christianity had to do battle
for its career as the universal religion—Jewish legalism,
pagan superstition, Greek speculation, Roman imperialism—
none, perhaps, placed it in sharper hazard than Gnosticism,
that strange, obscure movement, partly intellectual, partly
fanatical, which, in the second century, spread with the
swiftness of an epidemic over the Church from Syria to
Gaul.   The rise and spread of Gnosticism forms one of the
dimmest chapters in Church history ; and no attempt need
be or can be made here to elucidate its obscurities or
unravel its intricacies.   But one fact is clear: Gnosticism
was not, in the proper sense, a " heresy."   Although it
became a corrupting influence within the Church, it was
an alien by birth.   While the Church yet sojourned within
the pale of Judaism, it enjoyed immunity from this plague ;
but, soon as it broke through these narrow bounds, it found
itself in a world where the decaying religions and philo-
sophies of the West were in acute fermentation under the
influence of a new and powerful leaven from the East ; while

the infusion of Christianity itself into this fermenting mass only added to the bewildering multiplicity of Gnostic sects and systems it brought forth.

That this was the true genesis of Gnosticism,—that it was the result of an irruption of Oriental religious beliefs into the Græco-Roman world,—and that, consequently, it sought to unite in itself two diverse strains, Western intellectualism and Eastern mysticism, is generally admitted. Different views are held, however, as to which of these is to be regarded as the stock upon which the other was grafted. It has been the fashion with Church historians of the liberal school to glorify Gnosticism by giving chief prominence to its philosophical aspect. Oriental elements it admittedly contained, but these, in its most influential representatives at least, had been thoroughly permeated with the Hellenic spirit. In its historical result it was the " acute Hellenising " of Christianity. The great Gnostics were the first Christian philosophers; and Gnosticism is to be regarded as, upon the whole, a progressive force. More recent investigations and a more concrete study [1] of the subject have tended to discredit this estimate. Naturally, Gnosticism had to make some kind of terms with Hellenic culture, as Christianity itself had to do, in order to win a footing on which it could appeal to those who sought after " wisdom "; but by much the prepotent strain in this singular hybrid was Oriental Dualism. Many of the Gnostic sects were characterised chiefly by a wild, fanatical, and sometimes obscene cultus; and even in those which, like the Valentinian, made the most ambitious attempts to evolve a philosophy of the universe, Dualism was still the fundamental and formative principle. It is far truer to call Gnosticism a reactionary than a progressive force, and its most eminent leaders the last upholders of a lost cause, rather than the advance-guard of intellectual progress. [2]

[1] *v.* Bousset's *Hauptprobleme der Gnosis*, pp. 1–9.   [2] *v.* Bousset, *ibid.* p. 7.

But Dualism no less than Monotheism or Pantheism has its philosophy, its reading of the riddle of existence; and it is clear that it was by reason of its speculative pretensions that Gnosticism acquired its influence in the Church. The name by which the system came to be designated, the Gnosis, indicates a claim to a higher esoteric knowledge[1] of Divine things, and a tendency to reckon this the summit of spiritual attainment; a claim and tendency which St. Paul, as early as his First Epistle to the Corinthians, finds occasion to meet with stern resistance (1 Cor. 1^{19}–2^5 8^1 13^2), as engendering arrogance and unbrotherly contempt for the less enlightened (8$^{1.7-11}$). This Epistle, it is true, exhibits no trace of anything that can be distinctively called Gnosticism; but it does reveal into how congenial a soil the seeds of Gnosticism were about to fall. In the Epistle to the Colossians we find that the sower has been at work; in the Pastoral and other later Epistles, that the crop is already ripening. The innate pride and selfishness of the system became more and more apparent as it took more definite form (1 Tim. 6$^{3-5}$, 2 Tim. 3$^{2-5}$). Those who possessed the higher knowledge were distinguished from those who were incapable of its possession, as a superior order, almost a higher species, of believers. The latter were the unspiritual men, ψυχικοί, πνεῦμα μὴ ἔχοντες.[2] The highest Christian attainment was that of intellectual or mystic contemplation. To " know the depths "[3] was esteemed not only above the commonplace facts and moralities of the gospel, but above love, virtue, and practical holiness. When this, the general and most pronounced

---

[1] It is maintained, however, by Bousset (p. 277) that the name Gnosis primarily signified, not so much a higher intellectual knowledge, as initiation into the secret and sacramental mysteries of the Gnostic sects.

[2] Jude ^{19}, where the epithet is retorted upon those who used it.

[3] Rev. 2^{24}. Cf. Hippolytus, *Ref. Haer.* v. vi. 1.

feature of Gnosticism, is borne in mind, a vivid light is at once shed upon many passages in the Epistle. In those, especially, in which we find the formula "he that saith" (ὁ λέγων), or an equivalent (ἐὰν εἴπωμεν, ἐάν τις εἴπῃ), it becomes apparent that it is no abstract contingency the writer has in view, but a definitely recognised case. Thus in 2[4. 6. 9] we have what may be supposed to be almost verbal quotations of current forms of Gnostic profession (he that saith), "I know Him,"[1] "I abide in Him," "I am in the light";[2] and in each case the claim, unsupported by its requisite moral guarantee, is underlined with the writer's "roughest and blackest pencil-mark" as the statement of a liar. When we observe, moreover, the prominence which the Epistle gives throughout to the idea of knowledge, and the special significance of several of the passages in which it occurs, the conviction grows that one of the purposes chiefly aimed at is not only to refute the arrogant claims of Gnosticism, but to exhibit Apostolic Christianity, believed and lived, as the true Gnosis,—the Divine reality of which Gnosticism was but the fantastic caricature—the truth of experience to which it was the corresponding "lie" (2[4. 22] 4[20]). The confidence he has concerning those to whom he is writing is that they "know Him who is from the beginning," and that they "know the Father" (2[13]). The final note of exulting assurance upon which the Epistle closes, is that "we know the True One, and we are in the True One" (5[20]). This, the knowledge of the ultimate Reality, the Being who is the Eternal Life, is, for Christian and Gnostic alike, the goal of aspiration. But against the Gnostic conception of this as to be attained exclusively by flights of intellectual speculation or mystic contemplation, the Apostle labours, with the whole force of

---

[1] Cf. *Clementine Recognitions*, "Qui Deum se nosse profitentur." Holtzmann, *J. P. T.*, 1882, p. 320.

[2] To be of the "seed of the light" appears to have been a popular form of Gnostic pretension. Holtzmann, *ibid.* p. 323.

his spirit, to maintain that it is to be reached only by the lowlier path of obedience and brotherly love; and that by these, conversely, its reality must ever be attested. To speak of having the knowledge of God without keeping His commandments (2⁴) is self-contradiction. If God is righteous, then nothing is more certain than that "Every one that doeth righteousness is begotten of Him" (2²⁹), and that "Whosoever doeth not righteousness is not of God" (3¹⁰). "Whosoever sinneth hath not seen Him, neither *known* Him" (3⁶).

Still more strenuously, if that were possible, does the Apostle insist upon brotherly love as at once the condition and the test of the true knowledge of God. In Gnosticism knowledge was the sum of attainment, the crown of life, the supreme end in itself. The system was loveless to the core. St. Paul saw this with a prophet's eye (1 Cor. 8¹ 13²), and the contemporary witnesses bear testimony that it bore abundantly its natural fruit. "Lovers of self, lovers of money, boastful, haughty, railers, disobedient to parents, untruthful, unholy, without natural affection, implacable, slanderers" (2 Tim. 3², ³), are the typical representatives of the Gnostic character as it is portrayed in the later writings of the New Testament. "They give no heed to love," says Ignatius,[1] "caring not for the widow, the orphan, or the afflicted, neither for those who are in bonds nor for those who are released from bonds, neither for the hungry nor the thirsty."

That a religion which destroyed and banished love should call itself Christian, or claim affinity with Christianity, excites the Apostle's hottest indignation. To him it is the real atheism. Against it he lifts up his supreme truth, God is Love, with its immediate consequence, that

---

[1] περὶ ἀγάπης οὐ μέλει αὐτοῖς, οὐ περὶ χήρας, οὐ περὶ ὀρφάνου, οὐ περὶ θλιβομένου, οὐ περὶ δεδεμένου ἢ λελυμένου, οὐ περὶ πεινῶντος ἢ διψῶντος. *Ad Smyrn.* 6. 2.

to be without love is the fatal incapacity for knowing God. "Every one that loveth is begotten of God, and knoweth God" (4⁷); but, "He that loveth not knoweth not God: for God is Love" (4⁸). Spiritual illumination, apart from the practice of love, is the vaunt of a self-deceiver (2⁹). The assumption of a lofty, mystical piety, apart from dutiful conduct in the ordinary relations of life, is ruthlessly dealt with. "If any man say, I love God" (we can almost hear the voice of the self-complacent "spiritual") "and hateth his brother, he is a liar: for he that loveth not his brother whom he hath seen, how can he love God whom he hath not seen?" All these and numerous other passages (2⁷. ⁸. ¹⁰. ¹¹ 3¹⁰ᵇ. ¹¹. ¹⁴. ¹⁷⁻¹⁹. ²³ᵇ 4¹¹. ¹². ¹⁷. ¹⁸. ¹⁹. ²¹ 5¹ᵇ) receive fresh point when read in view of the unbrotherly aloofness inherent in Gnosticism. And, in general, it may be said that the uniquely reiterated emphasis which the Epistle lays upon brotherly love, the almost fierce tone in which the New Commandment is promulgated, is not adequately accounted for by any idiosyncrasy of the writer, on the supposition that he is writing in the abstract, but becomes vividly intelligible as the expression of a jealous wrath excited by actual tendencies that were powerfully assailing the life and fellowship of the Church.

But if Gnosticism was distinguished by this unethical intellectualism, its deeper characteristic lay in its dualistic conception of existence. Epiphanius tells us that Basilides began with the inquiry, πόθεν τὸ κακόν (*Haer.* 24. 6); Clement, that he ended by "deifying the devil" (θειάζων μὲν τὸν διάβολον, *Strom.* iv. 12, 87).[1] This may be taken as a compendious account of Dualism. It traces back into the eternal the schism of which we are conscious in the world of experience, and posits two independent and antagonistic principles of existence, from which, severally, come all the good and all the evil that exist.

[1] I admit that it is doubtful whether this particular phrase is to be understood in a thoroughly dualistic sense.

It is true that in those Gnostic systems which were most strongly touched by Hellenic influence, the fundamental dualism was disguised by complicated successions of emanations and hierarchies of æons and archons, bridging the gulf between absolute transcendent Deity and the material creation. These cosmogonies were broadly analogous to the materialistic theory of evolution; except that, while modern evolution is from matter upward to "whatever gods there be," Gnostic evolution was from divinity downwards. Invariably, however, the source and the seat of evil were found in matter, in the body, with its senses and appetites, and in its sensuous earthly environment; and invariably it was held inconceivable that the Divine Nature should have immediate contact with, or influence upon, the material side of existence.

To such a view of the universe Christianity could be adjusted only by a Docetic interpretation of the Person of Christ. A veritable incarnation was unthinkable. The Divine Being could enter into no real union with a corporeal organism. The Human Nature of Christ and the incidents of His earthly career were, more or less, an illusion. It is with this Docetic subversion of the truth of the Incarnation that the "antichrists" are specially identified in the Epistle ($2^{22.\ 23}\ 4^3$); and it is against it that St. John directs, with whole-souled force and fervour, his central thesis—the complete personal identification of the historical Jesus with the Divine Being who is the "Word of Life," the "Son of God," the "Christ." [1]

A further consequence of the dualistic interpretation of existence is that Sin, in the Christian meaning of Sin, disappears. In its essence, it is no longer a moral opposition, in the human personality, to good; it is a physical principle inherent in all non-spiritual being. Not

[1] See Chapters VI. and XIII.

the soul, but the flesh is its organ ; and Redemption consists not in the renewal of the moral nature, but in its emancipation from the flesh. And, again, it becomes apparent that no abstract possibility, but a very definite historical phenomenon, is contemplated in the repeated warning, " If we say that we have no sin, we deceive ourselves, and the truth is not in us." " If we say that we have not sinned, we make Him a liar, and His word is not in us " ($1^{8. \ 10}$).

With the nobler and more earnest spirits, the practical consequence of this irreconcilable dualism in human nature was the ascetic life. Only by the mortification of the bodily members and the suppression of natural appetite could the deliverance of the soul from its life-long foe be achieved. A rigid asceticism is ascribed to various Gnostic sects (Encratites, the followers of Saturninus, etc.), and has left distinct traces in the Epistle to the Colossians (2^{21}) and in the Pastoral Epistles (1 Tim. 4^3). But the same principle readily suggested an opposite method of achieving the soul's deliverance from the yoke of the material. Let the dualism of nature be boldly reduced to practice. Let body and spirit be treated as separate entities ; let each obey its own laws and act according to its own nature, without mutual interference.[1] The spiritual nature could not be involved in nor defiled by the deeds of the flesh ; and the power of external things was most effectually overcome when they were not allowed to disturb in anywise the tranquillity of the inner man. Let the flesh indulge every lust, but let the soul soar on the wings of lofty spiritual thought, no more hindered or harassed by the body and its appetites than is the skimming swallow by the barking dog that chases it. It is evident, from various references in the later New Testament writings (Tit. $1^{10. \ 16}$, 2 Tim. 3^{1-7}, 2 Pet. 2^{12-22}, Jude $^{4. \ 7-19}$, Rev. $2^{14. \ 15. \ 20}$)

---

[1] This was τὸ ἀδιαφόρως ζῆν. Clem. Alex, *Strom.* iii. 5. 40.

that Gnosticism, from its earliest contact with Christianity began to infect the Church with this leaven of all abominableness. And for the interpretation of our Epistle this Antinomian development of Gnosticism is of special importance. While there are no direct allusions to it, as there are in Second Peter and Jude, it is ever present to the writer's mind when he is on the ground of ethics. The moral indifferentism of the Gnostic sheds a vivid light upon such utterances as " sin is lawlessness " (3^4), and its converse, " every unrighteousness is sin " (5^{17}). Especially is it the key, as we shall find, to that difficult passage 2^{29}–3^{10}, the whole emphasis of which falls upon the " doing " ($\pi o \iota \epsilon \hat{\iota} \nu$), whether of righteousness or of sin. Every one that " doeth righteousness " is begotten of God (2^{29}). He that " doeth sin " " doeth also lawlessness " (3^4). He that " doeth righteousness " is righteous (3^7). He that " doeth sin " is of the Devil (3^8). Every one that is begotten of God " doeth not " sin (3^9), and every one that " doeth not " righteousness is not of God. Clearly, in all this trenchant reiteration of the same thought, St. John is not actuated merely by the consideration of the perpetual tendency in men to substitute profession, sentiment and vague aspiration for actual doing of the Will of God. The writer expressly indicates, indeed, a more definite object of attack (3^7); and the whole passage presupposes, as familiar to its readers, a doctrine of moral indifferentism, according to which the status of the " spiritual " man is not to be tested by the commonplace facts of moral conduct.

The detailed examination of this and kindred passages must be deferred to a later stage.[1] The purpose of the present chapter has been served if it has furnished a general view of the polemical scope of the Epistle, and if it has been shown that in it all the

[1] Chapter XI.

authentic features of Gnosticism, its false estimate of knowledge, its loveless and unbrotherly spirit, its Docetic Christology, its exaltation of the illuminated above moral obligations, are clearly reflected. It is true that the whole presentation of truth in the Epistle widely overflows the limits of the controversial occasion. On the one hand, the human tendencies that manifested themselves in Gnosticism are not of any one period or place. The Gnostic spirit and temper are never dead. On the other hand, St. John so little meets these with mere denunciation;[1] he so constantly opposes to the pernicious plausibilities of error the simple, sublime, and satisfying facts and principles of the Christian Revelation; he so lifts every question at issue out of the dust of mere polemics into the lucid atmosphere of eternal truth, that his Epistle pursues its course through the ages, ever bringing to the human soul the vision and the inspiration of the divine life. Nevertheless, for its interpretation, the polemical aim that pervades it must be recognised. The great tests of Christianity, the enforcement of which constitutes its chief purpose,—the tests of practical Righteousness and Love, and of Belief in Jesus as God Incarnate,—are those which are of perennial validity and necessity; yet it was just by these that the wolf of Gnosticism could be most unmistakably revealed under its sheep's clothing, and they are presented in such fashion as to certify that this was the object immediately aimed at.

One point more, though of minor importance, remains for consideration, namely, whether the polemic of the Epistle is directed throughout against the same persons, or whether, in its two branches, the Christological and the ethical, it has different objects of attack. The latter view has been widely held. It is admitted that it is Gnostic

---

[1] An instructive contrast, in this respect, is presented by the Epistle of Jude and its comparatively small influence in later times.

error that is controverted in the Christological passages, but not that it is Gnostic immorality that is aimed at in the ethical passages. On the contrary, it is maintained that the moral laxity against which these are so vigorously directed is within the Church itself. And on behalf of this view it is argued that, in the Epistle, no charge of teaching or practising moral indifferentism is brought against the "antichrists"; that, apart from the Epistle, there is no proof that Docetism in Asia Minor lay open to such a charge; and that the moral tendencies reflected in the Epistle are such as would naturally spring up in communities where Christianity had already passed from a first to a second generation and become, in some degree, traditional.[1]

But, as has been already said, the tone in which the writer of the Epistle addresses his readers lends no support to this supposition. He is tenderly solicitous for their safety amid the perils that beset them; but this solicitude nowhere passes into rebuke. It is plainly suggested, too, that the same spirit of error (4^6) which is assailing their faith is ready to make a no less deadly assault upon the moral integrity of their Christian life (3^7 "let no man deceive you," not, "let no man deceive himself"). Of necessity, Dualism led, in practice, either to Asceticism or to the Emancipation of the Flesh; and, in the absence of any allusion in the Epistle to the former, it is a fair inference that, with Gnosticism in Asia Minor, the pendulum had swung, at the date of the Epistle, towards the latter. This inference is confirmed by the historical data, scanty as these are. The name associated with the Epistle by unvarying tradition as St. John's chief antagonist is that of Cerinthus. It seems to be beyond doubt that the Apostle and the heresiarch confronted each

---

[1] Neander, *Planting of Christianity*, i. 407-408 (Bohn). With this view Lücke and Huther agree.

other in Ephesus.[1] Unfortunately, the accounts of Cerinthus
and his teaching which have come down to us are
fragmentary, confused, and, in some points, conflicting.
The residuum of reliable fact is that, according to his
teaching, the World and even the Law were created
not by the Supreme God, but by a far inferior power;
and that he deduced from this a Docetic[2] doctrine of the
Incarnation.

We do not know with equal certainty that he deduced
from it the other natural consequence of practical Antinomianism. But such testimony as we do possess is to that
effect. According to Caius[3] of Rome, a disciple of Irenæus,
Cerinthus 'developed an elaborate eschatology, the central
point of which was a millennium of bliss as sensual as that
of the Mohammedan paradise. This account is confirmed
by Dionysius of Alexandria (*c.* 260), who says that, as
Cerinthus was a voluptuary and wholly sensual, he conjec-
tured that Christ's kingdom would consist in those things
which he so eagerly desired, in the gratification of his sensual
appetites, in eating and drinking and marrying.[4] If such
was his programme of the future, we can more readily
believe, what is stated on good authority, that his position
approximated closely to that of Carpocrates, in whom
Gnostic Antinomianism reached its unblushing climax.
And although the only version of his opinions which we
have is that given by his opponents, there seems to be no
room for doubt as to their real character. Thus, so far as
they go, the historical data harmonise with the internal

---

[1] The well-known incident of their encounter in the public baths at Ephesus
has been discredited on the ground of its incongruity with the Apostle's character,
and of the improbability of the alleged visit of the Apostle to the public bath-
house. But Irenæus gives the story on the authority of those who had heard
it from Polycarp (*Adv. Haer.* iii. 3, 4 ; Euseb. *Hist. Eccl.* iii. 28, iv. 14) ; and
such evidence is not altogether contemptible.

[2] See, further, Chapters VI. and XIII.

[3] *Ap.* Euseb. iii. 28, vii. 25.

[4] *Ibid.* viii. 25.

evidence of the Epistle itself in giving the impression that the different tendencies it combats are such as were naturally combined in one consistently developed Gnostic system, and that the object of its polemic is, throughout, one and the same.

Note.—Regarding the False Teachers, and especially for the exhaustive account of all that is on record regarding Cerinthus, Brooke's *Commentary* (xxxviii–lii) ought to be consulted. His view, differing to some extent from that which is presented in the foregoing chapter, is that the Epistle is directed against various forms of false teaching, the writer summing up the tendencies in them which seemed to him most dangerous and most characteristic of the times. Amongst these, he is inclined to place the influence of the Jewish controversy. Although admittedly this is far less prominent than in the Fourth Gospel, the insistence on the confession that Jesus is the Christ makes it probable that one of the dangers which beset the first readers of the Epistle was to accept the view that " Jesus was indeed a prophet, sent by God and endowed with higher powers, but not the Deliverer of the nation, and not the unique Son of God, with whom the writer and his fellow-Christians identified Him." But it is to be observed that the truth insisted upon is not so much that Jesus is the Christ, as that He is the Christ " come in the flesh," and that this is a specific contradiction of the Docetic Christology rather than a reply to the Jewish assault. The supposition that the polemic of the Epistle is partly anti-Judaic gains no support from the fact that Judaizing tenets are ascribed (with doubtful accuracy, Mr. Brooke admits) to Cerinthus—as that he insisted on circumcision and keeping of the Sabbath ; for of the possible influence of such teaching among its readers the Epistle contains no suggestion. Mr. Brooke discredits the attribution of immoral practices to Cerinthus by later writers, like Caius ; but what the Epistle ascribes to the False Teachers is not so much gross immorality in practice, as an unethical intellectualism or pseudo-spiritualism which opened the way to this, since " doing righteousness" was for it no imperative requirement. The truth is that, with the help chiefly of Irenæus and Epiphanius, the situation in which the Epistle was written has to be reconstructed from the Epistle itself. The three great falsehoods it combats are moral indifferentism, lovelessness, and denial of the reality of the Incarnation. These may well have been combined in one type of Gnostic teaching, which also may well have been that which is traditionally associated with the name of Cerinthus ; and the natural conclusion is that the Epistle was elicited by some critical outbreak of such teaching in Asia Minor.

CHAPTER III.

The Writer.

Not only is the " First Epistle of St. John " an anonymous writing; one of its unique features, among the writings of the New Testament, is that it does not contain a single proper name (except our Lord's), nor a single definite allusion, personal, geographical, or historical. Untrammelled, therefore, by any question of authenticity, we are left to gather from tradition and from the internal evidence such facts, if such there are, as may furnish a warrantable conclusion regarding its authorship.

As to the general question of its antiquity, the evidence is peculiarly strong, and may be briefly stated. It is needless to come further down than Eusebius, by whom it is classed among the *homologoumena* (*c.* 325). It is quoted by Dionysius, bishop of Alexandria (247–265), by Cyprian, Origen, Tertullian, Clement of Alexandria, Irenæus, and the Muratorian Canon. Papias (who is described by Irenæus as Ἰωάννου μὲν ἀκουστής, Πολυκάρπου δ' ἑταῖρος) is stated by Eusebius (*H. E.* iii. 39) " to have used testimonies from John's former Epistle"; and Polycarp's Epistle to the Philippians (*c.* 115) contains an almost verbal reproduction of 1 John 4³. Reminiscences of it are found in Athenagoras (*c.* 180) (κοινωνία τοῦ πατρὸς πρὸς τὸν υἱόν, cf. i. 3), the Epistle to Diognetus (vi. 11), the Epistle of Barnabas (ἦλθεν ἐν σαρκί, cf. 4²; υἱὸς τοῦ θεοῦ ἐφανερώθη, cf. 3⁸), more distinctly in Justin (θεοῦ τέκνα ἀληθινὰ καλούμεθα καὶ ἐσμέν, *Dial.*

123), and in the Didache (cc. x., xi., τελειῶσαι αὐτὴν ἐν τῇ ἀγάπῃ σου; παρελθέτω ὁ κόσμος οὗτος; πᾶς δὲ προφήτης δεδοκιμασμένος, cf. Δ[18] 2[17] 4[1]). They are also alleged in Hermas. It is possible that the earliest of these indicate the currency of Johannine expressions in the Christian circles in which the writer moved rather than acquaintance with the Epistle itself. The evidence, however, is indisputable that this Epistle, though one of the latest, if not the very latest, of the books of the New Testament, won for itself immediately and permanently an unchallenged position as a writing of inspired authority.[1]

The verdict of tradition, moreover, is equally clear and unanimous that the Fourth Gospel and the First Epistle are both the legacy of the Apostle John, in his old age, to the Church. All the Fathers already mentioned as quoting the Epistle (excepting Polycarp, but including Irenæus) quote it as the work of St. John. And until the end of the sixteenth century this view was unquestioned.[2]

Proceeding to consider what light the Epistle itself sheds upon the personality of the writer, we note, in the first place, that, though writer and readers are alike left nameless, and any clue to the identity of either must be merely inferential, the writing before us is one in which a person calling himself " I " addresses certain other persons as " you," and is, in form at least, a letter. That it is more than formally so, has been denied by various critics, who have, in various ways, pronounced it deficient

---

[1] This statement requires no modification on account of the fact that the Epistle shared with the other Johannine writings the fate of rejection, for dogmatic reasons, by Marcion and the so-called Alogi.

[2] There are possible exceptions to this statement in the case of Theodore (Bishop of Mopsuestia, 393–428), who is said to have " abrogated " all the Catholic Epistles, and of the " certain persons " referred to by Cosmas Indicopleustes, the topographist (sixth century), as having maintained that all the Catholic Epistles were written by presbyters, not by apostles. Both statements are at second-hand; the latter, in addition, is very indefinite.

in genuine epistolary character, describing it as a treatise, a homiletical essay, or a pamphlet. This criticism is unwarranted. Although its topics are so broadly handled, the Epistle is not written in any abstract interest, theological or ethical; nor—though the movement it was designed to combat was one which threatened, on the widest scale, to imperil the very life of Christianity—is it even Catholic, in the sense of being addressed to the Church at large. From beginning to end the writer shows himself in close contact with the special position and the immediate needs of his readers. The absence of explicit reference to either only indicates how intimate was the relation between them. For the writer to declare his identity was superfluous. Thought, language, tone—all were too familiar to be mistaken. The Epistle bore its author's signature in every line.

Though the main characteristics of the Epistle are didactic and controversial, the personal chord is frequently struck, and with much tenderness and depth of feeling, the writer alternating between the "you" of direct address ($1^{3. 5}$ $2^{1. 7. 8. 12-14. 18}$ etc., $3^{5. 13}$ etc.) and the "we" in which spontaneous feeling unites him with his readers ($1^{6. 10}$ $3^{1. 2. 14. 16. 18}$ etc., $4^{7. 10. 11}$ etc., $5^{14. 15. 18-20}$). Under special stress of emotion his paternal love, sympathy, and solicitude break out in the affectionate address, "Little children"[1] (τεκνία, παιδία), or, yet more endearingly, "My little children" (τεκνία ἐμοῦ). Or, again, the prefatory "Beloved"[2] (ἀγαπητοί) gives proof how deeply he is stirred by the sublimity of his theme and by the sense of its supreme importance to his readers. He shows

---

[1] Expressing mingled confidence and anxiety (2^1), glad thanksgiving (4^4), fervent exhortation (2^{28} 3^{18}), urgent warning (3^7 5^{24}).

[2] Conveying in every case an *earnest appeal*, based upon the familiar and fundamental character of the doctrine advanced (2^7), the loftiness of the Christian calling and privilege (3^2), the urgent necessity of the case (4^1), the sense of special obligation ($4^{7. 11}$).

himself intimately acquainted with their religious
environment (2^{19} 4^1), dangers (2^{26} 3^7 5^{21}), attainments
($2^{12-14.\ 21}$), achievements (4^4), and needs (3^{19} 5^{13}). Further,
it is implied that the relation between them is definitely
that of teacher and taught, evangelist and evangelised
($1^{2.\ 3}$). The Epistle is addressed primarily to the circle
of those among whom the author has habitually exercised
his ministry in the gospel.[1] He is in the habit of
announcing to them the things "concerning the Word of
life" (1^1), that they may have fellowship with him (1^3);
and now [2] that his joy may be full he writes these things
unto them (1^4). He writes as light shines. Love makes
the task a necessity and a delight. That joy may have
its perfect fruition in aiding their Christian development,
in guarding them from the perils to which it is exposed,
in guiding them to the trustworthy grounds of personal
assurance of eternal life, he sets himself to draw out and
place before them the great practical implications of the
gospel, and the tests of genuine Christian discipleship which
these afford.

Thus the writer is a person who, to his readers, is of so
distinctive eminence and recognised authority that he does
not find it necessary even to remind them who he is. His
whole tone towards them is affectionate, solicitous, responsible. His relation to them is not necessarily that of
" spiritual father " in the Pauline sense, but it is, at any rate,

---

[1] This is worth noting for its bearing on the interpretation of the Epistle. It
has always seemed to me that such a passage as that on the " Three Witnesses "
contains merely a summary—" heads " of sermons, shall we say ?—intended to
recall fuller oral expositions of the same topics. Though this yields no help to
interpretation, there is a certain relief in the thought that what is so obscure to
us need not have been equally so to the original readers.

[2] ἵνα ἡ χαρὰ ἡμῶν ᾖ πεπληρωμένη. The words are almost a verbal reproduction of John 15^{24}. On critical grounds, it is not easy to decide between the rival
readings ἡμῶν and ὑμῶν (*v.* Westcott, critical note, p. 13). The former may be
preferred as less obvious, and as yielding the finer and more characteristically
apostolic sense. Cf. St. Paul's "Now we live if ye stand fast in the Lord"
(I Thess. 3^8, also Phil. 2^2).

that of spiritual guide and guardian, whose province it is to instruct, to warn and exhort with all authority, as with all tenderness. All this agrees perfectly with the traditional account of St. John's relation to the Churches of Asia Minor during the later decades of the first century. More than this cannot be said. Nothing has been, so far, adduced that points conclusively to an apostolic authorship. There is one passage in the Epistle, however, which has a special bearing upon the personality of the writer, namely, the Prologue (1^{1-4}); and this we shall now examine so far as it relates to this question.

1^{1-4}.

[1] " That which was from the beginning, that which we have heard, that which we have seen with our own [2] eyes, that which we gazed upon, and our own [2] hands handled, concerning the Word of Life (and the Life was manifested, and we have seen, and bear witness, and announce unto you the Life, the Eternal Life, which was with the Father and was manifested unto us); that which we have seen and heard we announce also unto you, that ye also may have fellowship with us. And these things write we unto you, that our joy may be full."

This is, in effect, a statement of the theme of evangelical announcement, an abstract of the report which the Christian apostle is sent to deliver " concerning the Word of Life." And, both for the interpretation of the passage itself and for its bearing on the question of authorship, the first point to be determined is what is signified by the " Word of Life." And here, at once, we enter upon controversial ground ; for the phrase may be taken as denoting

---

[1] For exegetical details, see Notes, *in loc.* ; for the doctrinal implications, Chapters VI., VII., and X.

[2] " Own " is not too strong for an adequate rendering of ἡμῶν in the phrases τοῖς ὀφθαλμοῖς ἡμῶν and αἱ χεῖρες ἡμῶν.

either the personal Logos of John 1¹⁻¹⁴ or the Christian Revelation.

Some of the Greek commentators, followed by Westcott and others, adopt the latter alternative. " The obvious reference is to the whole Gospel, of which Christ is the centre and the sum, and not to Himself personally" (Westcott, p. 7). But the immense difficulty of establishing this view (though it is said to be "obvious") is sufficiently illustrated by the acrobatic feats of interpretation to which its exponent is compelled to resort.[1] With the great majority of commentators, I conclude that the "Word of Life" here signifies the Personal Logos; and for the following reasons. (*a*) The parallelism between the Prologue to the Epistle and that to the Gospel is too unmistakable to permit of different significations for a word which is so cardinal in both. (*b*) In answer to the objection that elsewhere[2] λόγος τῆς ζωῆς is applied always to the Gospel, never to the personal Christ, it is to be observed that, while there is no reason why it should not be so applied, the form of expression is here determined by the verse following (καὶ ἡ ζωὴ ἐφανερώθη), which is

---

[1] The application of ὅ ἦν ἀπ᾿ ἀρχῆς to the Gospel is justified by the observation "of the grandeur of the claim which St. John here makes for the Christian Revelation, as, in some sense, coeval with creation." But, true as it is that the Gospel has an eternal being and operation in the thought and purpose of God, it is difficult to imagine that a truth so remote from the ordinary plane of thought was made the starting-point of the Epistle. Again, "What we have heard" has to embrace "the whole Divine preparation for the Advent, promised by the teaching of the Lawgiver and Prophets, fulfilled at last by Christ." "What we have seen with our eyes" connotes "the condition of Jew and Gentile, the civil and religious institutions by which St. John was surrounded, the effects which the Gospel has wrought, as revealing to the eye of the world something of the Life." It is acknowledged that ἐψηλάφησαν is a quotation of our Lord's own word ψηλαφήσατέ με (Luke 24³⁹); yet "While it is probable that the special manifestation indicated is that given by the Lord after the Resurrection, this is, in fact, the Revelation of Himself as He remains with His Church by the Spirit." In that case, the use of language surely is to conceal thought !

[2] Matt. 13¹⁹, Acts 20³², 2 Cor. 5¹⁹, Phil. 2¹⁶. It is to be observed that none of these parallels is Johannine. In John 6⁶⁸ ῥήματα, not λόγος, is found.

already in the writer's mind, and which requires τῆς ζωῆς
as a point of dependence. The theme of the whole Epistle,
moreover, is Life. Its whole scope is summed up in this:
" These things write I unto you, that ye may know that
ye have eternal life " (5¹³). What then more natural
than, at the outset, to place before the mind of the readers
their Lord and Saviour as the " Word of Life "? (c) There
is not a clause or a word [1] in the Prologue that does not
naturally and inevitably point to the personal Logos—Him
who in the beginning was with God, and was God, and who
" became flesh and tabernacled among us " (John 1¹·¹⁴).

The subject regarding whom the announcement
(ἀπαγγέλλομεν, 1²) is made being the Lord Jesus Christ,
the matter announced is " That which was from the beginning, that which we have heard, that which we have seen
with our (own) eyes, that which we beheld and our (own)
hands handled." From this, two inferences are obvious,
if the words " heard," " seen," " beheld," " handled " are
taken in their natural sense. The first is that the
Prologue does not in any way describe the contents of the
Epistle, but must refer to some other occasion or mode of
announcement. It is true that the reference to the historic
Gospel is here in absolutely the right place. The facts
in which the Divine Life has been personally revealed to
human perception are the fitting and firm basis for the
Epistle with all its theological and ethical developments;
and, doubtless, it is the purpose to impress this upon its
readers that underlies the Prologue. But, since the Epistle
itself contains no announcement whatsoever of such facts,
the reference (ἀπαγγέλλομεν ὑμῖν, 1²) can be only [2] either

---

[1] The single apparent exception to this statement is the use of the neuter ὅ,
instead of the masculine ὅς, in the relative clauses. As to this, see Notes,
in loc.

[2] Those who understand περὶ τοῦ λόγου τῆς ζωῆς as referring to the personal
Logos and yet regard the Prologue as a syllabus of the contents of the Epistle,
are reduced to extremities of exegesis. Rothe, *e.g.*, commenting on " con cerning

to the writer's habitual oral teaching, or to the literary record of it—that is to say, the Fourth Gospel.

The second inference is that the writer claims direct, first-hand acquaintance with the facts of the Saviour's life on earth. The terms in which he describes the substance of his announcement are these [1]—"what we have heard, what we have seen with our eyes," so that any suggestion of subjective, visionary seeing is set aside, "what we gazed upon" ($\epsilon\theta\epsilon\alpha\sigma\acute{\alpha}\mu\epsilon\theta\alpha$, deliberately and of set purpose to satisfy ourselves of its actuality), "what our hands handled" ($\epsilon\psi\eta\lambda\acute{\alpha}\phi\eta\sigma\alpha\nu$, the most incontrovertible evidence of physical fact that human sense can furnish). It is difficult to imagine words more studiously adapted to create the impression that the writer is one of the actual disciples of Jesus. But we are informed [2] that this "superficial impression is corrected" when the language is taken along with such expressions as John 1[14], 1 John 3[6], and 4[14]. Turning to these passages for the correction of our "superficial impression," all that we find is proof that $\acute{o}\rho\hat{\alpha}\nu$ (1 John 3[6]) may certainly, and that $\theta\epsilon\hat{\alpha}\sigma\theta\alpha\iota$[3] may possibly, be used of purely spiritual vision. This does not go far to alter the impression that when one speaks of "what he has seen with his eyes," he intends us to

the Word of Life," explains that the apostle is not (in the Epistle) in a position to announce the whole Word. "Only a drop from the ocean, not the ocean itself, will he give." To find this meaning in $\pi\epsilon\rho\acute{\iota}$ is to be, exegetically, *capable de tout*. Besides, the Epistle does not give even "a drop from the ocean." Haupt, on the other hand, idealises the meaning of $\acute{o}$ $\acute{\alpha}\kappa\eta\kappa\acute{o}\alpha\mu\epsilon\nu$, $\kappa.\tau.\lambda.$, and reaches the conclusion that "while it is the Logos who certainly is present to the writer's view, it is not the Person in Himself, and as such, that is the matter of his announcement, but only that quality in Him which is Life." Thus a mere abstraction, a quality belonging to the Person but considered apart from the Person, is "what we have heard, what we have seen with our eyes," etc.

[1] After $\acute{o}$ $\mathring{\eta}\nu$ $\mathring{\alpha}\pi'$ $\mathring{\alpha}\rho\chi\hat{\eta}s$, which, since it probably refers to the eternal pre-existence of the Logos, is not relevant to the point under discussion.

[2] Moffatt, *Historical New Testament*, p. 621.

[3] In John 1[14] a spiritual element is implied in the "beholding" ($\theta\epsilon\hat{\alpha}\sigma\theta\alpha\iota$), but it is the spiritual beholding of a Divine Glory revealed through facts of sense. In 1 John 4[12] the physical element is undeniable. No one would maintain that the meaning is, "No man has had spiritual perception of God at any time."

understand—well, just what he has seen, or supposes that he has seen, with his eyes.

It is asserted (*ibid.*) that even the "strange metaphor ἐψηλάφησαν is not too strong for the faith-mysticism of the early Church and its consciousness of possessing a direct experience of God in Christ." One desiderates some stronger proof for such a statement than a vivid phrase from so highly rhetorical a writer as Tacitus.[1] Assuredly, if one speaks of "what his hands have handled," meaning thereby his consciousness of a spiritual experience, it is one of the most bewildering uses to which human language has ever been put; and the ordinary mind may well despair of tracing, with any certitude, the meaning of a writer so elusive.

Besides these palpable obstacles to the adoption of the "faith-mysticism" interpretation, there are others, less obvious but not less insuperable. How, on that theory, can we explain the sudden change from the perfect tense[2] in ἀκηκόαμεν and ἑωράκαμεν to the aorist in ἐθεασάμεθα and ἐψηλάφησαν? The change of tense is quite naturally accounted for by referring the aorists to a definite occasion, that, namely, on which the Lord[3] invited His disciples to satisfy themselves of the reality of His Resurrection by the most searching tests of sight and touch (Luke 24^{39}, John 20^{27}). But can it be supposed that any definable diversities as to time or mode of *spiritual* perception are intended to be expressed by such variations of phraseology?

It is to be observed, moreover, that the writer assumes

---

[1] Moffatt quotes "mox nostræ duxere Helvidium in carcerem manus," from Tacitus, *Agricola*, 45, where the commentators debate whether he means his own hands or the hands of the senators. But I fail to perceive in this any analogy whatsoever to the faith-mysticism of the early Church.

[2] These perfects signify that the "hearing" and "seeing," though in the past, have been abiding in their results, one of which is the writer's present ability to bear witness to the facts seen and heard.

[3] ἐψηλάφησαν is a direct quotation of Our Lord's ψηλαφήσατέ με; while ἐθεασάμεθα is the natural response to the repeated ἴδετε in the same verse (Luke 24^{39}).

that, in announcing to his readers his experiences of the
Word of Life, he is communicating what they do not
fully possess (ἀπαγγέλλομεν καὶ ὑμῖν, 1^3).   But if these were
merely spiritual experiences, he could not and would not
write thus.   On the contrary, his constant assumption is
that his readers have full spiritual perception of the truth
($2^{13.\ 14.\ 20.\ 21.\ 27}$ etc.).   And, on the broadest exegetical
grounds, the "faith-mysticism" theory is inadmissible.
It eviscerates the words of precisely that (anti-docetic)
force of testimony they are intended to contain—not to the
ideal truth of the gospel nor to the consciousness of a
spiritual experience, but to the physical reality, certified by
the evidence of every faculty given to man as a criterion
of such reality, of the human embodiment by means of
which alone the glory of the Only-Begotten of the Father
was revealed to the spiritual perceptions of mankind.
Upon that testimony, together with the accompanying
testimony of the Spirit, the whole anti-docetic polemic
of the Epistle is based (2^{24} $4^{6.\ 14}$ 5^{6-8}); and it is incredible that the writer intended these words to be understood in a sense in which Cerinthus himself might have
appropriated them.

It is alleged,[1] however, that the words are susceptible of
an interpretation which, while preserving the natural sense
of "heard," "seen," "beheld," "handled," does not necessitate that the writer be held as making a strictly personal
claim to these experiences.   It is noted that here, in the
Prologue, the author writes in the plural number, while
elsewhere in the Epistle he speaks of himself in the
singular [2] (2^{12-14} 5^{13}), and uses the plural "we" only
when identifying himself with his readers.   And from
this it is argued that all he may have intended was to give

[1] Jülicher, *Introduction to N.T.* p. 247.

[2] There are exceptions to this statement, namely, 4^6 and 4^{14}. It might
be said, however, that in these the reference of "we" is involved in the same
ambiguity as here.

his Epistle the authority of "the collective disciples of Jesus," the emphasis being not on the persons, but on the actuality of the perception. At furthest, this would be possible, apart from unveracity, only if the writer were one who was recognised by the Church as so peculiarly identified with the original witnesses that, without creating a false impression, he could speak of the Apostolic testimony as virtually his own. But, except the presumption that the writer cannot have been one of the original witnesses, there is really nothing to urge in favour of this supposition. The use of the plural here perfectly harmonises with the dignity of the passage; and the same idiom is employed in the Prologue to the Fourth Gospel (1^{14}), where it is not denied that the testimony purports, at least, to be personal. And there are strong arguments to the contrary effect. The very emphatic phraseology—"what we have seen with *our eyes*," "what *our hands* handled"—makes it difficult, if not impossible, to suppose that the writer intends himself to be understood as merely producing the collective testimony of the Apostles, he himself not being of their number. No example of any such *modus loquendi* is found in the New Testament, or is alleged in the patristic literature.[1] And—what seems to be decisive—the author uses in the same passage the same "plural of majesty" of his present writing,[2] as well as

---

[1] This is scarcely accurate. A parallel is alleged from Irenæus (v. i. 1); but it is quoted without its context. The passage is—" Non enim aliter nos discere poteramus quæ sunt Dei, nisi magister noster, verbum exsistens, homo factus fuisset . . . Neque rursus nos aliter discere poteramus, *nisi magistrum nostrum videntes, et per auditum nostrum vocem ejus percipientes.*" It is a travesty of the meaning of this passage to say (as Holtzmann does) that Irenæus reckons himself, in any sense corresponding to our writer's, among those "whose ears have heard and whose eyes have seen." What Irenæus asserts, in both of the sentences quoted, is merely a general and necessary truth. As it was impossible for us to learn the things of God except by the Incarnation of the Word, so also it was impossible for us to receive the revelation of the Incarnate Word except through the medium of human sense. There is as little suggestion of a "collective testimony" as there is of "faith-mysticism."

[2] καὶ ταῦτα γράφομεν, 1^4. Cf. γράφω, 2^{12}; ἔγραψα, $2^{13.14}$ 5^{13}.

4

of the testimony on which he claims to found. So far from suggesting that the writer was merely one who could in some peculiar manner represent the original witnesses of the Incarnation, the language employed resists such an interpretation. He who writes these things" (1^4), is he who announces (1^3) his personal experiences of the incarnate "Word of Life" (1^1). Putting aside, as morally intolerable and inconceivable, the hypothesis of deliberate misrepresentation, we really seem to be shut up to the conclusion that the writer is one of the contemporary witnesses of the Saviour's life on earth.

To sum up, then, what has been gathered from the Epistle itself regarding the writer:—he was intimately acquainted with and profoundly concerned in the religious state and environment of his readers, their attainments, achievements, dangers, and needs; his tone and temper are paternally authoritative and tender; the relation between them is that of teacher and taught; and, finally, he claims that his testimony to the historic Gospel is based on first-hand observation of the facts. Thus the internal evidence agrees so completely with the ancient and un-broken tradition which assigns the authorship of the Epistle to the Apostle John that, unless this traditional authorship is disproved by arguments of the most convincing kind, it must be regarded as holding the field. Whether the arguments brought against the Johannine authorship possess this character is a question which involves the criticism of the Fourth Gospel even more than of the Epistle, and which cannot be investigated here.

Only a fragment of the Johannine problem—the relation of the Epistle to the Fourth Gospel—can be discussed in detail within the limits of this present study; and this discussion it will be well to reserve until we have completed our consideration of the Epistle itself.

Note to the Third Edition.

The Epistle does not fall under either of Deissmann's categories—the true letter, intended for the perusal only of the person or persons to whom it is addressed, and the Epistle, written with literary art and with an eye to the public. But it does possess that character of the N.T. Epistles in general, which is well described by Sir William Ramsay (*Letters to the Seven Churches of Asia*, p. 24): "They spring from the heart of the writer and speak direct to the heart of the readers. They were often called forth by some special crisis in the history of the persons addressed, so that they rise out of the actual situation in which the writer conceives the readers to be placed ; they express the writer's keen and living sympathy with and participation in the fortunes of the whole class addressed, and are not affected by any thought of a wider public. . . . On the other hand, the letters of this class express general principles of life and conduct, religion and ethics, applicable to a wider range of circumstances than those which called them forth ; and they appeal as emphatically and intimately to all Christians in all time as they did to those addressed in the first instance."

CHAPTER IV.

The Doctrine of God as Life and Light.

THE influence of the immediate polemical purpose of the Epistle is manifest in its doctrine of God—manifest not only in its contents, but, first of all, in its exclusions. For, though the conception and delineation of the Divine Nature are the crowning glory of the Epistle, and form its greatest contribution to New Testament thought, it may justly be said that this conception is a narrow one, or, at least, narrowly focussed. The limitations of the writer's field of vision are only less remarkable than the intensity of his perceptions within it. Throughout the Epistle, God is seen exclusively as the Father of spirits, the Light and Life of the universe of souls. His creatorship, His relation to the government of the world and the ordering of human lives, the providential aspects and agencies of His salvation, the working together of nature and grace for the discipline and perfecting of redeemed humanity,—all this is left entirely in the background. From beginning to end, the Epistle contains no direct reference to the terrestrial conditions and changes of human life, or to the joys and sorrows, hopes and fears, that arise from them. These do not come within the scope of the present necessity; it is not from this quarter that the faith of the Church is imperilled. The writer's immediate interest is confined to that region in which the Divine and the human directly and vitally meet —to that in God which is communicable to man, to that in man by which he is capable of participation in the Divine Nature.

From this point of view, the conception of God is presented under four great affirmations: God is Light (1^5); God is Righteous (2^{29}); God is Love (4^8); God is Life (5^{20}). And though, characteristically, St. John makes no endeavour to bring these ideas into an organic unity of thought, their inter-relation is sufficiently clear. Righteousness and Love are the primary ethical qualities of the Divine Nature; Life is the essence in which these qualities inhere; and that God is Light signifies that the Divine Nature, as Righteousness and Love, is self-necessitated to reveal itself so as to become the Truth, the object of faith, and the source of spiritual illumination to every being capable of receiving the revelation. Thus, while Gnostic speculation conceived the Divine Nature metaphysically, as the ultimate spiritual essence in eternal separation from all that is material and mutable, and while Gnostic piety aspired to union with the Divine Life solely by the mystic vision of the Light which is its emanation; with St. John, the conception of God is primarily and intensely ethical. A deity of mere abstract Being could never awaken his soul to worship. His homage is not given to Infinitude or Everlastingness. For him, God is in the least atom of moral good, as He is not in

> "the light of setting suns,
> And the round ocean, and the living air,
> And the blue sky."

For him, the Eternal Life, the very Life of God, brought into the sphere of humanity in the person of Jesus Christ, is Righteousness and Love; and with his whole soul he labours to stamp on the minds of men the truth that only by Righteousness and Love can they walk in the Light of God, and have fellowship in the Life of the Father and of His Son Jesus Christ.

God is Life.[1]

" This is the true God, and Eternal Life " (5^{20}). It is everywhere assumed in the Epistle that God is the absolute *final source* of that life—Eternal Life—the possession of which is the supreme end for which man, and every spiritual nature, exists. This is clearly implied in such a statement as " This is the witness, that God gave us Eternal Life " (5^{11}), and in all the passages, too numerous to be quoted, that speak of the existence of this Life in man as the result of a Divine Begetting. That God is also the *immanent* source of Life—that it exists and is maintained only through a continuous vitalising union with Him, as of the branch with the vine—is no less clearly implied in those equally numerous passages that speak of our abiding in God and God's abiding in us.

In all this it is further implied that God is the source of Life to men because He has Life in Himself. *Omne vivum ex vivo.* Eternal life may be spoken of as His gift (5^{11}, Rom. 6^{23}); but the gift is not extraneous to the Giver. It is nothing else than His self-communication to men, the transmission to us of His own nature. " This is the true God, and Eternal Life " (5^{20}).[2]

It must be observed, however, that St. John nowhere merges the idea of God in that of Life. God is the ultimate Eternal Life; Eternal Life is not God. God is personal,

[1] This part of the subject is treated very briefly. For fuller exposition of the Johannine conception of Life, see Chapter X.

[2] οὗτός ἐστιν ὁ ἀληθινὸς θεὸς καὶ ζωὴ αἰώνιος. See Notes, *in loc.* Even here, it is true, the thought is primarily soteriological. It is not of what God is in Himself, but of what He is in relation to us—the source of Eternal Life. This is clear from the contrast drawn between Him who is " the true God and Eternal Life," and the idols which cannot give life (cf. Jer. 2^{13}), and from which we are exhorted to guard ourselves (5^{21}). But, of course, the thought of what God is in relation to us inevitably passes up into the thought of what God is in Himself.

Life is impersonal; [1] and any manner of thinking by which God is reduced to a pantheistic *anima mundi* is as foreign to St. John as it is to every other Biblical writer. It is noticeable, indeed, that St. John nowhere carries his conception of God as the Life to its full cosmical expansion. It would be in full accord with that conception—it is its religious as well as its logical completion—to say that God, as immanent, is the principle of universal life; that life, throughout the whole hierarchy of creation, from the flower in the crannied wall to the archangel, is a pulse of God's own life, a stream not separated but ever flowing from Him as its fountain-head (Ps. 36[5]). For every finite being life is union with God according to its capacity. But the lower potencies of the creative Life do not come within the Apostle's horizon. Man alone, of terrestrial creatures, has capacity for the highest kind of life, which St. John calls Eternal Life; and his concern is exclusively with this.

What elements, then, are present in St. John's conception of the Divine Life? Primarily, as has been said, this conception is ethical. The activities in which the Life is manifested are those of Righteousness (2[29]), and Love (4[8]). The life God lives is a life absolutely righteous and loving. But the conception is also metaphysical. Essentially, the Eternal Life is nothing else than the Divine Nature itself, regarded, not as abstract being, but dynamically, as the ground and source of all its own manifold activities—as the animating principle [2] in virtue of which the Divine Righteousness and the Divine Love are not mere abstractions, but eternally active forces. And, finally, the Life of God is a principle of self-communication and self-reproduction. It is this by intrinsic necessity. Love cannot but seek to beget love (4[7]); and Righteousness to

---

[1] Even in 1[2], where ἡ ζωὴ ἡ αἰώνιος is, not the Logos, but the pre-incarnate life of the Logos. The Eternal Life is the common element in the personality of God, the Word, and those who are "begotten of God."

[2] *v.* Scott's *Fourth Gospel*, p. 257.

beget righteousness (2^{29}). In the Epistle, this generative activity of the Divine Life holds a place of equal importance with its ethical quality. No thought is more closely interwoven with its whole texture than that of the Divine self-communication. Eternally, the Father imparts Himself to His only-begotten Son (4^9), the Word whose life from the Beginning consisted in His fellowship with the Father (ἥτις ἦν πρὸς τὸν πατέρα, 1^2). To men, Eternal Life is communicated as the result of a Divine act, by which, in the terminology of St. John, they are "begotten of God" and become the "children of God" (τέκνα τοῦ θεοῦ). This actual impartation of the actual Life of God is the core of Johannine soteriology. It is this that makes the Gospel a gospel, and Christ the mediator of a real salvation. "This is the witness, that God gave us Eternal Life, and this Life is in His Son."

God is Light.

"And this is the message which we have heard from Him, and announce again unto you, that God is Light, and in Him is no darkness at all. If we say that we have fellowship with Him, and walk in darkness, we lie, and do not the truth" ($1^{5,\ 6}$).

The words "God is Light," though unrecorded in any of our Gospels, may quite conceivably contain the verbal reminiscence of an actual utterance of our Lord. This, however, is not necessarily implied in St. John's statement. What is asserted is that the whole purport of the Christian Revelation,[1] from a certain point of view, may be said to be this—God is Light. And our endeavour, in the first place, must be to determine the sense in which the symbol is here employed.

Light, the most beautiful and blessed thing in Nature,

---

[1] ἀγγελία is used with exactly the same import in 3^{11}. There the "message" is "that we love one another."

which seems as if created to be the emblem of all purity and splendour, of knowledge, safety, love and joy, and which fits the world to be the abode of the higher forms of life, has been inevitably associated by men of every race and religion with their conception of the Divine. It would lead far from our present purpose, however, to attempt an investigation of the typology of Light in the extra-Biblical religions, or even to examine minutely the symbolic meanings and uses of it that are scattered broadcast over the Scriptures themselves.[1] It will suffice to notice that there are two main lines along which the idea of Light is related, both in the Old Testament and the New, to the being, character and activity of God.

On the one hand, Light is associated physically or symbolically with the Divine *Essence*, and with the heavenly world. Everywhere in the Old Testament, Light is the actual medium of theophany, the physical accompaniment of Jehovah's presence.[2] In the New Testament also, the same conception of Light as pertaining to the essence of Deity—as the physical element, so to say, of the Divine nature—is abundantly present. God " dwells in light that is unapproachable " (I Tim. 6^{16}); and wherever the celestial world is projected into the terrestrial it is in a radiance of supernatural Light.[3] Following this line of analogy, we might infer that here in our Epistle the idea of Light is associated symbolically with the moral Being of God. That God is Light in which there is no darkness, signifies the spotless and radiant perfection of the Divine Holiness.

---

[1] The most comprehensive discussion, both of the Biblical and extra-Biblical typology of light, is contained in Grill's *Untersuchungen über die Entstehung des vierten Evangeliums.*

[2] In the visions of Ezekiel, *e.g.* (Ezek. 1^{28} 3^{23} 10^4 etc.), as the " Glory of the Lord "; which in the Priestly Code is localised, and assumes a definite uniformity as the Shekinah-Glory (Ex. 40^{34}, I Kings 8^{11} etc.).

[3] Cf. Matt. 17^2 28^3, Acts 9^3 12^7 etc. In these and other similar passages the conception is of a Light, supramundane, " above the brightness of the sun," but actual and in some sense physical, emanating from the Divine Presence.

In another class of passages the symbol is used to express the correlative facts of God's self-revelation and of the enlightenment it brings to man's spiritual perceptions. Thus, in the Old Testament, it is the symbol of the illuminative action of the Divine Word (Pss. 19^8 119^{105}), of the Divine Spirit (Ps. 36^{10}, Prov. 20^{27}), and of the witness of the people of God to the surrounding world (Isa. 42^6 49^6 60^{1-3}). In the New Testament this is the prevailing use. Christ is the ἀπαύγασμα of the Father's glory (Heb. 1^3); the Word in whom the Divine Life becomes the Light of men (John 1^4) and of the world (8^{12}); and the prophetic word is a "lamp shining in a dark place" (2 Pet. 1^{19}). The subjective illumination which is the counterpart of the external revelation is also Light. By the "Spirit of wisdom and revelation" the "eyes of the heart" are enlightened (Eph. 1^{18}); and as, in the first creation, God caused Light to shine out of darkness, so now He shines in the heart "to give the light of the knowledge of the glory of God in the face of Jesus Christ" (2 Cor. 4^6).

Now, for the interpretation of the Epistle, it is a question of some importance to determine with which of these ideas, essence or revelation, St. John's conception of the Divine Light comes into line. In my judgment it is with the latter. That God is Light expresses the self-revelation of God; first, as a necessity that belongs to His moral nature; secondly, as the source of all moral illumination. But while maintaining this interpretation I must admit that the exegetical authorities, almost with one voice, declare for the opposite view, namely, that Light here denotes the essential Being of God. "It is the innermost, all-comprehending essence of God, from which all His attributes proceed" (Haupt); "Absolute Holiness and Truth" (Huther); "the Absolute Holiness of God, especially as Love" (Rothe); "the new idea of God as unconditioned

Goodness, holy Love" (Beyschlag, ii. 450); "the Love which constitutes the essence of God" (Grill, p. 312). To this whole class of interpretations there is only one objection—a serious one, however—that they are irrelevant to the context. While this interpretation of the Light as absolute Holiness or Love serves admirably for this single sentence (1⁵), taken by itself, it will be found that it entirely dislocates the continuity of thought that runs through the paragraph (1⁵⁻²²). Examining this paragraph as a whole, we find that the unifying idea is not the Light, but is fellowship with God. St. John does not introduce the thought that God is Light as an independent thesis. He does not develop it, or even recur to it. It is introduced only for the sake of leading up to what follows, "If we say that we have fellowship with Him and walk in darkness, we lie, and do not the truth." In fact, it is the logical starting-point for the whole paragraph—the major premise from which the Apostle proceeds, in the course of the paragraph, to draw a number of conclusions regarding the conditions of fellowship with God. These conditions are, abstractly and summarily, that "we walk in the Light, as He is in the Light" (1⁷). Light is the medium in which fellowship between God and man is consciously realised; the first element which He and we may possess in common. The crucial question, moreover, is as to what this condition of fellowship—walking in the Light—signifies for *sinful men*; for, as St. John immediately proceeds to insist, to "walk in the Light" is, first and indispensably, to confess our sins (1⁸⁻¹⁰). Obviously, therefore, the Light cannot signify the absolute moral perfection of God. For sinners, fellowship with God cannot, initially, consist in sharing His moral perfection. The Light in which we, being yet sinful, can walk so as to have fellowship with God, is the Light of Truth, the Light which His self-revelation sheds upon all objects in the moral universe, and, first of all, upon ourselves and our sin. The clue to the whole passage, in short, is the idea of fellowship.[1]   As in nature Light is the medium of fellowship,—the social element in which all creatures, whatever their affinities or antagonisms, may meet and be revealed one to another,—so, in the spiritual sphere, the Light, the source of which is the self-revelation of God, is the medium of fellowship between all spiritual beings.   And especially is it the element in which we, though yet sinful, can have fellowship with God; because, when by confessing our sins we walk in the Light, "the Blood of Jesus, His Son, cleanseth us from all sin."

The single meeting-place of the Holy God and sinful men is, to begin with, the Truth; the only medium of their fellowship, a common view of spiritual realities.   And it is because God is Light that this is possible.   As it is said in the most Johannine of the Psalms, "In Thy Light shall we see light."

I. That God is Light signifies, therefore, in the first place, that the Divine Nature is, by inherent moral necessity, self-revealing.[2]   As Light, by its nature, cannot be self-contained, but is ever seeking to impart itself, pouring through every window and crevice, shining into every eye, bathing land and sea with its pure radiance ; so God, from His very nature of Righteousness and Love, is necessitated to reveal Himself as being what He is.   He is Light, and as such is always seeking to shine into the minds He has made in His own Image.   "And in Him is no darkness at all."[3]

---

[1] So Westcott (p. 14).   Yet, having grasped the clue, he does not follow it up.   Having struck the nail on the head, he proceeds to make a circle of dints all around it.

[2] So Weiss, though somewhat inadequately: "God is Light denotes the fact that He has become visible, namely, in Christ, in whom He is completely revealed."   "God is Light means in modern language that it is the nature of God to communicate Himself" (Inge, *Dict. of Christ*, i. 892b).   "The transcendent life streaming out on men, the absolute nature of God as Truth, as the Supreme reality for man to believe in " (Moffatt, *ibid.* ii. 34a).

[3] The idea of Light is one which plays a various but always prominent part in the Gnostic theologies and cosmogonies.   And it may very well be that the aim of the writer of the Epistle was partly, at least, to emphasise as supreme

In God there is nothing that hides, nothing that is hidden. In the Light of His self-revelation there is no darkness, because in His nature there is no inconsistency, no variableness, no secret reserve. God, as revealed in Christ, is knowable as no other Being is. His holiness, justice, and love are beyond knowledge, not because there is in Him anything that is not holiness, justice, and love, but because these, as they exist in Him, are beyond the measure of man's mind. The Divine character is utterly transparent —goodness without a shadow of evil. It is Light in which there is no darkness, to which there is no arresting horizon, that streams through the spiritual universe from Him who is its Sun, the Word of Life.[1]

II. But this thought of God's self-revelation carries with it, as its correlative, the thought of man's illumination thereby. As the light of the sun not only reveals the sun itself, but brings all things in their proper forms and colours to our vision, so the Light of God makes all things in the spiritual realm visible in their true character. As all truth is God's thought, and all finite intelligence is

the moral significance of the Divine Light, as opposed to the merely intellectual, or, on the other hand, semi-physical conceptions of Gnosticism. Westcott thinks that in the emphatic "in Him is no darkness at all" there is a reference to "Zoroastrian speculation on the two opposing spiritual powers." But Zoroastrianism did not teach that there are two opposing powers in *God*. Holtzmann, again, finds a protest against any idea of a σύγχυσις ἀρχική, such as was subsequently developed in the Basilidian system. But the doctrine of Basilides (Clem. *Strom.* ii. 20. 112), that the corruption of the human soul is due to an original confusion and mixture of Light and Darkness (κατά τινα τάραχον καὶ σύγχυσιν ἀρχικήν), has no perceptible relevance to St. John's dictum, "God is Light, and in Him is no darkness at all." The Antinomianism which the Epistle combats must have had as its basis a dualistic conception of the *Universe*; but there is no indication that it carried this dualism back into the Divine nature itself.

[1] In the Prologue to the Fourth Gospel, the concatenation of ideas is exactly parallel to that which I have endeavoured to establish in the Epistle. As here we have successively the ideas of the Word (1¹), the Life (1²), and the Light (1⁵); so there, "In the beginning was the Word" (1¹); "In Him was Life, and the Life was the Light of men" (1⁴). In the Gospel it is quite evident that the idea of Light is attached not to the Divine Essence, but to the self-revelation of God in the Word.

participation in the light of the Eternal Reason; so, in the moral sphere, the character that things have in the moral judgments of God and the view of them that is given in the light of His self-revealment constitute what is called, in Johannine phrase, ἡ ἀλήθεια the Truth.   And it is in their perception of the Truth, their illumination by the Divine Light, that there exists for all moral beings a medium of conscious fellowship with God.   For sinful men, especially, this is the only possible medium of such fellowship. We can come to the Light and walk in the Light, as He is in the Light (1⁷).   Light is the translucent atmosphere in which, even while still morally imperfect and impure, we can come to have a common perception of moral facts and a true fellowship of mind with Him who is the absolutely Good.   This, indeed, is the basis of spiritual religion; it is this that distinguishes Christianity from irrational superstitions and unethical ritualism.   It is no merely emotional, mystical, or sacramentarian fellowship with God that St. John declares to us; but a fellowship in the Truth, in thought and knowledge, and in all that springs from them.   God is not Life merely; He is Light also.   And the complete Johannine conception may be expressed in this, that Life is the medium of our sub-conscious, Light of all our conscious fellowship with God and with one another (1⁷).

The relation to God in which such fellowship is consciously realised is expressed throughout the Epistle, as in the Gospel, by the characteristic use of the verb " to know " (γινώσκειν).[1]

---

[1] To "know Him" (2⁴) is equivalent to "being in Him" (2⁵ᵇ), and to "abiding in Him" (2⁶). The children of God "know the Father" (2¹⁴). "Every one that loveth is begotten of God and knoweth God" (4⁷). "We have received an understanding that we should know Him that is true " (5²⁰). The antithesis of this relation is expressed as "not knowing" (3⁶ 4⁸); more emphatically by "lie" and "liar" (1⁶ 2⁴·²²). It must be observed that γινώσκειν invariably denotes knowledge, not by ratiocination, but by spiritual perception.

See, further, special note on γινώσκειν.

But the conception of spiritual knowledge, in all its presuppositions and in all its consequences, is equally remote from Rationalism and from Gnosticism. The perception of spiritual truth is as little attainable by logical faculty or common intelligence as it is by theosophic contemplation. Spiritual regeneration is the prerequisite of spiritual illumination. Those only who are "begotten of God" have the power to "see" and "know" Divine realities. God *is* Light; and had human nature been animated by a normal and healthy spiritual life, the Divine illumination would have flowed in upon it uninterruptedly by all its channels of affinity with the Divine nature. And, indeed, St. John's thought is that the Light never has been, never could be, wholly withdrawn. But "the Light shineth in the darkness, and the darkness apprehended it not" (John 1⁵). As the original state of every man is death (3¹⁴), so is it also blindness. And "Except a man be born from above, he cannot see the kingdom of God" (John 3⁸). The fundamental Johannine position is that the whole redemptive process has its origin, not in any conscious human act, but in an antecedent activity of the Divine Life in man; and the first fruit and manifestation of this activity is the power to "see," to "believe" on Him who is the Light, to "know" God whom He reveals.[1]

Yet, since Light is the element of conscious activity, of conscious obedience or disobedience (John 7²⁴), of sincerity or insincerity (John 3¹⁹⁻²¹), the Epistle strongly emphasises the office of human volition in the response made to it. The Light is a message in the imperative, not only in the indicative mood; and the Epistle speaks not of "seeing," but of "walking in the Light." The conception, in both Gospel and Epistle, is that, while the light, which shines around all men, becomes a power of saving illumination only in those who, as

[1] See, further, Chapters X. and XIII.

" begotten of God," are responsive to its influence, none can be entirely unconscious of its *being there*, or entirely insusceptible to its claims upon him. But men may close the shutters of the soul's windows against it. With an instinctive premonition of what it would constrain them to see and acknowledge, to do and forego, men may and do employ devices of various subtlety to fortify the mind against its entrance. As in the primeval story the covert of the trees of the garden is preferred to the Light of God's presence, so still " This is the judgment, that the light is come into the world, and men loved the darkness rather than the light, for their works were evil " (John 3^{19}).

A brief study of the paragraph (1^5–2^2) will show that this interpretation of the Light fits into the context like a key into its proper lock. The thesis of the whole paragraph is that " walking in the Light " is the one necessary and sufficient condition of fellowship with God. This is first stated in the most abstract form. " God is Light, and in Him is no darkness at all. If we say that we have fellowship with Him, and walk in darkness, we lie, and do not the truth " ($1^{5, 6}$). Here the affirmation is not merely (as in 2 Cor. 6^{14}) that two elements so opposite in nature as light and darkness, holiness and sin, purity and impurity, cannot mix and coalesce. What is in view is the irreconcilable *effect* of light and darkness. Light is that which reveals; darkness, that which conceals. Light is the medium in which we come to see as God sees, to have a true perception of all moral objects—qualities, actions, and persons. To " walk in the Light " is, therefore, to have, in the first place, the will to see all things in the Light of God, and to acknowledge and act up to what is thus seen to be the truth. To " walk in darkness " is the effort, instinctive or deliberate, not to see, or the failure to acknowledge and act up to what is seen ; to withdraw ourselves, our duties, our actions, our character, our relation to the facts and laws of the spiritual realm, from the light which God's self-revealment sheds upon them. And to do this is, *ipso facto*, to exclude the possibility of fellowship with God.

That this is the Apostle's meaning becomes still more apparent as we follow the concrete development of the thought in the remainder of the paragraph. This is composed of three parallel pairs of antitheses ($1^{6.\ 7}$ $1^{8.\ 9}$ 1^{10}–2^2), which may be arranged thus :

DARKNESS-SERIES.	LIGHT-SERIES.
1^6 "If we say that we have fellowship with Him, and walk in darkness, we lie, and do not the truth."	1^7 "If we walk in the light, as He is in the light, we have fellowship one with another, and the Blood of Jesus His Son cleanseth us from all sin."
1^8 "If we say that we have no sin, we deceive ourselves, and the truth is not in us."	1^9 "If we confess our sins, He is faithful and righteous to forgive us our sins, and to cleanse us from all unrighteousness."
1^{10} "If we say that we have not sinned, we make Him a liar, and His word is not in us."	2^1 "If any man sin, we have an advocate with the Father, Jesus Christ the righteous."

From this it is evident that to "walk in the Light" is, first of all, to confess sin ; to walk in the darkness, to ignore or to deny sin. All things assume a different aspect in the Light of God ; but nothing looks so different as we ourselves do. The first fact on which the light impinges is our sin. But, though it exposes sin in all its horror, we may loyally submit to and endorse the result— we may come to the Light and walk in it ; or we may "rebel against the Light" (Job 24^{13}) and "love the darkness." The "darkness," therefore, is not the "world," nor "sin, especially as impurity" (Rothe). It is, in this instance, self-concealment, the cloud of sophistry and self-deception which it is always the instinct of guilt to gather around itself. To "walk in darkness" is not necessarily, indeed, to live a double life under any of the deeper shades of deliberate hypocrisy. For the exclusion of the

5

Light, conscious dissimulation is comparatively ineffective. Simply to pursue the everyday life of business and pleasure, of purpose and achievement, without reference to the Will of God ; to live by the false and mutilated standards of the world ; to be blinded by the glare of its artificial illuminations—there are no more effectual and frequented ways than these of walking in darkness.

It is needless for our present purpose to pursue further the exposition of this paragraph.[1]   And it must suffice to indicate in a sentence how, in the remainder of this whole section of the Epistle (1^5–2^{29}), the contrast between walking in the Light and walking in darkness is developed.

The Light of God not only reveals sin (1^7–2^2), it reveals Duty (2^{3-6}) ; especially, it reveals Love as the highest law for the children of God (2^{7-11}) ; as it also reveals in their true character the " world and the things that are in the world," so that it is seen that " if any man love the world, the love of the Father is not in him " (2^{15-17}).   Finally, the light reveals Jesus as the Christ, the Incarnate Son of God (2^{18-28}).   He who denies the glorious reality of the Incarnation is a " liar," and is blind to the Light of God.

" God is Light " signifies the inward necessity of the Divine Nature to reveal itself, the fact of its perfect and eternal self-revelation in Christ, and the correlative fact of men's spiritual illumination thereby.   This is the only conception of the Light that fits into the train of thought running through this whole section of the Epistle.

[1] See Chapters VIII. and IX.

CHAPTER V.

THE DOCTRINE OF GOD AS RIGHTEOUSNESS AND LOVE.

God is Righteous (2²⁹).

GOD is Life, self-imparting; God is Light, self-revealing. But what, in itself, is the Divine Nature, the communication of which is Life and the revelation of which is Light? It is solely within the ethical sphere that the Epistle contemplates this question; and in the unity of God's moral being, two, and only two, elements are distinguished —Righteousness and Love. From these the whole moral activity of the Divine Life proceeds; and, as a necessary consequence, it is by the impartation of these same qualities to human nature that the whole development of the regenerate life is determined.

The words Righteous and Righteousness ($\delta i\kappa a\iota o\varsigma$, $\delta\iota\kappa a\iota o\sigma\acute{u}\nu\eta$) are used only in the broadest sense. They express neither the Pauline idea of forensic status nor the specific virtue of justice, the *voluntas suum cuique tribuendi*, but the sum of all that is right in character and conduct. Righteousness includes all of which sin is the negation. "Every one that doeth righteousness is begotten of God" (2²⁹), but "He that doeth sin is of the devil" (3⁸); and again, "Whosoever doeth not righteousness is not of God" (3¹⁰), but "Whosoever is begotten of God doeth not sin" (3⁹). Righteousness and sin divide between them the whole area of moral possibility.

That such Righteousness belongs to, or rather is, the

character of God, and that this is the basis of all Christian
Ethics, is everywhere implied, and is categorically asserted
in (2²⁹) ἐὰν εἰδῆτε ὅτι δίκαιός ἐστιν, γινώσκετε¹ ὅτι καὶ πᾶς
ὁ ποιῶν τὴν δικαιοσύνην ἐξ αὐτοῦ γεγέννηται. " If ye know
that He is righteous, know (or, ye know) that every one
also that doeth righteousness is begotten of Him."

The argument presupposes, in the first place, that
Righteousness in God and in man is one and the same.
Like begets like ; the stream has the quality of the fountain.
It presupposes, in the second place, that God, and He alone,
is originally and essentially righteous—there is no other
source from which human righteousness can be derived.

The Righteousness that belongs to the inward character of God extends also to His action; it ensures
rightness, unfailing self-consistency, in all that He does.
Thus, " If we confess our sins, He is faithful and
righteous (πιστός ἐστιν καὶ δίκαιος) to forgive us our
sins, and to cleanse us from all unrighteousness." When,
on the ground of Christ's propitiation, God forgives those
who by confession make forgiveness possible, He is
" righteous "; and because He is " righteous," He is
" faithful." He does not deny Himself (2 Tim. 2¹³). He
does what is according to His character, because He does
what is right.

But the activity of God's Righteousness, which is most
conspicuous in the Epistle, is that in which it is directly
and imperatively related to the whole moral action of His
creatures. The² Righteousness of God is that which

---

¹ The delicate differentiation of the two verbs to " know " is very noticeable
here. The εἰδῆτε of the first clause expresses the knowledge absolutely, as a
first principle assumed in all cogitation upon the subject ; the γινώσκετε of the
second clause expresses the art of mental perception by which knowledge, in the
particular instance, is acquired: The full sense of the verse is, " If ye know,
as ye do absolutely know, that He is righteous, recognise (or, ye recognise), as
implied in this, that every one also," etc. See special note on γινώσκειν and
εἰδέναι.

² On the whole subject of this paragraph, see, further, Chapter XI.

renders sin inadmissible in them; inadmissible *de jure* in all, inadmissible *de facto* in those who are "begotten of Him."

This the writer maintains with unexampled strenuousness and rigour. The Righteousness of God is Law for all men and for all their actions. "Sin is lawlessness; and every one that doeth sin doeth also lawlessness" (3^4). Nothing excites in St. John a warmer indignation than the supposition of compatibility between a life of actual wrong-doing and fellowship with the Righteous God. "He that saith, I know Him, and keepeth not His commandments, is a liar, and the truth is not in Him" (2^4). "Every one that doeth not righteousness is not of God" (3^{10}), but is "of the devil" (3^8). Not less absolutely is it insisted that all who are "begotten of Him" and in fellowship with Him partake of His Righteousness. "Every one that is begotten of God doth not commit sin, because His seed abideth in Him; and he cannot sin, because He is begotten of God" (3^9). "We know that every one that is begotten of God sinneth not; but he that was begotten of God keepeth himself, and the Wicked One toucheth him not" (5^{18}). It is an inveterate misreading of the Epistle that represents its author as being almost exclusively the "Apostle of Love." Intense as is St. John's gaze into the heavenly abyss of the Divine Love, it seems impossible that any writing could display a more impassioned sense, than this Epistle does, of the tremendous imperative of Righteousness—a more rigorous intolerance of sin. So long as the Church lays up this Epistle in its heart, it can never lack a spiritual tonic of wholesome severity.

It is true, however, that in its doctrine of Divine Righteousness, thoroughly spontaneous as it is, the Epistle makes no remarkable contribution to the development of New Testament thought. It does no more than restate, in a peculiarly forceful fashion, and with all the glow of an original intuition, that conception of the Divine Nature which is fundamental to the whole Biblical revelation. It must be conceded, moreover, that the assertion of the impeccability of the regenerate, into which the Writer, apparently at least, is led by the vehemence of the polemical interest, has tended to detract from the full usefulness of his teaching on this head. However effectively the unique form of expression employed may have been adapted to the peculiarities of the immediate situation, it has been to later generations a paradox and a puzzle rather than a source of instruction or a practical stimulus. It is far otherwise with the next of the great affirmations which constitute the Epistle's doctrine of God.

God is Love (4[8]).

Here the Epistle rises to the summit of all revelation; and, for the first time, enunciates that truth which not only is the profoundest, gladdest, most transforming that the mind can conceive, but is the beginning and the end— the truth in which all truths have their ultimate unity, the innermost secret of existence.

The New Testament word for Love, ἀγάπη, is virtually a coinage of Christianity. It may be that it is an old word reminted; but it is one of the curiosities, at least, of philology that, while the verb ἀγαπᾶν is fairly common in classical Greek from Homer downwards, the noun ἀγάπη is not found in any extant classical text; a single passage in Philo supplying the solitary instance of its extra-Biblical use.[1] This does not prove, indeed, that it was unknown to non-literary Greek; and Deissmann may be

---

[1] Even in the Septuagint there are only fifteen occurrences, eleven of them in Canticles, where the sexual tinge is unmistakable, as also in 2 Sam. 13[15] and Jer. 2[2]. In Eccles. 9[1. 6] it is opposed to μῖσος in a more general sense.

right in supposing it to have been current in the Egyptian vernacular.[1] The fact remains, however, that though the Greek language is rich in terms [2] answering to " love " in its various shades of meaning, the comparatively unused ἀγάπη was, as it were, providentially reserved to express that purely ethical love the conception of which Christianity first made current among men.

In the Epistle the words ἀγάπη and ἀγαπᾶν are used to express an energy of the moral nature in God towards men, in men towards God, in men towards one another. And one of its profound truths is that, in whatever relation it may operate, Love is one and the same. All love has its origin in God; and human love is the moral nature of God incarnate in man. " Every one that loveth is begotten of God " (4⁷). And, since nothing moral can exist merely in the form of action, Love is, primarily, a disposition, a permanent quality of the Will, an inherent tendency of the moral nature. The quality of this disposition is indicated by the fact that the object of Love in the human relation is invariably our " brother." [3] We may disregard the fact that brotherhood here denotes not physical but spiritual relationship ; for the spiritual presupposes the physical analogue. And though, in fact, it is not brotherhood that makes Love (2¹¹ 3¹²), but Love that makes brotherhood, Love may be said to be that mutual disposition which ideally exists among brothers in the same family — the disposition to act towards our fellow-men as it is natural for those

---

[1] The supposed discovery of the word in a papyrus of the second century B.C., announced by Deissmann in his *Bibel-Studien* (1895), has been abandoned (*Expository Times*, September 1898, p. 567). But its adoption instead of ἔρως by the LXX may be thought to lend probability to the supposition of its Egyptian origin.

[2] στοργή, the love that belongs to natural kinship ; ἔρως, with its predominant suggestion of sexuality ; φιλία, specially appropriated to friendship.

[3] 2¹⁰ 3¹⁰. ¹⁴. ¹⁶. ¹⁷ 4²⁰. ²¹.

to do who have all interests in common, and who instinctively recognise that the full self-existence of each can be realised only through a larger corporate existence. Love is the power to live not only for another, but in another, to realise one's own fullest life in the fulfilment of other lives.

Love is such a disposition, and such a disposition of necessity issues in appropriate action. In the Epistle nothing is more incisively dealt with than the fiction of a love that is inoperative in practice. "Whoso hath this world's good, and seeth his brother have need, and shutteth up his bowels of compassion from him, how dwelleth the love of God in him?" (3^{17}). That which terminates in the mere self-satisfaction of "feeling good," whatever it may be, is something else than Love. Love is the giving impulse. And it rejoices, not only in imparting benefits, the cost of which is imperceptible and the bestowal of which is a sheer luxury: it expresses itself most fully in sacrifice. It is that complete identification of self with another which makes it sometimes imperative, and always possible, to lay down even our lives for our brethren (3^{16}), and which, indeed, realises an exquisite joy in suffering endured for the beloved's sake.

In human history, Love has its one absolute embodiment in the self-sacrifice of Christ. "Hereby know we love," says the Epistle in one of its pregnant sentences, hereby do we perceive what Love is, "in that He laid down His Life for us" (3^{16}). This is the Absolute of Love—its everlasting type and standard. The world had never been without the dower of Love. It had known love like Jacob's, like David's and Jonathan's, the patriot's and the martyr's self-devotion. But till Jesus Christ came and laid down His Life for the men that hated and mocked and slew Him, the world had not known what Love in its greatness and purity could be.

And the Love of Christ in laying down His Life for us is the manifestation, under the conditions of time and sense, of the Love of God, eternal and invisible. God is Love; but what God is can be known only through His self-manifestation. Wherein does this consist? Not in word only. It was not enough that He should *say* that He is Love (cf. 3[18]). Not in the works of Nature and Providence alone. These are but starlight. The Epistle points us to the Sun (4[9. 10]).

" Herein was manifested the Love of God toward us, that God hath sent His Son, His Only Begotten, into the world, that we might live through Him. Herein is Love, not that we loved God, but that God loved us, and sent His Son (as) a propitiation for our sins." [1]

The first of these two verses emphasises the fact that God *is* Love, and exhibits the proof of it (" Herein was the Love of God manifested "); the second, the nature of Love itself, so manifested. But, taking both in one view, we perceive that there are five factors which here contribute to the full conception of Divine Love.

(1) First, the magnitude of its *gift* is set forth. " His Son, His Only Begotten." Elsewhere, the title of Our Lord is simply " the Son," the argument turning upon the relation of Father and Son; or " His Son," or the " Son of God," where the element of Divine power and dignity in the Sonship is made more prominent. Here only,[2] where he would display the infinite Love in the infinite Gift, does St. John use the full title, τὸν υἱὸν αὐτοῦ τὸν μονογενῆ. The essence of the manifestation is in the fact, not that God sent Jesus, but that Jesus, who was sent, is God's Only-Begotten Son. The full being of God is present in Him. Other gifts are only tokens of God's Love. Its all is given

---

[1] See Notes, *in loc.*
[2] In the Gospel, only in the parallel passage, John 3[16].

in Christ. It is His own bleeding heart the Father lays on Love's altar, when He offers His Only-Begotten Son (cf. Gen. 22^{12} and Rom. 8^{32}). (2) Secondly, the magnitude of the Love is exhibited in the person of the Giver. It was a father who thus sent his only-begotten son; but that father was God ($\dot{o}$ $\theta\epsilon\dot{o}\varsigma$, not $\dot{o}$ $\pi\alpha\tau\dot{\eta}\rho$, as in 4^{14}). It was the Divine Nature whose whole wealth was poured out in the sacrifice of Calvary. (3) Thirdly, the Love of God is manifested in the *purpose* of the mission of the Son. This purpose is "that we might live through Him,"[1] in which is implicitly contained the "should not perish" of John 3^{16}. The Love of God is thus seen to be His self-determination not only to rescue men from what is the sum of all evils, but to impart to them the supreme and eternal good, Life. (4) Fourthly, the Love of God is manifested in the *means* by which this purpose is achieved, God shrinks not from the uttermost cost of Redemption. His Son is sent as a "propitiation for our sins." He not only dies heroically on our behalf, as the good shepherd lays down his life in defending his helpless flock from the fangs of the wolf or the assault of the robber; but, as a father drinks a full cup of sorrow and humiliation in striving to make atonement for the criminal profligacies of an unworthy son, even so, Almighty God, in the person of His Son, humbles Himself and suffers unto blood for the sins of His creatures. Such is the Love of God to men; and what can be said of it, except that it is at once incredible that the fact should be so, and impossible that it should be otherwise? It is what never did, never could, flit within the horizon of man's most daring dream; it is that which, when it is revealed, shines with self-evidencing light. It needs no argument. Apologetic is superfluous.[2]

---

[1] $\tilde{\iota}\nu\alpha$ $\zeta\dot{\eta}\sigma\omega\mu\epsilon\nu$ $\delta\iota'$ $\alpha\dot{v}\tauo\hat{v}$. Cf. John 3$^{15.\ 16}$ 6$^{51.\ 57}$ 10^{10} 11$^{25.\ 26}$ 14^{19}.

[2]   " What doubt in thee could countervail
    Belief in it? Upon the ground

Such Love is *Divine.* The Being whose nature this is, is God.

But these statements ought, perhaps, to have been reserved until we had considered the final moment in the full conception of Divine Love, *its objects.* (5) "Herein is Love, not that we loved God, but that God loved us." The interpretation popularly put upon this verse, as equivalent to "Herein is love, that, although we did *not* love God, God loved us," is grammatically untenable,[1] and it misses the point in one of the profoundest sentences in the Epistle. The Apostle does not say that we have not loved God. What he says is that we *have* loved God, but that this is not love to call love. That we have loved God is nothing wonderful. The ineffable mystery of Love reveals itself in this, that God has loved us, who are so unworthy of His Love, and so repulsive to all the sensibilities, so to say, of His moral nature. The full glory of the Divine Love is seen in the fact that it is wholly self-created and self-determined.

It may be permissible to elucidate this truth somewhat more fully. As we have seen, Love is that mysterious power by which we live in the lives of others, and are thus moved to benevolent and even self-sacrificing action on their behalf. Such love is, after all, one of the most universal things in humanity. But always natural human

> That in the story had been found
> Too much Love? How could God love so?
> . . . . . .
> While man, who was so fit instead
> To hate, as every day gave proof,—
> Man thought man, for his kind's behoof,
> Both could and did invent that scheme
> Of perfect Love; 't would well beseem
> Cain's nature thou wast wont to praise,
> Not tally with God's usual ways."
>
> Browning's *Easter Day.*

[1] See Notes, *in loc.*

love is a flame that must be kindled and fed by some quality
in its object.　It finds its stimulus in physical instinct, in
gratitude, in admiration, in mutual congeniality and liking.
Always it is, in the first place, a passive emotion, determined
and drawn forth by an external attraction.　But the Love
of God is the ever-springing fountain.　Its fires are self-
kindled.　It is love that shines forth in its purest splendour
upon the unattractive, the unworthy, the repellent.　Herein
is Love, in its purest essence and highest potency, not in
our love to God, but in this, that God loved us.　Hence
follows the apparently paradoxical consequence, upon
which the Epistle lays a unique emphasis, that our love to
God is not even the most godlike manifestation of Love in
us.　It is gratitude for His benefits, adoration of His
perfections—our response to God's love to us but not its
closest reproduction in kind.　In this respect, indeed, God's
love to man and man's love to God form the opposite
poles, as it were, of the universe of Love, the one self-
created and owing nothing to its object, the other entirely
dependent upon and owing everything to the infinite
perfection of its object; the one the overarching sky, the
other merely its reflection on the still surface of the lake.
And it is, as the Epistle insists, not in our love to God,
but in our Christian love to our fellow-men, that the Divine
Love is reproduced, with a relative perfection, in us ($4^{12.\ 19.\ 20}$;
cf. Eph. 4^{32}–5^2).

Such is the conception of the Love of God that St.
John sets before us.　In this entirely spontaneous, self-
determined devotion of God to sinful men, this Divine
passion to rescue them from sin, the supreme evil, and
to bestow on them the supreme good, Eternal Life:
in this, which is evoked by their need, not by their
worthiness, which goes to the uttermost length of
sacrifice, and bears the uttermost burden of their self-
inflicted doom—in this, which is for ever revealed in the

mission of Jesus Christ, God's Only-Begotten Son—is Love.

This is at once the norm and the inspiration of all that is most truly to be called Love. Love is no merely passive, involuntary emotion awakened in one person by another. In the Epistle, as everywhere in the New Testament, it is a duty ($4^{7, 11}$), a subject of command-ment ($2^{7, 8}$ 3^{23b} 4^{21}), and is, therefore, a moral self-deter-mination which, in man, must often act in direct opposition to natural instinct and inclination. And this is a self-determination to do good, good only, and always the highest good possible (4^9), without regard to merit or attractiveness in the object (4^{10a}), and that even at highest cost to self[1] (4^{10b}).

Yet such a definition would be adequate only to one half of what Love is. Love is not solely benevolence issuing in beneficence. In its highest as well as in its lowest forms it contains the element of appetency. In its lower forms Love is predominantly an egoistic and appropriative impulse; in its highest form it becomes that marvellous power which reconciles and identifies the apparently opposite principles, egoism and altruism. One finds one's richest satisfaction in the happiness of others, one's own fullest self-realisation in promoting theirs. Love seeks not its own, yet makes all things its own. It is the utmost enrichment and enlargement of Life. " My beloved is mine "—a possession of which nothing can rob me. The more perfect the love, the more completely achieved is this mysterious result, this self-enlargement by self-communica-tion, this self-losing which is the real self-finding. If I love my neighbour as myself, I regale myself with his prosperity, even as I share the bitter cup of his adversity; I am honoured in his praise, promoted in his advancement, gladdened in his joy, even as I am humbled in his shame or

---

[1] Cf. J. M. Gibbon, *Eternal Life*, p. 106.

distressed in his sin.   In short, we might define the highest
Love as that state of the moral nature in which the egoistic
and the altruistic principles coalesce and are fused into one
living experience.   Such is the perpetual *miracle* of Love.
Such is it in man.   Such also is it in God, as it is delineated
in the New Testament.   No less than benevolence, God's
Love displays the element of infinite desire and yearning
quest.   It seeks the lost as the shepherd seeks the strayed
sheep upon the mountains ; as a father's heart yearns after
a wayward son.   It becomes the source of an infinite
Divine joy over the sinner that repenteth ; and because of
the joy, it endures the cross and despises the shame.   It is
in God's Love, and transcendently in His self-sacrifice for
the sinful and lost, that the Divine Life comes to its fullest
self-realisation.   And, though it is the self-communicating
aspect of Divine Love that alone is presented in the Epistle,
yet, always, Love is that for which self-communication
is the fullest self-assertion, and all that Love is, is
ascribed in its supreme perfection to God.   God is Love.

(1) He is Love *essentially*.   Like the sunlight which
contains in itself all the hues of the spectrum, Love is
not one of God's attributes, but that in which all His
moral attributes have their unity.   The spring of all
His actions, the explanation of all He does or ever can
do is Love.   (2) Therefore, also, His Love is *universal*.
If there were any of His creatures whom He did not
love, this would prove that there was something in His
nature that was not Love, but was opposed to Love.
Whatever be the mysteries of the past, present, or future,
God is Love.   That is St. John's great truth.   He does
not attempt to reconcile with it other and apparently
conflicting truths in his theological scheme ; possibly he
was not conscious of any need to do so.   But of this
he is sure—God is Love.   That fact must, in ways we
cannot yet discern, include all other facts.   No being is

unloved. Nothing happens that is not dictated or over-ruled by Love. (3) And if essential and universal, the Love of God is also *eternal and unchangeable*. It does not depend on any merit or reciprocation in its object, but overflows from an infinite fulness within itself. Our goodness did not call it forth; neither can our evil cause it to cease.

> "Love is not love
> Which alters when it alteration finds,
> Or bends with the remover to remove."

We may refuse to the Divine Love any inlet into our nature, may refuse to let it have its way with us, may so identify ourselves with evil as to turn it into an antagonistic force. This is the most awful fact in human life. But the sun is not extinguished, though shutters be closed and blinds drawn at midday; and though we may shut out God from our hearts, no being can by any means shut himself out from the great Heart of God. God is Love. It is the surest of all intuitions; the strongest corner-stone of the Christian Faith. Having known and believed the Love of God which is in Christ Jesus our Lord— the Love that came not by water only, but by blood also—we can tolerate no other conception of the Divine. (4) From all this it follows that we cannot ultimately con-ceive of God as a single and simple personality. Love, no more than Thought, can exist without an object. If we say that God was eternally the object of His own Love, we deny to Him the supreme prerogative of Love, self-communication. If we say that, either in time or from eternity, God created the universe in order to have an object for His Love, we make the Universe as necessary to God as God is to the Universe. His Love in creation was not the overflowing of the fountain, but the craving of the empty vessel. It is at this point that the Trini-tarian doctrine becomes most helpful. It enables us to think of the Life of God not as an eternal solitude of

self-contemplation and self-love, but as a life of communion :
—the Godhead is filled with Love, the Love of the
Father and the Son in the unity of the Spirit. So far
from being a burden to faith, the doctrine of the Divine
Trinity sheds a welcome light upon the mystery of God's
Eternal Being, both as self-conscious personality and as
Love. It is a mystery, but a mystery which "explains
many other mysteries, and which sheds a marvellous light on
God, on nature, and on man." It is the "consummation and
only perfect protection of Theism"; and it will be ultimately
found not only to influence every part of our theological
system, but to be the vital basis of Christian Ethics.

EXCURSUS

ON

The Correlation of Righteousness and Love.

God is Love ; God is Righteous. The two conceptions appear to be
equally fundamental ; and a problem of no small perplexity is presented
by the inevitable inquiry—what is their relation to each other ? When
it is said that God is Love, the only possible interpretation seems to be
that Love is that essential moral quality of the Divine Nature in which
all God's purposes and actions have their origin. But when it is said
that God is Righteous, it seems equally inevitable to regard His
Righteousness as determining all His purposes and ways. Both statements, moreover, are intuitively felt to be true. We can assert the one
and then, the next moment, assert the other without any sense of
contradiction. How, then, are we to think of the moral nature of God ?
Is it a unity, or is it a duality ? Is it, to use a mathematical analogy,
a circle having a single centre, or is it an ellipse formed around two
different foci ?

The latter solution of the problem has been most widely and
authoritatively maintained. Righteousness and Love, it is held, are
essentially different and mutually independent. They are not conterminous, Righteousness occupying the whole area of moral character
and obligation, while Love covers only a part of it. God is righteous
in all His ways ; in some only is He loving. Righteousness is a
necessity with Him ; Love is secondary, and can be exercised only
when it does not conflict with Righteousness. Let us consider whether
this view is tenable.

(1) In the first place, Love is included in Righteousness. A distinc-

tion is drawn between duties of Right and duties of Love. But there certainly are duties of Love. Love is not a mood or inclination that may or may not be exercised at one's option. The maxim is laid down by Dorner [1] that duties of Right precede duties of Love—"We must be just before we are generous." But in what is this precedence grounded? Assuredly, not in any essential difference in the nature of the obligation. We are not under one sort of obligation to be honest and under another and inferior obligation to be kind. It is a mere and inevitable fact, indeed, that is expressed by the axiom, "We must be just before we are generous." We cannot in reality be generous before we are just. If we act as if we could, we are generous with what is not ours but another's; that is to say, we are not generous at all. The apparent self-communication is altogether unreal. And it is because the temptation to forget this is, for many persons, peculiarly strong that the maxim, "We must be just before we are generous," is so needful. But morally it is no whit less imperative that a man be generous according to his real ability, than that he be honest; that he forgive an injury, than that he refrain from committing one. Such difference as exists between duties of Right and duties of Love is not qualitative but quantitative. To succour the needy is as truly a duty as to pay one's mercantile debts; but to be dishonest is a more flagrant violation of the law, "Thou shalt love thy neighbour as thyself," than to be ungenerous. The distinction between the two classes of duties is only a convenient expression of certain moral measurements, which experience has taught mankind to make, as to the duties that are the more universal and important, and the neglect of which works greater and wider injury.

The duties of love, then, are included in the area of Righteousness. According to all Christian Ethics, indeed, Love is the chief part of that sum of moral obligation which is Righteousness. (According to Matt. 22$^{35\text{-}40}$ and Rom. 13$^{8\text{-}10}$ it is the whole.) Love itself is the supreme duty, and the withholding of it the worst sin.

(2) But, further, it is clear that nothing that is truly called Love can be outside the area of Righteousness.

For since, *ex hypothesi*, Love always seeks for its object the greatest good possible to it, and cannot consent to sacrifice the greatest to any lower good, it seeks for moral beings always the same thing that Righteousness seeks—their highest moral excellence. Human love may be blind and mistake its way, and give instead of bread a stone; but when enlightened it cannot, if true to its own ends, seek aught less than the best. And, on the other hand, enlightened Love never becomes an impulse to undutiful conduct in the person who loves, never permits the supposition that we can promote another's good by means that involve inferior conduct on our own part; on the contrary, it

----

[1] *System of Christian Ethics*, p. 91 (Eng. trans.).

6

becomes the strongest impulse to realise the full moral worth of one's own personality.

All that is truly called Love is included in the area of Righteousness. (3) We come to a more disputed question when we ask—Is all Righteousness included in the area of Love? Can there be action that is righteous in which there is no Love? Or could there exist a person who, though destitute of Love, possessed the attribute of Righteousness? Without attempting to show in detail that all duties can be resolved into diverse applications of the law of Love, one may state the general question :—whether, if Love were non-existent, consciousness of any moral obligation whatsoever is conceivable. The answer it seems to me, is that it is not conceivable. If my *normal and proper* state of soul towards my neighbour were one of absolute indifference to his well-being, I could no more stand in any moral relation to him than to a stone. We find, in fact, that this is the case. In those abnormal natures in which benevolence seems to be completely extinct, the whole moral consciousness seems to be equally a blank. It is true, indeed, that there are social virtues, such as truthfulness, honour, equity, that are frequently regarded as existing in an entirely self-centred form—" I shall keep honour with that scoundrel, not because it is due to him, but because it is due to myself." But such an attitude (not to say that it is not that of Christian morality) is not really so self-centred as it seems. He who thus acts is importing into the particular instance a feeling derived from his sense of obligation to mankind in general. He acts upon a code and habit of honour which are to him of such worth that he would not be compensated for their violation by any satisfaction derived from paying a rascal in his own coin. But this code and habit of honour are not self-centred. The self-respect to which honourable dealing with our neighbour is felt to be due is reflex. We could not even be conscious that such conduct is necessary to self-respect, unless we were, in the first place, conscious that it is due from us to our neighbour.

It is in respect to Justice, and especially punitive Justice, that the question we are considering comes to its acutest point. And without discussing the ultimate origin of the idea of Justice, I again submit that if we were so constituted that the interests of our fellow-men were nothing to us, it would be impossible that we should be sensible of any obligation to justice, equity, or impartiality in our dealings with them. Whether or not the idea of Justice is directly derivable from Love as the distributive method by which Love deals with competing interests in such wise as to advance the best interests of all without detriment to any, it is at least evident that Justice is the instrument of Love. Love demands that we do justly. Nor is this less true of punitive Justice. In the popular understanding of the words, the Love of God is regarded as acting only in the direct communication of good ; while the judicial, punitive, and destructive energies of the Divine Nature, which are evoked by evil, are assigned exclusively to Righteousness. But this is a false antithesis, based upon an inadequate and one-sided conception of Love. Love, as seeking the highest good of its objects, is constrained to oppose, and to oppose passionately, all that works for the defeat of its purpose. Love is not merely a sweet, suave, and benignant disposition. Love has in it the sharpness of the sword and the fierceness of flame. Love hates—hates evil, which is opposed to Love. Love in the right-minded parent hates evil in the child ; in the right-minded ruler, hates evil in the society which he governs, and encounters it with the full force of his opposition and displeasure. Love cares for social as well as for individual well-being. The more truly loving a parent is, the more inflexible will he be in rebuking and correcting evil within the home ; in exercising justice, and preventing one member of the household from acting wrongfully towards another ; and, when the interests of the individual or of the whole family require it, in punishing and making an example of the wrong-doer, and even, should he prove incorrigible, in excluding him from the home. Yet all this Righteousness will he do for the ends and in the spirit of Love. Even so, the Love of God must assert itself in infinitely intense antagonism to all that works for the defeat of the eternal purpose of Love—Love that seeks the highest moral excellence of His creatures—for which He created and governs the universe. It is in accordance with that purpose that right shall be rewarded and wrong punished ; nay, this must be inherent in the constitution of a universe created and ruled by Love. In the interests of the sinner himself, sin must be punished. Even if there be no hope of his amendment, in the interests of the moral universe God must still encounter sin with the full force of His displeasure. Yet all this Righteousness God will do for the ends and in the spirit of Love.

It is a strong point in the Calvinistic tradition to maintain that punitive justice cannot be derived from Love. Yet it is not only consistent with, it is a necessity of God's changeless purpose of Love that wrong be punished. And I fail to conceive the nature of a Justice that has no connection with this purpose. There is, doubtless, a genuine moral satisfaction in the humiliation of triumphant wrong, in beholding the evil-doer receive the due reward of his deeds ; but this satisfaction is ultimately derived from sympathy with the central purpose of Love ; it is the satisfaction of beholding the beneficent moral order of the universe reasserting itself, repairing the breaches that have been made in it, and guarding itself against similar infringements in the future. And, again, I fail to conceive how, apart from such a purpose of Love, the punishment of wrong would be right or rational ; how, if the infliction of suffering—let us suppose the case—could be of no possible benefit either to the sinner himself or to any other being in the universe, present or future, there would still remain a ground of reason or of obligation for inflicting it. Nay more, I fail to conceive how a being without Love, wholly indifferent to the well-being of others, could ever be conscious of Justice as a moral obligation, or be capable of finding any moral satisfaction in it. If, indeed, this were possible, if there could exist a being of whose moral consciousness Justice were the sole content,[1] for whom Love did not exist, or existed only as a secondary and accidental attribute, of whom it could be said[2] that "Love is an attribute which he may exercise or not as he will," that "Mercy is optional with him," that "he is bound to be just, he is not bound to be generous," such a being would be morally of an infra-human type and vastly remote in character from the God who is revealed in Jesus Christ. This whole theory rests, in fact, upon the idea which, as has been already said, is the negation of Christian Ethics, that Love is something over and above what is strictly right, a work of supererogation, a comely adornment of character, but not the very fibre of which its robe is woven.

The conclusion, then, at which I arrive is that Righteousness and Love are conterminous in area; that as little can Righteousness exist without Love as Love, truly so called, without Righteousness. But the question remains, how we are to conceive their relation to one another.

An interesting and fruitful view—true, I believe, as regards the fundamental position, though I cannot find myself in agreement with the conclusion reached—is that presented by Dorner.[3] "The essence of morality consists in an unchangeable but also eternally living union of a righteous will and a loving will. The two together and inseparably one constitute a holy love." Dorner then construes Righteousness as the necessity of self-assertion in the Divine Nature, Love as the necessity of self-communication; and he has no difficulty in showing that without self-assertion ethical self-communication would be impossible. It would cease to be voluntary, and would become a merely instinctive benevolence, akin to a physical expansion like that of light or heat.

---

[1] One may try to imagine such a being, who should possess as his sole moral characteristic a passion for abstract Justice—for arriving at and executing equitable decisions regarding the merits of other beings—and who might find a peculiar satisfaction in thus administering Justice among men, or in a colony of ants, or a swarm of bees. But would such a characteristic be really moral? Would there be any ethical motive or value in such a passion for applying the rules of equity—there being no interest or sense of obligation to advance any one's well-being thereby—any more than in a passion for solving mathematical problems? Is there necessarily ethical value in the justice of a judge *qua* judge (the persons judged being to him but lay figures, representing so many judicial problems) any more than in the diagnosis of a physician? The crucial question is—Can any moral relation subsist between two persons apart from the obligation, recognised or unrecognised, to seek each other's good, that is to say, apart from Love? It does not seem possible. The prerequisite of all moral relationship is Love.

[2] See Steven's *Christian Doctrine of Salvation*, p. 178.

[3] *Christian Ethics*, pp. 76–79 (Eng. trans.).

But then it would seem to be equally true that, without self-communication, ethical self-assertion is impossible. The self-assertion or righteousness of God is that in all He does He must be true to Himself, must act according to the voluntary self-determination of His own moral nature. But that nature is *holy love*; and only by acting in holy love can God truly assert Himself. This, however, Dorner refuses to admit, maintaining that ethical self-assertion is possible without self-communication. And when we ask wherein this consists, he replies that it is in God's assertion of His non-communicable attributes—of His self-existence, His glory and majesty, of "Himself in the distinction which, to thought and in fact, exists between Him and the non-self-existing universe." "It is a guarding of the difference between Him and the world, even when He imparts Himself to it and wills to be self-imparting." But this is far from satisfactory. It amounts to this, that in communicating all of His own nature that is communicable,—life, physical, rational, and spiritual,—God is both loving and righteous; while in asserting what is incommunicable — His self-existence and supremacy as Creator and Lawgiver—He is not loving, but is exclusively righteous. But this does not seem to yield that living, inseparable union of a loving and a righteous will which Dorner rightly posits as "the essence of morality." For those of God's attributes that are not directly communicable may yet be *employed* for the ends of Love; as, for example, His self-existence for Creation, His power and omniscience for beneficent providential rule, His moral authority for the moral education and discipline of His creatures; and, if they were not so employed, His will would not be to its utmost possibility a loving will—God would not be Love. But if God's assertion of all His attributes is directed to the highest good of His creatures; if, as Christianity teaches, it is in blessing them, and, above all, in employing all His attributes, communicable and non-communicable, for their rescue from the death of Sin unto Life Everlasting; if Christ is the moral image of the Invisible God, and if it is in that He "counted it not a prize to be on an equality with God, but emptied Himself, taking the form of a servant," that the Divine Self is supremely asserted and the difference between God and the world supremely manifested,—then His fullest self-communication is also His highest self-assertion. The twain constitute that living and inseparable union of a loving and a righteous will which is the essence of all morality. And, in short, a moral nature cannot be thus divided into compartments. Separate attributes exist only as abstractions. If a person is perfectly loving, he is loving always and in everything; if he is perfectly righteous, he is righteous always and in everything; and if he is both perfectly loving and perfectly righteous, he is loving in his righteousness and righteous in his love.

The weakness of Dorner's argument lies in regarding Love as exclusively self-communication, and not rather as that in which self-communication and self-assertion coalesce. But accepting his definition of the essence of morality as the living, inseparable union of a loving and a righteous will, we may, perhaps, reach a conception of the correlation of the Righteousness and the Love of God along the following lines.

1. The perfect moral state is that in which self-communication is also self-assertion. This is the mind that was in Christ Jesus (Phil. 2$^{5-8}$). Such Love, therefore, is the content of all moral excellence (Matt. 22$^{35-40}$, Rom. 13$^{8-10}$). It is the inner principle without which even actions that are formally right are morally worthless (1 Cor. 13$^{1-3}$). All graces and virtues are either special manifestations of Love, as gentleness, compassion, reverence ; or are constitutional qualities of the will—as truthfulness, obedience, gratitude, perseverance, courage— or of the mind—as wisdom—which are ancillary to the perfect work of Love. All duties spring ultimately from the one duty of Love. Even the duty of justice or equity does so ; for, if we were so constituted as to be conscious of no obligation to seek the well-being of others, there would be no reason, except a prudential one, for doing to others as we would that they should do to us.

2. Because Love is that power by which self-communication and self-assertion coalesce in the unity of Life, it is not only the sum of all moral excellence, but the source of the highest moral satisfactions. It is by means of Love that Life runs its full circle, as if a river should carry back to its source all the wealth its fertilising influences have produced. And because it thus unites the egoistic and the altruistic principles, it is also the highest impulse to all duty. It is as much the supreme and universal power in the moral realm as gravitation is in physics.

3. As being, thus, the content of and the impulse to all moral excellence, and, at the same time, the source of the highest moral satisfactions, Love is the *summum bonum*. Without it no real good is possible ; and there is no blessedness conceivable beyond that of a society of persons all united in perfect love. Each communicates himself to all and all to each. Each seeks the joy and well-being of all, and, in turn, enjoys the joy and is blessed by the well-being of all. Such a society would be the perfect organism for the perfect life ; and such an organism God is fashioning and perfecting in the Body of Christ.

4. God is Love ; and, because He is Love, it is His Will to impart this highest good to all beings capable of participating in it. Because He is Love, it is His Will to make Love the law of His universe, His gift to all beings made after His own likeness, and His requirement from them. And this, I take it, is the Righteousness of God—that He asserts Love, the law of His own Life, as the law of all life that is derived from Him. This assertion necessarily acts in two directions ; in the communication of Love, the highest good ; and in antagonism to all that is opposed to it. These modes of action are not derived from conflicting or mutually independent principles, but are diverse applications of the same principle. If the eternal purpose of

God is to produce beings capable of the highest good and to impart it to them, then, by His very character as Love, He is also constrained so to order the universe that whatever tends to the defeat of that purpose shall meet His unceasing antagonism. This will take the form of what we call punitive Justice. And what makes the punitive Justice of God so terrible is that it is the Justice of one who is Love, and that even Infinite Love can find no alternative.

Thus, then, we may see that the moral nature of God is a unity, not a duality. Righteousness is Love in the imperative mood; is Love legislative and administrative; is the consistency of Love to its own high and eternal end. The Righteousness of God is that He makes Love the law of His own action, and that He, in His Love, can tolerate nothing less and nothing else as His purpose and requirement for His creatures than that what He acts upon they also shall act upon, and that the character He possesses they also shall possess. And nothing else than this is Righteousness in man. Duty is the obligation which is inherent in the very nature of Love and could not conceivably exist in a being destitute of Love, to seek the highest attainable good of all whom one's conduct affects, that is to say, to be faithful to Love's highest ends. And when, in popular language, Duty is contrasted with Love, the true significance of this is that Duty is the consistency of Love to its higher end, in the face of egoistic inclination or of temptation to decline upon some lower end.

It will be seen that the view here presented involves these fundamental positions. (1) All moral life is necessarily social. As self-consciousness is psychologically possible only by the distinction of the ego from the non-ego, so moral self-consciousness is awakened only in our relation to other personalities. An absolutely solitary unit (without God or neighbour) could have no moral consciousness. Our moral ideal of self is our conception of the ideal man in all his relations to God and his fellows; and apart from such relations moral self-love is inconceivable. (2) The supreme end is Life. All that we call moral excellence—Righteousness or Love—is the " Way of Life," the means to that fullest, highest Life which St. John calls Eternal. For it is only by our entering with that vivid, spontaneous response, which is at once self-communication and self-assertion, into all the relations, human and divine, amid which we have our being,

that Life is realised.   Hence, while it has just been said
that Life is the *summum bonum*, this may be also said of
moral excellence, that is, of Love.   Love is not only the
way to Life, it is the living of the Eternal Life.   (3) All
this implies, as has been shown, that the Divine Nature is
not a simple unity, but, in some ineffable sense, a fellowship.

CHAPTER VI.

The Doctrine of Christ.

THE centre of doctrinal interest in the Epistle is the Incarnation, in which St. John finds the single guarantee of a true manifestation of the Divine Life in man, and the single channel for its permanent communication to men. Before proceeding, however, to the study of the chief Christological passages, it will be convenient to advert to some few points that lie on the circumference of the subject, yet are of great interest.

The nomenclature of the Epistle is noticeably different in some respects from that of the Fourth Gospel. " Jesus Christ " has now become the proper personal name of our Lord (1^3 2^1 3^{23} 5^{20}). " Jesus " is not found except in conjunction with " Christ " or some other term of theological significance, such as " Son of God " (1^7), or where the sense requires some such term to be supplied (4^3). The absolute use of ἐκεῖνος (2^6 $3^{3.\ 5.\ 7.\ 16}$ 4^{17}) and of αὐτός ($2^{8.\ 12.\ 27.\ 28}$ $3^{2.\ 3}$ 4^{21}) almost as a name of the Saviour is peculiar [1] to the Epistle. Blending a certain idealising reverence with the allusiveness of familiar affection, this usage is singularly expressive of a state of mind to which, although the mists of time have gathered around the image of the historical Jesus, He is still the one ever-present living personality. As in old-style Scottish parlance, a wife would speak of her husband, present or departed as

---

[1] Unless we recognise the same usage in John 19^{35}.

"himsel"; [1] so with the Apostle it is needless to say who
" He " is.   There is but one " He."

Other designations applied to Christ are " righteous "
(δίκαιος, 2^1 3^7), " pure " (ἀγνός, 3^3), " the Holy One " (ὁ ἅγιος,
2^{20}).   The first of these (δίκαιος) expresses the broadest conception of His moral perfection.   In every aspect of character
and conduct He absolutely fulfils the idea of " right."   In
ἀγνός, again, the primary idea is that of freedom from moral
stain.[2]   The word may indicate a previous state of actual
impurity (Ps. 5 1^{12}), and it necessarily implies the thought of
possible impurity.   Broadly, we might say that Purity (ἀγνεία)
is the negative aspect of Love.   The command to " purify
oneself " (3^3) is equivalent to " love not the world, neither
the things that are in the world " (2^{15}).   Purity is that
element in holy character which is wrought out by the
discipline of temptation ; and thus the word imparts a
peculiar significance to the passage in which it is applied to
Christ.   Hoping in Him, we are to purify ourselves, even
as He Who, though tempted in all points like as we are, was
and is pure (3^3).

In ἅγιος (= קָדוֹשׁ) the same root-idea of separation from
evil has been merged in that of consecration to God.   The
sense is religious [3] rather than, *per se*, ethical.   To Christ it
is applied in a technical Messianic sense.   He is the " Holy
Servant " (ὁ ἅγιος παῖς, Acts 4^{30}), the fulfilment of the Old
Testament ideal of the Servant of Jehovah.   He is recog-

[1] Or a farm-servant, of his master.   In Theocritus (xxiv. 50), Amphitryon,
calling his retainers from their beds, cries, ἄνστατε δμῶες ταλασίφρονες, αὐτὸς
ἀὐτεῖ : " It is himself (your master) that is calling."   It is inevitable to compare
the Pythagorean αὐτὸς ἔφα.

[2] Biblically, ἀγνός is the equivalent of טָהוֹר=Levitically clean.   In classical
Greek, the prevalent sense is that of freedom from moral defilement ; more
specifically, chastity.   Thus in Homer ἀγνή is the epithet of the virgin goddesses
Artemis and Persephone.   This specific sense is frequently retained in the N.T.
(2 Cor. 6^6 7^{11} 11^2, Tit. 2^5, 1 Tim. 5^2, 1 Pet. 3^2).   The broader sense is exemplified
in 1 Pet. 1^{22} (τὰς ψυχὰς ὑμῶν ἡγνίκοτες) and Jas. 4^8 (ἁγνίσατε καρδίας, δίψυχοι).

[3] Thus the Father Himself is ἅγιος (John 17^{11}) ; the Divine Spirit is τὸ ἅγιον
πνεῦμα ; the angels are ἅγιοι ; Christians are ἅγιοι in virtue of their Divine calling
(1 Cor. 1^2, 2 Tim. 1^9).

nised by evil spirits (Mark 1²⁴, Luke 4³⁴), and confessed by disciples (John 6⁶⁹) as " the Holy One of God " (ὁ ἅγιος τοῦ θεοῦ). He is ὁ ἅγιος ὁ ἀληθινός (Rev. 3⁷), the " true " or " genuine" Holy One, who hath the Key of David—who wields all Messianic prerogatives. And it is obviously in the same sense that He is named " the Holy One" in the Epistle (2²⁰). It is as the Messiah, the Anointed, that He bestows upon the members of the Messianic community the " anointing " (χρῖσμα) of the Spirit.

Passing from these points, we proceed to consider the great Christological thesis of the Epistle. That thesis is *the complete, permanent, and personal identification of the historical Jesus with the Divine Being who is the Word of Life* (1¹), *the " Christ"* (4²) *and the Son of God* (5⁵); and it is characteristic of the author's method that this, which is to be the subject of repeated development in the body of the Epistle, is preluded in its first sentence. The abstract of the Apostolic Gospel which is there prefixed to the Epistle, as the fountain-head from which all its teaching is drawn, contains the two complementary truths: that Jesus is the " Word " in whom the Eternal Life of God has been fully manifested, and that this manifestation has been made through a humanity in which there is nothing visionary or unreal, and is vouched for by every applicable test as genuine and complete. The Incarnate Word has been " seen," " heard," " handled " (1¹⁻³).[1]

In the Epistle this thesis is maintained in the form of a vigorous polemic against certain heretical teachers whom the writer calls " antichrists," [2] in whom he discovers the true representatives of that arch-enemy of God and His Christ who figured so vividly in apocalyptic literature and in the popular belief. That we must recognise in these " antichrists" one or more of the many ramifications of Gnosticism, is beyond question. Though our knowledge of Gnosticism in the Johannine age is but dim and fragmentary,

---

[1] *v. supra*, pp. 46–48, 109.   [2] See Chapter XVI.

still, what we do gather from the scanty records of the Apostolic Fathers fits into the Christological passages of the Epistle so accurately that it renders their interpretation certain where otherwise it would be only conjectural. From the Epistle itself we learn that the heretical teachers denied that Jesus is the Christ (2^{22}), or, more definitely, " Christ come in the flesh " (4^3) ; they denied that Jesus is "the Son of God " (4^{15}); and they asserted that He came " by water only " and not " by blood also " (5^6). Plainly, what is here in view is, in the one or the other of its forms, the Docetic theory of Christ's Person ; for it appears that the theory existed in two more or less defined types. There was the crude unmitigated Docetism described in the Ignatian Epistles, according to which Jesus *was* the Christ, but was in no sense a real human being. It was only a phantom that walked the earth and was crucified. The Incarnation was nothing else than a prolonged theophany.[1] The other is specially associated with the name of Cerinthus,[2] of whom Irenæus reports (*Haer.* I. 26. i.) that he taught that Jesus was not born of a virgin, but was the son of Joseph and Mary, and was distinguished from other men only by superiority in justice, prudence, and wisdom ; that, at His Baptism the Christ descended upon Him in the form of a

---

[1] An interesting specimen of a Docetic Gospel of this type is extant in the recently published Acts of John, the date assigned to which is "not later than the second half of the first century" (*Texts and Studies*, vol. v., No. 1, p. x). According to this Gospel, our Lord had no proper material existence. He assumed different appearances to different beholders, and at different times. Sometimes His body was small and uncomely ; at other times His stature reached unto heaven. Sometimes He seemed to have a solid material body, at other times He appeared immaterial. It was only a phantom Christ that was crucified. During the Crucifixion, the real Christ appears to John on the Mount of Olives and says, " John, unto the multitude down below in Jerusalem I am being crucified and pierced with lances and reeds, and gall and vinegar are given me to drink ; but I put it into thine heart to come up unto this mountain, that thou mightest hear matters needful for a disciple to learn from his Master and for a man to learn from his God." The Lord then shows to John the mystic Cross of Light and the Lord Himself above the Cross, not having any shape, but only a voice.

[2] See Chapter II.

dove, and announced the unknown Father ; that, at the end
of His life, the Christ again left Jesus ; that Jesus died and
rose again, but that the Christ, being spiritual, remained
without suffering. According to this view, Jesus *was not*
the Christ, but only, for the period between the Baptism
and the Crucifixion, the earthly habitation of the heavenly
Christ. On either of the theories the Incarnation was only a
semblance. The one denied reality to the human embodiment of the Divine Life ; the other, admitting the reality of
the human embodiment, denied its permanent and personal
identification with the Divine. By some exegetes,[1] traces
of both forms of the Docetic theory have been discerned in
the Epistle. We shall find, however, that the Cerinthian
heresy alone offers a sufficient objective for all the Christological passages.

These passages are 2^{21-23} 4^{1-3} 4^{15} 5^{6-8}. And we shall,
in the first place, simply state the doctrinal content of each.

" Who is the liar, but he that denieth that Jesus is the
Christ ? " (2^{22}). Here the assertion or denial that Jesus is
the Christ has probably no relation to the early controversy regarding the Messiahship[2] of Jesus in the Jewish
sense.

In Gnostic nomenclature " Christ " was one of the æons
—spiritual existences emanating from the Godhead—who
appeared on earth in phantasmal or temporary embodiment
in Jesus ; and the Apostle also uses the name " Christ " as
equivalent to the " Word " or " the Son of God," to signify
the Divine pre-existent factor in the personality of Jesus.[3]

---

[1] For example, by Pfleiderer (ii. 433). Cerinthus was a contemporary of St.
John ; and if we accept Lightfoot's argument (*Apostolic Fathers*, i. 368), that the
more crudely Docetic view must have been the earlier, the natural tendency
being toward modification, it is evident that the polemic of the Epistle might, as
a matter of date, have been directed against either or both forms of the heresy.

[2] Cf. especially Acts 18^{28}, where the subject of controversy, though verbally
the same, is substantially quite different.

[3] Epiphanius attributes to Cerinthus the doctrine that Christ was τὸ κατελθὸν
ἐν εἴδει περιστερᾶς, καὶ οὐ τὸν Ἰησοῦν εἶναι τὸν Χριστόν,

Evidently, then, it is the Cerinthian heresy that is here repudiated. As to the manner in which this school of Gnosticism construed the personality of the composite Christ-Jesus during the period of union, we are ignorant; but the essential significance of the theory, truly and tersely stated, was that Jesus *was not* the Christ. There was only a temporary and incomplete association of Jesus with the Christ.

" Hereby recognise (or, ye recognise) the Spirit of God. Every spirit that confesseth Jesus (as)[1] Christ come in the flesh is of God; and every spirit that confesseth not Jesus is not of God " $(4^{2.\ 3a})$. Here the statement is more specific, but to the same effect; it is still the Cerinthian heresy that is combatted. The emphasis is not upon the real humanity of Jesus so much as upon the personal identity of the pre-existent Divine Christ with Jesus. There is no mere association, however intimate, between Jesus and the Christ. Jesus *is* the Christ, come in the flesh.

A third time the Apostle returns to the same theme. " Whosoever confesseth that Jesus is the Son of God, God dwelleth in him, and he in God " (4^{15}). Here the true con-

---

[1] ἐν τούτῳ γινώσκετε τὸ πνεῦμα τοῦ θεοῦ· πᾶν πνεῦμα ὃ ὁμολογεῖ Ἰησοῦν Χριστὸν ἐν σαρκὶ ἐληλυθότα ἐκ τοῦ θεοῦ ἐστίν, καὶ πᾶν πνεῦμα ὃ μὴ ὁμολογεῖ τὸν Ἰησοῦν, ἐκ τοῦ θεοῦ οὐκ ἐστίν.

Three different constructions of the crucial phrase in these verses are possible. (*a*) Ἰησοῦν Χριστὸν ἐν σαρκὶ ἐληλυθότα may be taken as one object after ὁμολογεῖ —" Every spirit that confesseth Jesus Christ, Who is come in the flesh ".(Huther, Westcott). Grammatically, this lies open to the objection that the article is (normally) demanded (τὸν ἐν σαρκὶ ἐληλυθότα); in point of sense, that it contains no definite statement—does not specify in what sense we are to confess Jesus Christ, Who is come in the flesh. (*b*) Ἰησοῦν Χριστόν may be taken as a proper name (cf. 1^3 2^1 3^{23} 5^{20}). Thus the confession would be expressly that Jesus Christ is *come in the flesh*; and would be opposed to that thoroughgoing Docetism which attributed to our Lord only the semblance of a human body (Weiss, Pfleiderer). But it is quite unnecessary to find here a reference to a different type of error. (*c*) For Ἰησοῦν alone may be taken as the direct object after ὁμολογεῖ, and Χριστὸν ἐν σαρκὶ ἐληλυθότα as a secondary predicate. "Every spirit that confesseth Jesus as Christ come in the flesh" (Haupt). This construction is rendered probable by so close a parallel as ἐάν τις αὐτὸν ὁμολογήσῃ Χριστόν (John 9^{22}), and, I think, certain by the fact that in the following clause Ἰησοῦν stands alone as object after ὁμολογεῖ.

fession, " Jesus is the Christ," appears as " Jesus is the Son of God." The terms are interchangeable, if not synonymous; and, in this instance, " Son of God " is preferred as bringing out the filial relation of Him who is sent to Him who sends (4^{14}), and thus exhibiting the immensity of the Divine Love manifested in the mission of Christ.

Finally, we have the much-debated passage, " Who is he that overcometh the world, but he that believeth that Jesus is the Son of God ? This is He that came by water and blood ; not by the water only, but by the water and by the blood " ($5^{5.\ 6a}$). The obscurity of the whole passage is due, doubtless, to the fact that the first readers of the Epistle, for whom it was written, were already familiar with the author's handling of the topics that are here merely indicated. Such expressions as the " water " and the " blood " are a kind of verbal shorthand, intended merely to recall to his readers the exposition of those themes which they had heard from his lips. Without attempting a full account [1] of the extraordinarily numerous and diverse explanations, ancient and modern, of these words, it must suffice to say that an interpretation based on a supposed reference to the sacraments was inevitable (so Lutheran commentators generally ; also, in part, Westcott). But, while Baptism and the Lord's Supper do exhibit sacramentally those elements in Christ's saving work that correspond respectively to His coming by Water and by Blood, to explain the text by direct reference to these is inadequate.[2] Equally inevitable was the effort to explain the passage by the account given in the Gospel of the efflux of water and blood from the Saviour's wounded side (Augustine and ancient commentators generally). But it may be said with consider-

---

[1] This may be found in Huther, pp. 456–458.

[2] This statement is made with reference only to the first mention (5^6) of the Water and the Blood. Subsequently ($5^{7.\ 8}$) there is, I think, a natural transition from the historical realities to their permanent memorials, the Christian Sacraments. See Chapter VII.

able confidence that while this passage in the Epistle may serve to explain the symbolical meaning which is apparently attached in the Gospel to that incident of the Passion, the incident in the Gospel sheds no light upon the passage in the Epistle. The clue to this is the Docetic tenet that the æon Christ descended upon Jesus at His Baptism, and departed again from Him before His Passion. Thus it is evident that the "water" here denotes our Lord's Baptism, the "blood," His death on Calvary. The Cerinthian heresy taught that the Christ came by "water," but denied that He came by "blood" also. Hence St. John's repeated and emphatic assertion that He came "not by the water only, but by the water and the blood."

As Westcott rightly points out, "He that cometh," "He that came" (ὁ ἐρχόμενος, ὁ ἐλθών), are terms used in the Gospels, and notably in St. John, as a technical designation of the Messiah.[1] When, therefore, it is said that Jesus the Son of God "came" by water and by blood, it is signified that first by His Baptism and then by His Death, Jesus entered actually and effectively upon His Messianic ministry. He "came" by water (δι᾽ ὕδατος).[2] In their own sense the Gnostics maintained that Christ "came" by water; in another sense, the Epistle asserts the same[3]—in what sense is clearly demonstrated in the Gospels, where the Baptism is invariably regarded as the actual beginning of His Messianic ministry (John 1[31], Acts 1[22]; Mark's Gospel *begins* with the Baptism). When Jesus definitely consecrated Himself in the full consciousness of His calling

---

[1] Cf. John 3[21] 6[14] 7[27] 11[27] 12[13], Matt. 11[3] 23[39], and cognate passages in the other Gospels.

[2] The exact significance of διά with ὕδατος and αἵματος is not easy to determine. The idea may be that of the door, so to say, through which Christ entered upon His mission.

[3] It might be supposed, were one to take this passage by itself, that the writer was half a Gnostic, that he held the view that Christ descended into Jesus at His baptism, while strenuously resisting the idea that the Christ departed from Jesus before His Passion.

(Matt. 3¹⁵); the Spirit was bestowed on Him "not by measure" for its accomplishment (Matt. 3¹⁶); and the voice from Heaven testified His predestination to it (Matt. 3¹⁷). But He came by Blood also. This the Gnostics denied; this the Apostle affirms.[1] He who was baptized of John in Jordan, and He whose life-blood was shed on Calvary is the same Jesus, the same Christ, the same Son of God eternally. For He "came" by blood. He did not depart by blood. He laid down His life only that he might take it again. Death was for Him only the entrance upon the endless career of His redemptive work, the unhindered fruitfulness of His life (John 12²⁴).

If the foregoing exposition of the chief Christological passages has been right, it has been made clear that these passages all promulgate the same truth in substantially the same way. If one might express it mathematically, there is on one side of an equation the Divine, or, at least, super-terrestrial, Being Who is the "Word of Life," the "Christ," the "Son of God"; on the other side, the human Jesus. But the two sides of the equation are not only equivalent, they are identical. Without ceasing to be what He is, the Son of God has become the human Jesus; and Jesus, without ceasing to be truly human, is the Son of God.

An investigation of the wider problems presented by the Johannine use of these titles, Logos, Christ, Son of God, cannot be undertaken here.[2] Only the more immediate theological implications of the passages that have been passed under review may be adverted to. It is at once

---

[1] "Not by the water only, but by the water and by the blood." Both the repetition and its form are directly determined by the repudiated error. The first member of the clause denies what Cerinthus affirmed, the second affirms what he denied.

[2] See on these topics, Scott's *Fourth Gospel*; especially the admirable chapter on "The Christ, the Son of God."

evident that, in the Epistle, these titles imply the pre-temporal existence of the Person to whom they are applied. Further, while for the abstract monotheism of the Gnostic the "Christ" could be nothing more than an emanation from the Eternal God, for the writer of the Epistle He is Himself Eternal and Divine. He is the "Word of Life" (1^1); and that this title implies relationship and fellowship within the Godhead itself is signified by the fact that the life manifested in Him is that Eternal Life which was in relation to the Father (ἥτις ἦν πρὸς τὸν πατέρα, 1^2). This relation is otherwise expressed by the terms "Father" and "Son"; and these terms are employed in no figurative or merely ethical sense, but in their full signification. The Son, no less than the Father, is the object of religious faith (5^{13}), hope (3^3), and obedience (3^{23}). He that confesseth the Son hath the Father also (2^{23}). Our fellowship is with the Father and with the Son, Jesus Christ (1^3). Believers are exhorted to "abide" in Christ (2^{28}), as elsewhere to "abide" in God. The very syntax of the Epistle testifies how the truth of the essential Divinity of Christ has become the unconscious presupposition of all the Apostle's thinking; for again and again [1] it is left uncertain whether "God" or "Christ" is the subject of statement, an ambiguity which would be reckless except on the presumption of their religious equivalence.

It would be a questionable proceeding, indeed, to read into the Epistle the full Trinitarian doctrine of the hypostatic Sonship. The problem of recognising personal distinctions within the Godhead and at the same time preserving its essential unity—a problem of which the Trinitarian doctrine is, after all, only the mature statement

---

[1] Thus in 2^{25} and 4^{21} the reference of αὐτός is quite ambiguous. In 2^3 αὐτόν ought grammatically to refer to Christ as the nearest antecedent, but does refer to God. In 2^{28} αὐτός is Christ; while in 2^{29}, without any note of transition, the unexpressed subject is God. In 3^{1-3}, again, αὐτός ought grammatically to refer to God (taking its antecedent from 2^{29}), but actually refers to Christ.

—has not yet been fully confronted. Yet it is not too much to say that all the elements of that problem are present here in the fundamental implication that Jesus Christ, in His pre-incarnate form of being, existed eternally in an essential unity of nature with God.

This, however, is only an implication. The crucial truth of the Epistle is Christological, not theological; its doctrinal emphasis is not upon the relation of Divine Father and Divine Son, but upon the relation of the Divine Son to the historic Jesus. And it will be well to look more closely at the most explicit of the various forms in which this relation is defined. " Every spirit that confesseth Jesus as Christ come in the flesh ('Ιησοῦν Χριστὸν ἐν σαρκὶ ἐληλυθότα) is of God " (4²). The statement, simple as it is, is of exquisite precision. The verb used (ἔρχεσθαι) implies the pre-existence of Christ. The perfect tense (ἐληλυθότα) points to His coming not only as a historical event, but as an abiding fact. The Word has become flesh for ever.[1] The noun (σάρξ) indicates the fulness of His participation in human nature, the flesh being the element of this which is in most obvious contrast with His former state of being[2] (John 1¹⁴). Even the preposition ἐν is of pregnant significance. It is not altogether equi-valent to "into" (εἰς). The Gnostics also believed that Christ came into the flesh. But the assertion is that He has so come into the flesh as to abide therein; the Incarnation is a permanent union of the Divine with human nature. Finally, this union is realised in the self-identity of a Person, Jesus Christ, who is at once Divine and human.

Again, however, we must not read into this the results of later Christological developments. It may be argued

[1] In 2 John 7 we find the unique expression ἐρχόμενον ἐν σαρκί, emphasising Christ's continuous activity, or, perhaps, His future coming, in the flesh.

[2] It is out of the question to understand by σάρξ " human nature as having sin lodged in it " (Haupt).

that the orthodox formula, " one Person in two natures for ever," is implied in the teaching of the Epistle; but there is nothing that asserts it. The truth taught in all its simplicity, and in all the majesty of its immeasurable consequences, is that of one Person in two states, a preincarnate and an incarnate state of being. Without change of personal identity, the Eternal Son of God is become and for ever continues to be Jesus. Jesus is the Son of God— the Christ—come in the flesh.

We next proceed to a most interesting and important part of our subject—the *practical significance* of the doctrine, as this is exhibited in the Epistle. For it is neither in the interests of abstract theology nor as the champion of ecclesiastical orthodoxy that St. John proclaims the truth of the Incarnation as the " roof and crown " of all truth, but solely from a sense of its supreme necessity to the spiritual life of the Church and the salvation of the world; because he perceives in the denial of it the extinction of the Light of Life which the Gospel has brought to mankind. Thus, in introducing the subject, he first of all sets himself to awaken in the minds of his readers an adequate perception of its gravity:—" I write unto you not because ye know not the truth, but because ye know it, and that no lie is of the truth " (2^{21}).[1] He writes because they know the truth. His aim is not to instruct their ignorance, but to arouse them to realise the significance of their knowledge. He has no actually new elements of Christian truth to impart, but would quicken their sense of the irreconcilable opposition of truth and falsehood, and of its stupendous import in this instance. It was no merely speculative antagonism that existed between the truth they had heard from the beginning (2^{24}) and the corrupt doctrine of the antichrists. The matter at issue was no mere difference of opinion. The alternative was between making truth or

---

[1] See Notes, *in loc.*

falsehood, and that on the greatest of all subjects, the guide of life. " Who is the liar," he passionately exclaims, " but he that denieth that Jesus is the Christ ?," and then, without conjunction or connecting particle of any kind, clause follows upon clause like the blows of a hammer, " This is the antichrist, (this is) he that denieth the Father and the Son. Whosoever denieth the Son hath not even the Father ; he that confesseth the Son hath the Father also " (2²². ²³).

Here we perceive the first of the great practical consequences which depend upon the Incarnation. (*a*) It alone secures and guarantees the Christian revelation of God, and with its denial that revelation is immediately cancelled, " He that hath not the Son hath not even the Father "¹ (2²³).

Contrary as it might be to the intention of the Gnostic teachers or to their interpretation of their own tenets, the result was that, by taking away the real Divine Sonship of Jesus, they subverted the Divine Fatherhood itself. It must be observed that the argument is not one of abstract logic, namely, that if there be no Divine Son there can be no Divine Father. It is concrete and experiential. What is in question is not God's absolute Being, but our " having "—not Fatherhood and Sonship as inherent in the Divine Nature, but the revelation to men of the Father in the Son. Refusing to recognise more than a shadowy and dubious connection between the historic Jesus and the Eternal Son of God, Gnosticism took away the one medium through which a sure and satisfying revelation of the Eternal Father has been given to the world. It was still true that no man had seen God at any time ; but it was not true that the Only-Begotten Son had declared Him ; not true that he who had seen Jesus had seen the Father. With the denial of Jesus as the full personal

---

¹ οὐδὲ τὸν πατέρα ἔχει. " Has not even the Father " ; or, at the least, " Has not the Father either." Cf. the translation quoted by Augustine : *qui negat Filium nec Filium nec Patrem habet.* For the intensive sense of οὐδέ, cf. Gal. 2³.

incarnation of the Divine, the whole Christian conception of God was but the " baseless fabric of a vision," having no point of contact with the world of known fact.   As regards Gnosticism, the Apostle's statement was entirely true.   Its God was a being so absolutely transcendent as to be incapable of actual relation to humanity ; and the gulf between absolute Deity and finite being remained unbridged by all its intricate hierarchy of semi-divine intermediaries.   But the Apostle's contention, that to deny the Son is to be unable to retain even the Father, is no less verified in the history of modern thought.   It is not matter of argument, but of fact, that the God-consciousness finds its true object most completely in Jesus Christ ; and that when God is not found in Christ, He is not ultimately found either in nature or in history.   Theism does not ultimately survive the rejection of Christ as the personal incarnation of God. The process of thought that necessitates the denial of the supernatural in Him has Agnosticism as its inevitable goal.[1]

(*b*) But, if the validity of the whole Christian Revelation of God is involved in the fact of the Incarnation, this is most distinctly true of that which is its centre.   It is highly significant that the writer whose message to the world is " God is Love " derives it so exclusively from this single source.   He has nothing to say of that benevolent wisdom of God in Nature, of that ever-enduring mercy of God in History, that kindled the faith and adoration of Old Testament psalmists and prophets.   His vision is concentrated on the one supreme fact, " Herein was the Love of God manifested towards us, that God sent His Only-Begotten Son into the world that we might live through Him " (4⁹). Compared with this, all other revelations are feeble and dim, are " as moonlight unto sunlight, and as water unto wine."   Here is Love worthy to be called

---

[1] See the convincing historical demonstration of this in Orr's *Christian View of God and the World*, pp. 37-53.

Divine.   And the one unambiguous proof of the existence
of such Love in God and of His bestowal of such Love
upon men absolutely vanishes, unless the Jesus who was
born in Bethlehem and died on Calvary is Incarnate God.
Here, again, it is in the practical significance of the Gnostic
theories that we discover the source of St. John's indignation.
It was not in the metaphysics of Gnosticism so much
as in its ethical presuppositions and consequences that
he discerned the veritable Antichrist.   Its theory of the
absolute Divine transcendence denied to God what, to the
Christian mind, is the "topmost, ineffablest crown" of His
glory—self-sacrificing Love.   It was, in fact, the translation into metaphysic of the spirit of the world, of the axiom
that the supreme privilege of greatness is self-centred bliss,
exemption from service, burden-bearing, and sacrifice.[1]
"They are of the world, and, therefore, speak they of the
world, and the world heareth them" (4[5]).   Ignorant of the
Divine secret of Love, having no comprehension that greatness is greatest in self-surrender, and that to be highest
of all is to be servant and saviour of all, unable, therefore,
to see the light of the knowledge of the glory of God in
the face of a crucified Jesus, Gnosticism fashioned to its
own mind a God wholly transcendent and impassible, a
Christ who only *seemed* to suffer and lay down His life
for men, a Gospel drained of its life-blood, a Gospel whose
Divine fire, kindling men's souls to thoughts and deeds of
love and righteousness, was extinguished.   And the result
of thus making man's salvation easy, so to say, for God—
salvation by theophany—was to make it easy for man also
—salvation by creed without conduct, by knowledge without

[1] "Omnis enim per se divum natura necesse est
    Immortali ævo summa cum pace fruatur,
    Semota a nostris rebus, seiunctaque longe.
    Nam privata dolore omni, privata periclis,
    Ipsa suis pollens opibus, nihil indiga nostri
    Nec bene promeritis capitur, nec tangitur ira."
                                        Lucretius, ii. 645–50.

self-denial for righteousness' sake, without self-sacrifice for love's sake.

For the Gnostic it was not " hard to be a Christian." The natural outcome of a Docetic incarnation was a Docetic morality; righteousness which consisted in the contemplation of high ideals ($2^{4.\ 6}\ 3^7$); love which paid its debt with fine sentiments and goodly words ($3^{17.\ 18}$). The actual meaning of Docetism could not be more truly touched than by the pathetic question of Ignatius, εἰ δὲ, ὥσπερ τινὲς ἄθεοι ὄντες . . . λέγουσιν, τὸ δοκεῖν πεπονθέναι αὐτὸν, αὐτοὶ τὸ δοκεῖν ὄντες, ἔγω τί δέδεμαι; [1]

And here again, the significance which St. John finds in the Incarnation is of undiminished validity for modern thought. That God is Love has for us the force of an axiom; it has become part of ourselves. If there be a God, a Being who is supremely good, He must be Love; for

> " A loving worm within his clod
> Were more divine than a loveless God
> Amid his worlds."

It may seem as if there were no intuition of the human spirit more self-evidencing than this; nor is there, when once it is seen. But, as a matter of history, the conviction, the idea, that God is Love, has been generated by nothing else than belief in Jesus Christ as Incarnate God, Who laid down His life for man's redemption. In the pre-Christian and non-Christian religions every quality, good and bad, has been deified except self-sacrificing Love. Power, beauty, fecundity, warlike courage, knowledge, industry and art, wisdom, justice, benevolence and mercy— the apotheosis of all these has been achieved by the human soul. The one deity awanting to the world's

---

[1] *Ad Trall.* 10: "But if, as certain godless men aver, His suffering was only in semblance, themselves being only a semblance, why, then, am I bound with this chain?"

pantheon is the God Who is Love. And if we inquire what, in the world of actual fact, corresponds to this conviction that God is Love, we to-day are still shut up to the answer, " Herein is Love, not that we loved God, but that God loved us, and sent His Son as a propitiation for our sins." With that as the key to the interpretation of the facts of life, we are able to read in them much that testifies, and are sure that, in the light of God's completed purpose, we shall find in them nothing that does not testify, that the universe is created and conducted by the Love of the Heavenly Father Who is revealed in Christ. Yet, even to those who are most jealous for the vindication of this, both nature and history are full of ugly and intractable facts. And, even at their clearest, the pages of natural revelation can give evidence for nothing more than a wise benevolence, a bloodless and uncostly love. If we ask what God has ever done for His creatures that it cost Him anything to do, the one *fact* which embodies the full and unambiguous revelation of this is that " the Father sent the Son to be the Saviour of the world " (4^{14}). Meanwhile, it may seem as if the Christian ethic could claim to exist in its own right, though severed from its historical origin and living root. The atmosphere is full of diffused light, and it may seem as if we might do without the sun. But if the history of thought has shown that, with the denial of the Incarnation, the Christian conception of the Being of God is gradually dissipated into the mists of Agnosticism, it begins also to appear that Christian ethics have no securer tenure. To Positivism, with the enthusiasm of humanity as its sole religion, succeeds neo-paganism, with the enthusiasm of self as the one true faith and royal law. Like the giant of mythology who proved invincible only when reinvigorated by contact with mother-earth, the Christian ethic, the ethic whose supreme principle is Love, maintains and renews its conquering energy only as it derives this afresh from Him who was historically its origin, and is for ever the living source of its inspiration.

(*c*) But, again, the Epistle exhibits the vital significance of the Incarnation for Redemption. The primary purpose of the Incarnation is not to reveal God's Love, but to accomplish man's salvation. God has sent His Son to be the Saviour of the World (4[14]); to be the Propitiation for our sins (4[10]). It is the same truth that underlies the more cryptic utterance of 5[6]: "This is He that came by water and blood; not by the water only, but by the water and by the blood." The reference to the Cerinthian heresy has been already explained; but the peculiar phraseology in which Christ's Passion is here insisted upon, the repeated assertion that He came by blood,—not by water only,—reveals the motive of St. John's energetic hatred of that heresy. For it is "the blood of Jesus, His Son, that cleanseth us from all sin" (1[6]). "Not by water only." The tragedy of human sin demanded a tragic salvation. And the Apostle's whole-hearted denunciation of the Docetic Christology was due to the fact that it not only dissolved[1] Christ, but took away from men their Redeemer.

(*d*) The final necessity of the Incarnation, for St. John, is that in it is grounded the only possibility for man of participation in the Divine Life, "He that hath the Son hath Life; he that hath not the Son of God hath not Life" (5[12]). When Christ came into the world, the most stupendous of all events took place. The Eternal Life, the Life that the Word possessed from the Beginning in relation to the Father (1[2]) was embodied in humanity, and became a fountain of regenerative power to "as many as received Him" (John 1[12] 3[16]). This is the ultimate significance of the Incarnation and the core of the Johannine Gospel,—a Christ who has power to place

---

[1] An ancient reading in 4[3]. λύει

Himself in a unique vital relation to men, to pour into their defilement His purity, into their weakness His strength, into their deadness His own spiritual vitality; reproducing in them His own character and experiences, as the vine reproduces itself in the branches—doing that, the ineffable mystery of which is only expressed, not explained, when we say that He is our "Life" (John $14^{19, 20}$ 15^5). And to deny the truth of the personal Incarnation, to dissolve the integrity of the Divine-human nature of Jesus Christ, is either, on the one side, to deny that human nature is *capax Dei*, or, on the other side, that it is the life of God that flows into humanity in Jesus Christ; on either supposition, to annul the possibility of that communication of the Divine Life to man in which salvation essentially consists. And here also the perspicacity with which the writer of the Epistle discerns the logical and practical issue is very notable. The history of theology, so far as I am aware, offers no instance in which the truth of the Incarnation has been rejected and a doctrine of Atonement or Regeneration, in anything approaching to the Johannine sense, has been retained.

Such are the practical[1] aspects of the fact of Incarnation which the Epistle brings out. The full impersonation of the Divine Life, the perfect effulgence of the Divine Light, the supreme gift of the Divine Love, is this—"Jesus Christ come in the flesh."

---

[1] It is interesting to compare what Harnack says of Athanasius. "It was not for a word or a formula that Athanasius was concerned, but a crucial thought of his faith, the redemption and raising of humanity to divine life through the God-man. It was only from the certainty that the divinity manifest in Jesus Christ possessed the nature of deity (unity of being), and was on this account alone able to raise us to a divine life, that faith was to receive its strength, life its law, and theology its direction. . . . Behind and beside him existed a speculation which led on a shoreless sea, and the ship was in danger of losing its helm. He grasped the rudder " (*History of Dogma*, iii. 140, 141).

CHAPTER VII.

THE WITNESSES TO THE DOCTRINE OF CHRIST.

THE doctrinal centre in the Epistle is, as we have seen in the preceding chapter, the Incarnation. The channel by which the full revelation of God and the gift of Eternal Life are conveyed to mankind is Jesus, the Son of God, the Christ "come in the flesh." Our present task is to examine the teaching of the Epistle as to the grounds on which this belief rests.

The correlative, intellectually, of Belief is "witness" (μαρτυρία, μαρτυρεῖν, 1^2 4^{14} $5^{6.\ 7.\ 9.\ 10.\ 11}$); and although the apologetic aim of the Epistle is fully disclosed only in the middle of the second chapter, the note of "witness" struck in the opening verses shows that this was in the writer's mind from the first.

The Apostolic Gospel, 1^{1-3}.

"That[1] which was from the beginning, that which we have heard, that which we have seen with our eyes, that which we beheld, and our hands handled, concerning the Word of Life (and the Life was manifested, and we have seen, and announce unto you the Life, the Eternal Life, which was with the Father, and was manifested unto us); that which we have seen and heard announce we unto you also, that ye also may have fellowship with us: yea, and our fellowship is with the Father, and with His Son Jesus Christ." Here the Epistle opens, as it likewise closes, in a strain

---

[1] For exegetical details, *v. supra*, pp. 43 sqq., and Notes, *in loc.*

of triumph. The complex periodic structure, unique [1] in the Johannine writings, expresses with stately rhetorical effect the writer's consciousness of the unequalled sublimity of his theme, and his exultation in the double apostolic privilege of having himself seen and believed, and of bearing witness to those who have not seen, that they also may have the blessedness of believing (John 20[29]).

First he plainly declares his personal acquaintance [2] with the facts of the Incarnate Life. He is not, like St. Luke, a sedulous investigator and recorder of the facts as certified by the most trustworthy witnesses; but is himself such a witness. His knowledge is derived from detailed and intimate observation; [3] and the testimony, certified by every faculty given to man as a criterion of objective reality, is that He who was from the Beginning and He who, in His earthly manifestation, lived and died and rose [4] again is (as against the Docetic conception) the same Person, embodied in the same form of actual human existence. But before completing the statement that all that has been outlined in 1[1] is the theme of apostolic testimony, the writer parenthetically anticipates the question how such testimony comes to be possible. Human sense has been made the medium of the knowledge of the eternal Divine Life. For "the Life was manifested, and we have seen and bear witness, and announce [5] unto you the Life, the Eternal Life which was

---

[1] The only parallel is the introduction to the washing of the disciples' feet (John 13[1-3]), where the motive is obviously the same as here.

[2] *v. supra*, pp. 46 sqq.

[3] The evidence is stated on an ascending scale — hearing, sight, touch. Herodotus had long ago made the observation, ὦτα γὰρ τυγχάνει ἀνθρώποισι ἐόντα ἀπιστότερα ὀφθαλμῶν, i. 8.

[4] ὃ αἱ χεῖρες ἡμῶν ἐψηλάφησαν—a verbal reminiscence of Christ's words to the disciples after the Resurrection.

[5] The fine logical precision with which the words are ordered is noticeable, ἀπαγγέλλομεν, emphasising the fact of communication; μαρτυροῦμεν, the truth, personally vouched for, of the communication made; ἑωράκαμεν, the experience on the strength of which the voucher is given.

toward the Father and was manifested to us." And
then in the following verse, which resumes and completes
1^1, there is repeated insistence upon the fact that the
testimony borne is based upon personal and first-hand
knowledge, "What we have seen and heard we announce
also unto you,[1] that ye also may have fellowship with
us." Having such a message to deliver he cannot refrain. His rejoicing in the Truth is such that he must
impart it to others also. For this Truth is the medium
of Christian fellowship;[2] nay, as he exultingly reminds
himself and his readers, it is the medium not only of
fellowship between Christians, but of their fellowship
with God—to have "fellowship with us" is to have
"fellowship with the Father and with His Son Jesus
Christ." Having himself been brought into living fellowship with God through his knowledge of the facts in which
the Son of God has been revealed to men, and the
Father in the Son, he would now, by making them full
partners in his knowledge, open to them the same door
of entrance into the same fulness of Divine Fellowship.[3]
"As every stream of water makes for the sea, every rill
of truth makes for fellowship of souls." But the crowning
joy of this communication is that by means of it men
are brought unto God and into the possession of Divine
Life.

The apostolic "witness" thus furnishes the permanent
content, the fact-material, of Christian belief. It is this—
"the word which ye heard from the beginning" (2^{24})—

---

[1] "Unto you also" (καὶ ὑμῖν) implies a contrast, not between former and
present recipients of the message, but between the Apostle himself and his readers.

[2] Upon the exegetical intricacies of the verse see Notes, *in loc.*

[3] It would be impossible to find a more spontaneous expression than these
words of the missionary spirit that is inherent in all truth, but, above all, in
Christian truth. The same Christlike and apostolic feeling breaks out afresh in
the verse that follows: "And these things write we unto you, that our joy may
be fulfilled." *v. supra*, p. 42, note 2.

that reveals the Son of God in the reality of the Incarnate Life. It is, therefore, the touchstone of truth, the Church's safeguard against all the freaks of human fancy and the vagaries of speculation:—" If it abide in you, ye also shall abide in the Son and in the Father" (2²⁴ᵇ). With unerring insight St. John declares the sovereign value of the Apostolic Gospel, and assigns its permanent function in the Church. As at the close of the Apostolic era the watchword of true advance is found to be "back to Christ," so always the historical manifestation of the Word of Life is at once the source and the test of all fruitful developments in theology or ethics. Whatever rights criticism may claim with respect to the literary medium by which the Apostolic Gospel has been transmitted, that Gospel has remained and must remain the "umpire and test" of truth in all emergencies, even as it is also the "good seed" of the kingdom of God.

The Testimony of the Spirit.

The knowledge of the Divine Revelation given to the world in Jesus Christ is derived ultimately from the testimony of the Apostles and a few other contemporary witnesses: and it is communicated by the same method as that by which information is ordinarily diffused among men: those who know tell it to those who are ignorant. But is the belief of those who "have not seen and yet have believed" inferior in point of certitude to that of the original witnesses? The Epistle assures its readers that they are in no such position of inferiority. They have the testimony and teaching of the Spirit.

In the first cycle of the Epistle the paragraph in which this topic is introduced is 2²⁰⁻²⁷.[1] Having in the preceding

---

[1] Regarding the exegetical difficulties of this passage, see Notes, *in loc.*

verses characterised the heretical teachers as the true anti-christs, St. John, before proceeding to exhort his readers to stand fast in the Faith, prepares the ground for such ex-hortation by reminding them of the living Witness they had in themselves—the Spirit God had given them, who both set the seal of immediate conviction upon the Truth itself and enabled them unfailingly to distinguish it from all its counterfeits (πᾶν ψεῦδος, 2²¹).

"And ye have an anointing (chrism) from the Holy One,[1] and ye know all things" (2²⁰). The word "chrism"[2] (not the act of anointing, but that with which it is per-formed) seems to be suggested here by the title "anti-christs" which has been applied to the schismatics. They were ἀντίχριστοι, counterfeits of Christ. The Apostle's readers had the true chrism, and, therefore, were able to detect their falsity. On the other hand, the use of the word without explanation assumes that it was familiar to both writer and readers as denoting the abiding gift of the Holy Ghost. Jesus is the "Anointed." It is He Who received the true Divine Anointing, "with the Holy Ghost and with power" (Acts 4²⁷ 10³⁸). And this anointing He received not for Himself alone, but for all the members of His spiritual Body. During His visible presence among men the conditions of His earthly ministry precluded the full com-munication of the gift. But when, having overcome the sharpness of death, He ascended the throne of His kingdom, the oil of His coronation in the heavens flowed down upon His people here on earth (Acts 2³³⁻³⁶). The precious ointment ran down to the skirts of the High priest's garments (Ps. 132²). The result of this "anoint-ing" is that "ye know all things." The specific office of the Spirit is to "guide into all the truth," to "take of Mine and declare it" (John 16¹³, ¹⁴).

---

[1] "The Holy One," that is, Christ. *v. supra*, p. 90.
[2] See special Note appended to this chapter.

This now leads the writer to reassert ($2^{7.\ 12-14}$) that the motive of his writing does not lie in the assumption of his readers' ignorance. He has no positively new elements to add to their Christian knowledge, " I write unto you, not because ye know not the truth, but because ye know it, and (know) that no lie is of the truth " (2^{21}). [1] . . . [2] " And, as for you, the anointing which ye received of Him abideth in you, and ye need not that any one teach you : but as the anointing from Him teacheth you concerning all things, and is true, and is no lie, even as it taught you, ye abide in Him " (2^{27}).[3]

The distinctive feature of this passage is that the testimony of the Spirit is regarded as a " teaching." And the question[4] that immediately arises is as to the conception of this " teaching " it implies. Examining this, we find, in the first place, that it is not regarded as superseding the Word, but as concurrent and co-operative with it. Their inter-dependence is signified, according to the Writer's habitual method, by alluding to them alternately ($2^{20.\ 21}$ the Spirit, 2^{24} the Word, $2^{26.\ 27}$ the Spirit). Their teaching is the same in

---

[1] See Notes, *in loc.*

[2] On the verses here omitted, see Chapter VI.

[3] " In Him." Not in the "anointing," but in Christ. The purpose of the Spirit's work, in all its aspects, is the believer's perfect and abiding union with Christ.

[4] In the parallel passage ($3^{24b}-4^6$) the action of the Spirit is charismatic and the testimony is objective, being given in the inspired confession of Jesus as the Christ come in the flesh (so also in 1 Cor. $12^{28.\ 29}$ and Eph. $4^{12.\ 13}$). Is the "teaching" here referred to also charismatic ? Is it given to the Church through inspired human utterance ; or is it the subjective enlightening action of the Spirit of truth upon the minds of all believers? The latter interpretation is assumed without question by Protestant commentators ("das fromme Gemeinde-bewusstsein," Holtzmann). The other view is implied in Catholic expositions, such as that of Estius (quoted by Huther), "Habetis episcopos et presbyteros quorum cura ac studio vestræ ecclesiæ satis instructæ sunt in iis quæ pertinent ad doctrinæ Christianæ veritatem." This interpretation is much too definitely ecclesiastical ; but, in view of the parallel passages, and of all we know regard-ing the place of inspired "prophets" and "teachers" in the N.T. Church, it seems to me that the "anointing" is here to be regarded as charismatic, and the "teaching" as given to the Church objectively, through those who were the organs of a special inspiration.

8

substance—Jesus is the Christ (2^{22}); and the result is the same—abiding in Him ("If that which ye heard from the beginning abide in you, ye also shall abide in the Son and in the Father" (2^{24}); and, again (2^{27}), "Even as it taught you, ye abide in Him"). The teaching, moreover, is continuous, shedding the light of truth upon all subjects as they arise in experience (2^{27} "The anointing abideth in you ... and teacheth you concerning all things"). But in another sense it was complete from the first (2^{27} "even as it taught[1] you"). When the Apostle's readers first received the gospel, the Spirit once for all led them to the centre of all truth. In that first "teaching," that first revelation to their faith of the Divine truth in Christ, lay enfolded all that, with the growth of experience and reflection, might afterwards be unfolded. Nothing at variance with it was admissible; nothing really new could be added to it:—"Even as it taught you, ye abide in Him."

The result of the Spirit's teaching is:—"Ye know[2] all things" (2^{20}), and "need not that any one teach you" (2^{27}).[2] These assertions cannot be understood as claiming infallibility for every believer (compared to this, Papal infallibility would be a trifle), or as denying all need of human agency in Christian instruction (so declaring the inutility of the Epistle itself). They must be interpreted in accordance with the general purport of the passage, which is to remind its readers that they already possessed in their fellowship a resource all-sufficient for discerning the real character of the antichristian doctrine. In view

---

[1] The aorist ἐδίδαξεν points to the definite occasion.

[2] οἴδατε πάντα. The reading is here uncertain. The alternative οἴδατε πάντες has strong authority (א, B, Theb. etc., *v.* Westcott, p. 93), and yields an excellent sense. Such knowledge is not the prerogative of an intellectual élite. Even if the "teaching" is a special spiritual gift, the knowledge imparted is the common property of the Christian fellowship (cf. 5^{20}, Eph. 4^{13}). It is certain that, on either reading, the passage contains a reference to and a repudiation of the esoteric pretensions of Gnosticism. Not the self-styled πνευματικοί are the taught of God. To be thus taught is the privilege of all believers. They are the true Gnostics.

of what they have " heard from the beginning," and of the " anointing " which abides in them, St. John can say, " Ye know all things—all that it is needful to know, and all there is to be known about this matter. It is not required that I write unto you as if ye were ignorant of the principles of Christian truth that are here in question. Ye are taught not only by the Word, but also by the Divine Teacher, who continually enlightens your understanding, strengthens your convictions, and ministers to you an invincible assurance of the truth of the Gospel. In this respect ye are independent of other teaching."

Thus the conception of the Spirit's teaching found here is in perfect accord with that of the Fourth Gospel and of the New Testament throughout. The Spirit is not a source of independent revelation, but makes the Revelation of Christ effectual. And this is done by a process that may be considered as twofold, teaching and testimony. There is an operation of the Spirit that is educative, ever extending the area of the spiritual understanding :—" His anointing teacheth you concerning all things." The Word —Christ in the Word—is the Truth ; the Spirit is the living Divine Teacher who works in us a progressive understanding of the contents of the Truth embodied in Him— unfolds its many-sided significance in relation to the various exigencies that arise for Christian thought and action. But the illumination wrought by the Spirit is also intensive. It is not only teaching, but testimony :—" He shall testify of Me " (John 15[26]). The Word—Christ in the Word—is the Light, the Truth ; it is the Spirit that makes the light light, and the truth truth, to the soul. The joyous assurance of faith is His gift. Both of these elements are included here in the thought of the " anointing." The former is the more prominent—the " anointing " teacheth. By means of it the Church unerringly detects as a " liar " every one who denieth that

Jesus is the Christ (2^{22}). But, underlying the whole
passage, there is also the thought of the Spirit's testimony,
" Ye have an anointing from the Holy One, and *ye know*
(οἴδατε)[1] all things " (2^{20}). The truth is placed beyond all
reach of controversy, and passes into absolute knowledge.
For it is not the proposition—Jesus is the Christ—*per se*
that is the bulwark against antichristian falsehood ; it is
the strength of conviction with which it is held. Not a
correct, clear-sighted orthodoxy, but a firm and fervent
assurance of the truth is the innermost citadel. " As His
anointing teacheth you, *and is true and is no lie*, even as
it taught you, ye abide in Him " (2^{27}).

Thus far, then, the teaching of the Epistle is that
Christian Belief is derived externally from the Apostolic
Gospel, internally and concurrently from the witness of the
Spirit. And each supplies a standard for its right development. Stated in modern language, the doctrine of the
Epistle is that all Christian theology must approve itself
as an interpretation of the historic Christ, and also as
satisfying the genuine spiritual instincts of the Christian
life. And no theology meets the one requirement that
does not also meet the other. The continuous development of Christian doctrine in the Church furnishes an ever-
growing testimony to the fulfilment of the twofold promise,
hindered as that fulfilment may be by human imperfection,
—" If that which ye heard from the beginning abide in
you, ye also shall abide in the Son and in the Father," and
" His anointing teacheth you concerning all things."

$$5^{5-12}.$$

This, the second passage of importance dealing expressly
with the grounds of Belief, is one of much difficulty and
obscurity.[2] We have already considered the meaning of

---

[1] Signifying absolute knowledge.
[2] As to the probable explanation of this, see Chapter III. p. 42 (note).

the unique phraseology in which the permanent reality of the Incarnation is here asserted. In opposition to the Cerinthian heresy, which taught that there was merely a temporary connection between the heavenly Christ and the human Jesus, beginning at the Baptism and terminating on the eve of the Passion, the Apostle testifies that Jesus *is* the Son of God (5⁵), and that He " came "—was manifested as the Christ, entered upon His Christly mission—both by the water of Baptism and the blood of the Cross. And, as warrant for this belief, he cites the testimony of five witnesses: the Spirit (5⁶ᵇ), the Water and the Blood (5⁸), God (5⁹), the believer's own experience (5¹⁰).

5⁶ᵇ.

The Witness of the Spirit.

" And it is the Spirit that witnesseth,[1] because the Spirit is Truth."

Almost as many explanations have been offered of the " Spirit " in this verse as of the " Water and the Blood " in the preceding verse. Undoubtedly, however, it is identical with the " Spirit " who inspires the confession of Jesus as the " Christ come in the flesh " (4²), and with the " anointing " that " teacheth you concerning all things,"—in short, is the Paraclete of the Fourth Gospel.[2]

As to the substance of the Spirit's testimony, it is not only that Jesus came by the water and by the blood; it includes the whole truth advanced, that the Jesus who thus came is the Son of God (5⁵, ⁶). As to the manner in

---

[1] τὸ μαρτυροῦν. The generic neuter (cf. πᾶν τὸ γεγεννημένον, 5⁴) emphasises that precisely this is the function of the Spirit. Everywhere in Johannine Scripture the office of the Spirit is to teach or testify (John 14²⁶ 15²⁶ 16¹³⁻¹⁵).

[2] The relation between the work of Christ and that of the Spirit is signified by a fine parallelism which is to some extent lost in translation, ἐστιν ὁ ἐλθών (5⁶), ἐστιν τὸ μαρτυροῦν (5⁷). Jesus is *He that came*, once for all fulfilling the Messiah's mission; the Spirit is *that which beareth witness*, ever authenticating its Divine origin, interpreting its purpose and applying its results.

which the testimony is borne, this may be conceived either
as direct or as indirect. In the Acts of the Apostles the
descent of the Spirit, with all its sensible manifestations,
is cited simply as a supernatural fact, bearing objective
testimony to Christ's Resurrection and Ascension (" This
which ye have seen and heard," Acts 2[33. 36]; cf. 1 Cor. 14[25]).
Such is the witness of the Spirit to the world; but to the
Church it is given by direct inspiration. The distinction is
clearly drawn by St. Paul, " Wherefore tongues are for a
sign, not to them that believe, but to them that believe
not; but prophesying is not to them that believe not, but
to them that believe" (1 Cor. 14[22]). It is the latter aspect
of the Spirit's testimony that is brought into prominence
in the Epistle. Whether acting charismatically through
the prophets or universally upon the minds of believers, it
is by direct inward "teaching" that the Spirit testifies of
Christ in the Church. Combining both aspects, we may
say that the permanent witness of the Spirit consists,
inwardly, in the Christian's intuitive assurance of the truth
revealed in Christ, and, externally, in the whole manifestation of a life of supernatural character and power in the
past and present of the Christian Church.

Next is added the reason why the Spirit is " that which
witnesseth " :—" because the Spirit is Truth." Again, this
might be understood as signifying simply that the Spirit
is an abiding reality. However the ideas and beliefs of
men may change and oscillate, the presence of the Spirit
is a permanent supernatural fact, and, therefore, is " that
which beareth witness." Probably, however, the meaning is
not different from that expressed in the familiar title, " the
Spirit of Truth "—the Spirit, that is, whose nature it is to
recognise and reveal the eternal Truth [1] of God. Perception

---

[1] There is an exact parallelism between what is said of Christ and of the
Spirit. Christ came into the world " to bear witness to the Truth " (John 18[37]).
And He is also Himself the Truth (John 14[6]), to which the " other Paraclete "
testifies.

implies kinship. Only Love can know Love. Only Purity can understand Purity. Only Truth can recognise Truth. And it is because "the Spirit is Truth" that He recognises and reveals Christ who is the embodiment of the Truth (John 15⁶). The statement, thus understood, points clearly to the personality of the Spirit; and, indeed, suggests the Trinitarian conception of the Godhead. The ultimate Truth is what God is. And as the Father is the Truth in its essence, and the Son is the Word or outgoing of the Truth, so the Spirit is the witness of the unity of the Essence and the Word,—the witness in the Father of His unity with the Son, and in the Son of His unity with the Father. And thus the Spirit, imparted to men, becomes the author of Faith,—becomes in us also the consciousness of God in Christ, and of the Christ in God.

5⁸.

The Witness of the Water and the Blood.

"For there are three that bear witness,¹ the Spirit, and the Water, and the Blood: and the three agree in one."

As regards the witness of the Water and the Blood, it is best to acknowledge that it is impossible to recover with certainty the precise conception in the writer's mind.² It is evident, however, that the controversial purpose of the passage must be taken as the starting-point towards any sound interpretation. Against the Docetic theory of

¹ "For there are three that bear witness." The connecting "for" (ὅτι) is loosely used. It seems to indicate that, though the Water and the Blood were not at their first mention (5⁶) cited expressly as witnesses, this was already in the writer's mind. Then the bringing forward of the Spirit's witness suddenly suggests to him that the witnesses attain to the significant number three, "For in fact, the witnesses are three in number," etc. It is probable that in the reiterated emphatic "three" there is an allusion to the requirement of the Mosaic Law, that only in the testimony of two or three witnesses should capital charges be held as proven (Deut. 17⁶; cf. Matt. 18¹⁶, John 8¹⁷ sqq.). This supposition is almost necessary to give point to "If we receive the witness of men" in 5⁹.

² See Chapter III. p. 42 (note).

a merely temporary habitation of the heavenly Christ in
the human Jesus, St. John asserts the truth of a real and
indissoluble Incarnation.   The Jesus Who was baptized in
Jordan and the Jesus Who was crucified on Calvary were
in every respect the same Divine-human person.   He
"came"—entered into the sphere of His Messianic action
—by Water and by Blood.   His Baptism was the initial
act, His Death the consummating act, of His self-conse-
cration to the work of the world's redemption.[1]   It is to
this that the Spirit bears witness (4^2); and since it is said
that the witness of the Water and the Blood is to the
same effect ($\epsilon i\varsigma\ \tau\grave{o}\ \overset{\text{v}}{\epsilon}\nu\ \epsilon i\sigma\iota\nu$), obviously this must be of such
a nature as to confute the Docetic annulment of the
Incarnation.   Now, since in 5^6 the Water and the Blood
undoubtedly refer to our Lord's own Baptism and Passion,
the natural course is to seek in these, and in the historical
facts connected with them, the "witness" of the Water and
the Blood.   Nor is it difficult to see how the Baptism of
Jesus, with its attendant circumstances (the testimony of
John the Baptist; our Lord's own consciousness of sinlessness, implied in the fact that, though John's baptism was a
baptism of repentance, He alone made no confession of
sin; the descent of the Spirit; the Voice from heaven),
testified to the Messiahship, which with St. John is equivalent to the Divine Sonship of Jesus.   But as to the witness
of the Blood there is serious difficulty.   To explain it
(Weiss) by those incidents of the Crucifixion to which the
Fourth Gospel attaches a special significance as fulfilments
of Scripture—"A bone of Him shall not be broken,"
"They shall look upon Him whom they have pierced"
(John $19^{33,\ 37}$)—is altogether inadequate.[2]

---

[1] See Chapter VI. pp. 96, 97.

[2] It is sufficiently remarkable that the Resurrection finds no place in the
apologetics of the Epistle, although the proofs of its reality are so carefully set
forth in the Fourth Gospel.   The reason probably is that Cerinthus and his
school did not deny the *resurrection of Jesus* (Irenæus, i. 26. 1).

The only interpretation left open is that the witness of the Water and the Blood is that of the Christian Sacraments. The objection to this is that it requires here in 5^8 a different sense for the Water and the Blood from what they have in 5^6. But in view of the extreme condensation of the whole passage, the objection is not insurmountable. The transition from the facts themselves to the appointed and familiar memorials of the facts is thoroughly natural. The witness of the Sacraments, moreover, would tell with destructive effect upon the position of the Docetists. Holding the truth that Christ "came" by Water, they would, no doubt, accept the Sacrament of Baptism ; but the Lord's Supper must have presented an insuperable obstacle to their theory of the Crucifixion. Whether they retained the observance of it we cannot tell ; but it is difficult to imagine what sacramental significance they could attach to this memorial of One Who before His Passion had been reduced to the level of common humanity.

On the other hand, the Apostle's words may suggest the question whether the worth of the Sacraments as permanent and, one might almost say, living witnesses to the historical reality, as well as to the ideal significance, of the facts they represent, is usually appreciated and emphasised as it ought to be. His declaration that Christ came by water, though not by water only, gives to Christ's own Baptism an importance that is not always recognised. It is evident that for the writer of the Epistle the Baptism (though it is not definitely recorded in the Fourth Gospel) was no mere incident in the life of Jesus, no merely formal inauguration of His Messianic ministry. It was by His Baptism "with the Holy Ghost and with power" that Jesus was qualified to be the Saviour of the world. The Holy Ghost by Whom His humanity was begotten in the Virgin's womb, Who formed and nurtured and trained in Him that

[1] Brooke takes the contrary view.

sinless manhood which brought back the lost image of God
to earth, was then first poured out upon Him "not by
measure," that from Him it might again proceed in life-
giving stream through the world of souls.   It was thus
that the Divine Life became in Him a perennial and overflowing fountain of regenerative power; and to this as
a fact of history, to say nothing more, the Sacrament of
Baptism is the abiding witness in the Church.   Christian
Baptism apart from the Baptism of Christ would be
meaningless.   Only He who has the fulness of the Spirit
can impart the Spirit.

But He came not by water only, but by the Water and
the Blood.   There was that in the Love of Christ—the
Love of God—which water could not, which only blood
could express.   There was that in the need of man which
water could not, which only blood could adequately meet.
By death the grain of wheat must be quickened and become fruitful.   The Life of Christ, endued with all fulness
of spiritual power, and with all its fulness of spiritual power
consecrated to God in His Baptism, must be poured out
in the uttermost sacrifice, that it might bring forth the new
life of the children of God.   And of this fact, that it was
the Christ, the Son of God, whose Body and Blood were
offered for us upon the Cross, the Lord's Supper is the
perpetual attestation.   The Sacraments are impressive and
incontrovertible witnesses to historical realities.   Every
successive generation of Christians has baptized, and broken
bread as the first company of believers did, and has received in these Sacraments the same testimony to the
foundation-facts upon which our salvation rests.   Older
than the oldest of New Testament Scriptures, of an
authenticity which no criticism can impugn, they lead us
back to the birth-hour of Christianity, and perpetuate in the
Church the historical basis of its Faith.   And not only does
one generation testify to another in the Sacraments; Christ

Himself testifies in them to His Church. If they are His ordinance, if it is by His appointment that we baptize in His name and "do this in remembrance" of Him, this is the surest evidence that He was conscious of being to men the one and ever-enduring source of regenerative virtue and propitiatory cleansing; and in them He is ever repeating that claim and pledging Himself anew to its fulfilment. But the Spirit also witnesses in the Sacraments. By them He has in all ages revived and strengthened faith, inspired love, awakened hope, and imparted new impulse to Christian lives—has, in short, made Christ a Real Presence, not in material elements, but in the hearts of His disciples. Materialised as the conception of the Sacraments has sometimes become, formal as their observance in many cases may be, the zealous affection and honour in which the universal Church has always held them, as the centre of its fellowship and, as it were, the very hearth of the household of faith, have written the best of commentaries upon the Apostle's words, " There are three that bear witness, the Spirit, and the Water, and the Blood."

Finally, the Apostle adds that these three witnesses " agree [1] in one "; they are to the same effect; they testify jointly to the truth which is the theme of the entire paragraph—that Jesus, who was baptized and crucified, is the Son of God. This combination of the historical (the Water, the Blood) and the ideal (the Spirit) is the strength of Christian apologetics. Without the one, Christianity becomes a mere Idealism, by which faith could no more conquer the world than the lungs could fill themselves in a vacuum. Without the other, the voice of truth awakens no inward response, lacks that self-evidencing power which alone makes it truth to the soul.

[1] εἰς τὸ ἕν εἰσιν " converge upon the same object." Cf. John 11[52] 17[23].

5⁹.

The Triple Witness considered as the Witness of God.

" If we receive the witness of men, the witness of God is greater: for this is the witness of God, because He hath borne witness concerning His Son."

The sentence, however it be construed,[1] is highly elliptical, requiring, for a full statement of the sense, to be supplemented thus: " If we receive the witness of men, the witness of God is greater (and, therefore, we ought the rather to receive it; and here this principle comes into operation), because this witness (of which I have been speaking) is the witness of God, because He has borne witness concerning His Son." Rugged and clumsy as the form of the sentence is, its intention is thoroughly clear,—namely, to set forth the threefold witness of the Spirit, the Water, and the Blood as being, in reality, the witness of God. In the facts which the Christian Sacraments commemorate, in the Baptism with the Spirit which inaugurated the Christly ministry of Jesus, and in the Death and Resurrection in which that ministry was consummated and by which it passed beyond all limitations of time, and place, and sense; in the testimony of the Spirit creating and establishing a world-conquering faith in the crucified Jesus as the victorious Son of God:—in these facts, if anywhere at all, God has uttered Himself in unmistakable testimony to mankind. And if we receive the testimony of men, as we do,—if nine-tenths of what we call " knowledge " is derived from the testimony of men,—the refusal to accept the testimony of God, thus given, is not due to any uncertainty in it. God has given to men no other testimony so explicit and convincing.

[1] See Notes, *in loc.*

$$5^{10}.$$

But there is still another Witness, that of Experience.

" He that believeth in[1] the Son of God hath the witness in himself: he that believeth[1] not God hath made Him a liar; because he hath not believed in the witness that God hath borne concerning His Son."

By " believing " the testimony of God, we " believe in " His Son. Our faith is directed towards the personal Christ, and rests in Him. And he who thus " believes in " the Son of God hath the witness (to the Divine Sonship of Jesus) in himself. To the historical evidence, even to the enlightening testimony of the Spirit, there is added in the believer a confirmatory witness in his personal experience of cleansing from sin and renewed life. He " tastes and sees "; believes and knows. He not only " sets to his seal " that the object of his faith is true: more and more he receives from it the experience of its truth. On the contrary, not to " believe in " Christ is equivalent to not " believing " God; and this is to " make Him a liar,"[2] because it is not to have believed in the witness that God hath borne concerning His Son. Here the deliberate and circumstantial repetition of what has been already said with emphasis in 5^9 brings out the gravity of the issue. The thought of making God a liar is an appalling one; and especially is it so when it concerns the witness that He hath borne concerning His own Son.

This argument, that the alternative to believing in Jesus as the Son of God is making God a liar, is one

[1] See Notes, *in loc.*, and special note on πιστεύειν, appended to Chapter XIII.

[2] " Hath made Him a liar." Cf. 1^{10}. The two ways in which men make God a liar are—" If we say that we have no sin," and if we do not believe " the witness He hath borne concerning His Son." The two are related as closely as possible. If we have no sin, the Gospel of the Water and the Blood becomes meaningless and incredible.

that gains cumulative force as the history of the Church and the world advances. To assert of the Christian gospel and the Christian Church—the mightiest of all beneficent influences in the life of men and the development of human history—that the one is the proclamation of a myth, and that the other is founded upon delusion and has grown up in an atmosphere of vain credulity,—this is to ascribe to falsehood, instead of to truth, the power to promote the most Divine ends; it is equivalent to saying that God, if there be a God, is a liar,—one whose chosen methods of accomplishing His Will are those of dissimulation and deceit.

From the summary thus made of the passages that treat of the basis of Belief, it will be apparent that the apologetic problem is handled, though in briefest compass, with no little breadth and fulness. And this chapter may be closed with a summary of the results. The whole Christian revelation is contained in the Person of Jesus Christ, who is known solely by the facts narrated in the Apostolic Gospel. These facts, embraced under the headings, the Water and the Blood, are themselves evidential (5^{6-8}). In them the Divine mission of Jesus is fully attested, and the eternal Life of God manifested on earth (1^2). Knowledge of these facts is conveyed through the normal channel of human communication (1^3)—by the Apostolic testimony, the trustworthiness of which is strongly asserted ($1^1\ 4^{14}$). Upon this, as its historical foundation, Christian Faith must always stand (2^{24}). But, though Faith is not apart from human testimony, its certitude is derived from the witness of the Spirit, which continuously attests the truth of the human testimony. (5^{6b}). All this is collectively the witness of God (5^9); for if God has spoken at all to men, it is in the Life, Death, and Resurrection of Christ, and in the witness that the Spirit of Truth bears to Him,

both in Christian Faith itself and in the whole influence
of that Faith on the world's history. And, finally, he
that believeth hath the witness in Himself. Christian
Faith carries with it the experience of a moral regeneration. While there is no elaboration of any of those topics,
it is with a quite amazing insight that the writer of the
Epistle seizes all the positions in which Christian apologetic
has ever since found its chief strongholds.

NOTE ON "ANOINTING" (χρῖσμα), 2²⁰.

This word is the last descendant of a long and interesting Biblical
lineage, the successive steps in which may be briefly indicated.

1. The anointing of the body with oil is practised as a means of
invigoration (upon infants, Ezek. 16⁹ ; upon the sick, Jas. 5¹⁴).

2. From the refreshing and pleasurable sensations thus produced,
anointing (especially with fragrant unguents) is an act of courteous
hospitality, betokening favour towards the guest (Ps. 23⁵). Failure to
observe this custom is a mark of perfunctory and ungenerous enter-
tainment (Luke 7⁴⁶).

3. Thus it naturally becomes a symbol of joy and strength (Prov.
27⁹, Isa. 61³, Matt. 6⁹), and is symbolically used in the appointment
of persons to high and sacred office as a mark of Divine favour and of
Divine endowment with the gifts and aptitudes required by the office. (a)
Kings are anointed (1 Sam. 10¹ ; the anointing being accompanied by
the gift of the Spirit) ; (b) Priests are anointed (Lev. 8¹². ³⁰, Ps. 133²) ;
(c) Prophets are anointed (1 Kings 19¹⁶, Ps. 105¹⁵, Isa. 61¹) ; (d) the
title "Anointed" (Messiah, Christ) is applied specifically to the kings
of David's line (Ps. 2² 84⁹) ; and becomes the title of the expected
Deliverer and Redeemer of Israel (Dan. 9²⁵. ²⁶, John 4²⁵ 7²⁷. ³¹).

4. It is given to Jesus and accepted by Him (Matt. 16¹⁶. ²⁰, John
6⁶⁹ 11²⁷, Luke 24²⁶ etc.), and becomes virtually a proper name of Jesus
(N.T. *passim*).

5. The χρῖσμα with which Jesus is anointed is the Holy Ghost (Acts
10³⁸ ; cf. Luke 4¹⁸, John 3³⁴).

6. This χρῖσμα is, after His Ascension, fully imparted to the Church
(John 16⁸, Acts 2³² ; cf. Acts 10⁴⁵, Eph. 4⁸ sqq., 2 Cor. 1²¹).

It does not at all follow from the use of the word χρῖσμα in 2²⁰ (which
is unique in the N.T.) that it was a technical ecclesiastical term, or
that the ceremony of actual Chrism, which very soon became a
recognised adjunct to baptism and the laying on of hands, was already
in use.

CHAPTER VIII.

THE DOCTRINE OF SIN AND THE WORLD.

THE Epistle presents no fully articulated doctrine of Sin; nor does it contain the material for such a doctrine. It suggests no exceptional preoccupation with the great Pauline problems of the inherence and operation of sin in human nature, or of its genesis and development in the individual and in the race. But if the Epistle adds little to the stock of New Testament ideas about sin, nowhere is the common Christian consciousness of sin and of its determining significance for man's relation to God more profoundly felt. Nowhere is the sense of sin as creating an antagonism in the moral universe that transcends all measurement more passionately expressed. Horror, hatred, fear, repudiation of sin pervade the whole Epistle. The essential tragedy of human existence is set forth in that single awful image of the world—"the whole world"—lying in the embrace of the Wicked One (5^{19}). It is against the dark background of sin that the innermost glory of the Divine Nature shines forth in God's sending His Only-Begotten Son as a propitiation for our sins ($4^{9.\ 10}$); and in nothing does the Apostle's own soul speak more intensely than in the fervid declaration, "My little children, these things write I unto you, that ye sin not" (2^1).

In the Epistle the nomenclature of moral evil contains but three words—ἁμαρτία, sin; ἀνομία, lawlessness; ἀδικία unrighteousness. We shall first consider those passages in which ἁμαρτία, or some cognate, is the prominent term.[1]

The idea of sin—the conception which the word calls up in every mind—is twofold. It denotes the character of an action as morally bad and in itself condemnable, and it implies the responsibility of the agent. The sinfulness of sin is the joint product of these two factors; and the consciousness of sin, universally and necessarily, contains both. Yet, in the actual view taken of sin, the one or the other is invariably the more prominent. According to the standpoint occupied, the emphasis may be either ethical or judicial—upon the quality of the act and of the moral nature displayed in it, or upon the culpability in which such act involves the agent. In the Epistle each of these aspects of sin is strongly presented. Of the two principal passages that have a direct bearing upon the subject, the first (1⁷–2²) contemplates sin as guilt, while in the second (3⁴⁻⁹) sin is contemplated in its ethical antagonism to the nature of God and of the children of God.

1⁷–2².

The judicial view of sin characterises the whole para-

---

[1] Logically, the following uses are to be distinguished :—

(*a*) ἁμαρτία without the article signifies a sinful act (5¹⁶·¹⁷); αἱ ἁμαρτίαι, sinful acts (1⁹ 2²·¹² 3⁵ 4¹⁰); ἁμαρτάνειν, to commit a sinful act (1¹⁰ 3⁶). The unambiguously concrete ἁμάρτημα is not found in St. John.

(*b*) ἁμαρτία without the article is used also collectively, signifying sin in its concrete totality (3⁵ ἁμαρτία ἐν αὐτῷ οὐκ ἔστιν=sin, as a whole, is excluded from the sphere of His being; 3⁹ ἁμαρτίαν οὐ ποιεῖ=sin, as a whole, is excluded from the sphere of doing).

(*c*) In the phrase ἁμαρτίαν ἔχειν (1⁸, John 9⁴¹ 15²²·²⁴ 19¹¹) the idea is more abstract, the phrase connoting not so much the act of sin as the culpability of the doer.

(*d*) With the article, ἡ ἁμαρτία is a pure abstract, signifying sin in its constitutive principle (ἡ ἁμαρτία, 3⁴·⁸, in direct antithesis to ἡ δικαιοσύνη, 2²⁹ 3⁷). So in 3⁸ ὁ ποιῶν τὴν ἁμαρτίαν=he who expresses in actual deed the essential principle of sin).

9

graph.[1]   According to the law of the moral universe, sin
committed constitutes an objective disability for fellowship
with God, which can be removed only by confession (1^9),
forgiveness (1^9), and propitiatory cleansing ($1^{7.\ 9}\ 2^2$).   It is
true that $1^{7.\ 8}$ are very generally interpreted from the
ethical standpoint.   But this is groundless.   With regard
to 1^7 (" The blood of Jesus His Son cleanseth us from all
sin "), the significations of " cleansing " and " sin " are
mutually dependent; and if, as I shall maintain in the
next chapter, " cleansing " ($\kappa\alpha\theta\alpha\rho\acute{\iota}\zeta\epsilon\iota\nu$) is here attributed to
the propitiatory power of Christ's blood, it follows that
" sin " is regarded primarily as guilt.   In 1^8 (" If we say
that we have no sin, we deceive ourselves ") the judicial
sense is unmistakable.   The phrase " to have sin " ($\check{\epsilon}\chi\epsilon\iota\nu$
$\acute{\alpha}\mu\alpha\rho\tau\acute{\iota}\alpha\nu$) is peculiar to St. John, and has a quite definite
sense.   Thus in John 15^{22} our Lord says, " If I had not
come and spoken unto them, they had not had sin; but
now they have no excuse for their sin."   Here, beyond
question, " to have sin " specifically denotes the guiltiness
of the agent.   In John 9^{41} 15^{24} 19^{11} the sense is equally
clear; and these parallels must be held as decisive for
the meaning[2] here.   " If we say that we have no guilt, no
responsibility for the actions, wrong in themselves, which
we have committed, we but deceive[3] ourselves."   In 1^9 (" If
we confess our sins,[4] He is faithful and righteous to forgive

---

[1] From the point of view of our present topic, that is.   The primary matter in
the paragraph is not sin, but the confession or denial of sin, regarded as walking
in the Light and walking in darkness.   See Chapter IV.

[2] Brooke admitting that $\check{\epsilon}\chi\epsilon\iota\nu$ $\acute{\alpha}\mu\alpha\rho\tau\acute{\iota}\alpha\nu$ accentuates the idea of responsibility,
yet holds (with Westcott and Plummer) that it chiefly connotes the presence of
sin as a principle.   The two ideas may, no doubt, be combined—responsibility
attaches not only to the sinful act, but to the stronger hold of indwelling sin
which follows.   But the interpretations by which Mr. Brooke discovers this
complex idea in the passages of the Gospel seem to me over-subtle.   And in
the absence of any good reason to the contrary, there is a strong presumption that
the phrase bears the same meaning in Gospel and Epistle.

[3] " Only when man recognises himself as sinner, can he believe in the nobility
of his manhood " (Rothe).

[4] The change to the plural form is significant.   We may deny sin as a whole

us our sins ") there is no ambiguity. To confess our sins is not only to acknowledge the presence in our life of wrong action, but is to confess this as needing *forgiveness* —to lay at our own door the full responsibility for it. In 1[10] (" If we say that we have not sinned, we make Him a liar ") the emphasis is directly on the fact of wrong-doing, the culpability of which has been asserted in the preceding verses. Again, in 2[1, 2] the judicial emphasis does not admit of doubt. Sin is that which needs God's forgiveness ; and, to this end, an Intercessor and a Pro-pitiation have been provided.

The doctrine of the paragraph may thus be stated in three propositions. (*a*) Sin is action for which the agent is primarily responsible. Whether his action contain more or less of the special elements of wrong,—rejection of light, treason to God, his neighbour, or himself,—his own evil will is the direct cause of its having existed. And if we say that such guilt does not belong to us, our error is worse than ignorance—we lead ourselves astray (ἑαυτοὺς πλανῶμεν) in outer darkness. It seems clear that the Apostle has here in view the doctrine of Gnostic Antinomianism, that the "spiritual" are free from sin, because sin is wholly of the flesh.[1] But this heresy is older and newer than Gnosticism. In manifold forms it reappears in modern thought. For the modern materialist, as for the ancient Manichee, sin is a question of physiology ; moral depravity only a manifestation of corporeal disorder. Or the evil in the world is due to the social environment, is the result of bad education and bad institutions. Against all such theories St. John lifts up the single word— Sin. " If we say that we have no sin, we deceive ourselves." (*b*) Sin is universal. " If we say that we have not sinned,

---

(1[8]), but confession must condescend upon particulars. Sin is known only by its concrete instances. The conscience does not deal with abstractions.

[1] *v. supra*, pp. 32–34.

we "—not only deceive ourselves—we " make God a liar "
(1^{10}). " All the institutions of the Divine economy, God's
entire government and work upon earth, the whole manifestation of the Son of God, based upon the presupposition
of human sin, are reduced to one comprehensive lie"
(Haupt). At the contemplation of such denial, be it blind
or wanton, the Apostle's soul is fired to passionate indignation. (*c*) The immediate effect of sin is to embarrass and
pervert man's relation to God, to disqualify him for that
fellowship with God for which he was created, and the loss
of which is death (3^{14} 5^{16}). The sole measure of its otherwise immeasurable evil is that only by the blood of Jesus,
God's Son, can there be cleansing from its stain and restoration to the Divine fellowship.

3^{4-9}.

In the paragraph we have just considered the leading
thought was that of walking in the Light; and by this the
view of sin was governed. Sin was regarded only in its
concrete manifestations—as a fact of observation and experience. In the second cycle of the Epistle the leading
thought is that of the Divine Begetting. The Christian
life is regarded as a Divine sonship—participation in the
essential nature of God. Consequently, sin is now contemplated in its absolute ethical antagonism to the nature
of God's children. " Every one that is begotten· of God
doeth not sin ; because His seed abideth in him : and he
cannot sin, because he is begotten of God " (3^9). Instead
of the concrete ἁμαρτία, the abstract ἡ ἁμαρτία, denoting sin
in its constitutive principle, becomes the distinctive term.
The phrase " every one that doeth sin " (ὁ ποιῶν τὴν ἁμαρτίαν,
$3^{4.\ 8}$) expresses the manifestation in actual deeds of the
essential principle of evil, which is called Sin. Sins are
multiform ; Sin is one. A sin is never an isolated act of
wrong-doing. If so viewed, it is not seen in its full

significance.   Individual sins are like islets, which appear as separate and casual specks on the surface of the ocean, but are, in reality, the mountain-peaks of a submerged continent.   He who "does sin" only gives particular embodiment to a universal principle, ἡ ἁμαρτία ; just as the right-doer embodies ἡ δικαιοσύνη (2²⁹), and as the truth-doer embodies ἡ ἀλήθεια (1⁶).   He shows, moreover, that this principle of evil is rooted in his own nature.   He is not a sinner because he commits sins; he commits sins because he is a sinner.   "Every one that doeth sin is of the devil; because the devil sinneth from the beginning" (3⁸).   The outward sin is the index to the inward nature.

The word by which St. John defines the essential principle of sin (ἡ ἁμαρτία) is "lawlessness" (ἡ ἀνομία). "Every one that doeth sin doeth also lawlessness; and sin is lawlessness"¹ (3⁴).   This conception of sin as being essentially lawlessness corresponds to the strong emphasis which the Epistle lays upon the commandments of God and their careful observance (2³·⁴ 3²²·²⁴ 5²·³).   But the thought is not to be limited by any of the historical deliverances of the Law.   Sin is fundamentally the denial of the absoluteness of moral obligation—repudiation of the eternal canon of Right and Wrong, upon which all moral life is based.   In other words, to sin is to assert one's own will as the rule of action against the absolutely good Will of God.   Thus it is but truth to say that every sin contains in germ the whole infinite of evil.   It embodies that principle which, given effect to, would

---

¹ The genuine use of the article with both subject and predicate (to which there is *no real parallel* in the N.T.) indicates how exactly convertible the two terms are.   There is no sin that is not lawlessness, and there is no lawlessness that is not sin.   ἀνομία, alike in classical Greek and in the N.T., signifies, not a state of being without law (though St. Paul uses ἄνομος in this sense in 1 Cor. 9²¹), but an act of opposition to law.   Elsewhere in our English versions it is translated "iniquity" (except in 2 Thess. 2⁷, where, as here, R.V. has "lawlessness").   In the N.T. it is used to translate various O.T. words ;—פֶּשַׁע (Rom. 4⁷), חַטָּאת (Heb. 10¹⁷), and רֶשַׁע (Heb. 1⁹).   Here it must be understood in its strict etymological sense as "lawlessness."

overthrow the entire moral order of existence. One little lie has in it that which would subvert the throne of God and extinguish the light of Heaven. All sins have sin in them, and "sin is lawlessness."

Though it does not occur in this paragraph, we may here consider another term by which an ethical significance is stamped upon sin—"unrighteousness" (ἀδικία). The word naturally suggests the negative aspect of sin—sin as declension from the standard of rightness (δικαιοσύνη). And this sense satisfactorily meets the requirements of the three passages in which alone it occurs in St. John (John 7^{18}, 1 John 1^9 5^{17}).

In the first of these, " He that speaketh of himself seeketh his own glory ; but he that seeketh the glory of Him that sent him, the same is true, and there is no ἀδικία in him," the meaning obviously suggested is " unfaithfulness to the trust imposed in one," or, more generally, " dereliction of duty." And the same sense admirably suits 1 John 5^{17}. The Apostle has been distinguishing between " sin unto death " and " sin not unto death "; but before leaving the subject he adds, " All unrighteousness is sin." The purpose of the addition is evident. The danger to be apprehended from emphasising the distinction between mortal and non-mortal sin is that we may fall into an attitude of comparative nonchalance toward the less heinous offences; and to obviate this danger we are reminded that every deviation from moral uprightness, however venial it may appear, is sin.[1] The same meaning is most appropriate also in 1^9, " God is faithful and righteous to forgive us our sins, and to cleanse us from

---

[1] This explanation seems much more natural than that according to which the purpose is to indicate how wide a field there is for brotherly intercession, even if the sin unto death is regarded as beyond its scope—because all unrighteousness, which is never awanting, is sin, and its presence an urgent call to prayer (Westcott, Haupt, Weiss). Westcott here takes ἀδικία as signifying "failure to fulfil our duty one to another." I am unable to perceive any ground for this limitation of the meaning.

all unrighteousness." As God is faithful to His own revealed character in forgiving our sins, so He is not unrighteous but righteous in "cleansing" us from every failure in righteousness, in relieving us, that is, from the religious disabilities imposed upon us by it.[1] Thus ἀδικία contemplates sin in its negative aspect as non-righteousness, unfaithfulness in the moral stewardship of life (cf. Luke 16[8]). And the Apostle emphasises the fact that all such unrighteousness, any morally inferior course of action, is sin, and contains the elements of positive guilt. This is continually overlooked. Men often think more of the distinctions and gradations of sin than of its essential wrongness. They speak of "peccadilloes," "foibles," "failings," of things that are "not quite right" (as if they were not *quite wrong*). The sinfulness of sin is wrapped around with euphemisms and circumlocutions. Concerning all this St. John has but one word to utter, "All unrighteousness is sin."

Thus far, then, the Epistle's doctrine of Sin may be summarised as follows. Sin is that which involves the culpability of the agent. Sins are of various kinds; but all failure in duty, all deviation from the right is sin. And all sin, in its real character, is repudiation of the supremacy of moral obligation—is revolt against the holy Will of God.

5[16. 17].

In the third cycle of the Epistle we encounter the perplexing topic of "sin unto death." It ought to be observed, however, that the introduction of this is merely incidental, and that the main subject of the passage is "sin not unto

---

[1] Here Westcott's interpretation is "the specific sins (αἱ ἁμαρτίαι) are forgiven; the character (ἀδικία) is cleansed." Thus an entirely different meaning is given to ἀδικία from that which he adopts in 5[17], the inconsistency being necessitated only by the determination to interpret καθαρίζειν in an ethical sense. See Chapter VIII.

death"; while its actual purpose is to use this as an example of those things regarding which we may pray with perfect confidence of success (5^{16}).

"If any man see his brother," to whom he is bound by the ties of Divine kinship (5^1), regarding whom he is persuaded that, at the root, he belongs to Him "in whom there is no sin" (3^5)—if he see this brother, nevertheless, "sinning a sin," plainly not abiding in Christ but taking the way that leads to certain separation from Christ, yet not so as to have irrevocably fallen from Him—if he see this, "he shall ask," and God will grant him in answer to his prayer, "life for them that sin not unto death." There is a sense in which every sin tends "unto death." Conscious or unconscious, it is fraught with injury and loss to life. It interrupts some channel of inter-communication between the Vine and the branch. But the Epistle has already declared the means by which the interrupted fellowship may be recovered. The renewed advocacy of Christ (2^1) and the renewed cleansing of His Blood (1^7), will unfailingly restore fulness of Life. But the condition of this is that we "walk in the light" (1^7), that is, in the present instance, that there be confession of sin (1^9). In the case contemplated, however, the erring brother has not fulfilled this condition. He is ignorant of his sin, or is impenitent, or is withheld from confession by fear or obstinacy (Ps. $32^{3, 4}$). It is in such an emergency that his brother may come to the rescue and do for him what he lacks the power or the will to do for himself—confess his sin and seek his restoration. And the Apostle affirms that such effort cannot be in vain; that God has so bound us together in the Body of Christ that one may by his prayer become the means of obtaining for another a fresh influx of "Life," by which he will be renewed unto repentance. Now, it is only by way of contrast with this that mention is made of the "sin unto death." The Apostle is jealous of misapprehension as to the Christian's assurance in prayer. It might be extended beyond its proper scope, with the inevitable result of its being weakened everywhere; and against this he will guard his readers. He will not forbid them to place in God's hands even him who has sinned unto death, with the fervent supplication that " if it be possible " he may yet be snatched from his doom. But he does view as a possibility, and assert as a fact, that there are those for whose restoration and salvation we cannot pray with unconditional confidence as for a thing "according to His will."[1] "There is a sin unto death: not concerning this do I say that he should make request."

What, then, are the characteristics of the " sin unto death," as we may gather them from this passage?

1. It is a sin which may be committed by Christians, and it is only as committed by Christians that it is here contemplated.

2. It is a sin which is visible, or, at least, recognisable. It is evident that the term " sin unto death " must have been one well understood by the first readers of the Epistle; and that it denoted a particular sin or kind of sin the characteristics of which were so definite that they were easy to perceive, and so familiar that they needed no description. On any other supposition the reference to this sin as an exception to the full exercise of brotherly intercession is entirely pointless.[2] It seems strange that

---

[1] This must be taken seriously, not as a mere concession to the infirmity of his readers' faith. It is not serious exposition to say that " some of St. John's disciples may have believed that when a man sinned a certain kind of sin it was contrary to God's will that he should ever be quickened to life again," and " that the Apostle does not pause to argue with them, does not even tell them that, in his own apprehension of it, the scope of the Divine mercy was far wider than in theirs, and must be of far wider scope than even he was able to conceive" (Cox, *Expositions*, 1885, p. 258).

[2] So Westcott, "Its character is assumed to be unquestionable, and its presence open and notorious" (p. 210). Plummer, on the contrary, strongly maintains that we must get rid of the idea that " sin unto death " is a sin that

what was so recognisable then is so unrecognisable now.
Yet it is conceivable that, in our own religious dialect and
modes of thought, there are phrases that to the Christian
of two thousand years hence will be no less obscure, and
conceptions no less difficult to locate in his religious and
ethical system, than the "sin unto death" is to ourselves.
The singular thing is that even to the earliest Patristic
writers who touch the subject the "sin unto death" is
already an enigma—its meaning as much a matter of
conjecture or inference as to us.

3. It is "unto death" ($\pi\rho\grave{o}\varsigma\ \theta\acute{a}\nu\alpha\tau\sigma\nu$). What does this
expression signify? (*a*) It is pointed out that the dis-
tinction of "sins unto death" and "sins not unto death"
is common with Rabbinic writers, and is based on the
Old Testament legislation, according to which the punishment for many offences (cf. Lev. $18^{29}\ 20^{9-21}$), especially for
those committed with a "high hand" (Num. $15^{30.\ 31}$), was
death, involving final "cutting off from the people."
This, however, while it may possibly indicate the origin
of the phrase, does not materially help towards an understanding of what it signifies in the atmosphere of New
Testament thought. The interpretations which have been
directly based upon the Old Testament usage—that "sin
unto death" is sin punished by the civil authorities with
death or by the Church with excommunication (thus the

can be recognised. "St. John's very guarded language points the other way.
He implies that *some* sin may be known to be not unto death; he neither says
nor implies that all sin unto death can be known as such." The commentator
does not state clearly what interpretation of the verse he deduces from this.
Apparently the thought is that we know that there *is* a sin unto death, but that
all we know of it is that it is not included among those which we *know to be
not unto death*; and the purport of the verse would be that we ought to inter-
cede with perfect confidence in cases of sin which we *know* are not unto death,
and that where this is not known the Apostle does not exhort to intercession,
because thus we might be interceding for one who has sinned beyond hope. But
if this had been the Apostle's meaning, I cannot conceive that he would have
expressed it by the simple positive statement, "There is a sin unto death; not
concerning it do I say that he should make request."

older Catholic theologians)—do not commend themselves. Of the former alternative nothing need be said; of the latter, that not every sin incurring excommunication is "unto death." In 1 Cor. 5[5] the offender is excommunicated "for the destruction of the flesh, that the spirit may be saved in the day of the Lord Jesus." In such a case brotherly intercession would be an urgent duty; and, in any case, excommunication does not constitute the "sin unto death," but is only the solemn recognition by the Church that it has been committed. (b) Nor is the proposal to interpret the passage by the aid of Jas. 5[14, 15], as referring to sin that is punished by God with bodily sickness or death (cf. 1 Cor. 11[30]), worthy of more consideration. In the whole usage of the Epistle θάνατος and ζωή have a spiritual significance, and there is nothing in the context to suggest that here "sin unto death" should be understood as sin punished by fatal bodily sickness. (c) And, if it is evident that θάνατος means spiritual death, —separation from fellowship with God,—it is also evident that sin πρὸς θάνατον means, not sin "tending towards death," but sin by which that fatal goal is reached.[1] Westcott[2] (p. 210) maintains that "St. John speaks of the sin as tending to death, and not as necessarily involving death. Death is, so to speak, its natural consequence, if it continue, and not its inevitable issue as a matter of fact." This view is quite untenable. Intended to put a humane and merciful interpretation upon the "sin unto death," how inhumane and unchristian a construction does it place upon the Apostle's directions regarding it! If there is a sin that does not already "necessarily involve death," but to which a *special* certainty attaches that, if it continues, death is the "inevitable issue," it is unimaginable that the

---

[1] Cf. John 11[4] αὕτη ἡ ἀσθένεια οὐκ ἔστιν πρὸς θάνατον.

[2] So Plummer, "Death is its natural, but not its absolutely inevitable, consequence."

Apostle should not enjoin the most urgent intercession, instead of positively saying that he does not enjoin it. Of all possible interpretations, this is unwittingly the most repugnant to Christian feeling. The only question which the Apostle's language leaves undecided is whether a resurrection even from this "death" is not possible. And concerning this his language is noticeably guarded. In the presence of such sin he does not command nor encourage intercession, neither does he forbid it. All he commits himself to is that for those who thus sin, Christian prayer cannot have that "boldness" which is its prerogative elsewhere. (*d*) The question remains—On what grounds can it be pronounced of any sin that it is "unto death"— that it effects a total severance from Christ? And the one answer which the first principles of Christianity permit to be given to this question is—final impenitence. Every sin that can be repented of can be forgiven ; every sin that is repented of finds forgiveness. We cannot, however, define sin unto death simply as the sin of those who are finally impenitent.[1] For this particular sin is recognisable now, and cannot be now *recognised from* final impenitence. The question, therefore, presents itself in this form—what sins are of such a nature as to render final impenitence, so far as we have reason to believe, their certain issue? In the New Testament there is allusion to two sins, if they are two, by which this dreadful condition is fulfilled.[2] There is the blasphemy against the Holy Ghost—that unpardonable sin—which our Lord's adversaries were, as He warned

---

[1] This is *one* of Augustine's explanations, "Si in hac tam scelerata mentis perversitate finierit hanc vitam," Westcott, p. 212.

[2] There is an approximation to such fulfilment in a third case—that pointed to in Matt. 18[37]—where wilful sin is so obstinately persisted in by the offender, against all brotherly efforts to bring him to repentance, as to involve his exclusion from the Christian fellowship ("Let him be unto thee as a heathen man and a publican"). But, as has been said, not every sin that involves excommunication is "unto death." Excommunication has in view not only the purity and self-protection of the Church, but the salutary discipline and ultimate restoration of the offender.

them, upon the verge of committing, when they accused Him of casting out evil spirits in the power of Beelzebub (Matt. 12²⁴⁻³²). In doing so they were deliberately outraging the eternal principle of goodness and truth, sinning against the Spirit of God, and extinguishing the light in their own souls; and this, because beyond repentance, would be beyond pardon. Intercession is silenced. Even the Saviour cannot plead, "Father, forgive them: they know not what they do." In this instance the blasphemy against the Holy Ghost (or perilous nearness to it) is ascribed to malignant unbelievers. Within the Church such sin can be manifested only in one certainly recognisable form— deliberate, open-eyed apostasy from Christ (Heb. 6⁴⁻⁶).

It is true that the same fatal result may be reached by other paths. The professing Christian may so wilfully and obstinately persist in heinous sin, or may have become so inveterately and whole-heartedly a lover of the world that, even in the judgment of charity, he has finally chosen his sin rather than his salvation. Yet, human nature being the same in New Testament times as now, to determine and pronounce upon the merits of such final hardening of the heart must have been so precarious, if not impossible, that one is constrained to believe that the "sin unto death" was the sin of those who by deliberate and avowed action severed themselves from Christ and from the Christian community. It does not follow that those who so acted necessarily reckoned themselves as apostates; and I think it probable that what St. John chiefly had in view was the sin of the "antichrists" and false prophets, who "went out from us that it might be made manifest that they were not of us" (2¹⁹). Once more, however, it is to be observed that all the Apostle says of "sin unto death" is that it does not present an object of *confident* intercession. And though it was perhaps inevitable, it is unfortunate that the mention of the perplexing "sin unto

death " has always awakened a livelier interest than that
which is the central truth of the passage—the Christian
prerogative of fearless and expectant prayer for a restora-
tive gift of Life to them that sin not unto death.

The Derivation of Sin.

According to the teaching of the Epistle, sin is not an
abnormality of *human* life alone—a phenomenon of the
κόσμος ; it belongs to a more gigantic system in which
it has its origin, and in which, again, it bears its final fruits
and reaches its goal.   There are organised kingdoms both of
Righteousness and of Sin, in the one or the other of which
every man has his citizenship.   The one has its prototype
in Christ (3^7); the other, in the devil (3^8).   As it is in Christ
alone that we see what Righteousness is when it becomes
the absolute principle of life, so it is in the devil only that
Sin is manifested to its last possibility.   Sin in its proper
nature is diabolical ; it is what has made the devil to be
the devil.

But the devil, ὁ πονηρός, is not only the prototype to
which all sin tends and is ultimately conformed, he is also,
in some important sense, the source from which all human
sin is derived.[1]   In what sense, we must more particularly
inquire.   The terms in which the relation of human sinning
to diabolic influence, and those in which the relation of
human righteousness to Divine influence are expressed, are
strikingly parallel.

He that sinneth is of the devil (3^8).	We are of God (5^{19}).
(ἐκ τοῦ διαβόλου ἐστίν.)	(ἐκ τοῦ θεοῦ ἐσμέν.)
The children of the devil (3^{10}).	The children of God (3^{10}).
Believers have God as their Father (2^{13} etc.).	Unbelievers, the devil (τοῦ πατρός ὑμῶν, John 8^{44}).

---

[1] In the Pauline scheme, sin is regarded chiefly as innate in humanity, as
having its temporal beginning and its hereditary source in the sin of Adam
(Rom. 5^{14}).   St. John has nothing to say of the Fall of man, but traces sin back
to a source external to human nature.

Is it to be inferred that the relations thus identically expressed are identical in fact? Some do not shrink from drawing the inference. " It is an appalling thought that man may enter into the same relation to the devil in which he originally stands to God" (Rothe). " The life that animates the sinner emanates from the devil" (Huther). But such statements are over-statements. That the devil is immanently and directly the source of all sin, as the Holy Spirit is of all holiness, is a thesis that cannot be seriously maintained. This is to ascribe to his agency an omnipresence and an omniscience which, so far as one can conceive, are impossible to a finite being. True, the Johannine phraseology might bear such an interpretation, nay, most naturally would bear it, if it could; but it does not absolutely demand it.[1]

On the other hand, more is signified than merely moral affinity or likeness. The devil is an active influence to which there is a corresponding receptivity in the life of the " world" (5^{19}). That he gave the first impulse to human sinning (John 8^{44}); that he still gives fresh impulse to it (John 13^2); that, directly or indirectly, all human evil may be described as the " works of the devil " (3^8), and that thus he is the father of all who do wickedly, is clear Johannine teaching :—" He that doeth sin is of the devil." He is of the devil's lineage, in the direct line of spiritual descent from him " who sinneth from the beginning."

Thus the personality of the Wicked One is not only recognised in the Epistle; it is related in no unimportant

---

[1] The analogous phrases, ἐκ τῆς γῆς, ἐκ τοῦ κόσμου, ἐκ τῶν κάτω, show that such rigidity of interpretation as requires ἐκ τοῦ διαβόλου to denote precisely the same relation as ἐκ τοῦ θεοῦ is not linguistically necessary. And while sinners are called τὰ τέκνα τοῦ διαβόλου, it is never said that they are "begotten" of the devil. Here, also, such expressions as τέκνα τῆς σοφίας (Matt. 11^{19}), τέκνα φωτός (Eph. 5^8), even τὰ ἐμὰ τέκνα (3 John ^{4}), tend to show that τέκνα τοῦ διαβόλου need not express more than moral affinity (though, in fact, it does express more). This is recognised by Haupt (" God can beget life, Satan cannot ").

sense to its doctrine of sin. Yet, regarding his person, St.
John is as reticent as other New Testament writers. In
the Epistle all that is said is that "he sinneth from the
beginning" [1] (3⁸ᵃ). Plainly, "from the beginning" is here
relative to human history. His is the sin from which human
sin is derived. When and why and how Satan became
Satan is to us unknown. He is the aboriginal sinner; and
what he became he still is. The first to sin, he still abides
in sin (ἁμαρτάνει). But, while there is in the Epistle no
attempt to account either for the existence of the Wicked
One or for his power (the "whole world" is his domain, 5¹⁹),
there can be no doubt that, underlying all the Apostle's
utterances on the subject, there is the ordinary assumption
that he is a fallen angel. Meagre as is the support which
the idea of the fall of Satan has in the New Testament
(2 Pet. 2⁴; Jude ⁶), speculation on the subject has no
other possible issue. Any other conception is "inconsistent with the absoluteness, or subversive of the goodness, of God" (Steven, *Johannine Theology*, p. 145).

The New Testament conception of diabolic agency is one
for which modern Christian thought has no small difficulty
in finding a place." [2] But, as presented in the Epistle, three
great thoughts—all, I believe, of permanent validity—are
contained in it. (*a*) Sin in its principle has that character
which we call diabolic. There is a darker strain of evil in

---

[1] "The devil sinneth from the beginning," ἀπ' ἀρχῆς ὁ διάβολος ἁμαρτάνει.
ἀπ' ἀρχῆς is emphatic by position, and with it may be compared the parallel
statement, "He was a murderer from the beginning" (John 8⁴⁴). The words
ἀπ' ἀρχῆς cannot be understood absolutely, since then we are stranded upon
an insoluble dualism (this interpretation, nevertheless, is maintained by Hilgenfeld and others); nor as "from the beginning of that being who is the devil,"
the intolerable consequence of which would be that God is the Creator of a
being inherently evil—dualism of the rankest sort. Nor is it satisfactory to
denude the words of all temporal reference, and to understand them as meaning
that "in him is the *principle* of all the sin of the world" (Rothe). This use
of ἀρχή, familiar in Greek philosophy, is unknown to the N.T. Not more
satisfactory is the interpretation, "from the devil's own beginning *as such*."

[2] In Clarke's *Outlines of Theology*, e.g., there is not a single reference to it.

the world than human weakness, ignorance and folly, or over-powering circumstance can account for. There is the manifestation of an essentially evil will, of opposition to good, enmity against God. (*b*) The great moral conflict of which human history always has been and will be the theatre—which is fought out around every human soul—is a conflict of personal agencies, not of abstract moral ideas. It may be said that of impersonal influences, or of actual moral force residing in impersonal laws, the New Testament knows nothing. And to this mode of conception modern thought is in some measure returning. Modern psychology tends at some points towards the New Testament standpoint. (*c*) The third truth is the ultimate triumph of Christ over His great adversary, in their conflict for the possession of humanity, "The whole world lieth in the wicked one"; but "to this end was the Son of God manifested, that He might destroy the works of the devil." The "strong man armed" has encountered an antagonist mightier than himself. Evil is overcome with good. On the downfall of the kingdom of the devil arises the Kingdom of the Son of God.

The World, the Social Organism of Sin.

In the Johannine writings the word κόσμος has a peculiar elasticity of application. Three chief uses (besides others more occasional) may be distinguished. When the κόσμος is material, it signifies (*a*) the existing terrestrial creation (*e.g.* John 1[10]), especially as contrasted with the sphere of the Heavenly and Eternal.[1] When it refers to the world of humanity, it is either (*b*) the totality of mankind as needing redemption and as the object of God's redeeming love (*e.g.* John 3[16]), or (*c*) the mass of unbelieving men, hostile to Christ and resisting salvation (*e.g.* John 15[18]). In the Epistle the word occurs in the first of these senses

---

[1] Frequently, ὁ κόσμος οὗτος (*e.g.* John 13[1]), but also ὁ κόσμος (John 16[28]).

(3^{17} 4^{17}), also in the second (2^2 4^9 4^{14}), but most frequently and characteristically in the third ($2^{15.\ 16.\ 17}$ $3^{1.\ 13}$ $4^{1.\ 3.\ 4.\ 5}$ $5^{4.\ 5.\ 19}$). Of the world in this sense it is said that it had no perception of the true nature and Divine glory of Christ (3^1; cf. John 1^{10}), and that it is equally blind to the true nature of the children of God (3^1); that it hates the children of God as Cain hated Abel (3^{13}; cf. John $15^{18.\ 19}$ 17^{14}); that the spirit of Antichrist dwells in it ($4^{3.\ 4}$), and that to it belong the false prophets and their adherents ($4^{1.\ 5}$); that it is wholly subject to the wicked one (5^{19}; cf. John 12^{31} 14^{30} 16^{11}); that whatsoever is begotten of God conquers it (5^4; cf. John 16^{33}) by the power of Christian Faith (5^5); that it is not to be loved (2^{15}); that the constituents of its life are "the lust of the flesh, the lust of the eyes, and the vainglory of life" (2^{16}); and that it "passeth away" (2^{17}). We shall for the present confine our attention to the last quoted passage:—

2^{15-17}.

"Love not the world, neither the things that are in the world. If any man love the world, the love of the Father is not in him. For all that is in the world, the lust of the flesh, the lust of the eyes, and the vainglory of life, is not of the Father, but is of the world. And the world passeth away, and the lust thereof; but he that doeth the will of God abideth for ever." I shall not attempt to thread the maze of various interpretations that have gathered around the term "world" in this passage. The real possibilities are only two. The word may be understood as signifying the whole content of material, sensuous, and therefore transient existence—"the sum of all phenomena, within the human horizon, which are sensuous, and which awaken sensuous desires" (Rothe). This interpretation, however, has serious difficulties, both logical and moral. How can it be logically affirmed that

" the lust of the flesh, the lust of the eyes, and the pride of life " which are subjective, constitute " all that is in the world " which is objective ?   And if this difficulty be waived, the more formidable moral objection remains :—How can it be said that the material and sensuous κόσμος, which God has created for man to dwell in, and between which and human nature He has established so many links of necessary and also delightful correspondence, has no other effect than to excite immoral desire and ungodly pride, or that the natural environment of human life is so ill-adjusted—so inimical to its supreme spiritual interest ;— that the one command regarding it must be an absolute " love not," and the one certainty, " If any man love the world, the love of the Father is not in him ? "   Had the writer been a Gnostic of the extreme ascetic type he might have been credited with such a thought, but it has no place in the New Testament.   Recognising this, the exponents of this interpretation import into it, in one way or other, a subjective element.   The " world " is the material and sensuous, not in itself, but in its relation to unregenerate human nature.   Westcott's definition—" The order of finite being regarded as apart from God "—may be taken as one now generally accepted.

This definition is admirable as giving the widest idea that underlies St. John's use of the word ; but it is by a process of logical abstraction that the idea is obtained. And it seems to me scarcely imaginable that the Apostle intended his readers to understand " the order of finite being regarded as apart from God " as the object of a command so terse and practical as " Love not the world." The same objection applies *à fortiori* to other varieties [1] of the same interpretation.

[1] "Quicquid ad præsentem vitam spectat, ubi separatur a regno Dei et spe vitæ eternæ " (Calvin). " The world, that is, godlessness itself, through which a man has not the right use of the creatures " (Luther). " It is not an entity, an actual tangible thing—it is spun out of these three abuses of God's glorious

The simple solution, and that which satisfies every requirement of the passage, is to understand the "world" as the mass of unbelieving and unspiritual men—the social organism of evil. This is the sense, except when another is clearly indicated by the context, which the word bears throughout the Epistle (and is by far the most frequent in the Fourth Gospel as well). To the Apostle's readers "Love not the world" would convey, as it does more or less to Christians in every age, a very definite and needful warning, and one that has many parallels in the Apostolic writings (*e.g.* 2 Cor. 6^{14-18}, Jas. 4^4), "Love not the world." Do not court the intimacy and the favour of the unchristian world around you; do not take its customs for your laws, nor adopt its ideals, nor covet its prizes, nor seek fellowship with its life. "Neither the things that are in the world." For what are the things that are in this "world." This aggregate of unspiritual persons, with their opinions, pursuits, and influences—what are the elements of its life? They are such that "If any man love the world, the love of the Father is not in him." God lays down one programme of life for His children; the world proposes another and totally incompatible programme to its servants. And in exact proportion as men are attracted by the world's programme—the life of fullest gratification for all · un-

gift of free will to man—the lust of the flesh," etc. (Alexander). "It is the reign of kingdom of the carnal mind—wherever that mind prevails, there is the world" (Candlish). "The world is whatever is ruled by selfishness" (Gibbon). "It is the place which we make for our own souls" (Alexander). There is, of course, profound truth in all this. We find the world of our own hue; it reflects our own image. But the word κόσμος, as here used, can scarcely signify such an abstract idea as the correspondence between the material and sensuous world and the unregenerate mind. On this interpretation, moreover, the only meaning that can be given to the Apostle's words is : "We must not love the world, because, owing to our evil subjectivity, the only effect it can have upon us is to excite the lust of the flesh, the lust of the eyes, and the pride of life"— which would be to render St. Paul's· "Unto the pure all things are pure" a futility, and would be a libel, not upon the world, but upon the power of Christian Redemption.

spiritual instincts and appetites — they are tempted to mistrust and dislike the absolutely different programme of self-denying love and obedience which God lays out for them, and by which He would make them trustful, pure, patient, and strong. For, as the Apostle with inimitable terseness proceeds to expound, the essential constituents of the world's life are these, " the lust of the flesh, the lust of the eyes, and the vainglory of life." This is literally " all that is in the world"; there is nothing nobler which it is in its power to give.

A. First, there is the " lust of the flesh " (the sensuous gratification which the flesh longs for). The evil signifi-cance of the phrase lies in " lust," [1] not in " the flesh." Least of all New Testament writers can the Apostle, whose message of Redemption begins with the announcement that the Flesh has become the organ of the Divinest life, be credited with the mystical bias which sees in the bodily organism an inherent and intractable element of evil.

The bodily appetites are in themselves absolutely wholesome; without them neither the race nor the individual could long subsist; nor can anything be more innocent than the pleasure that accompanies their legitimate satisfaction. Their degradation comes not from the body itself, but from the soul. And it comes because life is not dominated by these nobler aims and affections under the rule of which the lower fulfil their appointed purpose in the harmony of nature. It is when the love of God, the love of one's neighbour, and the love of one's nobler self

---

[1] The fate which the word ἐπιθυμία has suffered (and, similarly, "lust" in English) is an illustration of the degrading power of sin. ἐπιθυμία is occasionally found in the N.T. in its original unfallen sense of "desire" (Luke 22[15], 1 Thess. 2[17], Phil. 1[23]). But, distinctively, it characterises desire as evil, not necessarily because of the object desired, but because in the desire the higher nature is subordinated to the lower, instead of the lower to the higher. The "flesh" has not with St. John that special Pauline sense in which it comes to express the whole moral corruption of human nature, although, in certain passages, it naturally enough exhibits a tendency in that direction (John 3[6] 8[15]).

are shut out from the soul, that natural appetite becomes
the corrupt "lust of the flesh," asserting itself in sloth,
intemperance, and sensuality, or in the tyranny of the
anxious thought, "What shall we eat, what shall we drink,
and wherewithal shall we be clothed?"

> "What is he but a brute,
> Whose flesh hath soul to suit,
> Whose spirit works lest arms and legs want play?"

But, in truth, when the higher nature is thus made the
slave and minister of the lower, animalism is no name
for the level of degradation that is reached. The animal
body seeks only its natural food. The "lust of the flesh"
is in reality the hunger of the godlike soul deprived of
its proper nutriment and flying to the body for a substitute,
compelling it to devour "so many more of the husks as
will satisfy the starving prodigal within, and make a swine's
paradise for his comfort." [1]

B. The second element in the life of the "world" is the
"lust of the eyes." Here we rise from the merely animal [2]
into the region of the intellect and the imagination, to
which the eye, among the bodily organs, is the chief
ministrant. The most obvious example under this category
—the master-lust of the Eye—is Covetousness.[3] But the
phrase includes every variety of gratification of which
sight is the instrument, from the love of mere material
splendour and vulgar display in apparel and personal
adornments, pomp and luxury in the appointments of
public or private life, the spectacular excitements of the
theatre, the arena, and the racecourse, to the most refined
cult of the physically beautiful in nature or in art. Nay,

---

[1] Bushnell, *The New Life*, p. 32.

[2] The eye also may minister to the "lust of the flesh" (cf. Matt. 5[28]); but
the construction of the sentence, . . . καί . . . καί, shows that the ἐπιθυμία
τῶν ὀφθαλμῶν is not a subdivision of the more general ἐπιθυμία τῆς σαρκός.

[3] " Homo extra Deum quærit pabulum in creatura materiali vel per volup-
tatem vel per avaritiam," (Bengel on Rom. 1[29]).

if the Apostle's classification is to be regarded as at all exhaustive, we must give to the " lust of the eyes " a wider scope than the merely sensuous. It must include the craving for novelty of intellectual sensation (Acts 17²¹), the whole pursuit of knowledge, science, and art, when these are severed from the spiritual ends of life and are made, as in their own right, the object of man's devotion. The relation of intellectual and æsthetic culture to the spiritual life is a problem that did not urgently touch the Hebrew Christian, and probably did not gravely affect those classes of Greek and Roman society from which the members of the Church were chiefly drawn in the Apostolic age ; and it is scarcely touched upon in the New Testament. But the principle on which it must be determined is the same as that which assigns their right place to the bodily appetites. The Creator Himself is the original and perfect artist. The Eye and all that it desires and delights in are His thought and handiwork. We cannot behold the beauty with which He has dowered all His works, from the tiniest crystal to the constellations, without believing that in all this we see the passing gleams of an Ideal Beauty, which as truly belongs to the Divine Nature itself as wisdom or power. In our own nature, made in His likeness, the sense of beauty seems to be a fact as ultimate as the sense of truth or of right and wrong. It is of God and for God.

> " All earthly beauty hath one cause or proof
> To lead the pilgrim-soul to Heaven above ;
> Joy's ladder it is ; reaching from home to home."

But if the light of God be shut out from the desire for and the delight in beauty, whether physical or intellectual, it becomes merely " the lust of the eyes." The love of beauty divorced from the love of goodness, the art that is the gilding of idle, selfish lives, the love of knowledge that is merely the craving of an insatiable yet vain curiosity—these, so far from being a ladder that leads up, are, no less than vulgar avarice, chains by which the soul, which is made for the Infinite Good, is bound fast to the sphere of earthliness.

C. Next, the Apostle displays the obverse of the medal. He has designated the cravings of human nature when it is without the Knowledge and Love of God, as the "lust of the flesh" and the "lust of the eyes." Now he declares what results from the attainment of these—the "vainglory of life." Vainglory (ἡ ἀλαζονεία) does not so much signify arrogance towards one's fellows (ὑπερηφανία), as the fatuous pride of worldly possession and success, the vain sense of security that is based, like a house on the sand, upon a false estimate of the stability and worth of worldly things (cf. Dan. 4^{30}, Prov. 18^{11}, 2 Chron. 32^{25}, Acts 12$^{20-23}$). But these two varieties of pride, though distinguishable in thought, are inseparable in fact. The supercilious consciousness of superiority to one's fellow-men is possible only when the sense of dependence upon God has been lost (1 Cor. 4^7). And here the "vainglory of life" must be regarded as including both the egotistical and the atheistical attitude of mind. The same human life, the cravings of which, in those who are not animated by the love of God and the quest of Righteousness, are the "lust of the flesh" and the "lust of the eyes," has for its least transient satisfaction nothing better than this deluded self-security and empty self-satisfaction, against which all the facts of human experience offer in vain their unceasing protest. To live without looking up to God in dependence and submission, to live looking down on a larger or smaller number of one's fellow-men—this, which from the spiritual point of view is the worst and deadliest life can give, is, in the world's reckoning, its most enviable prize.

These, then, are the ideals the "world" of unspiritual men recognises; these are the marks that characterise it, the forces that govern it; these are its wants and its wealth; and plainly to every one who knows the God revealed in Christ, these things are "not of the Father," have not their origin in His will, have no affinity with His nature, are directly antagonistic to the life He intends for men and to which He calls men. They belong to a life which, if it could succeed in realising itself, would be without need of God, righteousness, purity, love or moral sense of any kind; in which the world, as the sum of all the "permanent possibilities" of enjoyment, would take the place of God as the object of trust and the source of all good; and whose heaven would be a paradise of sensuous and egotistical gratifications without limit and without end. Such a life, in the very idea and principle of it, is not "of the Father," but is "of the world." In no sense is it normal or natural. It exists only as a corruption and caricature. It is possible only to a nature that is made for fellowship in the highest order of life, but is used as an equipment for the rôle of a more highly-endowed animal. It is "of the world" —has no other basis or foothold in actual existence than the perverted human will. It has in it no principle of individual development; for it presents no object adequate to the greatness of human nature, has no outlet or outlook towards the infinite Good for which man is made. And it has in it no principle of social development. Selfishness can never make a Kingdom of Heaven; for, in the nature of the case, every man's selfishness must collide with every other man's. But the Apostle does not philosophise upon the theme. He sweeps the whole phantasmagoria of worldliness aside. "The world passeth away, and the lust thereof." [1] These words might well be understood as St. John's version of what has been the theme of preachers and moralisers from the beginning—"Tune to whose rise and

---

[1] "Thereof," αὐτοῦ, is not the objective genitive = the desire for the world, but the subjective = the desire felt by the world.

fall we live and die "—πάντα ῥεῖ.   But if our interpretation
of the passage is the true one, this is not the direct reference.   The world is still the world of human society which
is " in darkness until now."   " Love not the world " is the
sternly affectionate exhortation :   " for that world,—that
whole framework of society which is hostile to Christ and
His Kingdom,—imposing as it looks, stable and impreg-
nable and overpowering, is doomed.   With all that it
delights in and pursues, it is passing away.   Even while
I write it is moribund, its final dissolution is at hand." [1]
But over against this prophecy of doom, the paragraph
ends with the note of triumph—" He that doeth the will
of God abideth for ever."   Here the Will of God stands
as the absolute contrast to the Lust of the World.   The
Lust of the world degrades and desecrates all the best
things in life upon which it lays its hand,—renders them
trivial, ignoble, and evanescent.   But the Will of God
consecrates, glorifies, imbues with a Divine worth and
permanence even the lowest things of life, the humblest
gift, the most commonplace drudgery, the most unheroic
affliction, renders the lives of men day by day, unevent-
ful as they may seem, of imperishable significance.   The
Will of God alone is great, and it lays an equalising
touch upon all who truly serve it (Matt. 12[50]).   The Will
of God is the one Eternal Reality to which the life of the
creature can attach itself, the one bond of permanence
that makes human life and human history, not a thing of
fragments and patches, but a vital part of an ordered and
enduring whole.   If a man do the Will of God, his deeds
abide, his works " do follow him."   The fruit he brings forth

---

[1] Cf. 1 Pet. 4[7].   The statement is not to be understood as a prophecy of the
speedy conquest of the world by Christianity, or as pointing to the fact that
this conquest was already visibly beginning (Westcott).   The key to the sense
is given in the next verse, " Little children, it is the last hour."   The thought
in the Apostle's mind is that of the nearness of Christ's Advent and the world's
Judgment-day.

"neither withers upon the branches nor decays upon the ground. Angels unseen gather crop after crop as they are brought forth in their season, and carefully store them up in heavenly treasure-houses." Yet what the Apostle says is that he himself "abideth for ever." Already he has eternal life and is doing its works. What he is, that he will ever be. What he does, that he will ever do. The change will be only from the "few things" in which he has been found faithful to the "many things" of which he will be judged worthy. Doing the will of God, he has thrust his hand through the enclosing screen of the transient and laid hold of the abiding, and partakes of the immortality of Him Whose Will he does.

"And the world is passing away, and the lust thereof: but he that doeth the will of God abideth for ever."

In all literature there is no more solemn magnificence of effect than is produced by these few simple words; in all Scripture there is no more ringing challenge to the arrogant materialism of the "world" than sounds out of the depth of their calm.

CHAPTER IX.

THE DOCTRINE OF PROPITIATION.

MUCH that has been written on the Johannine theology shows a singular tendency to minimise its testimony to the specifically sacrificial and propitiatory aspect of Christ's redemptive work. It seems to be taken as axiomatic that, wherever it is possible, an ethical rather than a religious sense is to be assigned to any Johannine utterance regarding Redemption.[1] It is even asserted that the Johannine writings exhibit no trace of a doctrine of Redemption in the ordinarily accepted sense.[2] Nothing more than an unprejudiced study of the Epistle is needed to show how baseless these suppositions and assertions are. The fact of propitiation is placed in the forefront. The door through which we are conducted from the Prologue, with its announcement of Christ as the Life-giver, into the inner rooms of the ethical and Christological teaching, is sprinkled on its lintel and posts with the blood of Divine sacrifice.

The most comprehensive soteriological statement is that "the Father hath sent the Son to be the Saviour[3] of the

---

[1] "The Johannine theology emphasises *by preference* the moral bearings of the Atonement" (*DB* iv. 346). So far as the Epistle is concerned, this statement cannot be sustained.

[2] Reuss, *Hist. Christ. Theol.* ii. 443.

[3] ὁ πατὴρ ἀπέσταλκεν τὸν υἱὸν σωτῆρα τοῦ κόσμου. v. Notes, *in loc.* Although used in the first Apostolic preaching (Acts 5³¹ 13²³), the title σωτήρ does not seem to have found early currency in the Church. Its earliest use by St. Paul is Phil. 3²⁰, and it is characteristic chiefly of the later books, the Pastoral Epistles and Second Peter. Of the family of words, σώζειν, σωτήρ, σωτηρία, etc., σωτήρ alone is found in the Epistle; on the other hand, the full title "Saviour of the world" is exclusively Johannine, being found only here

world " (4¹⁴). Salvation, which culminates in the one supreme good, Eternal Life, includes, as a present possession, the forgiveness of sins (1⁹), cleansing from all sin and un-righteousness (1⁷· ⁹), being "begotten of God" (5¹ etc.), fellowship with the Father and with His Son Jesus Christ (1⁸), our abiding in Him and His in us (4¹⁵ etc.), the anoint-ing of the Spirit (2²⁰), fellowship one with another (1⁷), overcoming the world (5⁴· ⁵), righteousness of life (3⁶ etc.), love (3¹⁴ etc.), assurance towards God (3¹⁹ 4¹⁸), confidence in prayer (3²⁰· ²¹ 5¹⁴). As a possession perfected in the future, it includes boldness in the Parousia (2²⁸) and in the Day of Judgment (4¹⁷), complete assimilation to Christ as He will then be manifested (3²) and abiding for ever [1] (2¹⁷). Here the origin of Salvation in the love of God is exhibited in the twofold fact of the Father's having sent His Son, and of the Son's being sent as the "Saviour of the world" (emphasising, as this does, the human need that drew forth the manifestation of the Divine Love).

When we pass to the more specific question of the method by which Christ accomplishes His mission of saving the world, the answer, still general, is, "Ye know that He was manifested that He might take away sins" (3⁵).[2] Here the thought is only of the purpose for which Christ appeared on earth—the removal of sins; there is no re-ference to the definite means by which this is accomplished.

---

and in the confession of the Samaritans (John 4⁴²). In classical writers the title σωτήρ is applied to many deities, especially to Zeus; also, in later Greek, to princes of various dynasties, *e.g.* to Nero: Νέρωνι . . . τῶι σωτῆρι καὶ εὐεργέτηι τῆς οἰκουμένης (Inscr. quoted by Moulton). Both of these titles were regularly claimed by the Ptolemies. There is no reason, however, to believe that this current pagan usage at all influenced the Christian application of the term. In the Lucan passages (Luke 1⁴⁷ 2¹¹, Acts 5³¹ 13²³) it bears evident trace of its O.T. origin (cf. Deut. 32¹⁵, Ps. 24⁵ 25⁵, Isa. 17¹⁰ etc., where the LXX translate θεὸς σωτήρ).

[1] It is noticeable that the Epistle contains no direct reference to the Resurrection; nor does the cosmic view of salvation (Rom. 8²¹, Col. 1²⁰) come within its horizon.

[2] *v.* Notes, *in loc.*

The world can be saved only by the abolition of sin; and to this end all that Christ was and taught and did, by life, death, and resurrection—the whole human manifestation in Him of the unseen Divine Life (1^2)—was directed. This neither requires demonstration nor permits of argument. "Ye know,"[1] says the Apostle. In the Christian consciousness of Christ and His work this is the first principle.

Thus, from another point of view, the work of salvation may be regarded as one of destruction. "To this end was the Son of God manifested, that He might destroy[2] the works of the devil" (3^{8b}). The "works of the devil" signify human sin in its entirety regarded as the product of original Satanic agency; and Christ saves the world by breaking up and destroying from its foundations the whole system and establishment of Evil that dominates human life. This he does by "taking away sins." The Epistle contemplates no other means by which the destruction of the "works of the devil" is to be accomplished than the taking away of sin through the spiritual forces of the Kingdom of God. How, failing this, they are to be *destroyed*, is a question regarding which the Epistle has no message.

We come closer to the core of our subject when we ask by what specific mode of action Christ takes away sin—a result after which morality has toiled and religion agonised in vain, which has been at once the quenchless aspiration of conscience and its burden of despair. The first, though not the full, answer is, that the mode of action

---

[1] οἴδατε. Here in its most absolute sense. See special note on γινώσκειν and εἰδέναι.

[2] "Might destroy" (ἵνα λύσῃ). Here λύειν has its characteristic sense (cf. John 2^{19} 2 Pet. 3^{10-12}), the disintegration and dissolution of a compact body, the "works of the devil" thus being pointed to as presenting a solid, organised opposition to the Kingdom of God—a system to be broken up and destroyed. A better sense is thus obtained than when the "works of the devil" are understood as the works men do after the devil's pattern—works that are the works of men, yet, in principle, the works of the devil.

was that of self-sacrificing Love. The mission of Christ, while we must think of it as having its inception in the love of the Father, Who sent the Son as the Saviour of the world (4¹⁷), is achieved only by the same self-sacrificing Love on the part of the Son. " Herein know¹ we Love, because He laid down His Life for us " (3¹⁶). This is the absolute revelation of Love—the ideal to which all that claims that title must conform.² And it is only as exhibiting the fact and the magnitude of Christ's self-sacrifice on our behalf that the " laying down "³ of His Life is here contemplated. Reference to the Death of Calvary as a substitutionary⁴ ransom is excluded by the context, in which it is held up specifically as our pattern, binding on us the obligation to lay down our lives in like manner for the brethren. No necessity, save that of Love itself, is indicated for that infinite self-sacrifice. Nothing is said as to the conditions of human need or Divine law under which it was indispensable to our salvation and avails for it. All this, however, is done, with notable emphasis and unmistakable significance, in the group of passages that next come under consideration.

¹ See Chapter XII.

² Comparison with John 10¹¹·¹⁵·¹⁷ and 13³⁷ (it not the tense of the verb itself, ἔθηκε) renders it certain that the words do not denote the continuous self-sacrifice of Christ's life (Gibbon, Findlay), but the definite and final surrender of life through death.

³ "He laid down His Life" (τὴν ψυχὴν αὐτοῦ ἔθηκεν). This expression is peculiar to St. John. The Good Shepherd lays down His life for the sheep (John 10¹¹·¹⁵). Christ lays down His life that he may take it again (John 10¹⁷). Peter vows to lay down his life for his Master (John 13³⁷). The most illuminative parallel as to the precise meaning of "lay down" (τιθέναι) is John 13⁴ "He layeth aside His garments" (τίθησι τὰ ἱμάτια). As in the Upper Room Christ laid aside His garments, so on Calvary He laid aside life itself. *v.* Notes, *in loc.*

⁴ The substitutionary idea is not excluded, neither is it necessarily included by ὑπὲρ ἡμῶν. This idea is definitely expressed by ἀντί (*e.g.* Matt. 20²⁸). The distinction between ἀντί and ὑπέρ is well brought out by comparison of Matt. 20²⁸ λύτρον ἀντὶ πολλῶν, and the version of the same logion in 1 Tim. 2⁶ ἀντίλυτρον ὑπὲρ πάντων (Moulton, p. 105). Instead of ἀντί, St. John uses the (in this connection) virtually equivalent περί (2² 4¹⁰).

4¹⁰ " God loved us, and sent His own Son a propitiation for our sins."

2² "And He Himself (Jesus Christ the righteous) is the propitiation for our sins."

1⁷ᵇ " The blood of Jesus His Son cleanseth us from all sin."

1⁹ " God is faithful and righteous to forgive us our sins, and to cleanse us from all unrighteousness."

In these passages we have a concatenation of ideas— propitiation, blood, cleansing, forgiveness — which are directly derived from the sacrificial system of the Old Testament, which are expressed, indeed, in technical Levitical terms. To elucidate their meaning, therefore, it is necessary to examine them in the light of their Old Testament associations.

Here the primary term is ἱλασμός,[1] which with its congeners is used by the LXX. to translate the corresponding group, *Kipper* and its derivatives.[2] The root-idea of *Kipper* is that of covering over;[3] but its use in the Old Testament is restricted to the " covering " of sin ; and, like so many other ideas, it undergoes a remarkable process of moral elevation and religious development. The primitive conception is that found in the patriarchal narrative (Gen. 32²⁸), where Jacob proposes to " cover " Esau's face with a gift, that is, to render him blind to the injury done, by means of the gift thrust upon his

---

[1] Properly, the act, but in the N.T. the means, of propitiation. In the N.T. the word occurs only in this Epistle ; nor is the verbal family to which it belongs abundantly represented (ἵλεως, Matt. 16²², Heb. 8¹² ; ἱλάσκεσθαι, Luke 18¹³, Heb. 2¹⁷ ; ἱλαστήριον, Rom. 3²⁵, Heb. 9⁵). Etymologically, ἵλεως is connected with ἱλαρός, cheerful ; and in classical Greek signifies, as applied to men, kindly or gracious ; as applied to a deity, propitious.

[2] *Kipper* is rendered by ἱλάσκεσθαι (Ps. 65³ 78³⁸ 79⁹), but much more frequently by the intensive ἐξιλάσκεσθαι ; while ἱλασμός is the regular translation of *Kippurim*, "atonement." It also stands for " sin-offering " (Ezek. 44²⁷) and " forgiveness " (Ps. 130⁴).

[3] By some Semitic scholars the idea of *wiping away* is preferred. Driver suggests that both senses have a common origin in *wiping over* (*DB* iv. 128ᵇ).

attention. Crude as the instance is, it clearly exhibits the idea that runs through the whole complicated usage of the metaphor—that of rendering offence invisible, null, inoperative as a cause of just displeasure and punishment.[1]

The class of passages that shed the light of clearest analogy upon our present study are those that deal with legal or ritual propitiation. In this the agent is the priest; the means, usually, a sacrifice; the object, the person or thing on whose behalf the sacrifice is offered. Propitiatory efficacy is assigned to a large variety of sacrifices, but especially to the sin-offering and to blood as containing the " life." And it is peculiarly relevant to the exegesis of the Epistle to note the effects of propitiation, which are expressly the forgiveness[2] of sin (1[9]) and cleansing[3] (1[7b. 9]). Upon the whole subject, though one might quote from more recondite sources, a better statement could not be furnished of the action which, with its agents, instruments, and consequences, is denoted by propitiation than is given by Driver (*DB* iv. 131[b]). " It is to cover (metaphorically) by a gift, offering, or rite, or (if God be the subject) to treat as covered; the ideas associated with the word being to make (or treat as) harmless, non-existent, or inoperative, to annul (so far as God's notice or regard is concerned), to withdraw from God's sight, with the attached idea of restoring to His favour, freeing from sin and restoring to holiness—especially (but not exclusively) by the species of sacrifice called the sin-offering." Such is the word and such is the conception employed in the Epistle to express the mode of action by which Christ accomplished and still accomplishes His mission as the

---

[1] Thus Moses proposes to make propitiation for the sins of the people by intercession (Ex. 32[30]). Elsewhere it is God who " covers," that is, treats as covered, overlooks, pardons the offender (Ezek. 16[63]) or the offence (Ps. 65[3]).

[2] *e.g.* Lev. 4[20] ἐξιλάσεται περὶ αὐτῶν ὁ ἱερεύς, καὶ ἀφεθήσεται αὐτοῖς ἡ ἁμαρτία.

[3] *e.g.* Lev. 12[7] ἐξιλάσεται περὶ αὐτῆς ὁ ἱερεύς, καὶ καθαριεῖ αὐτήν.

11

Saviour of the world. " He is the propitiation for our sins ; and not for ours only, but for the whole world " (2^2). Two great truths emerge.　First, propitiation has its ultimate source in God.　Paganism conceives of propitiation as a means of changing the disposition of the deity, of mollifying his displeasure and rendering him literally " propitious."　In the Old Testament the conception rises to a higher plane ; the expiation of sin begins to supersede the idea of the appeasing sacrifice, and language [1] is chosen as if to guard against the supposition that a feeling of personal irritation, pique, or resentment, such as mingles almost invariably with human wrath, mars the purity of the Divine indignation against sin.　And this ascent from pagan anthropomorphism reaches the climax of all ethical religion in St. John's conception of the Divine atonement for human guilt :—" Herein is love, not that we loved God, but that God loved us, and sent His Son as a propitiation for our sins " (4^{10}).　The action of which, in some sense, God is Himself the object, has God Himself as its origin. Propitiation is no device for inducing a reluctant deity to forgive ; it is the way by which the Father in Heaven restores His sinning children to Himself.

Nevertheless, it is a real work of propitiation in which this love is exhibited and becomes effective for our salvation.　" And He Himself is the propitiation for our sins " (2^2).　To interpret the virtue of the ἱλασμός as consisting merely in its supreme exhibition of God's all-embracing, all-forgiving love, as if to assure men that no barrier to fellowship exists save in their own fears, is to empty the word of all that it distinctively contains. One may or may not accept the teaching of the New

---

[1] This is witnessed to (in the LXX.) even by grammatical construction.　In classical Greek the regular construction of (ἐξ)ιλάσκεσθαι is with the person (deity or man) in the acc., as the direct object.　This construction occurs only in a single O.T. passage (Zech. 7^2 ἐξιλάσκεσθαι τὸν κύριον), where the propitiation seems to be effected by prayer.

Testament; but it is, at any rate, due to intellectual honesty to recognise what that teaching is. And, beyond dispute, ἱλασμός can mean but one thing—that which in some way (we may not be able to say, and I do not here attempt to say, in what way or upon what principle) expiates the guilt of sin, which restores sinful offenders to God by rendering their sin null and inoperative as a barrier to fellowship with Him. The fundamental implication is that not until the moral fact of sin is thus dealt with, can the relations of God and man be established on a permanent, that is, on a moral basis. And because sin is thus dealt with by Christ, He is the " propitiation for our sins." The *ultima ratio* of propitiation lies at once in the Love of God and the guilt of man. It is at once the act in which alone the pure, spontaneous, all–forgiving Divine Love finds its total expression, and the act through which alone that Love, in consistency with its own highest aims and obligations, can go forth on its mission of reconciliation. It is through this channel of suffering and death, determined and cut out by human sin, that the life-giving stream which arises in the heart of the Eternal Love must find an outlet into the barren and unclean waste.

In saying so much, we have been guilty of a slight anticipation. In the statement that Christ is the propitiation for our sins, nothing more is implied than that, sin being a valid and by us insuperable obstacle to God's fellowship with us and ours with Him, the power by which this obstacle is removed springs from the Person of Christ.

This must now be considered in the light of the more definite statement, " If we walk [1] in the light as He is in the light, we have fellowship one with another, and the blood of Jesus His Son cleanseth us from all sin " (1⁷). In the Old

[1] *v. supra*, pp. 59, 60, 65.

Testament, propitiation was normally effected by the offering of an animal victim through death. Any other mode
of making over a life to God was unknown to the Levitical
ritual, and, indeed, to any pre-Christian conception of
sacrifice. And thus it is invariably assumed in the New
Testament that the sacrifice of Christ was consummated
and offered in the Death ot the Cross. That this is
St. John's presupposition is clear from this reference to
His Blood.

Neither here, however, nor anywhere in the New
Testament, is the Blood a synonym for the Death of Christ.
In the Levitical ritual the atoning virtue is assigned in
a peculiar degree to the blood as containing the "life"
(Lev. 17[11]). The warm, fluid blood was considered as the
life of the animal, not a symbol of the life, but the life
itself; and the essence, ritually, of the sacrificial act
consisted in the offering of the life-blood to God; so much
so that it might be regarded as a principle of the whole
ritual system that "without outpouring of blood there is
no remission" (Heb. 9[22]). The meaning of this manipula-
tion of the blood is variously explained; but the points of
real importance are these: that, according to the analogy
of the Old Testament, and in consonance with every type
of New Testament teaching,[1] the propitiatory virtue of all
Christ is and has done and does is here regarded as
concentrated in His Blood; and that what this term
connotes is the Life offered to God in His Death, not
death itself regarded as mere deprivation of life. And
now appears the immense significance of the words by
which the Blood is defined. For what manner of life is it
that is offered in this Blood? It is the life of perfect im-
maculate humanity—the life of Jesus; but it is at the same
time Divine life ("the Eternal Life that was with the
Father and was manifested to us")—the life of Jesus, His

---

[1] *e.g.* Rom. 3[25] 5[9], Eph. 1[7] 2[13], Col. 1[20], Heb. 9[12, 14], 1 Pet. 1[2, 19], Rev. 1[5].

Son.[1] It was this Divine-human life that was yielded up in spiritual sacrifice through physical death [2] in the Blood of the Cross.

The efficacy of this Blood is that it " cleanses from all sin " [3] (καθαρίζει ἡμᾶς ἀπὸ πάσης ἁμαρτίας). Here, again, the connection of ideas is strictly Levitical. In the Old Testament ritual, purification from moral or ceremonial uncleanness was constantly effected by expiatory sacrifice, and especially by blood.[4] One may almost say that, " According to the law, all things are purified with blood " (Heb. 9²²).

It is usually assumed without question, however, that, in this passage " cleansing " denotes not the removal of the guilty stain of sin, but cleansing of the character, deliverance from the power and defilement of sin itself (Lücke, Ebrard, Huther, Haupt, Rothe, Westcott; opposed, however, by Calvin, Weiss, Plummer). It is difficult to account for this; certainly there is no foothold in the Old Testament for such an interpretation of καθαρίζειν. There, the object of sacrificial cleansing is never the character; but is moral or ceremonial offence, regarded as leaving upon the offender a stain which makes covenant relations with God impossible till it is removed.[4] This impossibility is conceived either as objective, consisting in the re-action of the Divine purity against the uncleannesses of

---

[1] The addition of τοῦ υἱοῦ αὐτοῦ is a refutation of the Cerinthian doctrine that the Divine æon, Christ, departed from Jesus before the Crucifixion ; but the refutation consists in the assertion of the truth, which is the heart of Christianity, that it is by Divine sacrifice we are redeemed. " Early Christian writers use very extreme language in expressing this truth. Clement of Rome speaks of the παθήματα θεοῦ ; Ignatius of αἷμα θεοῦ and τὸ παθὸς τοῦ θεοῦ. Tatian has τοῦ πεπονθότος θεοῦ ; Tertullian, *passiones Dei* and *sanguine Dei*" (Plummer). Such language may be extreme, but it is more Christian than the doctrine of the impassibility of the Divine Nature.

[2] As it is in the Epistle, through the laying down of Christ's ψύχη (3¹⁶).

[3] Better, "from every (kind of) sin."

[4] *e.g.* Lev. 16³⁰ ἐξιλάσεται περὶ ὑμῶν καθαρίσαι ὑμᾶς ἀπὸ πασῶν τῶν ἁμαρτίων ὑμῶν.

men, or as subjective, consisting in man's consciousness[1] of such uncleanness, depriving him of confidence to draw near to God. Elsewhere in the New Testament the usage is identical with that of the Old.[2] Nor is there any support in the context for a different interpretation in the present case. True, it is the very glory of salvation by the Blood of Christ that it cleanses the character from evil affection at the same time as it removes the guilt of sin, that Divine pardon and moral renewal are organically inseparable. And this, moreover, is the truth to the assertion of which this Epistle is as a whole devoted. But the question here for the Apostle and his readers is still only this, how we, being such as we are,—we whose life and character, when brought into the Light of God, are only revealed in their actual deformity and guilt,—can nevertheless enter into immediate fellowship with Him in Whose Light we stand thus revealed. And the answer is that, when we walk in the Light, confessing our sins, "the Blood of Jesus His Son cleanseth us from all sin"—removes from us the stain of our guilt, and makes us clean in God's sight.[3]

The statement of this is varied and expanded in 1^9 "If we confess our sins, He is faithful and right-eous to forgive us our sins, and to cleanse us from all unrighteousness."[4] Still we are in the circle of Levitical

---

[1] Even in Ps. 51^{10} (according to Davidson, *Hebrews*, p. 206) a "clean heart" is a conscience void of offence, the result of forgiveness.

[2] The objective sense—cleansing from the guilt of sin in God's sight—is exemplified in Heb. 1^3 $9^{22.\ 23}$, Tit. 2^{14}, 2 Pet. 1^9; the subjective deliverance from an evil conscience, in Heb. 9^{14} 10^2, Acts 15^9. The only passages in which $\kappa\alpha\theta\alpha\rho\ell\zeta\epsilon\iota\nu$ has an ethical sense are 2 Cor. 7^1 and Jas. 4^8.

[3] This interpretation is confirmed by the parallelism of the whole passage. $1^{7.\ 9}$ $2^{1.\ 2}$ are parallels : "If we walk in the light" $(1^7)=$ "If we confess our sins" $(1^9)=$ "If any man sin" $(2^1$ implying, of course, the confession of sin). So, "the blood of Jesus cleanseth us from all sin" $(1^7)=$ "He is faithful and righteous to forgive us our sins, and to cleanse us from all unrighteousness" $(1^9)=$ "We have an advocate with the Father, and He is the propitiation for our sins" $(2^{1.\ 2})$.

[4] $\grave{\alpha}\delta\iota\kappa\ell\alpha$. *v. supra*, pp. 134–35.

ideas,[1] in which forgiveness and cleansing are as closely as possible related to each other, and both to propitiation. For, though unexpressed, the idea of propitiation is implicit here in the assertion that God is " faithful and righteous " in forgiving sin and cleansing from unrighteousness. Here " faithful "[2] is the wider concept, which includes the more specific " righteous." When upon our penitent confession (the psychological condition that makes forgiveness possible *de facto*) God sets us free from the sins and disabilities by which we stand debarred from His fellowship, He does what is according to His own unalterable character, because He does what is right. He is " faithful " to His own nature; and it is His nature to " delight in mercy " and to be " ready to forgive "; yet to forgive, not with a weak and injurious mercy, but only in such a way that no wrong is done, no truth slurred over, that sin is recognised and dealt with as being what it is. The human conscience itself, when truly awakened, has always declined to find a solution of the problem of sin in forgiveness granted either by arbitrary will or by a leniency that shrinks from inflicting pain more than from vindicating right and showing its abhorrence of wrong. The New Testament proclaims that God is faithful and righteous in forgiving sin (cf. Rom. 3[26]), because He first reveals in word and in action the true nature and guilt of sin; and then freely pardons all who, walking in the light of that revelation,—the light that shines with concentrated power from the Cross,—confess and forsake their sins. And the human conscience in every age has borne witness that where men

---

[1] Cf. Lev. 4[20. 26. 36. 35] 5[10. 13] etc. So also in Matt. 26[28] our Lord declares that His Blood is " poured out as an expiation for many, in order to the forgiveness of sins."

[2] πιστὸς καὶ δίκαιος. When faithfulness is ascribed to God, the sense is that He is faithful to Himself, acts in consistency with His essential attributes (2 Tim. 2[13]); or that, as a consequence, He is faithful in respect of His promises (Heb. 10[23]); or that He is faithful to those who trust Him (1 Cor. 10[13]). The first and radical sense is that which the word requires here

do thus walk in the Light, this result follows: the Blood of
Jesus cleanses away sin in the sight of God; to which He
bears witness in cleansing the conscience from its stain and
giving peace with Himself.

The last of this group of utterances speaks of Christ as
our Paraclete. Earnestly the Apostle affirms the aim of all
his writing to be "that ye sin not" (2^1). Nevertheless, the
present state being what it is, he contemplates the possibility—may we not say, the certainty?—of sin occurring
in the life even of those who are walking in the Light. In
such an event we are not left without a resource: "We
have a Paraclete with the Father, Jesus Christ the
Righteous" (2^1). The word Paraclete[1] is exclusively
Johannine (a statement which includes the LXX. as well as
the N.T.); and its meaning is everywhere the same. No
single English word, indeed, covers the whole breadth of
its various applications and suggestions; but these are
always different shades of the same meaning, not different
meanings. It may be said to signify in general a friendly
representative who defends one's cause, usually by influential intercession. In the Gospel the Holy Spirit, as
the Paraclete, maintains Christ's cause with the believer
(John 14^{20} 15^{26} 16^{14}), and champions the believer's cause

---

[1] The questions of etymology, sense and usage, have been very fully discussed,
and these discussions are so easily available (Westcott, *St. John* xiv. 16 ; *Epistles
of St. John*, p. 42 ; best of all, *DB* iii. 665) that they may be very briefly dealt
with here. The active meaning "Comforter" is nowhere tenable, the word
being by formation the passive verbal of παρακαλεῖν, to "call to one's aid,"
and being capable of no other sense than "one called in to aid the caller." The
term is most frequently associated with courts of justice, denoting a powerful
friend or learned "counsel" who pleads the cause or interposes on behalf of the
accused (Latin, "advocatus" or "patronus"); but the meaning is wider
than our "advocate"), and is distinctively the opposite of κατήγορος (cf. 2^2
with Rev. 12^{10}). It is used several times by Philo in the definite sense of
"advocate" or "intercessor" (Westcott, *St. John*, p. 212). In Lucian, *Pseu-
dol.* 4. (παρακλητεὸς ἡμῖν . . . ὁ Ἔλεγχος), the speaker summons the personified
Elenchus or Conviction to aid him in showing up his adversary in his true colours,
—a remote but somewhat interesting parallel to the office of the Paraclete
in John 16$^{8-11}$.

against the world (John 16$^{8-11}$); and here Christ is the penitent sinner's Advocate, and pleads his cause with the Father.

In this connection these words, "with the Father" (πρὸς τὸν πατέρα), are extremely significant. It is God's Fatherhood that renders such advocacy possible, and at the same time demands it. On the one hand, the words repudiate the caricature of Christ's Intercession as a process of persuasion acting upon a reluctant will. On the other hand, the writer could not by conscious intention have chosen words more directly contradictory of the assumption that the Divine Fatherhood, rightly understood, excludes all necessity or possibility of mediation and intercession. The all-forgiving Love of the Father is like the waves of a great reservoir, pulsing and throbbing against the barrier until the flood-gate is opened; when instantly the pent-up waters are sent bounding along the dried-up channel. That opening is, from the human side, repentance and confession (1^{9}); but, if New Testament teaching is unanimous on any point, it is regarding this, that from the Divine side also an opening of the flood-gate is needed, and that this is effected through Christ's work of propitiation and intercession. An Advocate with the Father! The words seem a paradox. Is not a father's heart the best advocate of an erring child? Will not a father's love have anticipated every plea that can be urged in his behalf? That must be understood. But it must be understood also that even the Father's love can urge nothing in apology for *sin*—nothing that is of force to absolve from its guilt. Yet there is One who can urge on our behalf what is at once the most appalling condemnation of our sin, and the only sufficient plea for its remission—Himself.

This Paraclete the Apostle now names and describes with reference to His personal qualifications for the office. He is Jesus Christ. Elsewhere the writer distinguishes between those two appellations, and brings out the proper and original force of each (2^{23} 4^2 $5^{1.6}$); but here Jesus Christ is used simply as a proper name, the full designation by which the Saviour of the World is known in history.

It is as Jesus Christ, the "Word made flesh," that He is our Paraclete. In virtue of His uniquely intimate union with humanity in nature, experience, and sympathy, He remains for ever its perfect and universal representative; and as, when He was on earth, He pled for friend (John 17, Luke 22^{31}) and foe (Luke 23^{34}), so still in the Heavenly places He upholds our cause.

But if it is as Jesus Christ that He is qualified to represent man, it is especially as Jesus Christ the Righteous [1] that He is fitted to be the sinner's Advocate. The epithet may apply directly to His advocacy. Not only without share in the sin of those for whom He pleads, He is untainted by any secret sympathy with it. He has resisted sin unto blood; He has suffered all things on account of sin. He sees it as it is, and confesses it as beyond apology or extenuation. His righteousness in interceding corresponds to the Father's righteousness in forgiving (1^9). Or we may, perhaps, better understand "righteous" as applying universally to the Advocate's nature and character. In Him the Father sees His own essential Righteousness (2^{29a}) revealed. In Him there stands before God the Divine Ideal of humanity (2^{29b}). It is as man in whom that ideal is consummated, as Jesus Christ the Righteous that He is qualified to undertake the cause of mankind before the Righteous Father (cf. Heb. $7^{26.27}$). This interpretation best agrees with what follows.

"And He [2] is the propitiation for our sins. And not for ours only, but also for the whole world" (2^2). Here a

---

[1] The proper sense of Ἰησοῦν Χριστὸν δίκαιον is, "Jesus Christ being, as He is, righteous." See Notes, *in loc.*

[2] He (αὐτός) is emphatic, "He Himself."

necessary relation between the office of Paraclete and the fact of propitiation is clearly indicated, again on Levitical lines.   As it was through the blood of sacrifice that the High priest [1] enjoyed the right of entering within the veil and making intercession for the sins of the people (Heb. 9[7]), so Christ's prerogative of advocacy is grounded on the fact that He has made propitiation (Heb. 9[12]).   On the other hand, as it was only in the High priest's appearing before God with the atoning blood that the act of atonement was completed, so it is by Christ's advocacy that the propitiation becomes actually operative.   The two acts not only are united in one Person, but constitute the one reconciling work by which there is abiding fellowship between God and His sinning people.

But the most notable point is that it is Himself—Jesus Christ the Righteous—who is the propitiation.   (So also in 4[10].)   St. John does not speak of Christ as " making propitiation."   He Himself, in virtue of all that He is, He who has lived the Life of God in man, in whom that Life has triumphed over the world and reached its last fulfilment in the self-surrender of death—He is the propitiation [2] for sin, and He is our Paraclete through whose permanent ministry before the Father, propitiation becomes salvation unto the uttermost (Heb. 7[25]).

What conception can we form of the reality denoted by Christ's office of Paraclete ?   It has sometimes been

---

[1] With regard to the identification here of the Paraclete with the High priest, it is interesting to note the statement that " Philo often uses it (Paraclete) of the High priest interceding on earth for Israel, and also of the Divine Word or Logos giving efficacy in heaven to the intercession of the priest upon earth " (Plummer).   The one passage usually quoted is not, however, quite to this effect. " It was necessary that the priest who is consecrated to the Father of the world should employ, as a Paraclete most perfect in efficacy, the Son, for the blotting out of sins and the obtaining of a supply of abundant blessings " (*De Vita Mosis*, III. xiv. 155).

[2] Or as the Epistle to the Hebrews has it, it is " through His own Blood " that " He entered once for all into the holy place, having obtained eternal redemption."

understood in a crassly anthropomorphic sense; and we must agree with Calvin, who repudiates the materialism of those "qui genibus Patris Christum advolvunt, ut pro nobis oret." Our Lord Himself negatives the idea of oral intercession (John 16[26. 27]).

On the other hand, His intercession is sometimes rarefied into a merely symbolical expression of the truth that His work of propitiation is of enduring validity. But no such abstract idea adequately represents the thought and the feeling of the Apostle's words, "If any man sin, we have an Advocate with the Father." The title Paraclete itself suggests, on the manward side, a ministry that is intensely personal and compassionate, intimately and sympathetically related to the moral crises of sin and temptation, distress and need, that arise in individual lives (Heb. 2[17] 4[15]). And if the New Testament understands by Christ's Intercession such a ministry toward men, it is also, without doubt, understood as containing a correspondent activity toward God. In what this consists — though it is not essentially more mysterious than Christ's intercession on earth—is necessarily beyond our conception. More we need not and cannot know than that Jesus Christ the Righteous—Propitiation and Paraclete—abideth for ever, and is the living channel through which the Eternal Love gives itself to sinful men, and all the spiritual energies of the Divine Nature stream forth to take away the sin of the world.

From the examination thus made of the principal passages in the Epistle that bear directly on Propitiation, it must be evident that its type of doctrine, under this category, exhibits a striking affinity with that of the Epistle to the Hebrews,—an affinity which does not, perhaps, imply direct derivation, but does imply that both are so far products of the same school of thought. For both, the fundamental religious concepts are those of the Levitical system. Both instinctively run Christian truth into Old Testament moulds. The entire theological scheme in *Hebrews* has as its nucleus the thought of "religion as a covenant, or state of relation, between God and a worshipping people, in which necessarily the high priest occupies the place of prominence" (Davidson, *Hebrews*, p. 197). St. John eschews the terms "covenant" and "High priest"—possibly because they were unfamiliar to those for whom he wrote, or, if familiar, debased by pagan associations. With him "covenant relationship" becomes κοινωνία (1³), filial fellowship with God, the mutual indwelling of God and His people.[1] And unmistakably this is the standpoint from which he approaches the problem of sin and its removal. St. John does regard sin ethically, and insists with startling emphasis upon its absolute antagonism to the nature of God and His children (3⁹); and it is open to any one to maintain that he *ought* to have adhered to this point of view throughout, and to have contemplated the removal of sin simply by ethical process, so that the atonement would be "the believer himself brought into harmony with the Divine mind, purpose, and will through the Mediator."[2] But this St. John does not do. Like the author of *Hebrews*, he contemplates sin primarily, in its *religious* consequences, as an objective disability for fellowship with God. As such, it can be removed only by "cleansing," which carries with it "remission"; and "cleansing" again is accomplished only by "propitiation" and specifically by "blood." For these ends a sacrifice and a priestly mediator are indispensable. The sacrifice is provided. The "Blood of Jesus His Son cleanseth from all sin"[3] (1⁷). And He who is the propitiation is Himself also the Priest (Heb. 9¹¹⁻¹⁴), who consummates the sacrifice by

[1] *v. infra*, pp. 195-6.
[2] Sears, *Heart of Christ*, p. 501 (quoted by Stevens).
[3] Cf. John 17¹⁹, where our Lord expressly represents Himself as the *covenant-sacrifice*, which consecrates His disciples as the People of God.

intercessory presentation of it before God ; for, though in
the nomenclature of St. John the Paraclete supplants the
Priest, the office of the Paraclete is indubitably identical
with that of the great High Priest of God's people, as it is
delineated in the Epistle to the Hebrews.

But it is maintained[1] that " The problem of sin, which
was central in the mind of Paul, to John appeared something secondary.   In the true Johannine doctrine there is
no logical place for the view of the death of Christ as an
atonement.   So far as that view is accepted we have to do,
not with John's characteristic teaching, but with the orthodox faith of the Church, which he strove to incorporate
with his own at the cost of an inner contradiction."   Now,
on any theory of its authorship, the Epistle must be regarded
as essentially a Johannine document ; and it is not going
beyond our province to consider how far, if at all, it
sustains these assertions.   It is true that we do not find in
it the same fierce grappling with the problem of deliverance
from sin as in the Epistle to the Romans ; that the truth
to which the earlier thinker fights his way, as with tears
and blood, the later gets not in possession by his own
sword, but finds and accepts as beyond all controversy.
And yet there is no lack of intensity in his statement
either of the problem of sin ($1^{8. \ 10}$) or of its solution ($1^{7. \ 9}$
$2^{1. \ 2} \ 4^{9. \ 10}$).   These words represent, no doubt, " the orthodox
faith of the Church " ; yet what words can possess a clearer
note of immediate spiritual intuition ?   What more fervent
and memorable expressions of the common doctrine of the
New Testament are to be found ?   What words are more
constantly used in the devotions of the Church, for the
confession of sin and the expression of confidence in its
removal by the Divine sacrifice, than the words of this
Epistle ?   It seems strange that these should be the words

---

[1] By the school of which Mr. Ernest Scott is the ablest as well as the most
recent representative among us.

of a writer who was only endeavouring to engraft the orthodox doctrine upon another truth that was vital to his own soul.

The doctrine of Propitiation has no " logical place " in St. John's " characteristic teaching," but is accepted " at the cost of an inner contradiction," *only if that can be true* of a doctrine which at the same time is for him the climax of all truth—the supreme revelation of the supreme principle of all moral life, human and divine. Organic relation cannot be closer than that which exists between St. John's doctrine of Propitiation and his doctrine of the moral nature of God. If " God is Love " is the master-light of all spiritual vision, this is the sole and perfect medium of its outshining : " Herein *is* love, not that we loved God, but that God loved us, and sent His Son as a propitiation for our sins " (4^{10}). This is no mere echo of an orthodox belief ; no repetition of a stock idea. St. Paul had already compared the love of God in the Death of Christ with the utmost men will do for one another (Rom. $5^{7, 8}$) ; but " St. John rises above all comparisons to an absolute point of view." [1] Christ's mission of propitiation not only has its motive in the Divine Love, it embodies and contains the complete fulness of that Love. Other acts and gifts are tokens and expressions of it ; but " Herein *is* Love "—the whole and sole equivalent in act of what God is in essence. In this passage we have a conception which, as it seems to me, surpasses anything to be found elsewhere in the Apostolic Scriptures,[2] of the sacrifice of God in Christ as a Divine act which, while it is free and optional, as being unsolicited and undetermined by anything external to the Divine nature itself, is an absolute self-necessity of that nature. St. John's doctrine of propitiation is related to his

---

[1] Denney, *Death of Christ*, p. 225.

[2] The only parallel is that which is *implied* in the parables of the Lost Sheep, the Lost Coin, and the Lost Son (Luke 15).

doctrine of God by the logic of moral necessity. If God is Love, nothing is more necessarily true than that He suffers on account of human sin; and to deny Him the power to help and save men by bearing their burden, is to deny to Him the highest prerogative of Love.

But it may be said that propitiation stands in no logical relation to the other and more prominent half of St. John's doctrine of Salvation—Regeneration. God saves men by the Divine Begetting, by the direct impartation of that Eternal Life which has been made communicable to them through the Incarnation of the Word. How and why, it may be asked, is this spiritual and ethical salvation from sin conditioned by the expiation of its guilt? We may not be able to answer this question. It is conceivable that St. John himself could not. But it does not follow that there is an inner contradiction. The difficulty does not attach itself to the Johannine theology exclusively. It belongs in some form to every type of theology in the New Testament. It only becomes specially obvious in St. John because with him the doctrinal centre is Life—the Life of the Word made Flesh becoming the new Life of mankind. And if we inquire, as we naturally do, why the Divine-human Life of Christ must pass through death, and thereby become a propitiation for human sin, before it could become the principle of new Life to men, St. John gives us no explicit answer. He tacitly presupposes the answer that in its various forms is given or assumed throughout the New Testament, that God, in bestowing the sovereign grace of pardon and sonship, must deal truthfully and adequately with sin as a violation of the moral order—as a fact, if we may say so, both of the Divine conscience and of the human conscience, which is its image. And with St. John, as with other New Testament writers, the necessity and the efficacy of *sacrifice* as the means by which this is accomplished are simply axiomatic.

But when we proceed to the endeavour to extract from the data of the Epistle the principle or principles upon which we may account for this, we encounter a task to which exegesis is not adequate, and which constructive theology has not yet finally achieved. It has become a commonplace to say that the New Testament contains no theory of the Atonement. Yet it is evident that the Apostolic writers were not only religiously conscious of reconciliation with God by the mediation of Christ, but were also intellectually interested in the mode of its accomplishment. The Epistles to the Romans and to the Hebrews abundantly witness that the fascination which the problem of Christ's Death has for the modern mind was no less intensely felt by the Apostolic mind. The tantalising feature of the case is that its need of explanation seems to have ended where ours begins. When the work of Christ was described as a propitiatory sacrifice, and was seen to embody the full truth which the sacrificial system of the Old Testament faintly and imperfectly expressed, no need of further elucidation suggested itself to the writers of the New Testament.

We are only driven back upon the further inquiries—what is the root-idea of sacrifice, and what is its relation to the end in view? How was it conceived by the earliest Christian teachers and their disciples? Did they feel that any *rationale* of sacrifice and its cognate institutions was either necessary or possible? What was to them the explanation has become itself the problem.[1]

One intensely illuminating ray St. John does shed upon it. The sacrifice of Christ is the sacrifice of God. This is the Epistle's great contribution to Christian thought—the vision of the Cross in the heart of the eternal Love. How

[1] See the admirable article "Sacrifice," *DB* (Paterson).

12

suggestive are these two statements when placed side by side : " Herein is Love—that God loved us, and sent His Son as a propitiation for our sins " (4^{10}), and " Herein do we know Love (recognise what it is), because He laid down His Life for us " (3^{16}) ! God's sending His Son and Christ's laying down His Life are moral equivalents. The Cross of Christ is but the manifestation of another Cross— that invisible Cross which the sin and folly, the trustlessness and ingratitude, of His children have made for the Father who is Love. How hard it has been for human thought to assimilate the ethics of Christ, needs no stronger proof than the fact that the impassibility of God had for so long the place of an axiom in Christian theology. When we speak of God as Father, when we say that God *loves* beings who are false, lustful, malicious, who are stubborn and impenitent, who in their blindness and perverse wilfulness rush upon self-destruction, what immeasurable sorrows do we imply in the depths of the Divine Love ! And it is out of those depths that the Cross of Christ emerges. He who bled on Calvary was first in the Bosom of the Father ; and what is the Gospel of a crucified Christ, but the proclamation of the infinitely awful, blessed truth that God Himself is the greatest sufferer from our sin ; that the Righteous Father drinks the bitter cup His children's unrighteousness has filled ? As in all things, Christ is in this the Word of the invisible God. He bore our sins in His sufferings and Death, not by any external infliction, but by the inward necessity of holy Love,—because He would live out the Life of God in this hostile world. In this there is nothing " transactional," " official," " forensic," nothing but inevitable spiritual reality. Holy Love cannot but bear sin, sorrow over it, suffer for it, and thereby, according to the redemp- tive law, become sin's propitiation.

What is that redemptive law ? There is no other problem over which Christian thought, since " Cur Deus

Homo," has brooded so intently; and there is no doctrine the history of which more clearly shows that ethical always precedes theological advance. Its history becomes an index to the moral development of Christendom, as we find each successive theory reflecting the moral standards and ideas of the time in which it arose. And it is idle to imagine that the theories that find favour in our day will prove more satisfying to our successors than those of preceding ages do to us. Always as the Spirit of Christ comes to more perfect fulfilment in the individual and in society, shall we come to a more perfect understanding of the sacrifice of Christ.

Yet the labour of past generations has not been fruitless.

There is not one of the great historical theories of the Atonement which, when its crudities and exaggerations have been carried away by the tide, does not leave some residuum of solid gain. There is no aspect under which the work of Christ has revealed itself to reverent minds but contains some element of essential value. This has not been sufficiently recognised. Criticism has been prone to seize upon incidental falsities and exaggerated expressions rather than upon abiding truths. It has been too generally assumed that the work of Christ is explicable by some single formula; and the part seen has been taken for the whole. We cannot doubt, indeed, that a unity there must be in which all its manifold aspects meet; one principle which is the master-key to all its complexities. "If we could find it, we might be surprised at its simplicity; we certainly should wonder at its Divine beauty and naturalness." Meanwhile, may we not recognise that the different aspects it reveals, when approached from different points of view, are not mutually destructive, but mutually complementary?

Inadequate as is the " moral influence " theory, when it

regards the work of Christ exclusively as the undoing of the effect of sin in the character, its essential truth is so obvious that it is the common element in all the theories. To make sinful men know that God grieves over them, that He longs to touch and win them to penitence and newness of life, that for this end He has willed to go to that length of self-sacrifice, the only measure of which is the Cross,—who does not acknowledge that this is supremely aimed at and achieved in the work of Christ?

And if there be taken away from the despised Anselmic theory its accidental taint of feudalism with its defective moral ideals, that theory also, when it contemplates the work of Christ in relation to the Divine personality, contains a profound truth. If we conceive of God as a Being to whom the notions of moral satisfaction and pleasure and their opposites are in any way applicable, must we not also conceive of the obedience of Christ—obedience not only flawless in will and deed, but obedience which exhausted the possibilities of obedience, which transcended all the obedience of earth because perfect as that of heaven, and which transcended all the obedience of heaven because wrought out through the pains, humiliations, and temptations of earth, obedience as perfect and divine as the Will to which it was rendered,—must we not conceive of that obedience [1] as a perfect satisfaction, "an offering and a sacrifice to God for a sweet-smelling savour," as, in literal truth, an atonement, a moral compensation for the sin of the world? If the race, which without Christ were a tragic moral failure, so that, to speak after the manner of men, it would have grieved and repented God that He had created it, becomes with Christ a moral triumph, so that looking upon that Face He can rejoice in having said, "Let us

---

[1] "Obedience" is intended here to include, and to include as its chiefest content, the Death of Christ. Anselm distinguishes between the two. My purpose is simply to give the essence of the "satisfaction" type of theory.

make man,"—is not Christ in a very real sense a propitiation for the sin of the world?

Is there not essential truth also in the so-called " governmental " theories by which the work of Christ is related specifically to the public moral interests of mankind and of the whole rational universe? In the universal Christian consciousness, the Cross of Christ is a solemn and unique testimony to the guilt of sin. It achieves in the realm of Divine government that vindication of moral law which it is sought to achieve in mundane communities by the infliction of adequate penalties for transgression. The Cross of Christ has made sin a vastly more appalling thing. Wherever its influence is felt it has inspired in the conscience a new sense of the enormity of sin. It becomes in experience a supreme factor in the moral administration of God's Kingdom; and can it be supposed that this lies apart from its essential purpose, or that there is not in this respect also a real propitiatory efficacy in the work of Christ?

And is there not essential truth also in the much-reprobated " penal " theory? More than any other, this theory has been wounded in the house of its friends. It has sometimes represented God as one with whom the quality of mercy is sadly strained, as a vindictive Shylock who must and will have a *quid pro quo*. But God is Love; and Justice, even punitive Justice, is one of the indefeasible functions of Love.[1] There is a law of retribution inherent in the very constitution of a universe created and governed by God who is Holy Love,—a law, that wherever sin is, suffering follows for the sinner himself or vicariously for others. And may we not conceive that there is an exactness in the operation of this law, whereby, whenever wrong is placed in the one scale, suffering is always accumulated in the other until the

[1] *v. supra*, pp. 82–84.

balance is adjusted; and that only by working itself out
in the full harvest of suffering can wrong exhaust its
power, and make way for the possibility of a new and
happy rightness? And may we not conceive that one truth
—the greatest truth—revealed in the Cross, is that in Christ
God Himself fulfils this law on behalf of His creatures, and
drains the bitter cup men's sin has filled? But, if such
a generalisation be too vast and venturesome, there are
still obvious and undeniable facts. Relieve the penal
doctrine of the forensic technicalities with which it has
been loaded, and the truth remains that God in Christ
has borne the penalty of human sin, as the worthy father
of an unworthy child, or the faithful wife of a profligate
husband bears its penalty, as by the inherent vicariousness
of Love the good always suffer for the bad. Does not
every Christian, whatever his theology, instinctively recognise
this, and say, when he looks to Gethsemane and Calvary,
"There is the true punishment of my sin; there in the
suffering flesh and spirit of my Saviour, I behold the
genuine fruit of sin; a Divine woe borne for me which I
shall never bear, but which, I pray, shall more and more
bear fruit in my penitence and devotion?" It is fact of
history that Christ has suffered for human sin; it is fact
of faith that God in Him has so suffered, fulfilling on our
behalf the retributive law that balances sin with suffering,
and that now no suffering is left save what is laden with
good to ourselves or to others. In this also we must
recognise a direct and vital element in Christ's work of
propitiation.

If, then, we find in every theory alike that the work of
Christ is the undoing of the work of sin, that in one
theory sin and its undoing are regarded in relation to the
moral disposition of man; in another, to the Personality
of God; in another, to the public interests of the Divine
government; in yet another, to the inherent constitution

of the moral universe,—we may conclude that none of these different conceptions will be lacking, whatever others may be present, in the final interpretation of the Apostle's words, " Herein is Love, not that we loved God, but that God loved us, and sent His Son to be the propitiation for our sins."

CHAPTER X.

Eternal Life.

In the foregoing chapter it has been made good, I trust, that the aspect of salvation in which sin is regarded as a fact of conscience and as a barrier to fellowship with God—the aspect denoted by the word propitiation—does not lack adequate and powerful presentment in the Epistle. But the theme which supremely engages the writer's thoughts, which he has most profoundly made his own, is the *terminus ad quem* of salvation—the Infinite Good, in the possession of which the reality of fellowship with God consists, and which is expressed throughout the Epistle by one word and by no other—Life (with or without the adjective "eternal"). With this theme the Epistle begins (1^2) and ends (5^{20}), while the purpose of the whole expressly is, "That ye may know that ye have Eternal Life" (5^{13}). Its predominance is complete; it is the centre to which every idea in the Epistle is more or less directly related. And, indeed, its unique development of the Christian conception of Life and Regeneration may be set beside its doctrine of the moral nature of God and its doctrine of the Incarnation, as one of the three great contributions of Johannine thought to the teaching of the New Testament.

Nowhere do the Scriptures furnish a definition of Life; but for the most part the Biblical conception of spiritual life is derived directly from experience. It denotes a rich complex of thought, emotion, and activity, in which man is conscious of that which fulfils the highest idea of his being. Life consists in the enjoyment of God's favour (Ps. 30⁵); it is the result of loving God and obeying His voice (Deut. 30¹⁹·²⁰); it is the fruit of true wisdom (Prov. 3¹⁸), and of the fear of the Lord (Prov. 14²⁷). Everywhere in the Old Testament, Life is conceived as the enjoyment of those blessings that flow to men from a vivid experience of God's favour and fellowship. It is upon these things men live, and altogether therein is the life of the Spirit (Isa. 38¹⁶). Nor is it otherwise in the New Testament. Life is an experience of the supreme and eternal blessings of the Kingdom of God. It is the goal toward which men are to struggle onward by the narrow way (Matt. 7¹⁴); for the attainment of which no sacrifice is to be deemed too costly, because in its possession every sacrifice is more than plentifully recompensed (Mark 10³⁰). The door of entrance to it is repentance (Acts 11¹⁸), and the way of attainment, patient continuance in well-doing (Rom. 2⁷). It is the end of that emancipation from sin and servantship to God of which holiness is the immediate fruit (Rom. 6²²); the harvest which they reap who sow unto the Spirit (Gal. 6⁸); the prize of which we are to lay hold by fighting the good fight of faith (1 Tim. 6¹²). In these and in all kindred passages the conception of Life is derived directly from the data of actual or anticipated experience. Life is a result, not a cause. It is conscious participation in the highest good for which man is made, which he can find only when his whole nature has been redeemed from the dominion of false ideals, and has been harmonised with the Divine order, by the perfect knowledge and love of God, and by unhampered and enthusiastic devotion to His will.

Now the definition of life, so conceived, will simply be a generalisation from its phenomena, that is, from its functions and characteristics as experienced and observed in the living organism. Thus in the physical sphere, the physiologist finds that such organisms invariably exhibit the phenomena of Assimilation, Waste, Reproduction, and Growth, and defines Life as the co-ordination of these functions. The biologist, again, regarding the phenomena from a different point of view, reaches the wider generalisation that life is correspondence to environment, " the continuous adjustment of internal to external relations " (Spencer).

In the same way, spiritual life may be defined as a correspondence of spiritual faculty to spiritual environment, the right relation of trust, love, and hope, of conscience, affection, and will, to their true Divine objects. " The mind of the flesh is death ; but the mind of the Spirit is life and peace " (Rom. 8[6]). Or it may be defined physiologically by the functions and energies with which it is identified ; it is " Righteousness, peace, and joy in the Holy Ghost " (Rom. 14[27] ; cf. Gal. 5[22. 23]). And our Epistle, more than any other New Testament writing, patiently places beneath our hands the material for such a definition of Life. Its subject-matter consists chiefly in the delineation of Eternal Life, positively and negatively, by means of its invariable and unmistakable characteristics,[1] Righteousness, Love, and Belief of the Truth. These are its primary functions. Confronted by the Truth of God in the person of Jesus Christ, every one in whom the Life is quickened believes— beholds in Jesus the Incarnate Son of God ; confronted by the Will of God, as moral duty or commandment, he obeys ; confronted by human need, he loves, not in word, neither in tongue, but in deed and in truth (3[18]). Life, accordingly, might be defined from the Epistle as consisting in Belief, Obedience, and Love, as the co-existence of these in conscious activity, carrying with it a joyful assurance of

---

[1] " Every one that doeth righteousness is begotten of God " (2[29]). " Every one that loveth is begotten of God " (4[7]). " Whosoever believeth that Jesus is the Christ is begotten of God " (5[1]).

present fellowship with God (3^{19-24} 4^{15-18}) and of its glorious consummation in the future (3^2).

Yet any definition from such a point of view would omit all that is most distinctive in the Johannine conception of Life. According to that conception, Life is cause, not effect; not phenomenon, but essence; not conscious experience, but that which underlies and produces experience. Eternal Life does not consist in the moral activities of Belief, Obedience, and Love, and still less is it a consequence flowing from the activities; it is the animating principle that is manifested in them, of which they are the fruits and evidences. Instead of "This do and thou shalt live" (Luke 10^{28}), St. John says conversely, "Every one that doeth righteousness is[1] begotten of God"; instead of "The just shall live by faith" (Rom. 1^{17}), "Whosoever believeth that Jesus is the Christ is[1] begotten of God." The human activity—doing righteousness, believing, loving—is the result and the proof of life already imparted, not the condition or the means of its attainment.

Thus the Johannine conception of spiritual Life is completely analogous to the commonly-held conception of physical Life. Physical Life, as has been said, may be defined from its phenomena. It is correspondence to environment; or it is the association, in a definite individual form, of Assimilation, Waste, Reproduction, and Growth. Such a definition covers all the phenomena that distinguish the organic from the inorganic; and if no other existence than that of phenomena is recognised, it represents the furthest limit of thought on the subject. But the mind does not naturally rest in such a definition. We intuitively assume a something behind the phenomena, an entity of which they are the manifestation. To the ordinary way of

---

[1] ὁ ποιῶν . . . γεγέννηται (2^{29}); ὁ ἀγαπῶν . . . γεγέννηται (4^7); ὁ πιστεύων . . . γεγέννηται (5^1). The tenses sufficiently show that in each case the Divine Begetting is the necessary antecedent to the human activity. But this is the presupposition of the Epistle throughout. See Chapters XI., XII., XIII.

thinking, the " continuous adjustment of internal relations
to external relations " is not a definition of what Life is,
but merely a highly generalised statement of what Life
does. Life is not correspondence to environment; it is
what determines such correspondence. What Life is in
itself we may not be able to say. Indeed, we cannot say.
It is the mystic principle, the *natura naturans*, of which
Nature is at once the revelation and the veil. Science
fails to throw a ray of light across the gulf between Life
and Death. But the idea of Life as an animating principle,
the essence in which inhere all the potencies developed in
the living organism, is one which, though it expresses
what science is confessedly ignorant of, is necessary to
science itself.

This conception of physical Life is by no means foreign
to Biblical thought. The " life," the animating principle of
the bodily organism (נֶפֶשׁ), is in the " blood " (Gen. 9^4,
Lev. 17^{11} etc.). God is the fountain of all Life (Ps. 36^9);
and to every creature (Ps. 104^{30}), as to man (Gen. 2^7), it is
a direct impartation by God's own quickening Breath.
But it is not until we come to the Johannine writings that
we find this mode of conception expressly applied to the
spiritual Life. And we shall now proceed to consider how
it is expressed and applied in our Epistle.

The designation most frequently employed is simply
" the Life " (ἡ ζωή, $1^{1.\ 2}$ 3^{14} $5^{12.\ 16}$). Elsewhere the Life
is qualitatively described as " eternal " (ζωὴ αἰώνιος, 3^{15} $5^{11.\ 13}$.
Twice (1^2 2^{25}) the form ἡ ζωὴ ἡ αἰώνιος is used, by which the
separate ideas of " life " and " eternal " are more distinctly
emphasised. A comparison of these passages makes it
certain that these forms of locution are used quite interchangeably. The ideas of duration and futurity which are
originally and properly expressed by the adjective αἰώνιος [1]

---

[1] αἰώνιος = belonging to an æon—specifically, to " the coming æon," αἰὼν
ὁ μέλλων.

have become in Johannine usage only one element, and that not the primary element, in its significance. Always Life is regarded as a present reality (*e.g.* 3^{14} 5^{12}); and the adjective "eternal" is added even when the reference to its present possession is most emphatic (3^{15} "Ye know that no murderer hath eternal life abiding in him)." Eternal Life is not any kind of life prolonged *ad infinitum*. The life of a Dives, though he should be clothed in purple and fine linen, and fare sumptuously through everlasting ages, would come never one inch nearer to the idea of Eternal Life. The category of time recedes before that of moral quality. Eternal Life is one kind of life, the highest, the Divine kind of life, irrespective of its duration. It is the kind of Life that is perfectly manifested in Christ (1^{2} 5^{11}). Every hour of His history belonged to the eternal order. Every word He spoke, every deed of obedience and love He did, was an outgoing of Eternal Life. The Divine nature was in it. And in whomsoever it exists, whether in heaven or on earth, the possession of that nature which produces thoughts, motives and desires, words and deeds, like His, is Eternal Life.

But though, abstractly, the idea of Eternal Life might be considered as timeless, it would not be accurate so to describe the Apostle's actual conception of it. It was from "the Beginning" in the "Word" (1^{1}). It is the absolute Divine Life (5^{20}), therefore imperishable. It stands in triumphant contrast to the pathetic ephemeralities of the worldly life (2^{17}). And while there is no passage in the Epistle (not even 2^{25}) where Life, with or without the adjective "eternal," does not primarily signify a present spiritual state rather than a future immortal felicity, the latter is not only implicit in the very conception of Eternal Life as the *summum bonum*, but comes fully to light in the vision of the impending Parousia (2^{17} 2^{28} 3^{2} 4^{17}).

Of this Life, God, the Father revealed in Christ, is

the sole and absolute source. He is the true God and Eternal[1] Life (5^{20}). Eternal Life is His gift[2] to men; potentially, when He "sent His Son into the world that we might live through Him" (4^9); actually, when we believe in His name (5^{13}). For of this Life, again, Christ is the sole mediator. If "the witness is that God gave us Eternal Life," this is because "this Life is in His Son" (5^{11}). By the Incarnation of the Only-Begotten Son the Eternal Life in its Divine fulness became incorporate with humanity, and remains a fountain of regenerative power to "as many as receive Him" (John 1^{12}). And here St. John's doctrine of the Logos enables him to carry New Testament thought on this subject a step further than the Pauline view of Christ as the Second Adam and the "Man from heaven" (1 Cor. $15^{22.\ 45-49}$). In what sense the Life of God is in Christ and is mediated through Him, is unfolded in the opening verses of the Epistle, where it is said that the subject of the entire Apostolic announcement is "the Word of Life" ($\pi\epsilon\rho\grave{\iota}\ \tauο\hat{\upsilon}\ λόγου\ τ\hat{η}ς\ ζω\hat{η}ς$, 1^1), this announcement being possible because "the Life was manifested, and we have seen, and bear witness, and declare unto you the Life, the Eternal Life, which was in relation to the Father, and was manifested unto us" (1^2).

Here the mediation of Life through the historic Christ (1^1) is grounded in the relation, eternally subsisting within the Godhead itself, of the Word to the Father (1^2). For, whatever be the exact interpretation of the title, "the Word of Life,"[3] the main intention of the whole passage is to identify the Life manifested and seen in Christ with "the Life, the Eternal Life, which existed in relation to the

---

[1] *v. supra*, p. 54.

[2] 5^{11} ζωὴν αἰώνιον ἔδωκεν ἡμῖν ὁ θεός. The force of the verb διδόναι and of the aorist tense is as here stated. The tense points to the definite historical act, the Incarnation, by which Eternal Life was communicated to humanity; the verb asserts comprehensively that "God has sent His Only-Begotten Son into the world that we might live through Him."

[3] See Notes, *in loc.*

Father" (ἥτις ἦν πρὸς τὸν πατέρα).[1] And that this refers
to the Life of the pre-incarnate Logos, is plain from the
exact parallelism of expression employed regarding the
Logos Himself (ὁ λόγος ἦν πρὸς τὸν θεόν, John 1[2]). In
the Gospel it is said that the Logos existed " toward " (πρός)
God, that is, as a personality distinct from God, yet eternally
and by necessity in relation to God. Here the same statement is made with regard to the Life that is in the Logos.
That " the Logos existed in relation to God," and that " the
Life existed in relation to the Father," are practically
equivalent statements.[2] The latter interprets the former.
The Logos is that Person whose Life from everlasting was
found in His fellowship with the Father, in that continual
perfect recipiency toward the Father which corresponds to
the continual and complete self-impartation of the Father
toward Him. It is thus that Christ is the one and only
mediator of the Divine Life. It is His own relation to the
Father that He reproduces in men (John 1[12] 17[23]). The
Life that was manifested in His Incarnation and that is
given to men through Him is no other than that which He
had as the pre-incarnate Word in His eternal fellowship
with the Father.[3]

We proceed next to the teaching of the Epistle
regarding the communication of this Life to men.
(*a*) The necessity of Regeneration is fundamental to the

---

[1] See Notes, *in loc.*

[2] This by no means implies that the Logos and the Life are equivalent terms,
or that the Life is here hypostatised. The Life is impersonal—the common element in the personality of God, of the Logos, and of the "children of God."

[3] The distinction between the Logos and the Life, and their mutual relation,
are well brought out by the exquisite precision of the Apostle's language in the
parallel statements, " The Word became flesh " (John 1[14]) and " The Life was
manifested " (1 John 1[2]). It could not have been said that the " Life became
flesh," because the Life in both states of the Logos was the same, and just in
this consisted the reality of the Incarnation. Nor could it have been said that
the " Word was manifested " ; for the Person of the Logos was not revealed, but
rather was veiled. But it was when the Divine Person became flesh that the
Divine Life was first fully revealed.

whole theological scheme. Life, which consists in union with God—which is nothing else than participation in the Divine Nature—is not inherent in man as he is naturally constituted. The state of every man is *a priori* that of death, of spiritual separation from God; and those who know that they have Eternal Life know that it is theirs because "they have passed from death into life"[1] (3^{14}). For those to whom the Apostle is writing, and with whom he includes himself, the recognition of their present state as one of Life is heightened by the remembrance of a former state which they now see to have been one of Death. And the same contrast between an original self-nature that is averse to the highest good and a new nature that desires and ·pursues it, is present in all Christian consciousness, though it may not be connected with the memory of a definitely marked transition. Between these opposite poles, Death and Life, all Christian experience moves. Always it is an experience of *salvation*; of Life as haunted by the shadow of Death; of good as a triumph over potential evils, a "following" which is also a "fleeing" (1 Tim. 6^{11}).

(*b*) This transition from Death into Life is effected by that act of Divine self-communication which in the Epistle is constantly and exclusively expressed by the word "beget" (γεννᾶν).[2] The word, nowhere defined or expounded, is in

---

[1] μεταβεβήκαμεν ἐκ τοῦ θανάτου εἰς τὴν ζωήν. τοῦ θανάτου, the Death that is death indeed ; τῆς ζωῆς, the Life that is life indeed.

[2] The invariable formula is γεγέννηται, or γεγεννημένος, ἐκ τοῦ θεοῦ (or ἐξ αὐτοῦ). The perfect tense denotes at once the past completion of the act, and its abiding present result. " Is begotten " is the inevitable translation ; yet "has been begotten" would be, in every case, less ambiguous, making it clear that the Divine Begetting is the antecedent, not the accompaniment or consequence, of the action associated with it in the sentence. The phraseology is varied in 5^4, where we find πᾶν τὸ γεγεννημένον ἐκ τοῦ θεοῦ ; and, very remarkably, in 5^{17}, where the normal ὁ γεγεννημένος in the first clause becomes ὁ γεννηθείς in the second. On both, see Notes, *in loc.*

A practically equivalent phrase is εἶναι ἐκ τοῦ θεοῦ=to have the source of one's life in God. This phrase, however, is of wider significance than the former, and is applied not only to regenerate men (3^{10} $4^{4, 6}$ 5^{19}), but to a "spirit" ($4^{1, 2, 3}$) to Love (4^7), and, negatively, to the "things that are in the world" (2^{16}).

itself of far-reaching significance. It implies not only that salvation—Life—has its ultimate origin in God, but that its communication, by whatsoever means, is directly and wholly His act. The human subject of this act cannot, indeed, be regarded as merely passive; but only because the gift communicated is itself the gift of Life, of power, and activity.

Whatever human response of faith, love, and obedience there is to Divine truth and grace, the power to make that response is "begotten" of God. It is not the product of man's own character, but of the new life imparted to him. Whatever action of the human will there is in passing from death into life, the human will is necessarily moved therein by the Divine Will. Death cannot make response to life. The Divine Begetting is antecedent to all else (cf. John 1[13]).

(c) As to the instrumentality, Divine or human, through which this regenerative act is wrought, the Epistle is silent. And at this point there is a gap in its system of thought which, so far as I am aware, has not been adequately recognised. For while, on the one hand, the Divine Begetting is everywhere regarded simply as the immediate act of God as the Father, on the other hand the Son has been sent "that we might live through Him" [1] (4[9]), and the Life which God gave to men is "in Him" (5[11]); but no attempt is made to supply the requisite link of connection between the mediating of Life by the Son and the immediate begetting of Life by the Father.

If it be asked how God begets in men that Life which is "in His Son," or what necessity or efficacy the Incarnation of the Son has in relation to the Divine Begetting,

---

[1] It is never said that Christians are "begotten of Christ" or are "of Christ." Christ is the medium, not the source of Life. The distinction is clearly marked by the prepositional phrases, εἶναι ἐκ τοῦ θεοῦ and ζῆν δι' αὐτοῦ (4[9]). Cf. 1 Cor. 8[6], where the same precision of language is noticeable, ὁ πατήρ, ἐξ οὗ τὰ πάντα . . . Ἰησοῦς Χριστός, δι' οὗ τὰ πάντα.

13

the Epistle supplies no answer.[1]   The truth is that here
we find the most noticeable *lacuna* in the theology of the
Epistle—its silence regarding the work of the Spirit as the
immediate agent in regeneration.   The Johannine thought
of the Father as the final but also the direct source of Life,
and of the Son as its sole medium, leads on imperatively to
the Trinitarian doctrine of the Spirit proceeding from the
Father and the Son, and given to men as the Spirit of
Christ.   The same Holy Ghost who was the author of the
Incarnation, who begat the full Life of God in the humanity
of Jesus, is now given by Him to men to beget and foster
in them the same Life that is in Him.   This is the
supreme gift of the Incarnation, that by the power of the
Divine Spirit the Life of God has received perfect and permanent embodiment in our humanity in the person of
Jesus Christ, and that by the power of the same Divine
Spirit acting upon men through the revelation of Christ,
and breathed into their souls by Christ, they are " begotten
of God " unto Life Eternal.

(*d*) Those who are " begotten of God " are *ipso facto* the
" children of God " (τέκνα θεοῦ).   This τέκνα θεοῦ is peculiarly
Johannine,[2] and is to be distinguished from the Pauline " sons
of God "[3] (υἱοί), which is never applied by St. John to Christians.   While the latter title emphasises the *status* of sonship
(υἱοθεσία) bestowed on believers, the Johannine τέκνα[4] connotes, primarily, the direct communication of the Father's
own Divine nature ; and, secondarily, the fact that the nature

---

[1] In the Gospel we read (John 5[21. 26]) that " As the Father raiseth the dead
and quickeneth them, even so the Son also quickeneth whom He will. . . .
For as the Father hath life in Himself, even so gave He to the Son to have life
in Himself."   But this passage itself stands in need of elucidation.   For, while
it asserts for the Son a power of " quickening " equal to and co-ordinate with the
Father's, the Father's " quickening " and the Son's cannot be conceived of as
separate Divine activities.

[2] John 1[12] 11[52], 1 John 3[1. 2. 10] 5[2].   But it is also Pauline, Rom. 8[16. 17. 21],
Phil. 2[12].

[3] Rom. 8[14. 19], Gal. 3[26] 4[6. 7].

[4] τέκνα ; from the root τεκ-, to beget.   Cf. the German *zeugen*.

thus communicated has not as yet reached its full stature, but contains the promise of a future and glorious development. We are children of God, but what it fully is to be children of God is not yet made manifest (3^2).

It is, indeed, the surpassing dignity thus bestowed upon us, the sublimity, beyond all understanding, of the privilege, that first calls forth the Apostle's exclamation of amazement (3^1). That we should be called the children of God [1] —"Behold, what manner of love!" But instantly the subjoined "and such we are" (καὶ ἐσμέν) arises from the Apostle's heart, asseverating that the title, magnificent as it is, is no more than the truth. And in how completely literal a sense the Apostle's conception of the Divine Begetting is to be taken appears very strikingly in 3^9. "Everyone that is begotten of God doeth not sin, because His seed abideth in him." This unique σπέρμα αὐτοῦ ("His seed") has been variously [2] explained; but unquestionably it signifies the new life-principle which is the formative element of the "new man," the τέκνον θεοῦ. It is the Divine germ that enfolds in itself all the potencies of "what we shall be," the last perfection of the redeemed and glorified children of God.

This abides in him who has received it. It stamps its own character upon human life, and determines its whole development.[3]

(*e*) This Life, as it streams through humanity, creates a family-fellowship (κοινωνία) at once human and Divine. In its human aspect this fellowship is conceived on spiritual much rather than on ecclesiastical lines. It is realised in the actual Christian community, and there only. But there spurious elements may intrude themselves; as is proved when schism reveals those who, though they have

---

[1] Not αὐτοῦ, which, grammatically, would have sufficed, but θεοῦ, emphasising the wondrousness of the fact.

[2] See Notes, *in loc.*   [3] *v. infra*, pp. 221, 226–8.

belonged to the external organisation, have never been genuinely partakers of its life (2^{19}).[1]　Only among those who walk in the same Light of God does true fellowship exist (1^7).　These are truly "brethren," and are knit together by the duties (3^{16}) and the instincts (5^1) of mutual love, and of mutual watchfulness and intercession (5^{16}).

But this human relationship grows out of a Divine. It is the fellowship of those who are in fellowship with the Father and with His Son Jesus Christ—who "abide" in God, and God in them.　No thought is more closely interwoven with the whole texture of the Epistle than this of the Divine Immanence, by which the Life of God is sustained and nourished in those who are "begotten" of God; and no word is more characteristic of the Johannine vocabulary, alike in Gospel and Epistles, than that by which it is expressed—"abide" ($\mu\acute{\epsilon}\nu\epsilon\iota\nu$).[2]

Between the Fourth Gospel and our Epistle, however, there is a noticeable difference in the statement of this great doctrine.[3]　In the Epistle the formulæ almost exclusively employed and constantly repeated are these— "God abides in us," "We abide in God," "God abides in us and we in Him."　In the Gospel, on the other hand, the reciprocal indwelling is that of Christ and His disciples (John 15^{4-10}), which has its Divine counterpart in His "abiding" in the Father (15^{10}) and the Father's abiding in Him (14^{10} 17^{23}).　This diversity is consistent with the point of view occupied in the two documents respectively. The Gospel is Christocentric, the Epistle Theocentric.　In the Gospel we ascend from the historic revelation, the

---

[1] See, further, Chapter XVI.

[2] $\mu\acute{\epsilon}\nu\epsilon\iota\nu$ occurs some forty times in the Fourth Gospel as against twelve times in the Synoptics; twenty-five times in the Epistles, which is as often as in all the other N.T. Epistles collectively.　Its use to express the fact of God's (or Christ's) mystical union with His people is peculiar to St. John.

[3] For details, see Chapter XVII.

visible Christ, to that conception of the invisible God which He embodies. In the Epistle we start from that conception. Instead of the concrete presentment of the living Christ, there is an immediate intuition of the Divine nature revealed in Him. While the theme common to both is the " Word of Life," the special theme of the Gospel is the Word who reveals and imparts the Life; in the Epistle it is the Life revealed and imparted by the Word. To discover in this traces of the Monarchianism [1] of the second century is unwarrantable. For here Christian thought is merely following its natural and inevitable course. It has not been able to rest in any merely Messianic conception of Christ's Person and character. It has realised that the question of questions still is—What is God? and that the ultimate significance of the life lived from Bethlehem to Calvary is the answer which it supplies to that question—" He that hath seen Me hath seen the Father." Thus, while the aim of the gospel is to display the divinity of Christ, it is the converse of this which is chiefly presented in the Epistle; instead of the metaphysical God-likeness of Christ, it is the moral Christ-likeness of God. And it is the writer's immediate contemplation of the moral nature of God and his governing idea of salvation as participation in that nature that inevitably cause him to carry up the thought of the indwelling Christ to the ultimate truth of the indwelling God.

Yet, while this diversity of view exists, there can be no doubt, it seems to me, that the whole conception in the Epistle has had its origin in the Gospel similitude of the Vine and the branches (John 15$^{1-10}$). According to the analogy there presented, the vitalising union by which the influx of Divine Life is maintained in those who are " begotten " of God, consists in two activities, not identical,

---

[1] Holtzmann, *J. P. T.*, 1882, p. 141 ; followed by Pfleiderer (ii. 392, 446, 447), and by Grill (p. 303) but not by Häring (*Theologische Abhandlungen*, p. 191).

not separable, but reciprocal—God's abiding in us, and our abiding in Him. These are two distinct actions, Divine and human, yet so bound up together in the unity of life that either or both can always be predicated regarding the same persons and certified by the same signs—the three great tests of Righteousness, Love, and Belief which meet us everywhere in the Epistle.[1]

The "abiding" of God in us is the continuous and progressive action of that same self-reproducing energy of the Divine nature the initial act of which is the Divine Begetting. By the same power and mode of Divine action Life is originated and sustained. The Epistle, it is true, seems to give two slightly diverse conceptions of this matter. As the human parent once for all imparts his own nature to his offspring, so, in virtue of the Divine Begetting, the Divine nature is permanently imparted to the children of God (3^9 "His" *i.e.* God's, "seed abideth in him"). But, whereas in the human relationship the life-germ thus communicated is developed in a separate and independent existence, in the higher relationship it is not so. The life imparted is dependent for its sustenance and growth upon a continuous influx of life from the parent-source. Thus the analogy followed is taken from the facts of

---

[1] It may be useful to exhibit this in tabular form.
  I. That God abides in us is certified—
    (*a*) by our keeping His commandments (3^{24a}) ;
    (*b*) by our loving one another (4^{12}) ;
    (*c*) by our confessing that Jesus is the Son of God (4^{15}), or by (the exact equivalent of this) the Spirit God hath given us (3^{24b} 4^{13}).
  II. That we abide in God is certified—
    (*a*) if we walk as Christ walked (2^6), if we sin not (3^6), if we keep His commandments (3^{24a}) ;
    (*b*) if we abide in Love (4^{16}) ;
    (*c*) if we have the Spirit that confesses Jesus as the Son of God (4^{13}).
  III. The full reciprocal relation, that God abides in us and we in Him, is certified—
    (*a*) if we keep His commandments (3^{24b}) ;
    (*b*) if we abide in Love (4^{16}) ;
    (*c*) if we have the Spirit of God (4^{13}), the Spirit, namely, that confesses that Jesus is the Son of God (4^{15}).

vegetable rather than of animal life; originally, as has been said, from the similitude of the Vine and the branches. The branches of a tree are actually children of the tree. Structurally, a branch is a smaller tree rooted in a larger. Even a single leaf with its stalk is simply a miniature tree, exactly resembling what the parent tree was in its first stage of growth, except that it derives its sustenance from the parent tree instead of from the soil. Thus a great vine is, in fact, an immense colony or fellowship of vines possessing a common life. It is the sap of the parent vine that vitalises all the branches, " weaves all the green and golden lacework of their foliage, unfolds all their blossoms, mellows all their clusters, and is perfected in their fruitfulness." So does the Life of God vitalise him in whom He abides, sustaining and fostering in him those energies—Righteousness, Love, and Truth,—which are the Divine nature itself. The language used is in no sense or degree figurative. Rather are the Divine Begetting and Indwelling the realities of which all creaturely begettings and indwellings are only emblems. Though the manner of it is inexplicable, as all vital processes are, this actual communication of the actual Life of God is the core of the Johannine theology.

But this abiding of God in us has as its necessary counterpart our abiding in Him. In this reciprocity of action, priority and causality belong, as always, to God, without whom we can do nothing; yet not so that the human activity is a mere automatic product of the Divine. We can invite or reject the Divine Presence; keep within or avoid the sphere of Divine influence; open or obstruct the channels through which the Divine Life may flow into ours. Hence, "abiding in God" is made a subject of instruction and imperative exhortation ($2^{27.\ 28}$; cf. 2^{15} $5^{18.\ 21}$). And when the word "abide" ($\mu\acute{\epsilon}\nu\epsilon\iota\nu$) is thus used, the idea of persistence or steadfast purpose, which is inherent in it, comes into view. As the abiding of God in us is the persistent and purposeful action by which the Divine nature influences ours, so our abiding in God is the persistent and purposeful submission of ourselves to that action. The only means of doing this which the Epistle expressly emphasises is steadfast retention of and adherence to the truth as it is announced in the Apostolic Gospel (2^{24}; cf. John 8^{31}) and as it is witnessed by the Spirit (2^{27}). Yet, although "keeping God's commandments," "abiding in love," and "confessing" Christ are exhibited primarily as the requisite effects and tests of our abiding in God, these effects become in their turn means. It is by these that practical effect is given to the message of the gospel and the teaching of the Spirit; and thus only is the channel of communication kept clear between the source and the receptacle of Life.

This study of the Epistle's doctrine in detail entirely sustains the preliminary view of the Johannine conception of Life with which we began. Life is conceived, fundamentally, not as the complex of phenomena observable in the living organism, but as the principle or essence that underlies and produces these. So spiritual Life is not simply the collective whole of the qualities, activities, and experiences of the spiritual man; it is the essence in which these qualities inhere, and from which these activities and experiences proceed.

But now we can advance to a more concrete conception. What is this Life? The Apostle says only that God, the true God revealed in Christ, is Eternal Life. And only this can be the ultimate definition. Life of every grade is the result of a Divine Immanence; and Eternal Life is the Immanence of God in moral beings created after His own likeness. And, although the Epistle does not directly represent the Holy Spirit as the agent of this Divine Immanence, Christian Theology in doing so has only taken the next step in an inevitable process of thought. Eternal Life is the Divine nature reproducing itself in human nature; is the energy of the Spirit of God, of the Father and of the Son, in the spiritual nature of man.

This whole Johannine conception of Life as an essence or animating principle is subjected to vigorous criticism. From the Ritschlian standpoint it is objected that this idea of Life is purely philosophical, that it is not given in religious experience, but seeks to interpret it in accordance with certain philosophical presuppositions.[1] This is so far true. Life in St. John's sense is not an object of conscious experience, but is an inference from experience. It is like the wind which is known only by the sound thereof (John 3[8]). But it is true also that the philosophy presupposed is not the philosophy of the schools. The idea of Life as an essence or principle is natural to the thought, and is presupposed in the ordinary language of all mankind. To this extent, we are all naturally metaphysicians. It is to produce a pure phenomenalist that a philosophical discipline is needed.

Thus, while it is true that early Christian thought was, in certain directions, influenced and fertilised by contact with Hellenism, and while it may be true that the Johannine doctrine of Life, in particular, has been formed under the influence of principles and modes of thought indirectly borrowed from Greek philosophy,[2] it is to be remembered that the tendency to infer causes from effects and to reason from phenomena to essence was not the peculiar property of the Greek intellect. St. John's conception of Life was certain, sooner or later, to emerge in Christian theology; for New Testament thought it lies in the natural line of development.

It is implicit in that whole strain of thought in our Lord's Synoptic teaching which regards doing as only

---

[1] See, *e.g.*, the chapter on Life in Scott's *Fourth Gospel.*
[2] *v.* Scott's *Fourth Gospel*, pp. 243 sqq.

the outcome of being, and which is emphasised in such
utterances as " Either make the tree good and its fruit
good ; or else make the tree corrupt and its fruit corrupt:
for the tree is known by its fruit " (Matt. 12^{33}).   It is implicitly contained, moreover, in the whole Pauline doctrine
of the new creation and of the mystical indwelling of
Christ in the members of His Body.   And it is not
difficult to imagine how, as the fruit of further reflection
upon the facts of Christian experience, it became with
St. John a clear and dominant idea.   Just as we have in
the Johannine doctrine of the Logos the last result, within
the New Testament period, of the Church's endeavour to
furnish a *rationale* of its own experience in relation to the
Person of Christ, so the Johannine doctrine of the Life is
the ripest fruit, within the same period, of the Church's
reflection upon its own characteristics, of its endeavour
to find a conception intellectually adequate to the new
experiences of faith, holiness, and love which it possessed,
and which it was conscious of as forming the one essential
distinction between its own life and the life of the world.
When the Christian compared himself with his former
self, how were the new vision of truth, the new aims and
affections that arose out of the depths of a new nature to
be accounted for ?   Or, when he compared himself with
the " World lying in the Wicked One," how came it that
he saw where others were blind, worshipped where others
scoffed ; that he stood on this side, others on that, of a
great gulf going down to the foundations of the moral
universe ?   Christian instinct had from the first repudiated
personal superiority of nature as the answer.   St. Paul
had found the solution of the riddle in a Divine predestination, fulfilling itself in the operation of a supernatural
Divine grace.   The Johannine conception of regeneration
combines and transcends both.   The efficient source of
all faith, righteousness, and love is a new life-principle

which is nothing else than the Life of God begotten in the centre of the human personality. In this alone the children of God differ from others. It is not because they believe, do righteousness, and love their brother, that they are " begotten of God," but because they are begotten of God that they believe, love, and do righteousness. The Life is behind and within all.

Finally, the question remains as to the nature of the change wrought in man by the Divine Begetting. On this point also the Johannine doctrine has been vigorously criticised. Thus Dr. Scott in his *Fourth Gospel* distinguishes two strains of doctrine in St. John : one which is purely ethical and religious and in the line of Synoptic teaching, according to which " the power of Christ when it takes hold of a human life effects a renewal of the whole moral nature," so that he " enters on a new life under the influence of new motives and thoughts and desires " (p. 280); another which is mystical and philosophical, according to which " not so much his mind and will as the very substance of which his being is formed must be changed " (p. 281). In the one view the birth from above is regarded as " a moral regeneration answering to the μετάνοια of the Synoptic teaching," in the other, as " a transmutation of nature," " a magical and semi-physical change." [1] Without discussing the alleged two-

---

[1] On this topic Dr. Scott writes with less than his usual lucidity. Some definition of terms would be desirable. He describes the doctrine which he approves as a " renewal of the whole moral nature," which is otherwise expressed as renewal of the " moral temper," as a " radical change of mind," more definitely as " entering on a new life under the influence of new motives and thoughts and desires." But this is not to use the term " moral nature " in its commonly accepted sense. In that sense a man's " moral nature " does not consist in the influence which particular thoughts and motives have over him ; it is what makes him susceptible, in this or that way, to their influence. According as his moral nature is good or bad, good or bad motives, thoughts, and desires find a response within him. The thoughts, motives, and desires that appeal to a man do not, in the first instance, determine his moral nature ; they only reveal what it is, and call it into action.

fold strain of doctrine, but accepting what Dr. Scott calls the mystical and philosophical as being the peculiarly and genuinely Johannine, we take so different a view of it as to maintain that the renewal of the whole *moral nature* (due weight being given to both words) is the very truth it teaches with singular emphasis and precision.

It implies a renewal of *nature.* Dr. Scott is right in asserting that according to this doctrine more is required for man's moral renewal than the presentation of new truths and motives. The very capacity of response to these is required; and the only possible alternative to the Johannine doctrine is the familiar one, that this capacity is inherent in the constitution of human nature itself (although this only leads back to the *impasse*—how it comes that the possession of a common capacity displays such diversity of result). But this alternative St. John emphatically rejects, "That which is born of the flesh is flesh." The chord in man's moral nature that responds to Christ and to the truths and motives of His gospel is silent, is broken. It must be restrung; and it is restrung in those who are "begotten of the Spirit." Only by this direct Divine agency is a renewal of the "moral temper," a "radical change of mind," effected. This for St. John, as for the profoundest Christian thought of subsequent times, is the unique feature of the moral regeneration of which Christ is the author. Character is renewed, not as in other religions and ethical systems, by the sole influence of new truths and motives, but by the renewal of the soul, the moral nature itself. All presentation of truth is unavailing without this concurrent Divine operation from within. Admittedly, there is no prominent development of this view in the Synoptics. The Synoptic attitude is that of the evangelist who delivers his message to men, trusting that it may awaken a responsive chord in their hearts, and who presses it home in urgent endeavour to touch that chord. St. John's attitude is that of the theologian. His doctrine is the result of reflection upon the diverse and opposite issues of evangelism—that result being that man's response to the Truth and Grace of Christ is due, in every instance, to a higher will than his own, is, indeed, the sign and proof that he is " begotten of God."

But the Divine Begetting is the renewal of the *moral* nature. It can by no means be conceded that it implies a change in the very substance of which man's being is formed;[1] not, at least, if by this is meant an organic change in the constitution of human nature, or that the regenerate man is something more or other than man. The children of God are distinguished by no superhuman deeds or capacities. Instead of walking in darkness they walk in the Light; instead of doing sin they do right-eousness; instead of hating they love; instead of denying, they confess Jesus as the Divine, and seek to walk even as He walked, and to purify themselves as He is pure. But these things they do because their *moral* nature has been renewed. The wineskin, so to say, remains the same, but is filled with new wine. No new faculty is created, but every faculty becomes the organ of a new moral life; faith, hope, and love rest upon new objects; conscience receives new light, and the will a new direction and force. And what St. John really teaches is that this transforma-tion of moral character is explicable only by a renewal of the *moral nature*—is due to a change in the sub-conscious region of personal being, which is wrought directly by Divine

[1] This view of regeneration as consisting in a change in the substance of the soul has never been accepted by any Christian Church. It was advocated by Flacius Illyricus, one of the most prominent theologians of what is called the Second Reformation in Germany; but it was universally rejected, and was definitely condemned in the Form of Concord as virtually a revival of the Manichæan heresy.

influence, and which can be conceived only as the communication of a new life-principle. The point at issue is
clearly brought out by the criticism which Dr. Scott
brings against the Johannine view of regeneration as
implying a change which is "semi-physical." The
epithet does not seem happily chosen. If by "physical"
is meant what is of the material or corporeal order, the
statement cannot be admitted (cf. John 3^6 4^{24}). But
if it is intended to signify that which constitutes and
conveys the φύσις, the nature or life-principle of the
subject, the modification of the adjective is uncalled for.
St. John's conception of life is not semi-, but wholly
"physical." It is the conception of a vital essence in which
inhere all the energies that form right moral character,
just as there is a corporeal life-principle by which the
development of the body, with all its characteristics and
functions, is determined. It may be said, indeed, that
the crucial truth of the Johannine conception of Life and
Regeneration is, that it is at once spiritual or ethical and,
in the sense which has just been defined, physical.[1] The life
communicated is a new moral life; a life which is manifested
in a new view of sin and righteousness; in a new view of
Christ and of God; in new desire and power to do the
Will of God, to love one another and to conquer the
world. And the doctrine of St. John is the fullest
recognition in the New Testament that the conscious

---

[1] The use of the word "physical" lies open to the objection that, in modern
use, it has become exclusively associated with the non-spiritual. But it has
been the word chosen by theologians of repute to express the direct action of
the Divine Spirit upon human nature. Thus Owen in his *Pneumatologia* says,
"There is a real *physical* work whereby He infuseth a gracious principle of
spiritual life into all that are really regenerated"; and, again, in speaking of the
work of the Spirit in and through the Word, "God works immediately by His
Spirit on the wills of His Saints—that is, He puts forth a real *physical* power
that is not contained in those exhortations, though He doeth it with them and
by them." So Turretin also, "Ad modum physicum pertinet quod Deus Spiritu
suo nos creat, regenerat, cor carneum dat et efficienter habitus supernaturales fidei
et charitatis nobis infundit."

experiences and activities of the Christian life are ultimately rooted in that deeper region of human personality where God works His own mysterious and inscrutable work of begetting in human nature, and of renewing and replenishing in it, the energies of the Divine Life.

CHAPTER XI.

THE TEST OF RIGHTEOUSNESS.

ONE peculiarity of the Epistle among the writings of the New Testament is that the practical purpose for which it is avowedly written is a purpose of testing. To exhibit those characteristics of the Christian life, each of which is an indispensable criterion, and all of which conjointly form the incontestable evidence of its genuineness, is the aim that determines the whole plan of the Epistle, and dictates almost every sentence: "These things I write unto you, that ye may know that ye have Eternal Life" (5¹³).

As we have seen, Life, according to the Johannine conception, is the essence or animating principle that underlies the whole phenomena of conscious Christian experience, and cannot itself be the object of direct consciousness. Its possession is a matter of inference, its presence certified only by its appropriate effects. It may be tested simply as life, by the evidence of those functions—growth, assimilation, and reproduction—which are characteristic of every kind of vital energy.

Or it may be tested generically, by its properties, as the kind of tree is known by the kind of its fruit. The Epistle adopts exclusively the latter method. It bids its readers try themselves, not as to the fulness and fruitfulness of their spiritual life, but as to their exhibiting those qualities which belong essentially to the Life of God. God is righteous, therefore whosoever has the Divine Life in him doeth righteousness. God is Love, therefore His life in men exhibits itself in love. God is conscious of Himself in His only-begotten Son Jesus Christ, therefore His life is manifested in men by their Belief,—their perception of the Divine in Jesus.

But God is not only Life, He is Light; and fellowship with Him is not only essential participation in the Divine Life; it is also conscious and ethical—"walking in the Light, as He is in the Light" (1^7). It is this thought of "walking in the Light" that governs the first Cycle of the Epistle as a whole;[1] and it is from this point of view that the three cardinal tests—Righteousness, Love, Belief—are applied in it.

Righteousness the Test of Walking in the Light.

2^{3-6}.

This paragraph stands in intimate relation to that which immediately precedes (1^7-2^2).[2] There the same test has been applied *negatively*. We have been brought under the searchlight of God's righteousness, and it has been seen that the first effect of honest submission to this self-revelation is the confession of sin. Now follows the *positive* application. Though the immediate effect of the light is to expose sin, its primary purpose is to reveal duty. The confession of sin must not be regarded as an equivalent for actual well-doing (Ps. 119^4, Matt. 7$^{21. 24}$). To have

---

[1] We must acknowledge and obey the light that God's self-revelation sheds upon every object within our moral horizon; ourselves and our sins (1^{7-10}); our duty (2^{3-6}); our relation to our brother (2^{7-11}) and to the world (2^{15-17}); the Person of Christ (2^{18-28}). *v. supra*, pp. 7-11.

[2] The progression of thought is clearly marked by the recurring phrase, "if we say" or "he that saith," both marking the possibility of a spurious profession :

1^6 "If we say that we have fellowship with Him."
1^8 "If we say that we have no sin."
1^{10} "If we say that we have not sinned."
2^4 "He that saith, I know Him."
2^6 "He that saith that he abideth in Him."
2^8 "He that saith he is in the Light."

14

fellowship with God, we must not only acknowledge what the light reveals as true; we must realise in action what it reveals as right.

"And hereby we perceive that we know[1] Him (God),[2] if we keep His commandments.

"He that saith, I know Him, and keepeth not His commandments, is a liar, and the truth is not in him. But whoso keepeth His word, in him verily is the love of God perfected.

"Hereby perceive we that we are in Him. He that saith he abideth in Him ought himself also so to walk, even as He walked."[3]

The paragraph contains a threefold statement both of the matter to be tested and of the test appropriate to it, and of both on an ascending scale.

Walking in the Light.	The Test.
$2^{3, 4}$　We know God.	That we keep His Commandments.
2^{5a}　The love of God is perfected in us.	That we keep His word.
$2^{5b, 6}$　We abide in Him.	That we walk even as Christ walked.

The first expression of the fact to be ascertained is the knowledge of God; and, as has been pointed out in an earlier chapter, it is used here with evident reference to the pretensions of Gnosticism.[4] "He that saith, I know Him" is not an arrow shot at a venture, but has a definite mark in the Antinomian intellectualist for whom his self-assured knowledge of Divine things superseded all requirements of commonplace morality. Yet, with St. John himself, there is no more distinctive expression than "knowing God," for all that constitutes the essence of true religion—the soul's sincere response to God's revelation of His character and will (cf. $2^{13, 14}$ $4^{6, 7, 8}$ 5^{20}, John $17^{3, 25, 26}$). In this he allies

---

[1] See special note on γινώσκειν.　　　　[2] See Notes, *in loc.*

[3] The logical structure of the paragraph is somewhat obscured by the verse-division. It consists of a thesis (2^3), an antithesis ($2^{4, 5a}$), and a restatement of the thesis ($2^{5b, 6}$).

[4] *v.* pp. 28 sqq.

himself with Old Testament thought (cf. Jer. 31³⁴, Isa. 11⁹ 54¹³, Hos. 4¹ 6⁶); and though contact with the influences of Hellenic speculation and Gnostic theosophy did, no doubt, contribute to give to the idea of knowledge that prominence which it has in his conception of religion, this was by way of recoil as much as of assimilation. To "know" God is not to have a speculative notion of the Being and Attributes of God; it is to have a spiritual perception of the Divine Father (2¹³), whose moral personality is revealed in His Son (5²⁰); it is to have this perception as an abiding possession (ἐγνωκέναι) that is part of oneself, and is made the actual basis of life.

The proof of this "knowing" God is active sympathy with His will,—keeping His commandments. The word translated "keep" (τηρεῖν) expresses the idea of watchful, observant obedience. It is habitually used, for example, of seamen who carefully observe the direction of the winds or ocean-currents and shape their course accordingly. So ought we to keep a heedful eye on God's commandments. The word "commandments" (ἐντολαί), again, emphasises the idea of surrender to moral authority. The "commandments" are the clear, precise orders that God has laid down, dealing with conduct in detail, peremptory as military instructions. And although much more than this is included in the Christian idea of righteousness, yet with profound wisdom is this made the first test—that we make conscience of keeping God's commandments. Other services and tributes may express more vividly the spontaneous impulses of the soul; but with these it is always possible that something of self-pleasing and self-display may mingle. In vain do we break the alabaster box, if we do not obey. Zeal that is not zeal for keeping God's commandments is but egotism subtly disguised. On the other hand, "To know that I know God, I need not aspire to mystic insight, or

visionary rapture, or sublime ecstasy.   A lowlier path by
far is mine" (Candlish).

For "Whoso keepeth His word, in him verily is the
love of God perfected."   Here the unity of the "word" is
substituted for the multiplicity of the "commandments."
The Christian commandments are not a miscellany of
arbitrary requirements or by-laws; they are practical applications of the one Divine Law to the outstanding facts
and situations of human life.   Though many, they are one
in principle and authority — outgrowths from one root;
so Christian Righteousness also, though manifested in
numberless details, is a moral unity.   It is to do the will
of God—the revelation of which is His "word" (cf.
Jas. 2^{10}).

The apodosis of the sentence, instead of taking the
anticipated form, "This man verily knoweth God," introduces a characteristic variation and enrichment of thought.
"In him verily is the love [1] of God perfected."   Here the
"love of God" is usually understood as our love to God,
not God's love to us.   And plainly it must be taken in such
a sense as to indicate a right moral state in us.   But, interpreted in the light of the parallel passage 4^{17} (where we find
simply ἡ ἀγάπη, "the Love"), the "Love of God" is neither
God's love to us nor ours to Him, separately considered,
but that which unites both in one common conception,—
the Love which is the nature of God (4^8), and which is the
nature also of those who are "begotten of Him" (4^7).
That this Divine Love dwells in any man is witnessed by
the fact that he keeps God's "word."   For God's "word"
is nothing else than the revelation in Christ of the Divine
character and will as Love, and to keep that "word" is
nothing else than to embody that Divine character and
will in human deed.   And in this it is "perfected."   "Perfected" love, in the phraseology of the Epistle, signifies, not

---

[1] Cf. $4^{12, 17, 18}$.   See, further, Chapter XIV.

love in a superlative degree, but love that is consummated in action.   Bearing fruit in actual obedience, Love has been perfected : it has fulfilled its mission, has reached its goal.

 " Hereby perceive we that we are in Him.   He that saith that he abideth in Him ought himself also so to walk, even as He [1] walked."   Here, again, the thought is restated in varied form.   Instead of " knowing God," we have " being in Him " (2^{5b}) and " abiding in Him " (2^6) as expressing the fact of fellowship with God.   These expressions are synonymous, denoting from the human side the reciprocal indwelling of God and man, which is for St. John the deepest underlying fact of the Christian life.   The fact is indicated more generally by the phrase " to be in Him " (cf. 5^{20}) ; while the " abiding " in Him may emphasise the element of persistent purpose that is necessary on man's part to continuance in union with [2] God.   From the union of nature there springs an ethical union of will ; and of this the test is that we " walk even as Christ walked." [3] We cannot observe without admiration the exquisite outblossoming of the thought.   As the " commandments " find their ideal unity in the " word," the " word " finds its actual embodiment in Him who wrought

> " With human hands, the creed of creeds,
>   In loveliness of perfect deeds,
>   More strong than all poetic thought."

The ideal, and the power no less than the ideal, of all holy obedience are contained in His word, " Follow Me."   And as His " walk " was the proof of His union with God (John 6^{38} 17^4), so to " walk even as He walked " is the inevitable test of ours.   For it is to be observed that the idea of

---

[1] ἐκεῖνος=Christ.   *v. supra*, p. 89.   [2] *v. supra*, pp. 199, 200.
[3] "Even as He walked."   For St. John the words could not but be tinged with tender personal reminiscences (John 7^1 10^{23}).   He had seen with his eyes the "walk" of his Master in love and holiness ; and it had been the purpose of his Gospel that his readers might as with his eyes behold it (1^3).

the *test* is still dominant. The clause, " He that saith that he abideth in Him, ought himself also so to walk even as He walked," is not hortatory but predicative. It is strictly correlative to the " Hereby we perceive " of the preceding clause. The whole antithesis between truth and falsehood is compressed into the ominous " He that saith " and the incisive " ought " (ὀφείλει, more stringent than δεῖ). The assertion is not only that he who makes this profession incurs this obligation, but that the obligation is of such a nature that its fulfilment or non-fulfilment is decisive of the truth or the falsehood of the profession.

This paragraph as a whole, if the structure of the Epistle has been rightly apprehended, is governed by the thought of " walking in the Light." If we keep not God's commandments, if we keep not His word, if we do not walk as Christ walked, we forsake the path of Light and enter the region of darkness. The necessity of Righteousness is grounded on the requirements of fellowship with God, " Who is Light, and in Whom there is no darkness at all."

In the second Cycle of the Epistle the test of Righteousness is differently presented. It assumes more distinctly the character of a direct polemic against Gnostic Antinomianism ; and its necessity is found not in the revelation of God's Will, but in the Divine nature itself. Through the whole paragraph devoted to the subject there runs the idea, not of Light, but of Life. It is an exposition not of the conditions of ethical fellowship with God, but of the evidence of the Divine Begetting.

Divine Sonship tested by Righteousness.

$$2^{29}-3^{10a}.$$

" If ye know (as absolute truth) that He (God) is righteous, know (take note) that every one also that doeth righteousness is begotten of Him " (2^{29}).

This, the opening sentence of the paragraph, announces the purport of the whole. It introduces (for the first time in the Epistle) the subject of the Divine Begetting, and indicates that this is to be expounded in all the rigour of its ethical demands. The Divine nature, to whomsoever it is imparted, is Righteousness; therefore the test of possessing it is *doing* [1] Righteousness.

Having thus stated his thesis, the Apostle is immediately swept away into rapturous digression. The full magnificence of the thought that sinful men should be brought into such a relation to God smites his soul with amazement: "Behold, what manner of love the Father hath bestowed upon us!" (3[1, 2]).[2] But though these verses to a certain extent interrupt the sequence of thought, they lead off into no side-issue. Like the eagle, the Apostle has soared to the heights, only that he may with mightier impetus swoop down upon his quarry. We have been led to contemplate the Christian life in the glory of its future consummation, only to be brought back once more to the test: "Every one that hath this hope in Him purifieth [3] himself, even as He is pure" (3[3]). This sentence, again, is not hortatory but predicative. It is the statement not of a duty, but of a fact. The hope of perfect likeness to Christ's glory hereafter is not held out as a *motive* to strive after present likeness to His purity; but, conversely, to strive after His purity is the inexorable *test* of having the hope of His glory. Thus "hope" must be taken here in an objective, not a subjective, sense. Not every one who cherishes the hope of glory, seeks the life of purity; but he alone [4] who aims at the absolute purity of Christ (καθὼς ἐκεῖνος)

---

[1] *v. infra*, p. 219.　　　　　　　　　[2] *v.* Chapter XVI.

[3] On ἀγνός, ἀγνίζει, ἐκεῖνος, *v. supra*, pp. 89, 90.

[4] "Every one that hath this hope." πᾶς ὁ ἔχων is more stringent than the simply descriptive ὁ ἔχων. It hints at the "exceptional presumption of men who regarded themselves as above the common law" (Westcott). In most instances of its use (cf. 2[23] 3[4, 6, 9, 10]) the phrase πᾶς ὁ . . . has a distinctly polemical suggestion.

and can be satisfied with no lower aim, possesses it in fact. He alone has in him that Life which will blossom out in immortal perfection when it is brought into the full sunshine of Christ's manifested presence. This is involved in the unity of the Eternal Life here and hereafter. And were one to argue [1] that it is idle (so different are the conditions of the future from those of the present) to aim at the purity of Heaven while here on earth, the answer is that the Life which is begotten of God is by innate necessity, and in whatever environment, a life of truceless antagonism to sin. This the writer proceeds to maintain: (1) in the light of what Sin is; (2) in the light of Christ's character and mission; (3) in the light of the Divine origin of the Christian Life; (4), in the light of the fact that all that is of the nature of sin is of diabolic origin.

3[4].

"Every one that doeth [2] sin doeth also lawlessness; and sin is lawlessness." [3]   It is noticeable that this verse exactly corresponds in thought as well as in position to 2[3. 4]. As there Righteousness was exhibited first of all as the "keeping of God's commandments," so here Sin is, first of all, repudiation of the whole authority and aim of

---

[1] As Bishop Blougram does in his cynical vision :
> "Of man's poor spirit in its progress, still
> Losing true life for ever and a day
> Through ever trying to be and ever being—
> In the evolution of successive spheres—
> *Before* its actual sphere and place of life,
> Half-way into the next, which having reached,
> It shoots with corresponding foolery
> Half-way into the next still . . .
> . . . Worldly in this world
> I take and like its way of life."

[2] "Every one that doeth sin." The direct antithesis to the "purifieth himself" of 3[3]. Instead of refraining himself (ἀγνίζει ἑαυτόν) from sin, he does it.

[3] For fuller discussion of "sin" and "lawlessness," *v. supra*, p. 133.

God's moral government. This is expressed with singular emphasis. Sin, in its constitutive principle (ἡ ἁμαρτία), whatever be the act in which the principle is embodied, is essentially lawlessness (ἡ ἀνομία), no matter what be the form in which the Law is delivered. It is to set up, as the rule of life, one's own will instead of the absolutely good will of God. The inference does not require to be explicitly drawn, that to do so stands in fundamental contradiction to the Life that is begotten of God. But this argument against moral indifferentism,—that every act of sin is the assertion of a lawless will and a defiance of moral authority—while it is a truth that lies at the basis of Christianity, is not the specifically Christian expression of that truth. This the Apostle next gives. Indifference to sin, in whatever degree, on whatever pretext, is the direct negation of the whole purpose of Christ's mission and the whole significance of Christ's character.[1]

3[5].

" And ye know that He was manifested to the end that He might take away[2] sins ; and sin in Him there is not." He "was manifested." The Being and Work of Christ are the manifestation of the Eternal in the sphere of history, of the Unseen Divine Life in the world of our humanity. And the whole Being and Work of the Incarnate Word— word and deed, influence and example, action and suffering, life and death—are directed to this one end, the taking away of sins. It was for this purpose that He was manifested at all, and by this purpose that His manifestation was governed throughout. "And in Him is no sin." The sinlessness of Christ is one of the intuitions of the

---

[1] Again we may observe that the argument follows exactly the same course of development as in 2[3-6] ; 3[5. 6] here corresponding to 2[6] there.

[2] *v. supra*, p. 158, and Notes, *in loc.*

Christian. It is not, in the nature of the case, capable of complete logical demonstration; but *we know* that in Him is[1] no sin. Sin is altogether excluded from the sphere of what He was, and is, and is to be.

The inevitable conclusion from these premises is the " inadmissibility[2] of sin."

3⁶.

" Every one that abideth in Him sinneth not; every one that sinneth hath not seen Him, neither knoweth Him." The impossibility of maintaining at the same time the same kind of connection with Christ and with sin is immediately evident. Any other attitude towards sin than that of absolute repudiation and self-denial is fatal disproof of our living union with Him, and, indeed, of our ever having had the faintest perception of what Christ is, and of what He stands for. But here the Apostle's words seem to assert much more than this;—not only the inadmissibility in principle, but the non-existence in fact, of sin in the regenerate life. This assertion, which constitutes one of the crucial difficulties in the exposition of the Epistle, recurs in 3⁹; and we shall place ourselves in a more advantageous position for examining the problem by first completing the survey of the whole paragraph.

3⁷.

" Little children, let no man deceive you. He that doeth righteousness is righteous, even as He is righteous." Here, for the first time, the polemical import of the whole passage is clearly disclosed, and the clue is given that leads to the solution of its difficulties. The point of

---

[1] " In Him *is* no sin." The tense is to be taken strictly. The sinless Lamb of God is still the object of our faith, because what He was He is eternally.

[2] To borrow Professor Findlay's admirable phrase.

prime importance is that we now discover the precise significance of the phrase ὁ ποιῶν ("whosoever doeth"), which is so characteristic of the paragraph (2^{29} $3^{4.7.8.9.10}$). When it is said, "Little children, let no man deceive you : he that doeth righteousness is righteous," and when the same warning is continued in the words, "He that doeth sin is of the devil" (3^8), the implication clearly is that there were persons who taught the contrary doctrine, namely, that one may be truly righteous apart from the *doing* of righteous deeds, and that, on the other hand, the mere *doing* of sinful acts is no disproof of inward spirituality, nor incompatible with the status of Divine sonship. It is evident that the same persons who held that there is an essential righteousness which is superior to the "doing" of righteous deeds would also hold that there may be a "doing" of sin that does not imply essential depravity in the agent. These are inseparable aspects of the same doctrine.

Thus the point of the argument is missed when ποιεῖν τὴν ἁμαρτίαν (and, *mutatis mutandis*, ποιεῖν τὴν δικαιοσύνην) is taken as signifying to sin habitually, to live a sinful life.[1] It is not the frequency or the unbroken habitualness of the "doing" that is in view, but the fact that Being is to be tested and known by Doing, the inward spiritual nature by the outward conduct which is its product. The object of attack is the Gnostic Antinomian, to whom, in his proud intellectualism or his overstrained spiritualism, the prosaic requirements of common morality were of small moment. It is true that the tendency to exempt religious claims from moral tests is not confined to any heretical sect. "We are too often content with the consciousness that we stand in some special relation to the Lord, and come to regard sin as an unavoidable evil which is not so very harmful as might be thought" (Haupt). This is the ubiquitous and

---

[1] Steven, *Johannine Theology*, p. 136. Likewise Huther—"whose life is a service of sin," "who lives in sin as his element."

inextinguishable heresy. But it was not this universal tendency that gave occasion to the pointed, tremulously affectionate appeal, "Little children, let no man lead you astray." Doing is the test of Being:—"He that doeth righteousness is righteous, even as He is righteous." This was and is the manner of Christ's righteousness. Immeasurable in its perfection, it was and is wholly translatable and translated into deed. In Him the outward life is wholly commensurate with the inward. And in vain do men prate of union with the True Vine if they do not in like manner bring forth fruit.

3⁸.

"He[1] that doeth sin is of the devil; because from the beginning the devil sinneth. To this end was the Son of God manifested, that He may destroy the works of the devil."

The proof already advanced of the incompatibility of sin with the life of the children of God, first from its own nature (3⁴), then from the character of Christ and the purpose of His mission (3⁵·⁶), is reinforced by the further consideration, that the source from which all that is of the nature of sin is derived is not uncertain. And we cannot but recognise an intentionally *terrific* force in the point to which the Apostle here brings matters. He who self-tolerantly commits sin can have no kinship with Christ. But what then? He is not without spiritual kinship. He has a spiritual father—the Devil—who "sinneth from the beginning." And "to this end," the Apostle adds, "was the Son of God manifested, that He might destroy the works of the Devil." With pregnant force the majestic title "the Son of God" (used for the first time in the Epistle) marks the true character of the works of the Devil.

[1] For fuller discussion of this verse, *v. supra*, pp. 142–4, 158.

" Judge ye what they are," the Apostle would say. " It was no other than the Son of God whose task it was to destroy them. So abhorrent to God are the works of the Devil that it was worth His while, yea, He was necessitated by His own Holiness and Love, to send even His own Son into the deadly fight for their complete undoing."

3^9.

" Whosoever [1] is begotten of God doeth not sin ; because His seed abideth in him : and he cannot sin, because he is begotten of God." The Apostle advances the fourth and last proof of the unqualified antagonism to sin that is inherent in the life of the children of God. As the seed of physical generation stamps upon the offspring an ineffaceable character, and nothing in after years can alter the inherited basis of life, so does the germ of spiritual life from the spiritual Father set the impress of a permanent organic character upon the God-begotten. On this the Apostle finally grounds the certainty that the Christian Life, in its inmost eternal essence ($\sigma\pi\acute{\epsilon}\rho\mu\alpha\ \alpha\mathit{\grave{v}}\tau o\mathit{\hat{v}}$), is a life of perfect righteousness ; that is, under present conditions, a life of continual opposition to sin, and victory over it.

3^{10a}.

" In this the children of God are manifest, and the children of the devil : whosoever doeth not righteousness is not of God." In our " doing " and also in our " not-doing " the spiritual affinities, which are in their essence secret, become manifest—manifest, that is, to all men of spiritual discernment (cf. Matt. 7^{20}, Gal. 5^{19-23}). With the solemn words, " Whosoever doeth not righteousness is not of God," the argument concludes. The end of the paragraph reverts

[1] *v. supra*, pp. 195, 198.

to and logically completes the assertion with which it began. That assertion was :—" Every one that doeth righteousness [1] is begotten of God "; here the complementary negative is set forth, " Every one that doeth not righteousness [1] is not of God " (2²⁹).   The test of righteousness is enforced on every side.   No gap is left in the circle drawn around the " begotten of God."   All who do righteousness are included ; all who do not are excluded.

The writer has thus, with four-fold argument, enforced the truth that the life of Divine sonship is a life that necessarily expresses itself in righteousness and in irreconcilable antagonism to sin ; and, further, that there can be no righteousness apart from right-doing, and, conversely, no evil-doing apart from the principle of sin, which has its arch-embodiment in the Devil.   It must be admitted, however, that the manner in which this truth is presented is fitted rather to puzzle the exegete than to edify the reader.   By an apparently overstrained identification of persons with the principles they represent, and by neglect of the fact that there is in human nature, as it actually exists, a commixture of incongruous elements, the writer seems to spurn the solid ground of experience and to soar into a region of mere abstract dialectic.   Had he asserted in the strongest terms the impossibility of maintaining the same kind of relation to Christ and to sin,—that to believe in Christ and to believe in sin, to love Christ and to love sin, to live in Christ and to live in sin as one's element, is as unthinkable as that one should face North and South at the same moment,—to this every Christian heart would instantly respond.   But when he says :—" Whosoever abideth in Him sinneth not : whosoever sinneth hath not seen Him, neither knoweth Him " (3⁶); " Whosoever is begotten of

---

[1] Westcott distinguishes between $\tau\grave{\eta}\nu$ $\delta\iota\kappa\alpha\iota\sigma\acute{\nu}\nu\eta\nu$ in 2²⁹ and $\delta\iota\kappa\alpha\iota\sigma\acute{\nu}\nu\eta\nu$ here, as, respectively, the abstract—" the idea of righteousness in its completeness "— and the concrete—" that which bears a particular character, viz., righteousness. I find it impossible to realise any exegetical value in the distinction.

God doeth not sin ; because His seed abideth in him : and he cannot sin, because he is begotten of God " (3⁹) ; and, again, " We know that whosoever is begotten of God sinneth not " (5¹⁸),—he seems to contradict not only the universal testimony of the Christian conscience (which much rather assents to Luther's paradox, " He who is a Christian is no Christian ") and the general doctrine of Scripture, but his own explicit teaching. Has he not said, " These things I write unto you that ye sin not " (2¹), thereby recognising the possibility of what he declares impossible ? Has he not set forth, in view of that possibility, the Divine provision for it, " If any man sin, we have an Advocate with the Father " (2¹) ? Does he not expressly contemplate the contingency of our seeing " a brother sinning a sin not unto death " and prescribe the course to be followed in that event (5¹⁶) ? Undesirable, therefore, as it is, even for the sake of vindicating a writer's self-consistency, to seek another meaning for plain words than they carry on their face, the inconsistency here is of such a nature that we are compelled to look for some interpretation by which the discord may be resolved.

We return, therefore, to the consideration of 3⁶ " Whosoever abideth in Him sinneth not : whosoever sinneth hath not seen Him, neither knoweth Him." Attempts to untie the knot have been made from many sides. (*a*) A solution is sought in the Apostle's " idealism " (Candlish, Weiss). As to St. Paul, all Christian believers, notwithstanding their abundant imperfections, are saints, κλητοὶ ἅγιοι ; so to St. John every genuine Christian, regarded in the light of his divinely-begotten nature, " sinneth not." This in no way meets the requirements of the passage. The writer's purpose is not to exhibit an ideal, but to apply a *test* ; and it is precisely against the dangers of a false or vague idealism that his argument is directed.[1] (*b*) Help has been

---

[1] See on 3⁷ *supra*.

sought in the word μένει. When the Christian sins, he is not, for the moment, abiding in Christ. "*In quantum in Christo manet in tantum non peccat*" (Augustine and Bede, quoted and adopted by Westcott). But, even if this were a satisfactory explanation of the first clause (which it is not), it is unavailing with respect to the second, "Whosoever sinneth hath not seen Him, neither knoweth Him." (*c*) The verse refers to mortal sin. But any distinction between mortal and venial sins is resolutely debarred by the context, the argument of which is that every sin, of whatever description or degree, is "lawlessness" (3[4]). (*d*) ἁμαρτάνει is explained as meaning a life of unbroken and impenitent sin—following sin "as a calling" (Stevens, Gibbon). But this only empties the word of its proper meaning: ἁμαρτάνειν in 3[6], cannot be other than synonymous with ποιεῖν τὴν ἁμαρτίαν in 3[8]; and this (*v. supra* on 3[7]) connotes not the frequency or other characteristic of the sinning, but its simple actuality. (*e*) Finally, a solution is most commonly sought on the lines of Rom. 7[20].[*] "A Christian does not *do* sin, he suffers it" (Besser). "It is no longer sin, but opposition to it, that determines his conduct of life" (Huther). "*Etsi infirmitate labitur, peccato tamen non consentit, quia potius gemendo luctatur*" (Augustine). Here, however, the Apostle is not distinguishing between a man and his deeds; on the contrary, he is in the most rigorous fashion identifying them (πᾶς ὁ ποιῶν, 3[4. 7. 8. 9. 10]). With Rom. 7[20], as a contrite acknowledgment of sinful weakness, St. John might have had no quarrel. But it is against that text abused—made an apology for sin, and a pretext for moral indifferentism—that the concentrated fire of his artillery is directed.

I venture to suggest that a more satisfactory explanation of this perplexing passage is to be found in

---

[*] "But if what I would not, that I do, it is no more I that do it, but sin which dwelleth in me."

the obvious fact that it is written in view of a definite controversial situation and in a vehemently controversial strain, the absoluteness of its assertions being due to the fact that they are in reality unqualified contradictions of tenets of unqualified falsity. The polemical reference which underlies the whole paragraph becomes explicit in 3[7-8] :—" Little children, let no man lead you astray. He that doeth righteousness is righteous, even as He is righteous. He that doeth sin is of the devil." Clearly, as we have seen, this is aimed against a pseudo-spiritualism for which mere conduct was of minor concern; and here, if anywhere, we get the desired clue. Let it be supposed that the Apostle and his readers were familiar with a class of teachers who maintained that true righteousness is entirely of the spirit, while *doing*, whether of righteousness or of sin, has its sphere solely in the flesh, and that, therefore, the truly spiritual man is no more affected by the deeds of the flesh than are the sunbeams by the purity or the filth on which they shine; let it be supposed that it is against such a doctrine, disseminating itself like a plague, that the passage is directed, and its apparent exaggeration and over-emphasis are naturally accounted for. Suppose that it were maintained that one may commit outward sins without injury to his spiritual connection with Christ, the reply would naturally be the strongest possible assertion that the very proof of any one's connection with Christ is his *not sinning*,— " Whosoever abideth in Him sinneth not." Suppose that it were affirmed that the man whose spirit is occupied with the inward vision and knowledge of Christ need not lose his equanimity over such trivial and transient phenomena as his deeds of sin, the fitting reply would be, that such an one has not the faintest apprehension of what Christ and Christianity stand for (3[6b]); that, indeed, his real affinities are with the Devil. I have put the case as a supposition; but

15

there is abundant evidence [1] that such tenets and practices were characteristic of Gnosticism in both its earlier and its later developments; they were, indeed, the inevitable off-spring of its fundamental principle of dualism.   And it is from this quarter, I submit, that an explanation of the Apostle's language in this verse is to be found.   It is the language not of calm and measured statement, but of vehement polemic.

The same explanation holds good for the equally un-qualified dictum of 3^9: "Whosoever is begotten of God doeth not sin, because His seed abideth in him; and he cannot

---

[1] Irenæus informs us that the Gnostics imagined three classes of men, the material, the psychical, and the spiritual.   They themselves, who had the perfect knowledge of God, were the spiritual.   "Hence they affirm that good moral conduct is necessary for *us*" (*i.e.* for ordinary Christians), "because without it we cannot be saved; but they affirm that they themselves will unquestionably be saved, not from moral conduct, but because they are by nature spiritual.   For, as the material are incapable of receiving salvation, so the spiritual are incapable of receiving corruption, whatever moral conduct they may practise; for, as gold when deposited in mud does not lose its beauty, but preserves its own nature, the mud not being able to injure the gold; so also they say of themselves that, whatever may be the character of their material morality, they cannot be injured by it nor lose their spiritual substance.   Hence the most perfect among them perform all forbidden things without any scruple, and some of them, obeying the lusts of the flesh even to satiety, say that carnal things are repaid by carnal, and spiritual things by spiritual" (*Contra Haer.* i. 6. 2).

Of the followers of Simon Magus it is reported: "They even congratulate themselves upon this indiscriminate intercourse, asserting that this is perfect love.   For (they would have us believe) they are not overcome by the supposed vice, because they have been redeemed. . . . They do whatsoever they please, as persons free; for they allege that they are saved by grace" (Hippolytus, *Refutatio* VI. xiv.).

Of the Nicolaitans it is said: "They quote an adage of Nicolaus, which they pervert, 'that the flesh must be abused' (τὸ δεῖν παραχρῆσθαι τῇ σαρκί). Abandoning themselves to pleasure like goats, as if insulting the body, they lead a life of self-indulgence" (Clem. *Strom.* II. xx.).

"These quotations I have add⸺ ⸺ in reproof of the Basilidians, who do not live rightly, either as having power (ἐξουσίαν) to sin because of their perfection, or as being altogether assured by nature of future salvation, although they sin now, because they are by dignity of nature the elect" (*Strom.* III. i.).

Of the Prodicians the same writer says: "They say that they are by nature children of the supreme God; but, abusing that nobility and liberty, they live as they choose, and they choose lasciviously; judging that they are bound by no law as 'lords of the sabbath,' and as belonging to a kind of superior race, a royal seed.   And the law, they say, is not written for kings" (*Strom.* III. iv.).

Such quotations might be indefinitely multiplied.

sin, because he is begotten of God." He in whom a seed
of Divine Life thus abides and determines development
not only does not do sin, he does not because he cannot.
To him it is as impossible as it is, say, for the embryonic
bird to acquire the habits of a serpent. Theoretically this
is true. It was true of Christ; and if in our case the
Divine Begetting were not a re-begetting, if there were
no other element than the seed of God present in our
nature,—no "old man" to put off, but only the "new man"
to put on,—this would be actually true of us also. As the
case stands, nothing is more certain to the consciousness of
those who are "begotten of God" than that, while they
ought to be incapable of sin, they both can and do sin.

An outlet from the *impasse* is usually sought in the
explanation that the *regenerate* element in the regenerate
man is sinless, and that the Christian is here spoken of only
in so far as the Divine nature has attained supremacy in
him. "As long as the relationship with God is real, sinful
acts are but accidents. They do not touch the essence of
the man's being" (Westcott). "With his proper self, his real,
completely independent personality, the regenerate man
cannot sin; and so his sinning can never be a sinning in the
full and proper sense of the word, but takes place only
when his proper personality is overcome by the power of
evil—is always sin of infirmity" (Rothe).

These are statements which, to say the least, cannot
be assented to. It is true that the sins of a good man are
foreign to that element in his nature which is deepest and
most permanent, and which will ultimately assert its
supremacy. Nevertheless, there necessarily are elements
in his personality to which his sins are due; and this the
good man sincerely recognises and penitently confesses.
True it is, also, that the good man does not sin spontaneously and gratuitously, but only because he is overcome by the power of temptation. But this is no less

true of most of the sinning of unregenerate men. No one, moreover, is overpowered by evil except by his own consent. The will, though non-resisting, is not non-existent even in sins of infirmity. This explanation, so far from realising the Apostle's intention, rather, it seems to me, reverses it. The whole paragraph is a protest against the doctrine that, in the regenerate man, sin is to be regarded as an " accident," or that his " proper self " is to be held blameless of his actual deeds. Again, I submit, the explanation is that the statement is not theoretical but practical, moulded and warmly coloured by the exigencies of controversy. St. John's οὐ δύναται ἁμαρτάνειν is not the calm dictum of the theologian, but a word suffused with holy passion, a vehement repudiation of the adversary's false δύναται. For it depends upon who the speaker is, and how it is said, and with what motive, whether it be true or false to say that the " begotten of God " can sin. Suppose it to be *claimed* that he can, that he may be a liar, a glutton, or unchaste, yet none the less " begotten of God "; suppose it to be said that his very prerogative is this—that he can sin without prejudice to his high standing as a spiritual and enlightened man—" No ! " would be the unhesitating reply, " that is what he *cannot* do." What the fact of his being " begotten of God " means, is just that this has become to him morally impossible. " Can a woman forget her sucking child, that she should not have compassion on the son of her womb ? " It must be admitted that there are such monstrosities as mothers who can. But if it be *claimed* that a mother can be cruel and neglectful, and that without losing her character as a mother, the right answer, the morally true answer, is an indignant denial. In the same sense it is true that the Christian, because he is " begotten of God," *cannot* sin ; and to assert the contrary is to assert a blasphemy, a calumny upon God.

In the third Cycle of the Epistle the writer recurs finally to the Test[1] of Righteousness in 5[18] "We know that every one that is begotten of God sinneth not; but he that was begotten of God keepeth himself, and the wicked one toucheth him not." Nothing needs to be added to the explanation already advanced of the unqualified language in which this last protest is made against the idea that declensions from actual righteousness are of small moment or none to the spiritual man. But the second clause introduces new matter, "He that was begotten of God taketh heed[2] to himself,[3] and that wicked one toucheth him not." This is added obviously as a safeguard against a perverse application of what has just been said, "Every one that is begotten of God sinneth not." Might this truth be made a pillow for laziness instead of a stimulus to action? Might some one, saying in his heart that he was "begotten of God," and that to him, therefore, righteousness was assured, fold his hands and go to sleep? Let him remember that righteousness is possible to man only as victory over a powerful and sleepless foe ("the wicked one"); that this victory is won only by man's own vigilant effort ("taketh heed to himself"); and that, while both this vigilant effort and its victory are assured by the forces of the Divine Life operating in the regenerate, it is the effort made and the victory won that give the required proof of regeneration.

In this practical motive of the clause we may find, perhaps, the reason for the strange substitution of the aorist form γεννηθείς for the usual perfect γεγεννημένος.[4]

---

[1] Also in 5[3], where the test of love to God is keeping His commandments. See Chapter XII.

[2] τηρεῖ. *v.* p. 211.

[3] ὁ γεννηθείς . . . ἑαυτόν. For discussion of the reading, see Notes, *in loc.*

[4] ὁ γεγεννημένος = "He who has been begotten of God and who still retains that character," the perfect tense connoting the act and its abiding result. ὁ γεννηθείς = "He who was begotten of God," the aorist merely pointing to the act as having taken place.

It is in this γεγεννημένος that danger may lurk. "Begotten of God, therefore now and for ever, whether working out my salvation with fear and trembling, or living in somnolent security, I am a child of God." But with the unique γεννηθείς the Divine Begetting is for the moment regarded as a past event, not necessarily of present efficacy. "Were you once begotten of God? Rest not on that; but take heed to yourself! It is the very mark of the God-begotten that he takes heed to himself." A greater might, a more ceaseless and penetrating vigilance than his own must be his salvation; and will be, but only on condition of his obedience to the Master's command γρηγορεῖτε καὶ προσεύχεσθε.

Then, "the wicked one layeth not hold of him"[1] As it was true of the Master, so shall it be true of the watchful disciple—"The ruler of this world cometh and hath nothing in me."

---

[1] The translation "toucheth him not" goes beyond the true sense. The "wicked one" may, indeed, touch him; but there is nothing by which he may lay hold of him who is thus on his guard.

CHAPTER XII.

The Test of Love.

As has appeared very clearly in the preceding chapter, the purpose of the Epistle is not to exhibit in the abstract that view of Christianity which may be distinctively called Johannine, but, by holding up the true standard of Christian faith and ethics, to expose the antichristian character of contemporary Gnosticism. And in pursuance of this object, the subject-matter of the Epistle consists mainly in the presentation, from various points of view, of those three crucial characteristics of all that is genuinely Christian— Righteousness, Love, and true Belief. In both the first and second cycles of the Epistle the test of Righteousness is followed immediately by that of Love. The writer nowhere correlates these two conceptions of the ethical principle. Broadly, however, it may be said that Righteousness stands for its negative aspect. Righteousness is to "keep the commandments," to "walk even as Christ walked"; but it is to do so in respect of not sinning. It is to "purify oneself as He is pure," to "guard" oneself as the begotten of God. The positive element in the Christian ethic is Love. And, according to the plan of the Epistle, this is first presented as the condition and test of "walking in the Light."

Love the Test of Walking in the Light.

$$2^{7-11}.$$

" Beloved,[1] no new commandment write I unto you, but an old commandment which ye had from the beginning; the old commandment is that which ye heard.   Again, a new commandment write I unto you, which thing is true in Him and in you; because the darkness is passing away, and the true light is already shining " ($2^{7,\ 8}$).

By a certain stateliness in the introduction of his theme the writer shows how strongly he is moved by the sense of its greatness.   His desire to come very close to the heart of his readers breaks out spontaneously in the affectionate and appealing " Beloved "; while, with deliberate skill, he uses the rhetorical device of reticence in order to whet their interest.   He announces his subject only by suggesting that there is no need to announce it—wraps it up in half-revealing, half-concealing paradox.   " No new commandment write I unto you, but an old commandment. . . . Again, a new commandment I write unto you." But he has sufficient confidence in the perspicacity of his readers to assume that they will at once recognise in the commandment which is both " old " and " new " the familiar precept, " Love one another " (cf. 2 John [5]).

In this identity, though it has been denied or missed by some exegetes,[2] lies the fine significance of the antithesis. The commandment is " old," because it is what " ye heard from the beginning."   It is " new," because it is " true (has its vital realisation) in Him and in you."   The commandment is " old."   It is no novelty the Apostle is about to urge upon them.   The test of walking in the light is

---

[1] These verses have been found susceptible of a bewildering variety of interpretations. *v.* Notes, *in loc.*

[2] *v.* Notes. *in loc*

nothing erudite or far-fetched. To the readers of the Epistle it is "old" as the familiar fundamental law of Christianity which they had been taught among the first rudiments of the Gospel ("from the beginning," cf. 2²⁴). But in a wider sense it is old as humanity itself, nay, older. It is the law God has impressed upon all creature-life; which is seen in the self-sacrificing care of the tigress for her whelps, of the mother-bird for her nestlings. It is the Eternal Law—the law of God's own Being. God is Love. And, therefore, it is always "new," a fresh and living commandment. Other laws become archaic and obsolete. Like the ceremonial law of Judaism, for instance, they are now fossils, relics of modes of thought and of religious and social conditions that no longer exist. But never can age antiquate or custom stale this commandment. Never can the time come when men shall appeal to tradition or to statutory authority as a reason for loving one another. This commandment is always "new," instinct with vital force, a spark from the Divine fire that kindles every soul into being.

But to the Christian it is "new" in another and a special sense :—" which thing¹ (not the law itself, but the fact that it is a new and living law) is true in Him and in you." There are times when the Law of Love shines out with a morning splendour, when it reveals a new significance to the human conscience and enters upon a further stage in its predestined conquest of human life. And this was supremely the case when it was embodied in Christ, and when He infused into the precept, "Love one another," the new dynamic, "as I have loved you" (John 13³⁴). The Love of Christ, typified by His washing the disciples' feet (John 13¹⁻¹⁷), and completely realised in the laying down of His life for those whom only His love made His "friends" (John 15¹³), created a new commandment—gave

¹ *v.* Notes, *in loc.*

to mankind a new conception, and imposed a new obligation. And this commandment is still " new " in Him. His whole Love expressed but did not exhaust itself in one act. He laid down His Life that He might take it again. The Love of Calvary is an ever-flowing fountain. But also in " you "—in the Christian life—the commandment is always " new." It is " old,"—a word once for all heard and accepted,—but it is also a law continually realising itself in the movements of life, daily imparting fresh light and impulse in the experience of all upon whose heart it is written by their entering into and abiding in that life-transforming relation to Christ which is declared in the great words, " as I have loved you " (cf. 2 Cor. $5^{14.\ 15}$).

The following clause, " because the true ($\dot{a}\lambda\eta\theta\iota\nu\acute{o}\nu =$ real) Light is already shining," may be regarded as stating either the reason why the commandment is " new " in the experience of the Apostle's readers, or the reason why he writes to remind them of this. The sequence of thought, in either case, is far from obvious; but it is less obscure and more forcible on the latter [1] supposition than on the former. The " true Light " that is vanquishing the darkness is not the dawning light of the Parousia (Huther) but the light of the Gospel. It points back to the announcement on which this whole section of the Epistle is based, " God is Light " (1^5). The Light, which is the self-revelation [2] of God, is now shining forth as never before. In former times it had shone dimly and fitfully : in the Gentile world only as starlight ; in the Old Testament only as a prophetic dawn. In Christ it is as the sun shining in its strength. The greater, then, is the necessity that men assure them-selves of their walking in the Light of God, and the more is it necessary to remind them that, since the central

---

[1] On this interpretation, " which thing is true in Him and in you " is treated as a parenthesis, and the clause, " because the darkness passeth away," etc., is attached to " a new commandment write I unto you." *v.* Notes, *in loc.*

[2] *v.* p. 56 sqq.

glory of that Light is now seen to be the Divine Love, the inevitable test of fellowship with God is that the commandment of Love—the law of God's own Being—be fulfilled in them.

"This old commandment, which ye heard from the beginning, is, nevertheless, a new, fresh, living commandment—a fact that is realised first in Christ and then in you; and of this commandment I once more put you in remembrance, that ye may assure yourselves thereby that ye are walking in the true Light which now is shining in the world."

In the following verses (2^{9-11}) we have the application of the test.

"He that saith he is in the Light, and hateth his brother, is in the darkness even until now" (2^9).

The ominous "He that saith" (cf $2^{4. 6}$) points unmistakably to the Gnostic, who, glorying in his superior enlightenment, despised the claims and neglected the duties of brotherly love. With regard to such an one, the Apostle, instead of saying "He lies," states the plain, concrete inference, "He is in the darkness even until now." The light that does not reveal the obligation and impart the impulse of love is but a barren phosphorescence. Even though the true light is now shining, he that lives in hate walks in darkness; for God, who is Light, is Love.

"He that loveth his brother abideth in the Light, and there is no stumbling-block in him" (2^{10}). From the connection between the two clauses, it is evident that here the stumbling-block ($\sigma\kappa\acute{\alpha}\nu\delta\alpha\lambda\text{ov}$ [1]) is conceived, not as a temptation that a man puts in another's way (Haupt), but that in his own disposition, which is a source of temptation to himself (Rothe; Westcott characteristically attempts to

---

[1] $\sigma\kappa\acute{\alpha}\nu\delta\alpha\lambda\text{ov}$. Cf. Ps. 119^{165} "Great peace have they that love Thy law, and nothing shall offend them" ($o\mathring{v}\kappa\ \mathring{\epsilon}\sigma\tau\iota\nu\ a\mathring{v}\tau o\hat{\iota}s\ \sigma\kappa\acute{\alpha}\nu\delta\alpha\lambda\text{ov}$, LXX.).

combine both ideas). As in broad daylight obstructions over which one might trip and fall are seen and avoided, so, if we live in the habitual disposition of Love, we are not liable to be taken unawares by any temptation to sin against our brother. Not only does Love remove such σκάνδαλα as pride, envy, jealousy, revenge; it is the one sure light for the path of duty, the one infallible guide in all our complex relations to our fellow-men. It is because self-seeking governs men that life becomes so entangled. Love is that power of moral understanding [1] which, almost with the certainty of instinct, discovers the way through the maze to those "good works which God hath before ordained that we should walk in them." There is nothing in love to entrap into sin.

On the contrary, "He that hateth his brother is in the darkness, and walketh in the darkness, and knoweth not whither he goeth, because the darkness hath blinded [2] his eyes" (2[11]).

The antithesis is complete in every item. Towards a brother, not to love is to hate.[3] There is no third possibility. And he that hateth is ignorant of the stumbling-blocks that are in him.

His whole moral being and doing are enveloped in darkness. Without the guiding light of Love, he knoweth not whither he goeth [4]—does not perceive the true character of his own actions. The selfish man is innocent of any notion that he is selfish; the quarrelsome person thinks

---

[1] The same thought is finely brought out in Phil. 1[9. 10] "And for this I pray, that your love may abound more and more in knowledge, and in all perception" (ἐπιγνώσει καὶ πάσῃ αἰσθήσει).

[2] Literally, "blinded" (ἐτύφλωσεν). *v.* Notes, *in loc.*

[3] "*Ubi non est amor, odium est; cor non est vacuum*" (Bengel). To "hate" expresses, not instinctive dislike, but a state of moral perversion—an evil will. It is thus the opposite of ἀγαπᾶν not of φιλεῖν (Westcott).

[4] The clause is almost a *verbatim* reproduction of John 12[35] καὶ ὁ περιπατῶν ἐν τῇ σκοτίᾳ οὐκ οἶδεν ποῦ ὑπάγει. Cf. Prov. 4[19]: "The way of the wicked is as darkness; they know not at what they stumble." ἐν σκοτίᾳ οἴχεσθαι οἷς ἂν τύχωμεν προσπταίοντες, is quoted as a proverb in Lucian, *Hermotimus*, 49.

that every one is unreasonable except himself; the revenge-
ful, that he is animated only by a proper self-respect.
"His whole life is a continual error." Even if he does
observe that his relation to his brother is somehow out of
joint, he goes on imputing to him all the wrong and the
mischief, the roots of which are really in himself—"Because
the darkness hath blinded his eyes." The penalty of
walking in the darkness is the extinction of vision. The
Word of God is full of this truth.[1] He who will not see,
at last cannot.

The thought that gives unity to the second Cycle of
the Epistle is Divine Sonship (2^{29}–4^6); and here, accordingly,
Love is enforced as a test of participation in the Life of
God. In the previous paragraph, to love one's brother is
the proof of having passed from darkness into Light (2^{10}),
here, of having passed from death into Life (3^{14}). The
paragraph, however, is not so regular in structure, nor
are its contents knit so closely to the leading thought as is
the Writer's wont. But the leading thought itself is clearly
fixed at the beginning, "Whosoever loveth not his brother
is not of God."

Divine Sonship tested by Love.

$3^{10b-24a}$.

"Whosoever doeth not righteousness is not of God,
neither he that loveth not his brother."

Here the first clause sums up the preceding paragraph;
the second unobtrusively effects a transition to the new[2]

---

[1] Cf. the fontal passage Isa. 6^{10}; also Matt. $6^{22.\ 23}$, John 6^{39}.

[2] "He that loveth not his brother" (καὶ ὁ μὴ ἀγαπῶν) in the second clause
may be regarded as a further definition of "whosoever doeth not righteousness"
in the first (καί = "namely"). "It carries forward to its highest embodiment the
righteousness which man can reach" (Westcott). Love is the fulfilling of the
Law (Rom. $13^{8.\ 9}$). But this correlation of Righteousness and Love is not characteristic of the Epistle. It is better, therefore, to regard the two clauses as
strictly co-ordinate.

paragraph and propounds its thesis: "Whosoever loveth not his brother is not of God." The ultimate ground for this assertion is, of course, the impossibility of the loveless soul's having any community of life with God, Who is Love. This, however, is advanced only in the third cycle ($4^{7.8}$); and, meanwhile, the Apostle is content to base his argument upon the primacy of Love, not in the Divine nature, but in the revelation of the Divine will.

"Whosoever loveth not his brother is not of God. For this is the message which ye heard from the beginning, that we love one another" (3^{11}). What was formerly announced as a "commandment" (2^7) is here expressed as a "message." [1]   "Love one another" is not only a definite Christian precept (John 13^{34}), it is the sum of Christian ethics. All that Christ was and did says to men this one thing, "Love one another" (John $15^{12.13}$). This the Apostle's readers had heard "from the beginning." [2]   No one can learn the Gospel at all without learning this.

In what follows, the Apostle, instead of developing his theme dialectically, does so pictorially. He sets before us two figures, Cain (3^{12}) and Christ (3^{16}), as the prototypes of Hate and Love, and, therefore, of the children of the Devil and the children of God.

In John 8^{44} the Devil is represented as the "murderer from the beginning"; but here a more vivid image of the diabolical spirit is displayed in Cain, the firstborn of darkness, in whom that spirit, like Minerva from the brain of Jove, sprang immediately to full growth.

"Not [3] as Cain was of the [4] evil one, and slew his brother. And wherefore slew he him? Because his own works were evil, and his brother's righteous" (3^{12}).

---

[1] On the identical import of ἀγγελία in 1^5, *v.* p. 56.

[2] Cf. 2^7.

[3] The construction of the clause is elliptical and irregular; but the meaning is clear. We are to love one another, and not do as Cain did. *v.* Notes, *in loc.*

[4] "Was of the evil one." Cf. 2^{13} $3^{8.10}$ 5^{19}.

The word translated " slew " (ἔσφαξεν) [1] suggests the brutality of the deed. But it was not in the manner of the deed, it was in its astounding motive that the essentially diabolic spirit of brother-hatred was manifested. This is brought out by the vivid interrogation and answer :—" And for what reason was it that he slew his brother? Incredible as it may seem, it was because his brother's works were righteous, while his own were evil." His brother's works were righteous, and he, therefore, hated and slew him. The goodness he refused to emulate was unendurable ; it goaded his self-love to madness. A sentence was surely never penned that sheds a more horrifying light upon the evil capability of the human heart. If we did not know as a fact and an experience the envy " which withers at another's joy and hates the excellence it cannot reach," it would seem a thing entirely preposterous—a fantasy from some grotesque nightmare world. Yet, that man can become such a child of the Devil as to be filled with envy—what is this but proof that he is made to be the child of God? How insatiable must the heart be that seeks to allay its thirst with the wine of Hate !

" Marvel not, brethren, if the world hateth you " (3[13]). This is most simply and logically taken in close connection with the verse preceding.[2] " Cain still lives, and still hates Abel for his righteousness' sake. The causeless and inexplicable hate that the world manifests towards you need awaken no surprise. You are to it what Abel was to Cain. It hates you because its works are evil and yours are righteous " (cf. John 15[18, 25]).

" We know [3] that we have passed from death into

---

[1] ἔσφαξεν, "butchered." Originally, the word meant to " kill by cutting the throat," and the idea conveyed by it is always that of brutal slaughter. In the N.T. it is found only here and in the Apocalypse. Cf. σφαγή, Rom. 8[36], Jas. 5[5].

[2] v. Notes, *in loc.*

[3] ἡμεῖς οἴδαμεν. ἡμεῖς is emphatic in itself and also by position, " As regards ourselves, we know."

life,[1] because we love the brethren.   He that loveth not abideth in death " (3[14]).

The primary stress of the sentence falls upon the emphatic "We know."

As Cain, because he was of the evil one, hated and slew his brother, whose works were righteous, and as the world, because it is subject to the evil one (5[19]), still hates the children of God ; so, on the contrary, the proof that we are begotten of a different spirit—that we have passed from death into life—is that we love the children of God—" the brethren." The point of immediate emphasis is not that " we have passed from death into life " (though this also is necessarily emphatic), but that the test by which this is ascertained in our own case, is love to the brethren.[2]

" We have passed from death into life because we love," contains a profound truth.   " The life which is the highest good is that which enters with ever quick and fresh responsiveness into the personal relationships in which our humanity is realised " (Newman Smyth).   By Love the soul lives and grows.   Selfishness spends for the poorest returns the noblest capacities of human nature. The gold it lays its hands upon turns to dross ; the flower it plucks withers.   Love alone discovers and possesses the highest good that is in all things human and Divine.   It has the magic wand that changes even dross into fine gold.   To love the least of our brethren is to enrich the soul from the treasury of God.   To love is to live.[3] " He that loveth not abideth in death."   The statement is more than simply antithetic to what precedes.   There is no clearer proof of the great transition from life to death than love of the brethren ; but the absence of such love is not only the absence of such proof, it is

---

[1] " Have passed from death into life."   *v. supra*, pp. 191–2.

[2] For a different view of the sequence of thought, *v.* Notes, *in loc.*

[3] In the same spirit as St. John, Philo points out that Cain slew, not his brother, but himself (Plummer).

proof that the transition has not taken place. This strong, severe statement is defended and confirmed in the verse following, "Whosoever hateth his brother is a murderer; and ye know that, no murderer hath eternal life abiding in him." Here the "not loving" of the preceding verse becomes "hate" (cf. $2^{10, 11}$). In the absence of Love, Hate is always potentially present. "We often reckon want of love as mere indifference. But such it is only while there is no rivalry or collision of interests. As soon as this occurs indifference reveals its true character; it becomes actual hate" (Rothe). You have but to irritate a man's self-love, to render yourself disagreeable to him; and, if there be no love in him toward you, there will presently be hate. "And every one that hateth his brother is a murderer." The proposition is stated as one of inherent necessity ($\pi \hat{a}_s \; \dot{o} \; \mu \iota \sigma \hat{\omega} \nu$). "Hates any man the thing he would not kill?" Literally, of course, this is not true. Many hate who do not commit murder, nay, for whom the desire or dream of doing so is beyond the limit of the imaginable. Yet, morally, the proposition is true; not merely because hate is the invariable precursor of murder, but because both reveal essentially the same moral attitude, and differ from each other only as a mild differs from a virulent attack of the same malady, or as a homicidal maniac under restraint differs from the same maniac at large. In actual manifestation, hate may proceed no further than the feeling of a certain satisfaction in the discovery or report of what redounds to the hated person's discredit; but let hate be released from all the adventitious restraints of circumstance, of the conventional morality which sanctions hate but forbids overt injury, of the sensibilities engendered by civilised life, to which bloodshed or violence is æsthetically abhorrent; let hate act out its spontaneous impulses, and infallibly it would—as with the savage or the tyrant

16

it does—kill.[1]   In spite of seeming exaggeration, it is a profoundly true moral judgment—" He that hateth his brother is a murderer."   *A fortiori* is this true of the man, if such there be, who hates *the brother* beside whom, as he at least imagines, he lies in the bosom of the same Divine Love.   " And ye know that no murderer hath eternal life abiding in him."   Comment is unnecessary.   The word translated " ye know " ($o\emph{ἴδατε}$)[2] signifies that the matter requires neither demonstration nor even reflection (cf. Rev. 21[8]).

So stringent, so inevitable, in its negative aspect, is the test of Love.

The development of the subject that now follows (3[16–18]) differs in two respects from that which has preceded.   The presentation, which thus far has been negative, becomes positive—Hate as personified by Cain gives place to Love as personified by Christ (3[16]).   And the test, which thus far has been applied in the abstract, is now brought closer to the facts of life (3[17. 18]).

" In this, that He[3] laid down His life[4] for us, have we learned what Love is, and we ought to lay down our lives for the brethren " (3[16]).   Virtues are best illustrated by their contraries ; and now we discover that the sinister figure of Cain has been introduced only the more perfectly to reveal the glory of Another Who is fairer than all the children of men.   Cain sacrificed his brother's life to his

> " Of the million or two, more or less
>   I rule and possess,
> One man, for some cause undefined,
>   Was least to my mind.
> I struck him, he grovelled, of course—
>   For, what was his force ?
> I pinned him to earth with my weight
>   And persistence of hate . . .
> . . . I soberly laid my last plan
>   To extinguish the man."
>
> Browning, *Instans Tyrannus.*

[2] $\kappa\alpha\grave{\iota}$ $o\emph{ἴδατε}$.   *v.* special note on $\gamma\iota\nu\acute{\omega}\sigma\kappa\epsilon\iota\nu$ and $\epsilon\emph{ἰδέναι}$.

[3] " He," $\emph{ἐκεῖνος}$ = Christ.   *v. supra*, p. 89.   [4] *v. supra*, p. 159.

own wounded self-love; Christ sacrificed His own life in love to His brethren. Cain slew his brother because his own works were evil and his brother's righteous; Christ's works were righteous and His brethren's evil, yet He took on Himself the burden of their evil deeds, and laid down His sinless life for their sakes. And every man belongs to the brotherhood either of Cain or of Christ. "In this we have learned to know [1] what Love is" (3[16a]). The fine point of the statement is lost by the insertion of any supplement—" of God " or " of Christ "—after " Love." This—this devotion of Jesus Christ to sinful men—is Love; and in this we have for the first time recognised what deserves the name. " And we ought to lay down our lives for the brethren " (3[16b]). We lay claim to Love. What the nature of Love truly is, we have learned by this, that He laid down His life for us. And Love must reproduce [2] in us what it was and did in Him. If we have, so to say, a drop of the blood of Jesus Christ in our veins, we are under bond and pledge ($\dot{o}\phi\epsilon\dot{\iota}\lambda o\mu\epsilon\nu$),[3] whensoever the call comes to us, to manifest our Love in the same way of uttermost sacrifice. For, though to think of Christ's Love to us, and then to think after what fashion it may be repeated in our relations to our fellow-men, is to compare the infinite with the infinitesimal—the sun with a flickering candle; yet, as light is light whether in the candle or the sun, as it has the same properties and the same laws of action, so Love is Love whether in Christ or in us. Our lives must exhibit the same properties, obey the same spiritual laws, must be built upon the same ground-plan, as that Life of which the Cross was the perfect expression. This is the test of our union with Him and of our Divine sonship in Him.

[1] $\dot{\epsilon}\gamma\nu\dot{\omega}\kappa\alpha\mu\epsilon\nu$ = have recognised, learned to know. $\tau\dot{\eta}\nu$ $\dot{\alpha}\gamma\dot{\alpha}\pi\eta\nu$ = Love in its essence, what Love is.

[2] The same necessity that the life of Christ be reproduced in us has already been asserted with regard to Righteousness (2[6] and 3[4]).

[3] Cf. 2[6].

But, though this obligation to lay down our lives for the brethren ever rests upon us, though our lives are mortgaged to this extent, opportunity for a full discharge of this obligation rarely comes (and, necessarily, it cannot yet have come to any living man, unless he have proved a recreant). And we must, above all, beware of crediting to ourselves as Love what is but the mouthing of well-sounding phrases, the play of the imagination upon lofty ideals, or the thrill of merely emotional sympathies. This is a danger which besets Christianity, most, perhaps, of all religions. Its ideals are so sublime, the emotions they awaken are so lofty and satisfying, that we are apt to regard our appreciation of those ideals and our susceptibility to those emotions as entitling us to a high place in the moral scale—to feel as if we had paid every debt to Love when we have praised its beauty, felt its charm, and experienced its sentiment. There needs some homelier test of Christian Love than the laying down of life.

" But whoso hath the world's goods, and beholdeth his brother in need, and shutteth up his compassion from him, how doth the Love of God abide in him ? " (3^{17}). The word "beholdeth" ($\theta\epsilon\omega\rho\hat{\eta}$) implies, not a casual glimpse, but a more or less prolonged view. The case supposed is that the rich brother's sympathy is naturally drawn out by the spectacle of his poor brother's necessitous condition, but, when sympathy is on the point of becoming an impulse to action, the thought of the price in " the world's goods " causes him suddenly to call it back and, as it were, turn the key ($\kappa\lambda\epsilon i\sigma\eta$) upon it. Then, with vivid and even contemptuous interrogation, the niggard is held up before our eyes—" In what fashion does the Love of God dwell [1] in

---

[1] " How dwelleth . . . ? " ($\pi\hat{\omega}s$ . . . $\mu\epsilon\nu\epsilon\iota$). Neither here nor in 3^{15} does $\mu\epsilon\nu\epsilon\iota$ contain the idea that the person contemplated is a backslider in whom the Love of God has formerly been, but is not now, abiding (Haupt, Rothe). Cf. John 5^{38} $\kappa\alpha\iota$ $\tau\dot{o}\nu$ $\lambda\dot{o}\gamma o\nu$ $\alpha\dot{v}\tau o\hat{v}$ $o\dot{v}\kappa$ $\ddot{\epsilon}\chi\epsilon\tau\epsilon$ $\dot{\epsilon}\nu$ $\dot{v}\mu\hat{\iota}\nu$ $\mu\dot{\epsilon}\nu o\nu\tau\alpha$, where a previous indwelling is excluded by the context.

" such a man [1] as that ? " By the " Love of God " we are
to understand neither the love of God to us (Rothe, " How
can God do otherwise than turn away His love from such
a man ? ") nor our love to God (Huther, Haupt), but the
Love which is the nature of God, which He has manifested toward us in Christ (3^{16}), and in the possession of
which consists our community of nature with Him.[2] To
have " the Love of God abiding in us " is equivalent to
having " Eternal Life abiding " in us (3^{15}), to being
" begotten of God " (4^7) and to having God Himself
" abiding in us " ($4^{12.\ 16}$).

The Apostle next sums up the paragraph with an affectionate exhortation to the practice of the truth which has
been elucidated (3^{18}), and a restatement of its reality as a
test of our Divine sonship ($3^{19.\ 20}$).

" Little children, let us not love in word, neither in
tongue; but in deed and in truth " (3^{18}).[3] It is true, of
course, that " words " are sometimes the best " deeds " of
Love; and also that, as St. Paul insists (1 Cor. 13^3), there
may be " deeds " without the " truth " of Love. St. John
is content to put the contrast broadly and strongly (cf.
Jas. $2^{15.\ 16}$).

" And by this shall we recognise that we are of the
truth, and shall assure our hearts before Him, whereinsoever
our heart condemn us ; because God is greater than our
heart, and knoweth all things " ($3^{19.\ 20}$).

This statement seems to resile from the settled
certainty asserted in 3^{14}. " We know that we have
passed from death into life, because we love the
brethren." But this knowledge must still be sustained
by the testing fact—that " we love the brethren "; and
how this testing fact is to be established has just been
shown (3^{18}). The future tense, " we shall recognise "

---

[1] *ἐν αὐτῷ*, emphatic by position.   [2] Cf. 2^5. *v. supra*, p. 212.
[3] *v.* Notes, *in loc.*

(γνωσόμεθα), points not to the future fulfilment of the conditions laid down in 3[18] (Westcott),—that, of course, is assumed,—but to the future possibility of some shadow falling upon the clear mirror of the soul, as when our own heart condemns us. Even then, if we have loved "in deed and in truth" we shall recognise by its proper marks the fact that our lives are, in their measure, an expression of that Divine Truth of which Christ is Himself the full embodiment (cf. John 14[6] 18[37]). But this verse and those that follow (3[19-22]), in which the effect of Love in "deed and in truth" upon the consciousness of our relation to God is exhibited, will come under consideration in a later chapter. [1] We proceed, therefore, to the third Cycle of the Epistle. Here the place of primacy, which in the first and second Cycles is held by Righteousness, is given to Love.

Love the Test of Union with God.

4[7-12].

In the first Cycle, Love has been exhibited as the great "commandment" of the Christian Life (2[7. 8]). In the second, it is regarded as the sign and test of Divine sonship (3[10b. 14. 17]); but this, though assumed, has not been clearly grounded. That the life begotten of God is essentially a life of Righteousness has been expressly deduced from the nature of God:—" If ye know that He is righteous, know that every one also that doeth Righteousness is begotten of Him" (2[29]). But no parallel statement has hitherto been made with regard to Love; and it is this development of the subject, therefore, that occupies the present paragraph. Here the Epistle rises to its sublimest height. It is impossible to conceive that the theme which is the ethical heart of Christianity could be more nobly enshrined than in these few sentences of gold pure and unadorned. Brief as the paragraph is, it is

---

[1] *v. infra*, pp. 281 *seq.*

worthy to be set beside the Prologue to the Fourth Gospel, as the loftiest that man has ever been inspired to indite.

"Beloved, let us love one another, because Love is of God" (4[7a]). Again the prefatory "beloved" (cf. 2[7]) reveals how warmly the Apostle's affections are stirred towards his readers by his thought of the truth he is about to declare (cf. 2[7]). It urgently commends to their thought the "old commandment,"—an exhortation so familiar that it might be in danger of being accepted and neglected as a truism.

"Let us love . . . because Love is of God." This, as has been said, is a new connection of ideas. It has been implied, but not hitherto expressed.

Up to this point Love has been regarded as duty rather than as disposition (2[7. 8] 3[23]). The duty of active Love has been urged as indispensable to "walking in the Light" (2[10]), as an obligation bound upon the Christian by the example of Christ (3[16]), and as a tangible proof that we are "of the truth" (3[19]). But now the deeper underlying thought, "Love is of God," reveals a deeper motive for the duty, "let us love." Let us express in word and deed the Divine nature which is ours—let us cultivate the disposition of Love and bring forth its fruits. Thus the verse emphasises equally the Divine source of Love and its manifestation in human activity.[1] The "exceeding greatness of His power toward us who believe" does not supersede, but only heightens the power of volition (Phil. 2[12. 13]). Therefore, "let us love one another, because Love is of God."

"And every one that loveth is begotten of God, and knoweth God" (4[7b]). The redemptive relation to God is here presented in its double aspect as the being "begotten of God," and as "knowing God"[2] (cf. 2[3. 4] 4[6], John 17[3]).

---

[1] The urgent imperative, "Beloved, let us love one another," is, therefore, to be given its full force, and is not to be regarded merely as an introductory formula (Haupt) or as a resumption of 3[23] (Weiss).

[2] *v.* Chapter IV. pp. 62–63.

And as the reality of this has been already tested, in both aspects, by Righteousness and Belief (the Divine Begetting by Righteousness, 2^{29}, by Belief, $4^{2. 3}$; the knowledge of God by Righteousness, $2^{2. 3}$, by Belief, 4^6), so now it is subjected, in both aspects, to the test of Love.   The inter-relation of these terms—" loving " " begotten of God," " knowing God "—has been variously [1] construed.   But it is quite clear that the relation of " loving " to each of the other two is that of the test to the thing tested.   Love is the test, because the invariable consequence of the Divine Begetting. And it is the test of the knowledge of God, either because it is its invariable consequence, or because it is its indispensable condition.   We may say that only he who loveth knoweth God, because like is known only by like.   Love is the organ of spiritual insight—the Divine in us which enables us to apprehend the Divine ($2^{9. 11}$).   But it is equally true that Love is the effect and, therefore, the test of all true knowledge of God.   We may choose either form of the argument, or adopt both.   The resulting truth is that every one who lives the life of Love has therein the realisation of the fact that he has been made partaker of the nature of God, and that he has a continuous and progressive perception (γινώσκει) of what God's nature is.

On the contrary, " He that loveth not has no knowledge of God, because God is Love " (4^8).   Here the negation is heightened in proportion as the affirmation is strengthened. It was said of " every one that loveth " that he has a continuous perception of what God is (γινώσκει) ; but what is said of him " that loveth not " is that he has never had any perception of God at all (οὐκ ἔγνω).[2]   The reason is that God *is*

---

[1] *v.* Notes, *in loc.*

[2] The R.V. is curiously inconsistent in its translation of ἔγνων. In John 16^3 "have not known"; in John 17^{25} "knew"; here "knoweth." Here the sense is perfective, but this may be rendered in English by the simple past tense, as in Greek by the aorist. " I never knew such a man " is good colloquial English for " I have never known such a man." So here we might translate, " He that loveth not never knew God."

Love.   There is nothing in Him that is not Love.   Otherwise it might be claimed for "him that loveth not" that he has *some* perception of God, though not of His love.   But God is Love; and the blindness of the unloving is unbroken by a single gleam.

The exposition of the next two verses has been given in an earlier chapter.[1]   Here, it is enough to indicate their place in the sequence of thought.   The first (4^9) is closely linked to the idea of knowledge; the second (4^{10}), to the idea of Love.   Begotten of God and loving one another, we have the faculty for spiritually apprehending the nature of God, Who is Love.   But wherein is God fully revealed for our apprehension?   "Herein was the Love of God manifested toward us, that God hath sent His Only-Begotten Son into the world that we might live through Him."   And what is the essence of this manifestation, the nature of the Love thus revealed?   "Herein is Love, not that we loved God, but that He loved us, and sent His Son as a propitiation for our sins."

From this sublime contemplation of the Divine Love, the Apostle returns to his main theme.   "Beloved, if God loved us, we also are bound [2] to love one another" (4^{11}).   If it was thus that God loved us, if His love was so transcendently great, and so independent of all worthiness or attractiveness in us that our very sinfulness became the occasion of its supreme activity: then we, if we are partakers of His nature, are bound,—for us it is a moral necessity—to love even as He loved (cf. Matt. 5^{43-48}, John 13^{34}).   But by what is this debt to be paid?   The answer to this question is highly significant.   Instead of the anticipated "We ought to love God," it is "We ought to love one another"; and why it must be so is immediately explained.

"God (in Himself) no man hath ever seen; if we love one another, God abideth in us, and His Love is perfected

---

[1] *v. supra*, pp. **73-77**.   [2] ὀφείλομεν, stronger than δεῖ; cf. 2^6 3^{16}.

in us " (4^{12}). God is invisible.[1] We cannot directly do Him any good. We can make no sacrifice for His immediate benefit. He has no need of our help. We cannot give to Him, but can only receive from Him blessings upon blessings, numberless as the sand of the shore. We cannot, in short, love God after the same fashion in which He has loved us. Yet, if we are " begotten of God " we have in us the same nature of Love that He has manifested toward us in Christ. And there is provision by which this nature may be manifested and exercised in us. " If we love one another God dwelleth in us, and His Love is perfected in us."

If we have the Love[2] that is not merely liking for the likeable, admiration for the admirable, gratitude to the generous—Love whose will to bless men is undeterred by demerit or unattractiveness, that bears another's burden, dries another's tears, forgives injuries, overcomes evil with good,—Love which is prompt to help those who need our help (hoping for nothing again), instead of those who need it not (hoping for much in return)—then the Love that manifests itself in us is that Divine *kind* of love which is most worthy of the name; yea, it is God Himself within us, acting out His Life in ours. It is His Love that is " fulfilled "[3] ($\tau \epsilon \tau \epsilon \lambda \epsilon i \omega \tau a \iota$) in us. Thus the end of the paragraph answers to the beginning. The Apostle's exhortation and its ultimate ground are: " Beloved, let us love another—If we love one another, the Love of God is perfected in us."

The same theme is resumed and developed in the final paragraph on Love (4^{20}–5^{3a}).[4]

In all that has been said, the necessity and the sufficiency of Love as a test of genuine Christianity have

---

[1] Almost all the commentators, I have to admit, take a quite different view of the sense of this verse. *v.* Notes, *in loc.* The exposition I have given agrees in some measure with Rothe's.

[2] *v. supra*, pp. 75–77.

[3] *v. infra*, pp. 286–7.

[4] On $4^{18.\ 19}$ *v. infra*, pp. 288–95.

been established. But before leaving the subject the Apostle will once more remind us of the tests by which Love itself is to be recognised as genuine (cf. 3^{16-18}). These are found, first, in its action towards our fellow-men ($4^{20}-5^1$); and, secondly, in its moral integrity ($5^{2.\ 3a}$).

Love to God tested by Love to Man.

$$4^{20}-5^1.$$

" If any man say,[1] I love God, and hateth[2] his brother, he is a liar: for he that loveth not his brother whom he hath seen, cannot love God whom he hath not seen " (4^{20}).

The argument is, at first sight, one which it is difficult to maintain. For, while it is true that visibility and neighbourhood conduce to love, that " If the object to be loved incites to love by the immediate impression it makes upon us, love is easier than when we have no sensuous perception of it at all " (Rothe, so also Huther and Weiss); it is no less true that the impression made may be such as by no means to incite to love. To love my brother may be to love one in whom there is little that is amiable, one, perhaps, who has done me grievous wrong; to love God is to love Him Who first loved me, Who has forgiven me a thousand wrongs, Who is Himself all that is glorious, beautiful, and good. The Apostle must not be held guilty of making a statement so preposterous as that it is easier to love such a brother,[3] because he is visible, than to love God, since He is invisible. The truth is that this interpretation is based on an erroneous notion of what, in the

---

[1] "If any man say." Cf. "If we say" (1^6); "He that saith" ($2^{4.\ 6.\ 9}$). "Saying" is, throughout, the writer's target.

[2] As always, St. John recognises no third possibility between Love and Hate. See on 2^9 and 3^{15} *supra*.

[3] Calvin, Ebrard, and Westcott understand "brother" as signifying what is Godlike in man. If we do not love the image of God in our brother, we cannot love God Himself. Cf. Jas. 3^9. This thought, however, is given in 5^1, not here.

mind of St. John, Love is. With him, Love does not stand for a passive emotion awakened by the impression that others make upon us. It is an active principle, a determination of the will to do good, the highest good possible, to its object.[1] This being borne in mind, the argument here is both intelligible and absolutely cogent. It is, in fact, the same argument, in more explicit form, as we have already found in 4^{12}. Visibility and invisibility signify the presence or absence, not of attraction or incitement to love, but of *opportunity* for loving. Your brother is in sight; and when you will you may do him good. But God is invisible; your beneficence, your sympathy, cannot reach unto Him Who is the bearer of all burdens, the giver of all good gifts (cf. Ps. 50^{9-12}, Matt. 26^{11}). In the nature of the case there is no other medium through which our love to God, who first loved us, can be realised than by loving our brother, especially if he have *not* first loved us.

It is now asserted, moreover, that our relation to our brother is ordained for this very end. "And this commandment have we from Him, that he who loveth God love his brother also" (4^{21}). The first reason why love to God is necessarily realised in love to men is the consideration of opportunity (4^{20}). The second is the express revealment of the Divine purpose for man. The ultimate end for which all social relations exist is that they may be, so to say, the arteries through which the Divine Life of Love shall flow.

In the following verse a third reason is adduced— affinity of nature. The commandment that "He who loveth God love his brother also" is based on the deep universal law of kinship. "Whosoever believeth that Jesus is the Christ is begotten of God: and whosoever loveth Him that begat loveth him also that is begotten of Him" (5^1). Here the first [2] clause is strictly introductory

---

[1] *v. supra*, p. **77.**　　　　　[2] On the first clause, see *infra*, p. **270.**

to the second. The statement, "Whosoever believeth that Jesus is Christ is begotten of God," is made only in order to define the persons to whom the brotherly love of Christians is due, and the grounds on which it is due. In opposition to Gnostic exclusiveness it claims for all believers the full measure of brotherly love; and it does so, because all are children of the One Father—"Every one that loveth Him that begat loveth him also that is begotten of Him."

He who loves the parent who is the source of his own life, must love those whose life is derived from the same origin. Fraternal love follows by psychological necessity from filial love. He that is "begotten of God" cannot but love those who share with him the life that unites men in their deepest convictions, dispositions, aspirations, and hopes.

Love tested by Righteousness.

$5^{2. 3a}$.

In the next brief sub-section, containing the Apostle's last word on this theme, Love, whether towards God or towards man, is finally tested by Righteousness.[1] Genuine Love must be holy. "Herein we know (recognise) that we love the children of God, when we love God and do His commandments" (5^2). This is a verse the great significance of which is apt to be overlooked. Its statement of the necessary relation of love to God and love to man is the exact converse of that which is given in the preceding verses. There it has been shown that by a threefold necessity—necessity of opportunity (4^{20}), of obedience to express ordinance of the Divine Will (4^{21}), of the instincts of spiritual kinship (5^1)—love to God

---

[1] The correlation of Love with Righteousness has been suggested by simple collocation of the ideas in 3^{10} and in $3^{22. 23}$. Here the bonds are drawn closer. *v.* Chapter I. p. 15 sqq.

can only realise itself in love to man. Here, on the other hand, it is maintained that love to man is truly love only when it is rooted in and governed by love to God. Piety without philanthropy is unreal; philanthropy without piety may be immoral—may instead of a fish give a serpent,—at best, it is impotent to bestow the highest good, and instead of bread gives a stone. It is a great ethical principle that St. John here enunciates. We cannot truly bless our fellow-men,—unless in our personal lives we follow after the highest good—"love God and do His commandments." The man who does many generous actions but lives a licentious or an impious life does, upon the whole, more, and more enduring harm than good. The Kingdom of Heaven is like unto leaven, and "the true philosophy of doing good is, first of all and principally to have a character that will of itself communicate good." The love of Christ had its supreme activity, not in His feeding the hungry or giving sight to the blind, but in this—"For their sakes I consecrate Myself, that they also may consecrate themselves" (John 17^{19}). The highest service that any man can render to humanity is to "love God and keep His commandments."

"For this is the Love of God,[1] that we keep His commandments" (5^{3a}). The Apostle re-echoes his Master's words (John 14$^{15, 21}$) in asserting that to speak of a love to God that does not essentially signify moral integrity is to speak of what does not and cannot exist. To love God is not only a motive impelling to obedience; it is, in itself, assimilation to the Divine. To love God is to love all that is of "righteousness and true holiness." It has no other meaning than this.

Thus it has been shown that from love to God there

---

[1] In 2^5 probably, and in 4^{12} certainly, "the love of God" is a true possessive (= the love that is God's own). Here unmistakably it is a genitive of the object (= our love to God).

necessarily issue both love to our brother (5^1) and moral integrity ($5^{2, 3a}$). Hence also it follows that neither of these can genuinely exist without the other (cf. 3^{10}). "By this we recognise that we love the children of God, when we love God and keep His commandments" (5^2). This is the Apostle's last word on Love.

Of the various themes which are so wonderfully intertwined in the Epistle, that to which it most of all owes its imperishable value and unfading charm is Love. There are portions of it that are seldom read and more seldom expounded in our churches; but there are few passages of Scripture more familiar than those in which St. John has been so divinely inspired to write of the Eternal Life, in God and in man, as Love. This is due to nothing concrete or dramatic in the presentation; and insistent as he is that Love is essentially a practical energy, yet as an exponent of the practical implications of Love he does not come into competition with St. Paul. There is nothing in the Epistle that is comparable to the thirteenth chapter of First Corinthians, with its delicate analysis, or to the twelfth chapter of Romans, with its masterly exposition of the manifold applications of the New Commandment to the actual relations of life. On the other hand, St. John's development of the theme, according to his peculiar genius and for his special purpose, is unapproachable and final. He has demonstrated from every point of view that Christianity without Love is a contradiction in terms. Do we think of the Christian life as a walking in that Light which is the self-revelation of God, then the central ray of that Revelation is Love; and to walk in Light is to walk in Love. Do we think of it as that Life of which Christ is the Archetype and Mediator, then His spirit of absolute self-surrender must be reproduced in it. Do we think of it as participation in the Divine Nature itself, then God is Love, and every one that loveth, and none else, abideth in

God and God in Him. Finally, would we be assured that that Love which is the nature of God is operative in us, then this must be made manifest in our conduct toward our fellow-men.

But it is just here that a feature emerges in which St. John's conception of Love seems to be strangely circumscribed and defective—its rigid limitation to the love of Christians toward their fellow-Christians. The urgency with which every argument and plea is plied to enforce love to our "brother," to the "children of God," only makes the fact more glaring, that from first to last there is not the suggestion of an outlook beyond the Christian community. By the modern reader this limitation is scarcely noticed, for we instinctively give the widest scope to the language used, and interpret our "brother" as our fellow-man. But by the exegete the fact has to be recognised that, in the teaching of the Epistle, there is no hint that ἡ ἀγάπη—the Love that is the replica in man of the Love of God—is due from us to any other than our fellow-Christian. The point is one that has received little consideration. It is not enough to say that it is "only through the recognition of the relation to Christ that the larger relation is at last apprehended" (Westcott). How shall we explain the absence of anything to indicate that the larger relation has been at all apprehended by the Writer? Or, again, if all that can be said is that "other members of the human race are not excluded, they are not under consideration" (Plummer), it must be admitted that, in point of Christian insight, the Epistle lags far behind the Parable of the Good Samaritan. Nor is it inconceivable that this should be the case. But as we have found, I hope, a key to some of the perplexities of the Epistle regarding its doctrine of Righteousness in its immediate polemical purpose, it is from the same quarter, probably, that we must seek light upon the present difficulty. For it must be observed that it is exclusively as a *test*, that the idea of Love is employed in the Epistle. Even when the utterance is most positive and hortatory, the underlying thought is that of the test supplied by the obligation enforced. And if we think of the circumstances of a Christian community in the Apostolic age, it is very evident that the most immediate, practicable, and certain test of Christian Love was to be found, not in its widest extension, but in the sphere of its most definite and obvious obligation. This difference of purpose must be allowed for in comparing the teaching of the Epistle with our Lord's great parable. There, He holds up to us the Samaritan as a pattern of the Love that makes neighbours, and says, "Go and do likewise." Here, St. John holds up the Priest and the Levite as specimens of the lovelessness that declines the claims even of brotherhood, and says: "If you can thus shut up the bowels of your compassion from a needy brother, you are a Christian only in name" (3^{17}). And even this he does with direct polemical aim. He is striking, not at a universal tendency, but at a special manifestation of that tendency. As has been shown in a previous chapter,[1] the utterances of the Epistle regarding Love are as directly anti-Gnostic in their aim as those regarding Righteousness and Belief. The task thrust upon the writer was not to urge the truth, "*Homo sum ; humani nihil a me alienum puto*," but to insist, in view of the arrogant and loveless [2] intellectualism of the Gnostic character, that Love is of the essence of the God-begotten Life ; and, in view of its esoteric and separatist tendencies, that Christian Love must be extended to the whole Body of Christ—must comprehend without distinction all the children of God.[3]

---

[1] *v. supra*, pp. 30, 31.
[2] *v.* quotation from Ignatius, p. 30 (footnote).
[3] *v.* Brooke on 3^{10}, pp. 90, 91.

CHAPTER XIII.

THE TEST OF BELIEF.

ONE peculiarity of the Johannine vocabulary is the frequency [1] with which the verb πιστεύειν appears in it; and another is that, in contrast with the usage of other New Testament writers, the object of this verb is much more commonly a fact or a proposition than a person, and that consequently the result of its action is to be expressed in English by the word Belief rather than Faith or Trust.[2] Thus the Epistle speaks only once of " believing in " Christ [3] (ὁ πιστεύων εἰς τὸν υἱὸν τοῦ θεοῦ, 5¹⁰); whereas in other passages the object of belief is a truth concerning Him, as that He is the Christ (5¹) or the Son of God (5⁵); or a testimony (God's, 5¹⁰; a spirit's, 4¹); or a fact of the spiritual order, such as the " love which God hath towards us " (4¹⁶). This does not signify that the personal Christ has been in any degree supplanted by Christology; it only reveals the fact that the writer uses a phraseology and a mode of thought peculiar to himself. If St. Paul says, " That life which I now live in the flesh I live in faith, the faith which is in the Son of God " (Gal. 2²⁰), St. John expresses the same truth when he writes, " And now, little children, abide in Him " (2²⁸), or " Our fellowship is

---

[1] The Johannine writings furnish more than a half of the whole occurrences in the N.T. of πιστεύειν (57 out of 100). Singularly, the cognate name πίστις is found only once (1 John 5⁴). This avoidance of πίστις may have been due to the fact that it was already finding a place in the terminology of Gnosticism.

[2] See special note on πιστεύειν appended to this chapter.

[3] Elsewhere, of " believing in His Name " (εἰς τὸ ὄνομα, 5¹³; τῷ ὀνόματι, 3²³).

with the Father, and with His Son Jesus Christ" (1³). The fact remains, however, that with him, "believing" denotes less frequently the action of the will in trust and self-committal, more frequently the perception of a truth or the crediting of a testimony which is the prerequisite to such action; less frequently a direct personal relation to Christ, more frequently a theological conception of Christ. And thus, to the modern reader, with whom credal interests are apt to be at a discount, the tone of the Epistle, in some of its utterances, may appear to be unduly or even harshly dogmatic.

In estimating this dogmatism, however, we must take into account several explanatory—I do not say, modifying —factors.

(a) In the Epistle the writer reveals himself as one whose mind is dominated, in an exceptional degree, by the idea of Truth. To him Christianity is not only a principle of ethics or even a way of salvation; it is both of these, because it is, primarily, the Truth—the one true disclosure, without a competitor,[1] of the realities of the spiritual and eternal world. The adjective ἀληθινός,[2] describing that which both ideally and really corresponds to the name it bears, and the substantive ἀλήθεια, denoting the reality of things *sub specie æternitatis*, are conspicuous expressions of Johannine thought. The light of the Gospel is the "true light" (τὸ φῶς τὸ ἀληθινόν, 2⁸), no dim symbolic light like that of the Old Testament, no illusory phosphorescence, like Gnostic speculation, but the light of the Eternal Mind shining out in Christ upon every object in the spiritual world. The God revealed in Christ is the "true God"

---

[1] "St. John does not treat Christianity as a religion containing elements of truth, or even more truth than any religion which had preceded it. St. John presents Christianity to the soul as a religion which must be everything to it, if it is not to be really worse than nothing" (Liddon).

[2] τὸν μόνον ἀληθινὸν θεόν (John 17³); τὸ φῶς τὸ ἀληθινόν (1⁹); τὸν ἄρτον τὸ ἀληθινόν (6³²); ἡ ἄμπελος ἡ ἀληθινή (15¹); ὁ ἅγιος ὁ ἀληθινός (Rev. 3⁷).

(ὁ ἀληθινὸς θεός, 5²⁰), the God who is, and who is all
that God ought ideally to be; or, again, He is simply the
"True" (ὁ ἀληθινός, 5²⁰), the ultimate eternal Reality.
No words are more characteristic of St. John than that
"No lie is of the truth" (2²¹). Everywhere we find the
same rigorous sense of reality, the same insistence upon
the primary necessity of squaring conduct with facts—of
"doing the truth" (1⁶); and, in order to this, of knowing,
believing, and confessing the great facts in which all true
life is rooted. A mind like St. John's, for which the ideal
is the only real, and by which every matter of practice is
so clearly seen in the light of its ultimate principles and
issues, necessarily lays a weighty emphasis upon Belief,
and displays an intense dread and hatred of error. "No
lie is of the truth." Truth and untruth cannot blend.
They have no common factor; they are opposite in origin
and issue. Whatever be the subject in question the
"truth" concerning it is one, and is the sole path by seeing
and following which we are "made free" (John 8³²)—are
brought into saving contact with the universe of realities.

(*b*) In the Epistle this idiosyncrasy has its edge
sharpened by the controversial situation. If the writer is
vehement in his denunciation of all teaching that subverts
the orthodox doctrine of the Incarnation, it is because
this doctrine is in his conviction the centre and compendium
of all Truth.[1] Nor is this dogmatic attitude one that
stands in need of apology. It is true that "the Gospel
centres in a Person and not in any truth, even the greatest
about that Person" (Westcott). But it is true also that
the Gospel cannot consist merely in the narrative of a life
and the delineation of a character, apart from the question
who the Person is whose life is narrated and whose
character is pictured. A creedless or merely biographical

---

[1] As to the practical significance attached by St. John to the Incarnation,
see Chapter **VI.**

Gospel is impossible. The baldest humanitarian, no less than the fullest Trinitarian, conception of Christ implies a creed. The picture of the historical Jesus has one significance, if we can say—That is the ideal man; another, if we can say—That is very God; still another, if we can say—That is at once the true God and the true man. But unless we can say one or other of these things about Jesus, His personality remains only a picture or a dream; our knowledge of Him is reduced to that of a mere phenomenon, standing in no known relation to the facts of life; and no Gospel of any kind can centre in Him. But it has been only in process of time, and chiefly under the stimulus of conflict with antichristian or defectively Christian estimates of the significance of Christ, that Christian Faith has become conscious of its own intellectual contents. In the first generation it had instinctively given to Christ the significance of true God and true man; but now, as Hellenic speculation and Oriental theosophy sought to draw it into their own strangely blended currents and to assimilate it to their peculiar genius, Christian Faith was compelled to realise the implications of its own consciousness of Christ, and, in repudiating the fantastic *eidolon* that Gnosticism substituted for the Christ of the Gospel, to develop and formulate those "beliefs" about Christ which, from the first, were implicit in its "believing in" Him. This was the especial task of the Johannine Theology; and this explains in part the stringent dogmatic tone of the Epistle.

(c) But there is still another factor to be kept in view,— the most important of all in estimating St. John's conception of Belief and the emphasis he lays upon it,—Belief is the touchstone of spiritual life. Belief in itself is an intellectual judgment regarding the truth of a proposition; yet Christian Belief is essentially more than this. It is an act of the intellect which has moral and spiritual presuppositions, which is the response not of the reasoning faculty alone, but of the whole moral personality, to the data presented. It is not belief under coercion of logical proof; it has its deeper source in the spiritual perception of spiritual realities. Such perception is ultimately a power bestowed by the Divine Begetting (5^1)—a function of the Divine Life therein imparted. Yet it is conditioned also by moral sincerity—the will to do the will of God (John 7^{17}). Thus Belief is the subject of commandment: "This is His commandment, That we should believe on the name of His Son Jesus Christ, and love one another, as He gave us commandment" (3^{23}). No more than Christian Love is a merely instinctive or passive emotion, is Christian Belief a matter either of sheer intellectual compulsion or of involuntary impulse. It is the gift and the work of God (Eph. 2^8, John 6^{44}); at the same time it is a work of man (John 6^{29})—the work in which self-determining will at its highest is displayed (John 5^{40} 7^{17}).

$$2^{18-28}.$$

The paragraph in the first Cycle of the Epistle in which the subject of Belief is treated is 2^{18-28}. The chief interest this paragraph has for us lies in its exposition both of the content and the basis of Christian belief; and these topics have been dealt with in preceding chapters.[1] But it must not be overlooked that the writer's purpose is not exposition; his interest is wholly in the practical application of his cardinal doctrine as the decisive test of Christian and antichristian tendencies. The warmth of his indignation breaks out in such an abrupt and peremptory interrogation as, "Who is the liar, but he that denieth Jesus is the Christ?" (2^{22}). There are many lies and many liars; but he who utters this lie is *the* liar. To St. John himself the perception of Jesus as the Christ, the Divine Redeemer,

---

[1] *v. supra*, pp. 93, 94, 111–116. Regarding the "antichrists," *v. infra*, pp. 318–324.

is the ultimate certainty; and he cannot conceive that any one should be able to deny this truth, unless he has, at the same time, lost all sense of truth whatsoever.

But the passage which chiefly demands our attention in this chapter is the important paragraph in the second Cycle of the Epistle.

$$3^{24b}-4^6.$$

Comparing this with the corresponding paragraph 2^{18-28}, we find that the Apostle is by no means covering the same ground a second time.

Here we are confronted by the phenomenon of false as well as of true inspiration; and while in the former paragraph the Spirit of Truth was seen to be the source and guarantee of the True Belief, here, conversely, the "spirits" are themselves tested by the belief to which they give utterance.

The paragraph is introduced by the customary formula, "Hereby we perceive" (ἐν τούτῳ γινώσκομεν). What is to be established is that "God abideth in us"; and the reality of this is to be tested "by the Spirit which He hath given us" (3^{24b}).[1] But the Apostle is drawn somewhat aside from the direct line of his argument by consideration of the actual facts with which he has to deal. The argument in its essence is, "God abides in all to whom He has given His Spirit; but only the spirit that confesses

---

[1] That is to say, the possession of the Spirit of God—the Spirit that confesses Jesus as the Christ (4^2)—is the objective and infallible sign that God is abiding in us. I have to admit that a different view is taken by the commentators whom I have consulted (except, in part, Holtzmann), who, though by various interpretations of the words, understand the Spirit as the source of our subjective assurance that God dwelleth in us. But this is because the connection between 3^{24b} and what follows has been missed. When it is recognised that 3^{24b} really introduces the new paragraph, $3^{24b}-4^6$, and when this is compared with the parallel paragraph 4^{13-16}, it becomes apparent that the Spirit, throughout these passages, is regarded simply as the inspirer of the True Confession of Jesus. If we make this confession, it is evidence that the spirit in us is the Spirit of God. Thus "we know that God abideth in us by the Spirit He hath given us." *v.* Notes, *in loc.*

Jesus as the Christ come in the flesh is the Spirit of God;
if, therefore, the spirit in us inspires this confession of
Jesus, we know that God abideth in us." But the writer
and his readers have to reckon with the fact that there
are in their midst spirits that testify to the contrary effect;
and, therefore, he continues, " Beloved, believe not every
spirit; but try the spirits, whether they are of God; because
many false prophets are gone out into the world " (4^1). The
reference, of course, is to the psychical manifestations with
which, from whatever cause, the atmosphere of the Apostolic
age was charged in a degree quite unfamiliar to modern
experience. The " spirits " on either side are many, yet
have one head and represent one character—the Spirit
of Truth and the Spirit of Error (4^6). It is not to be
assumed (as by Huther and Haupt) that the plurality of
spirits consists in nothing more than the manifestations of
the one personal Spirit, as these are diversified by the
individuality of the human " medium "—that, in other words,
the " spirits " are simply the " prophets " themselves as the
inspired organs of the Spirit. On the contrary, all that
we learn from the New Testament regarding this matter
points to the Spirit of Truth and the Spirit of Error as
acting upon men through a hierarchy of subordinate
spiritual agents.[1] Thus, as the Church had its " prophets,"
who were inspired by spirits of heavenly origin, the adherents of antichrist had their pseudo-prophets, the subjects
of a dæmonic inspiration. The Apostle accordingly warns
his readers not to believe every spirit simply because it is
a spirit, but to " test the spirits, whether they be of God ";
this being the more necessary " because many false [2]

---

[1] Cf. 1 Cor. 12^{10} $14^{12, 32}$; more remotely, Matt. 18^{10}, Heb. 1^{14}, Rev. 1^4
3^1 22^6. On the other side, abundance of spiritualistic manifestations seems
to have been characteristic of the heretical sects. 2 Thess. 2^9, 1 Tim. 4^1,
Rev. $16^{13, 14}$.

[2] Both in the Old Testament and in the New, false prophets are frequently
referred to (*e.g.* Deut. $13^{1, 5}$, Acts 13^6, Rev. 19^{20}). In some instances these are

prophets," not merely false teachers, "have gone out" as ambassadors from their native sphere "into the world." This warning to practise a wise incredulity is not super-fluous at any time. The tendency to yield a facile homage to whatever is characterised by violent emotion and dis-turbances of human nature, to regard anything that is extraordinary and sensational, rather than what is calm and normal, as possessing in itself the credentials of truth, is one that has borne much evil fruit in the religious world. Enthusiasm is no guarantee of truth.

According to 1 Cor. 12^{10} there was in the primitive Church a special charism of "discerning spirits." Here, however, this is regarded as within the competency of all Christians. And, indeed, the Apostle immediately proceeds to ensure this by furnishing one crucial test by which the Spirit of Truth is to be at once distinguished from the Spirit of Error. "Hereby recognise the Spirit of God.[1] Every spirit that confesseth[2] Jesus as the Christ come in the flesh[3] is of God" (4^{2}).

It is by the substance of the confession, not by its publicity, that the Divine character of the inspiration is to be tested. To introduce here the idea of contrast between open confession of Christ and inward faith (Haupt, Westcott, following Augustine), is entirely beside the point. It is of "spirits," not of believers, that the passage speaks; and the antichristian testified no less openly than the Christian spirits. And, to state the matter with full logical exhaustiveness: "Every spirit that confesseth not

described as mere impostors, but, for the most part, are regarded as the subjects of a real inspiration.

[1] τὸ πνεῦμα τοῦ θεοῦ. The individual "spirits" are said to be ἐκ τοῦ θεοῦ (4^1). But it is from the Divine Spirit that they derive their character and their message. In their manifestations, therefore, it is the agency of the Spirit of God that is discerned.

[2] The confessing here spoken of refers to the inspired testifying of the pro-phets in the congregation (1 Cor. 12^3 14$^{1-6}$).

[3] As to the exegesis and doctrinal content of the confession, *v. supra*, pp. 94, 99.

Jesus[1] is not of God"; but, on the contrary, is to be identified with Antichrist[2] (4[3]). There is no third possibility.

The Apostle then proceeds to congratulate his readers upon the faithfulness and success with which they have hitherto resisted and overcome the enemy of their faith. "Ye are of God" (in contrast with the spirits that "are not of God"), "my little children, and have overcome them." And this victory is assured of permanence, because "greater is He that is in you than he that is in the world" (4[4]). The spirit that has been identified with Antichrist is further characterised as having its sphere of operation and dominion "in the world." They (the spirits who are agents of him "who is in the world") "are of the world." And their spiritual affinities determine the character of their teaching. "They speak as of the world"; and the character of their teaching reveals the character of their hearers; "Therefore the world heareth them" (4[5]); for the world "loveth its own" (John 7[7] 15[19]) and "listens to those who express its own thought"[3] (Westcott). In direct opposition to this description of the false spirits and prophets, the writer asserts of himself and of those whom he associates with himself as truly unfolding the word of life, that "We are of God," and that "Every one that knoweth[4] God heareth[5] us";[6] while, on the contrary, the mark of "Whosoever is not of God," is that he "heareth not

---

[1] τὸν Ἰησοῦν. The article defines Jesus in the full sense of the formula in the preceding verse, which the writer does not deem it necessary to repeat. The only valid confession of Jesus is that He is "the Christ come in the flesh."

[2] See Notes, *in loc.*　　　[3] *v. supra*, p. 103.

[4] "Every one that knoweth God"—γινώσκων τὸν θεόν—He who has a true perception of what God really is, who recognises the Divine when it is presented to him. This, not progressiveness of knowledge (Westcott, "The Christian listens to those who teach him more of God") is what the word denotes.

[5] ἀκούει; cf. John 10[3, 16, 20, 27].

[6] The claim of Apostolic authority is based solely upon the inherent truth of the Apostolic message. Cf. 1[1-3], Acts 1[8] 2[32] etc., John 14[26] 15[26, 27] etc., 1 Cor. 2[16], Gal. 1[6-9, 11, 12], 2 Tim. 1[11-13].

us" (4⁶). Finally, he sums up the purport of the whole argument in the words: " From this we recognise the Spirit of Truth " (*i.e.* the Spirit given by God, 3²⁴), " and the Spirit of Error." [1] The inferential phrase " from this " (ἐκ τούτου) is to be understood, not as referring exclusively to the last-mentioned test, the " hearing " or " not hearing " of " us " (Huther, Weiss), but as indicating the accomplishment of the writer's purpose in the paragraph as a whole. That purpose, as stated at the outset, was to urge upon his readers this test of God's dwelling in them, namely, the presence and operation in them of the Spirit of God. But the very office of the Divine Spirit, the promised Paraclete, is to testify to Jesus as the Christ come in the flesh. Every spirit, therefore, that bears witness to this is of God ; and every spirit that does not bear witness to this is not of God. This test is decisive for the " spirits " themselves. It is decisive also for those who speak by their inspiration, distinguishing the false prophets from those who, like the Apostle himself, are the messengers of the Truth. But it is decisive also for their hearers. And this is the point at which, in reality, the paragraph is aimed. Not all had the prophetic afflatus. There were those who gave utterance to the Church's confession and moulded its doctrine ; and there were those who only associated themselves therewith by approval and adherence. For the majority, the actual test consisted in the confession they received as true and adopted as their own, and in the teaching to which they approvingly listened. For all alike, teachers and taught, their attitude towards the truth of the Incarnation was decisive of the spirit that was in them, whether it was the Spirit of Truth or the Spirit of Error.

---

[1] τὸ πνεῦμα τῆς πλάνης. This designation, unique in the N.T., is naturally accounted for by the contrast with the " Spirit of Truth." But cf. 2²⁶, Matt. 24¹¹, Mark 13⁵, Rev. 12⁹ 20¹⁰.

$$4^{13-16}.$$

In the third Cycle of the Epistle the corresponding paragraph [1] is 4^{13-16}. And, in fact, this paragraph reproduces in the simplest and directest form the argument which in $3^{24}-4^6$ was somewhat complicated by the reference to the different " spirits " and their human organs.

" In this, that [2] He hath given us of His [3] Spirit, we perceive that we abide in Him, and He in us " (4^{13}).

Here, as everywhere in the Epistle, the Spirit is regarded exclusively as the Spirit of Truth—the Witness to Christ, and the Author of true Belief.

The first-fruit of this endowment with the Spirit is the Apostolic testimony itself—" And we [4] have beheld and bear witness [5] that the Father sent the Son (as) the Saviour of the world "; (4^{14})—its full result is the continuous re-production of the same testimony in others also. Not only the Apostles have in their vision and testimony the infallible sign of God's dwelling in them; but " Whosoever shall confess that Jesus is the Son of God, God abideth in him, and he in God " (4^{15}). In 4^2, the true confession was, " Jesus is the Christ come in the flesh "; here, it is " Jesus is the Son of God." The two formulæ are equivalent; and here the

---

[1] Having for the third time exhibited Love as the sign and test of Life ($2^{7, 11}$ $3^{10b-24a}$ 4^{7-12}), the writer again advances the test of Belief, likewise for the third time ($2^{18, 28}$ 3^{24b} 4^6; and now, 4^{13-16}).

[2] *v.* Notes, *in loc.*

[3] ἐκ τοῦ πνεύματος αὐτοῦ. Cf. ἐκ τοῦ πληρώματος, John 1^{16}. The phrase is peculiar and, taken by itself, might justify the contention that the personality of the Spirit is not fully realised in the writer's conception. But it does not necessitate this conclusion. Though the Spirit dwells personally in all who are "begotten of God," yet, according to the measure of His working in them, they may be said to have more or less of the Spirit. With this thought the common N.T. expressions, "full of" or "filled with" the Spirit, agree. *v. infra,* pp. 351–52.

[4] " And we." The writer and his fellow-witnesses. See Notes, *in loc.*

[5] The Apostolic testimony is not a mere recital of the facts which constitute the historical manifestation of Christ; it is also a Spirit-taught interpretation of their significance—that " the Father sent the Son to be the Saviour of the World." See Notes, *in loc.*

latter is preferred as suggesting more directly the revelation of the Divine Love in the mission of the Son, and as thus leading up to the statement in which the thought of this whole section is summed up, "We have perceived and believed [1] the Love which God hath toward [2] us. God is Love; and he that abideth in Love abideth in God, and God in him" (4^{16}).

It ought to be observed that in this paragraph the ideas of Belief and Love are knit together in closest relation. At the beginning (4^{13}), the mutual indwelling of God and man is said to be certified by the presence of that Spirit Who, alike in the Apostles (4^{14}) and in the whole company of the faithful (4^{15}), testifies to the true Belief. In the end, the same mutual indwelling is certified by our "abiding in Love" (4^{16}). And the transition is naturally effected through the fact that the whole weight of our assurance that God is Love, and that, consequently, to abide in Love is to abide in God, hangs upon the fact that Jesus is the Son of God, sent by the Father to be the Saviour of the world. St. John does not say or imply that Love is the fruit of Belief, or Belief of Love. Their correlation consists in this, that both Love and Belief are necessarily and concomitantly wrought in men by the Divine Begetting and Indwelling. Because God is Love, the new nature of the God-begotten also is Love (4^7). But the fulness of the Divine Love is manifested only in the mission of the

---

[1] "We have known and believed"; —ἐγνώκαμεν καὶ πεπιστεύκαμεν τὴν ἀγάπην. The two verbs form one compound idea. They are found in the same conjunction, but in the reverse order, in John 6^{69}. I cannot agree with Westcott that the addition of πεπιστεύκαμεν is due to the conscious imperfection attaching to the ἐγνώκαμεν. "We know the Love of God, but we believe that it is greater than we know." (So also Abbott, *Johannine Vocabulary*, 1629, where a reminiscence of Eph. 3^{19} is suggested.) It cannot be insisted too strongly that γινώσκειν signifies spiritual perception, πιστεύειν the resultant intellectual conviction. Thus ἐγνώκαμεν καὶ πεπιστεύκαμεν might be translated; we have recognised (in the fact that Jesus is the Son of God) the Love which God hath toward us, and are firmly persuaded of its truth.

[2] "Toward us"=ἐν ἡμῖν. See Notes, *in loc.*

Son (4$^{9, 10}$), and those who are "begotten of God" necessarily have the power to perceive this when it is presented to them,—to recognise in the Incarnation and the Saviourship of the Son of God, the supreme divinity of Love. Therefore, "Every one that loveth is begotten of God" (4^{7}); therefore also, "Whosoever confesseth that Jesus is the Son of God, God abideth in him and he in God" (4^{15}).

Here, then, the characteristic doctrine of the Epistle with regard to Belief is unmistakable. Belief is the outcome, therefore the test, of life. The truth asserted is not that our abiding in God and God's abiding in us are the result of our belief in Christ and confession of Him, but, conversely, that the confession is the result of the abiding. The same position is categorically affirmed in 5^{1} "Every one that believeth that Jesus is the Christ is begotten of God." Here the tenses (πιστεύων—γεγέννηται) make it clear that the Divine Begetting is the antecedent, not the consequent, of the believing; that, in other words, Christian Belief, which is essentially the spiritual recognition of spiritual truth, is a function of the Divine [1] Life as imparted to men. This is the most distinctive element in the Johannine conception of Belief; and, unless it is firmly grasped, the most characteristic utterances of the Epistle regarding Belief will appear to be the assertions of a hard, scholastic dogmatism that interprets intellectual assent to an orthodox formula as the equivalent of spiritual union with God. Fuller consideration than has yet been given to this point will, therefore, not be out of place.

The conception of Belief just indicated is most fully developed in the Fourth Gospel, which it dominates from beginning to end. A few passages out of many may be

---

[1] Hence, it may be observed, the Epistle nowhere proposes to test Belief by its fruits in good works, after the fashion of St. James (2$^{14-16}$). Belief, Righteousness, and Love are all concomitantly tests of having Eternal Life.

quoted. " Unto this end have I been born, and to this end have I come into the world, that I might bear witness to the truth ; every one that is of the truth heareth My voice " (18³⁷). " Ye believe not, because ye are not of My sheep. My sheep hear My voice . . . and they follow Me " (10²⁶· ²⁷). " I have manifested Thy name unto the men whom Thou gavest Me. Thine they were, and Thou gavest them Me " (17⁶; cf. 3¹⁹⁻²¹ 12³⁷⁻⁴¹ 5⁴⁴ 6⁴⁴ 8⁴²· ⁴⁷). " Every one that hath heard from the Father cometh unto Me "; " No man can come unto Me except it be given him of My Father " (6⁴⁵· ⁶⁵). In these and all similar passages, in the Gospel and the Epistle, belief or unbelief, when Christ is presented, depends upon antecedent spiritual predisposition. The Gospel does not create the children of God ; it finds them, attracts them, reveals them, draws them forth from the mass of mankind. Thus St. John can speak of those who have not even heard the Gospel as being, at least potentially, the " children of God " (John 11⁵²). And this is otherwise expressed in the favourite Johannine view that Christ's work among men is a work of judgment, of sifting and separation (κρίσις, John 9³⁹ 3¹⁸· ¹⁹). Christ comes as a Light into the world ; and those who, though they dwell in darkness, are lovers of the Light, come unto Him. Christ comes as the voice of Eternal Truth, and all who are " of the truth " hear His voice. Christ is thrust as a magnet into the midst of mankind, and draws to Himself all who have an affinity with Him. Others He repels ; they " see no beauty in Him, that they should desire Him." Men believe or disbelieve according to the spirit that is in them. By their attitude to the Revelation of God they reveal themselves ; according as they pronounce their judgment upon the Truth, it pronounces judgment upon them. To recognise or not to recognise God in Christ—there lies the boundary-line between spiritual life and spiritual death.

Pfleiderer, however, gives a quite inconsistent statement of the Johannine doctrine, when he interprets it to the effect that "The manifestation of Christ brings nothing absolutely new into the world, but develops and matures the Divine and undivine germs that already lie implanted in men" (ii. 490). As well might one say that the spring-sunshine brings nothing new into the world, because autumn sowed and winter stored the seeds it brings to germination; or that the dawn brings nothing new into the world, because it comes to those who, though sitting in darkness, yet have eyes. What the Johannine doctrine avers is, that there exists in some men what is lacking in others, a power of spiritual vision by which Christ is recognised and welcomed in His true character—a capacity and a predisposition to receive Him (John 1[12, 13]).

This is, in fact, St. John's equivalent to the Pauline doctrine of predestination.[1] Pondering the question why the Gospel reveals so profound a cleavage among men, St. Paul answers it by the thesis of a direct Divine predestination; St. John, by that of a personal spiritual predisposition. But St. John's predisposition is no more inherent in the natural character than St. Paul's predestination. He refuses to find its source in the human personality (John 1[13]; 1 John 5[1]). The children of God are not a superior species of the genus *homo*. They are men who "have passed from death into life" (3[14]); and who have done so because they are "begotten of God." And the motive of St. John's doctrine is precisely the same as that of St. Paul's. Partly, it is apologetic. It is the assertion, as against the unbelieving world, of the inward ground and the intuitive certainty of Christian Belief. As we need no proof that light is light when the eye beholds it, so the soul, begotten of God, beholds and recognises eternal truth (5[20]). Partly, the

[1] Cf. Scott's *Fourth Gospel*, p. 278.

motive is religious. It is to satisfy the innermost Christian consciousness that, not even for this vision of the truth, not even for the appropriation of God's gift in Christ, can believers take credit to themselves; that in nothing can the human will do more than respond to the Divine; and that, in the last resort, this power itself is of God.

It is far-fetched to find, as Pfleiderer does (ii. 490), a historical kinship between this doctrine and the Gnosis of Basilides. The connection he suggests with Philo's doctrine of the separative activity of the Logos is more credible. But the historical roots of the Johannine conception lie nearer at hand—in the Old Testament, in the Synoptic Gospels, in the Epistles of St. Paul. They are plainly to be traced in the great prophecy (Isa. 6[10. 11]) quoted in St. John (12[37-41]), and so often elsewhere in the New Testament; in such Pauline passages as 2 Cor. 2[15. 16] 4[3-6]; in such Synoptic utterances as Luke 2[34. 35], Matt. 11[25. 26] 16[17]. But, in truth, it is not necessary to deduce the doctrine from any remoter source than the meditation of a thoughtful Christian mind upon the facts of life. And when we consider what the facts are;—that, among men of the same race, traditions, education, manners, and morals Christ is, on the one hand, the supreme and enduring attraction, and on the other, an object of frigid indifference or of keen hostility; that, as when of old He was crucified between two malefactors, the Cross itself became a throne of judgment on which He sat separating the sheep from the goats, so still, under all the apparent identities and diversities of human life, Christ shows Himself the great divider of men: when we consider, further, that we can know and be attracted by that only with which we have some affinity, that the soul cannot kindle in recognition admiration and desire of what is alien to its own nature,—we are constrained to ask whether any truer word can be spoken concerning all this, than that of the Epistle,

18

—that a believing response to the Revelation of Christ, in whomsoever it is found, is due to the fact that he has been " begotten of God." " Can you tell why the needle trembles to the pole, why the buds feel their way to the spring, the flowers to the sunlight? They are made for it: and souls are so made for Christ."

The Conflict and Victory of Belief.

Of Divine contents and origin, Christian Belief is also a Divine power in men, victorious over the evil and falsehood of the World. The first of the passages that tell of this victory is that in which the Apostle congratulates his readers upon their having quitted themselves like true soldiers of Jesus Christ, by their resolute and successful resistance to, the enemies of their faith. " Ye are of God, little children, and have overcome them: because greater is He that is in you, than he that is in the world " (4⁴). Here the conflict is expressly between Truth and Error; and, indeed, between the personal Spirit of Truth and the personal Spirit of Error. As it is said " ye are of God," so " He that is in you " can be none other than God,[1] acting by " the Spirit He hath given us " (3²⁴ᵇ)—the " Anointing" which " teacheth concerning all things " (2²⁷). And " He that is in the world " can be none other than the διάβολος [2] of 3⁸, ¹⁰. The human combatants are identified on both sides with a superhuman personality whose instruments they directly are and in whose power they contend. And the victory of Truth is won, and its permanence is ensured by the fact that its Divine protagonist is greater than the opposing Spirit of Error. Great as is the power of falsehood to captivate and to mislead, the

---

[1] The thought leads back also to the "Son of God Who was manifested that He might destroy the works of the Devil " (3⁸).

[2] ὁ τοῦ κόσμου ἄρχων, John 12³¹ 14³⁰ 16¹¹. ὁ θεὸς τοῦ αἰῶνος τούτου, 2 Cor. 4⁴, Eph. 2² 6¹². ὁ κόσμος ὅλος κεῖται ἐν τῷ πονηρῷ, 1 John 5¹⁹.

convincing power of Truth is always, in the end, greater (John 16$^{8-11}$). This $\mu\epsilon\acute{\iota}\zeta\omega\nu$ [1] is the Christian's sheet anchor of hope when he contemplates the power of falsehood in the World.

$$5^{3b-5}.$$

" And His commandments are not burdensome, because everything that is begotten of God overcometh the world. And this is the victory that overcometh the world, even our faith. Who is he that overcometh the world, but he that believeth that Jesus is the Son of God?"

Here, as elsewhere [2] in the Epistle, the " World " is not the order of the seen and temporal considered as a power to hold the soul in bondage and to render it insensible to spiritual realities; it is the world of ungodly persons, with the opinions, sentiments, and influences—the " lust of the flesh, the lust of the eyes, and the vainglory of life "— which they embody. The " World " is, therefore, a prolific source of temptations that inevitably tend to make God's commandments burdensome to those who strive to obey them fully. Its hostility may take the form of overt persecution; but always the world brings to bear against those whose aims are spiritual, a force of ideas and estimates—as of " success," " happiness," " honour "—and of social influences, which he must conquer or to which he must succumb. Such an environment would necessarily render the requirements of the Christian Life a grievous and a galling yoke but for this,[3]—" Whatsoever is begotten of God overcometh the world." As the human body is unaffected by an external atmospheric pressure that would crush it to a pulp, but for the fact that there

---

[1] Cf. John 16$^{8-11}$, Eph. 1$^{19-23}$, Col. 1^{11}.   [2] *v. supra*, pp. 145–9.

[3] $\pi\hat{a}\nu$ $\tau\grave{o}$ $\gamma\epsilon\gamma\epsilon\nu\nu\eta\mu\acute{\epsilon}\nu o\nu$. The abstract $\pi\hat{a}\nu$, instead of the concrete $\pi\hat{a}s$, seems to emphasise, not the persons who conquer, but the Divine energy by which they conquer. It brings out the thought that whatsoever is of Divine origin has *ipso facto* a power mightier than the world's.

is an equal expansive pressure within the body itself; so, since " Greater is He that is in us, than he that is in the world," the world's hostile pressure is more than neutralised, and God's commandments are not burdensome.   " And this is the victory that overcometh (hath overcome,[1] R.V.) the world—our Belief."   Belief itself may be regarded as the victory.   Simply to believe in Christ is, in principle, complete victory over the world.   This alone puts the world, with its false ideals and standards, under our feet. But the battle has to be fought out in detail; and our Belief is necessarily the spiritual weapon [2] by which every successive temptation is met and overcome.   What this Belief is the next verse declares: " Who is he that over-cometh the world, but he that believeth that Jesus is the Son of God ? "   The union of the human name " Jesus " with the full title " the Son of God," expresses vividly the world-conquering power of this belief.   For, from the worldly point of view, no one was ever more manifestly over-whelmed by defeat and disaster than was this " Son of God."   To believe that, living and dying, Jesus of Nazareth was the Son of God,—that to do the will of God and to finish His work as Jesus did is the one true victory life can give—that to minister rather than to be

---

[1] ἡ νίκη ἡ νικήσασα.   The aorist is difficult, and has been variously explained; —as indicating that from the beginning (Heb. 11) Faith overcame the world (Huther.   But why then the emphatic ἡ πίστις ἡμῶν ?) ; as referring definitely to the victory already mentioned (4⁴) over the false teachers (Weiss.   This is tenable, but the reference seems too remote, and far too narrow for the context) ; as referring to the victory of Christ (John 16³³), in which believers are by their faith made partakers (Westcott.   There is, without doubt, a reminiscence of John 16³³ ; but to make the text mean, "We are by our faith made partakers in the same victory as Christ once gained over the world," seems beyond the limits of possible exegesis).   But the aorist tense does not necessarily indicate a definite point in the past ; and here νικήσασα seems to be a genuine example of the " constative" aorist, by which " the whole action is comprised in one view," or " the line is reduced to a point by perspective " (Moulton, pp. 108 sqq.).   In English idiom this has often to be translated by the perfect, as here by the " hath overcome " of the R.V.

[2] Thus, by a strong metonymy, the victory itself is identified with the means by which it is won.

ministered unto, and to give oneself a ransom for many, is its "topmost, ineffablest crown," is to be, in thought at least, emancipated from the "lust of the flesh, the lust of the eyes, and the vainglory of life." But it is not only by its loftier ideal that Christian Belief conquers the world. It combines with the purely ethical ideal both the power of Love ("This is the Love of God, that we keep His commandments," 5³) and the assurance of immortality; setting over against the world that "passeth away" the vision of another where the Divine Ideal is in fact, as here it is in right, supreme. Above all, Belief is victory because it is the proof of union with Christ Who, Himself victorious over the world, is the source of all-conquering power to them in whom He abides (John 16³³). "He that hath the Son hath Life" (5¹²); and, while surrounded by the world's hostile influences, he is made partaker in Christ's own triumph over them.

> " Remember what a martyr said
>   On the rude tablet overhead !
>   ' I was born sickly, poor and mean,
>   A slave : no misery could screen
>   The holders of the pearl of price
>   From Cæsar's envy ; therefore twice
>   I fought with beasts, and three times saw
>   My children suffer by his law.
>   At last my own release was earned :
>   I was some time in being burned,
>   But at the close a Hand came through
>   The fire above my head, and drew
>   My soul to Christ, whom now I see.
>   Sergius, a brother, writes for me
>   This testimony on the wall—
>   For me, I have forgot it all.' "

NOTE ON πιστεύειν.

In the Johannine writings this word has the same leading significations as in classical Greek. In one instance it means to "entrust" (ἐπίστευεν αὐτὸν αὐτοῖς, John 2²⁴). Elsewhere it means (a) to "believe" a fact (with the noun in the accusative, as in 4¹⁶ πεπιστεύκαμεν τὴν ἀγάπην) or the statement of a fact (introduced by ὅτι, as in 5¹· ⁵);

(*b*) to "believe" or credit the testimony of a person or thing ; (*c*) to "believe in" or trust a person or thing. Confining attention to the last two of these usages, we find that in classical Greek πιστεύειν in either sense has the object in the dative, never being followed by a prepositional phrase.

But it was indispensable that N.T. Greek should possess the means of distinguishing ideas that are so different for Christian thought as "believe" and "believe in." In St. John to "believe in" or "trust" (=בְּ הֶאֱמִין) is, as a rule, πιστεύειν εἰς (5¹⁰). In the three cases in which πιστεύειν εἰς has a thing, not a person, as its object (εἰς τὸ φῶς, John 12³⁶ ; εἰς τὴν μαρτυρίαν, I John 5¹⁰ ; εἰς τὸ ὄνομα, I John 5¹³), it may be argued that the sense is still to "trust," the reference being really to the person who is the source of the light, the author of the testimony, the possessor of the name.

On the other hand, to "believe" is, as a rule, πιστεύειν, c. dat. Moulton (p. 67), like Westcott and Abbott, will have it that the rule is invariable for the New Testament. But in Acts 16³⁴ 18⁸ much the more natural sense of πιστεύειν, c. dat., is "believe in." In St. John, also, the two constructions are sometimes used interchangeably (cf. John 6²⁹·³⁰ and 8³⁰·³¹). And, in the Epistle, it is impossible, without pedantry, to assign different shades of meaning to πιστεύειν τῷ ὀνόματι (3²³) and πιστεύειν εἰς τὸ ὄνομα (5¹³). The truth is that, in the nature of the case, the two ideas "believe" and "believe in" frequently run into and blend with each other, belief of the thing testified resting upon trust in the person testifying (cf. John 5²⁴·³⁸ with 12⁴⁴).

CHAPTER XIV.

THE DOCTRINE OF ASSURANCE.

IN the foregoing chapters we have seen with what urgency St. John sets before his readers the three fundamental and inseparable tests by which they may satisfy themselves that they have Eternal Life (5^{13}): "He that keepeth His commandments dwelleth in Him, and He in him" (3^{24}); "He that dwelleth in Love dwelleth in God, and God in him (4^{10}); "Whosoever confesseth that Jesus is the Son of God, God dwelleth in him, and he in God" (4^{15}). And, in general, it has to be asserted that the Epistle acknowledges no certitude of personal salvation other than is based on the fulfilment of those tests. In its scheme of thought no place is provided for any immediate, self-certifying consciousness of regenerate life. The possession of this is to be recognised (γινώσκειν) from the presence of its appropriate fruits, and thus only. "We know that we have passed from death into Life, because we love the brethren" (3^{14}). But while thus the effect of the Epistle is, upon the whole, extremely heart-searching, there are passages in which the writer pauses in his persistent probing and testing of souls, and dwells upon the heart-pacifying aspect of the truths he enunciates.

$$2^{28}.$$

"And now, little children, abide[1] in Him; that, if He

---

[1] "Abide in Him . . . that we may have boldness." The sense is not (as 1 Thess. 2^{19}, Phil. 4^1, Heb. 13^{17})—"Do ye abide in Him that we, as your responsible guide and teacher, may give in our account with joy." The

shall be manifested, we may have boldness, and not shrink from Him in shame (αἰσχυνθῶμεν ἀπ' αὐτοῦ) at His coming."[1] The phrase to "have boldness" (παῤῥησίαν ἔχειν), here introduced, is destined to further service (3[21] 4[17] 5[14]). In classical usage παῤῥησία denotes that outspokenness or fearless declaration of personal opinion which was especially the cherished privilege of Athenian freemen.[2] In the Epistle to the Hebrews and in our Epistle[3] it signifies the confidence of open childlike speech with our Father in prayer, or, as here, the fearless trust with which the faithful meet Christ. Its peculiar force is finely brought out by the contrasted "shrink from Him in shame." Both are phrases of graphic power, vividly suggesting the picture of the judgment-seat before which all must stand, and of the frank confidence with which men turn to their Judge and look upon His face, or the speechless confusion in which they avoid His gaze (cf. Matt. 22[12]). The ground of this "boldness in His Parousia" will be that men, though much exposed to the plausibilities of pseudo-Christian teaching, have held fast the truth that Jesus is the Christ, the Son of God (2[22-24]), as this is witnessed by the Apostles (2[24]) and taught by the Spirit[4] (2[27]). The ascription of this ultimately decisive value to Belief has been already discussed.[5] However remote it may seem to be from the purely ethical grounds of final judgment foretold by our Lord (Matt. 25[31-46]), it is not, in the mind of St. John, incompatible with these; on the contrary, they are its necessary implicates. To believe that Jesus is Incarnate

---

Apostle violates grammatical construction rather than seem to exclude himself from what he enjoins on his "little children." He identifies himself with them as a Christian man "still struggling to effect his warfare" in a world of temptation (cf. 1[9] 2[2] 3[19. 20. 21] etc.).

[1] ἐν τῇ παρουσίᾳ αὐτοῦ. See Chapter XVI.

[2] See additional note, p. 415.

[3] In the Fourth Gospel the word is used somewhat differently, signifying plain as contrasted with mystic (5[24] 11[14] 16[29]), or open as contrasted with secret utterance (7[26] 18[20]).

[4] *v. supra*, pp. 108-16.   [5] *v. supra*, pp. 261-2, 270-4.

God, is to accept Love as the law of life, as is made evident by the passage that next comes under consideration.

$$3^{18-20}.$$

" Little children, let us not love in word, neither in tongue; but in deed and in truth.[1] And herein shall we know (= ascertain) that we are of the truth, and shall assure our heart before Him, whereinsoever our heart condemn us; because God is greater than our heart and knoweth all things." [2] It is necessary to distinguish at the outset between the absolute and the conditional ground of confidence toward God, as these are here set forth. The former is that we are " of the Truth " [3]—that we belong to the kingdom that is Christ's (John 18[37]); that our life is based upon and our character moulded by the Divine and eternal Reality, the full expression of which is Christ, Who is " the Truth." But in our own particular case this must be established by the fact that we " love not in word, neither in tongue; but in deed and in truth."

This question, whether we are " of the truth," is here figured as the subject of a trial in which a man's own " heart " (conscience; that is, the faculty of moral self-judgment) is the accuser and he himself the defendant, which is carried on in the presence of Omniscient God, and is finally referred to His decision. There are thus three elements to be considered in the case. (*a*) Our own heart [4]

---

[1] On the first clause, *v. supra*, pp. 245-6, and Notes, *in loc.*

[2] On the exegetical difficulties of this *locus vexatissimus*, see Notes. In the present exposition, I assume the conclusion to which I have come—that, without emendation of the text, the R.V. best meets the requirements both of grammar and of sense.

[3] To be " of the Truth " denotes substantially the same thing as to be " of God " (3[10]). Regarding ἀλήθεια, *v. supra*, pp. 62, 259-60.

[4] " Heart " (καρδία) is rarely found in St. John. In John 13[2] it signifies the source of impulse to action, in 14[1, 27] 16[6, 22] the seat of thought and emotion. συνείδησις, which in the N.T. exactly covers our " conscience," both as the faculty of self-judgment and in the wider sense of moral discernment, does not occur in St. John.

may condemn us. We believed that we had passed from death into life (3^{14}); but to ourselves this has become almost or altogether doubtful.[1] When Conscience summons us to the tribunal within, it declares us guilty. We have failed in doing the " righteousness " of the children of God (3^{10}), or our faith has faltered—our vision of the Truth has become dim. The evidence of our union with Christ is obscured by the consciousness of inconsistencies which, regarded in themselves, compel us to question whether we are " of the truth " or have been self-deceived (cf. $2^{4,\ 6,\ 9}$ etc.). This is the first element in the case. (*b*) The second is, " In this we shall recognise that we are of the truth." When conscience brings forward these allegations of insincerity, to what shall we appeal? To this, says St. John: that we have loved, and that " not in word, neither in tongue; but in deed and in truth." There are actual things we can point to—not things we have professed or felt or imagined or intended, but things that we have done, and that we know we would never have done but for the Love which God has put into our hearts. Of ecstatic emotions, heaven-piercing vision, we may know nothing; but if, in the practice of Love—in bearing another's burden, in denying ourselves to give to another's need (3^{17}), we are sure of our ground, hereby we shall tranquillise our self-accusing hearts—yea, even in the presence[2] of God. (*c*) " Because God is greater than our heart, and knoweth all things." But here a difficulty meets us. What may be called the popular inter-

---

[1] This is the explanation of the future " we shall know " ($\gamma\nu\omega\sigma\dot{o}\mu\epsilon\theta a$). It does not merely point to the fulfilment of the conditions laid down in 3^{18},—that, of course, is assumed,—it contemplates the possibility of some shadow having fallen on the clear mirror of the soul—some future occasion on which our own heart accuses us.

[2] " Before Him " ($\ddot{\epsilon}\mu\pi\rho\sigma\sigma\theta\epsilon\nu$ $a\dot{v}\tau o\hat{v}$). The thought is not of the Day of Judgment, but that the self-examination is brought about by the sense of God's Presence, and under the sense of the same Presence is carried on.

pretation:[1]—" Since even our own imperfectly enlightened heart accuses us, how much more must we dread the judgment of the All-knowing "—is directly opposed to the requirements of the context. Plainly the fact that " God is greater than our heart, and knoweth all things," must be a reason for pacifying the heart, not for increasing its alarm. Almost all modern exegetes, accordingly, take " greater than our hearts " as referring to the greater tenderness of God. Conscience is a " recording chief inquisitor," who notes without pity all that is done amiss. God is Love, and, reading in our hearts the Love He has put there, blots out the handwriting that is against us. But this is irrelevant. The question under consideration is not one of merciful judgment, but solely one of *evidence* as to whether we are or are not " of the truth." When it is said that " God is greater than our heart," what is meant is simply that " He knoweth," that is, takes cognisance of " all things." Our own heart does not take cognisance of all things. On the supposition made, its rôle is solely that of accuser. It is regarded as occupying itself exclusively with those facts that cast suspicion upon the reality of our Christian life, while it needs to be reminded of those that tell in our favour. But God takes note of all—both of the inconsistencies that conscience urges against us, and of the deeds whose witness we can cite in reply to its accusations. And for this very reason that He knows all, we can persuade and pacify our hearts *before Him*. To the hypocrite, who only seeks a cloak for his sin, the thought of the All-seeing is full of dread ; but to him who, though conscious of much that may well be thought to falsify his Christian profession, is also conscious that it is

[1] This interpretation is still maintained and powerfully defended by Professor Findlay. Granted the right to emend the text as he does, his view is obviously sound ; and the emendation is tempting. *v.* Notes, *in loc.* But the explanation here given of the text as it stands is, I think, tenable.

in facts of a different kind that his deepest life has found true expression, it is full of comfort. The appeal to Omniscience is his final resort; his hiding-place is in the Light itself (Ps. 139²³· ²⁴). Thus it was with Simon when not only his own heart accused him, but his Master so persistently voiced its accusations—" Lord, Thou knowest all things; Thou knowest that I love Thee " (John 21¹⁷). And it is not difficult to suppose that the γινώσκει πάντα of the present passage is a reminiscence of that memorable incident (κύριε, πάντα σὺ οἶδας, σὺ γινώσκεις ὅτι φιλῶ σε).

Looking at the passage as a whole we find two notable features in it. On the one hand is the emphasis placed upon objective facts as the only valid evidence of our being " of the truth "; on the other hand is the principle that positive outweighs negative evidence[1]—that deeds of love rightly prevail against the consciousness of inconsistency and defect. In part, doubtless, this emphasis is due to the historical situation. It is a repudiation of the loveless intellectualism of the Gnostic; and it is also an assurance and consolation of those " little ones " who were liable to be " offended " by those who based their claim to be " of the truth " upon a profounder knowledge of the spiritual universe than was attainable by the simple believer. Not philosophy, but Love has the title to the Kingdom of Heaven. Not on the boast of fruitless illumination, but on the Christ-life of self-sacrificing Love was the stamp of the Truth impressed. Yet the Apostle's doctrine has respect to the deep common needs of the Christian life. To the man of self-accusing heart in every age he speaks. To the man whose belief seems to himself little more than a struggle with unbelief, who is more conscious of darkness and doubt than of triumphant faith, he says: " Your life,

---

[1] It needs, perhaps, to be emphasised that the matter under consideration is wholly one of *evidence*. There is no question of setting the merit of good deeds over against the demerit of evil deeds.

your actual indubitable deeds in which you embody the spirit that is in you—what is their testimony? Are these the fruit of faith or of unbelief?" To the man who mourns defects of character and lapses of conduct that seem to vitiate his title to be of those who have the seed of the Righteous God abiding in them (3⁹), he says: "These may be the negations and failures of your life, what are its affirmations and achievements? Is the goal towards which you strive the goal of Love?" The test is absolutely valid. Not the presence of evil, but the absence of good, is the fact of fatal omen. It is the invariable test of our Lord Himself, with whom the irremediable sin is ever the sin of lovelessness, fruitlessness, slothfulness,—the damning accusation, "Ye did it not." He who loves not in word, neither in tongue, but in deed and in truth; who lays down his life for the brethren, if not in one crowded hour of glorious self-surrender, yet, perhaps, more nobly, in the patient well-doing and helpful kindness and unselfish service which enrich the years as they pass, this man verily bears the marks of the Lord Jesus. Let no man trouble him; let him not trouble himself; but herein let him recognise that he is "of the truth," and humbly assure his heart before God.

The following verses (3²¹·²²) introduce the subject of assurance in Prayer, and so, postponing them, we proceed to a passage which is as closely as possible allied to that which we have just considered.

4¹⁷⁻¹⁹.

"Herein is love made perfect with us, that we may have boldness in the Day of Judgment; because as He is, even so are we in this world. There is no fear in Love; but perfect love casteth out fear; because fear hath punishment; and he that feareth is not made perfect in love. We love, because He first loved us."

Logically, 4¹⁷ contains three members:—The purpose

achieved—"That we may have boldness in the Day of Judgment"; the ground upon which this confidence is established—"Because as He (Christ) is, so are we in this world"; the proof that we are entitled to occupy this ground—"Herein is Love perfected with us." We shall, however, consider these clauses in the order in which they occur. (*a*) "Herein [1] is Love [2] perfected (fulfilled) with us." By the word "herein" the sentence is linked on to the immediately preceding one: [1] "He that abideth in Love abideth in God, and God in him" (4^{16}). What that Love is and how it is "perfected" is unmistakably defined in 4^{12}: "If we love one another, God abideth in us, and His Love is perfected in us." The only variation in the phraseology is that, instead of the "perfected in us" (ἐν ἡμῖν) of 4^{12}, we have here "perfected with us" (μεθ' ἡμῶν),[3] the latter being probably intended as a stronger expression of the fact that it is in the social relations of the Christian community that the Divine life of Love has its fullest human realisation.

Clearly, then, it is in the exercise of brotherly love that Love is here said to be perfected. Further, if we inquire why this is so,—what specific idea the Apostle intends to convey by the "perfecting" of Love,—this also becomes clear when we compare the two passages in which this "perfecting" is described: "Whosoever keepeth His word, in him verily is the love of God perfected" (2^5); and "If we love one another, God abideth in us, and His love is perfected in us" (4^{12}). Manifestly, the conception common to "keeping His word" and "loving one another" is the embodiment of Love in actual conduct. The assertion of perfectness refers, not to the strength or purity of Love as a sentiment, but solely to its bearing fruit in deeds which prove its reality and fulfil its purpose. The idea is

[1] *v.* Notes, *in loc.*

[2] ἡ ἀγάπη. Not the Love of God to us, nor specifically our Love to God or to our brother, but that moral nature which is called Love. Cf. *supra*, p. 212.

[3] μεθ' ἡμῶν. *v.* Notes, *in loc.*

that, not of qualitative, but of effective perfection; and τετελείωται might be translated more unambiguously by "fulfilled" or "accomplished" than by "perfected." That is τετελειωμένον which has reached its τέλος, has achieved its end, has run its full course.[1]   And the end of God's Love to us is attained in our loving one another.   As the seed reaches its goal in the fruit, so the Love of God has its fulfilment in reproducing itself in the character and conduct of His children.   But, as we have[2] seen, the Love of God to us cannot be directly reproduced in our relation to Him.   It is only when we love one another with the love of God—the love which is His own, and which He begets in us—that His love is *fulfilled* in us.   Then Love's circuit is complete, from God to us, from us to our brother, and through our brother back to God (cf. Matt. 25[40]).

Next, the Apostle states a special purpose achieved by this fulfilment of Love—"that we may have confidence in the Day of Judgment."[3]   This is not the only end, but it is an end; in the present view, indeed, the ultimate end of all action.   All that life most profoundly signifies is contained in the thought of our final responsibility to God (2 Cor. 5[9. 10]).   This confidence is a present possession (ἔχωμεν),[4] not only because the Apostle thinks of the Day of Judgment as at hand, but because the thought of that Day and of its issue for us is, or ought to be, present to our minds.

Finally, the Apostle supplies the necessary connecting link between "perfected Love" and this "confidence." Our love, however truly fulfilled, does not in its own right

---

[1] A comparison of other Johannine occurrences of τελειόω confirms this. Jesus "accomplishes" or "fulfils" the work of the Father (John 4[35] 5[36] 17[4]); the Scripture is "accomplished" or "fulfilled" (19[28]). Cf. Acts 20[24] τελειῶσαι τὸν δρόμον μου; Jas. 2[22] ἐκ τῶν ἔργων ἡ πίστις ἐτελειώθη = "in works faith found fulfilment." "To make perfect (τελειόω) is to bring to the *end*, that is, the appropriate or appointed end, the end corresponding to the idea" (Davidson, *Hebrews*, p. 65).

[2] *v. supra*, pp. 76, 250–52.

[3] The Day of Judgment. See Chapter XVI.

[4] ἔχωμεν. *v.* Notes, *in loc.*

furnish confidence against the Day of Judgment. It does so, " because as He is,[1] so are we "—because it is the proof that we are spiritually one with Christ.

The statement is, that what Christ is we also are, though He has gone to the Father and we are still in this world.[2] The sign and test of our union with Him has been stated as "walking even as He walked " (2[6]), " purifying ourselves as He is pure " (3[3]), being " righteous as He is righteous " (3[7]). Here, finally, it is that " Love is fulfilled in us." The heart of all Christ's doing and suffering was the intense longing He had to make Himself the channel through which the Love of God might reach men. To this end He followed the path of love to the crowded city, to the wilderness, to the Cross and the grave. In Him Love had its absolute fulfilment. And if we also seek to be channels through which the Love of God reaches our fellow-men, then, in our small measure and degree, we are " as He is "; and Love, feeble and poor though it be, has herein reached fulfilment in us, that we may have boldness in the day of judgment. Love will be on the Judgment-seat. Love will be before the Judgment-seat. And Love cannot be condemned or disowned of Love.

4[18].

" There is no fear in love ; but perfect love casteth out fear, because fear hath punishment : he that feareth is not made perfect in love."

In the preceding verse it has been asserted that Love " fulfilled " establishes the Christian in confidence toward God, as being the fruit and the test of his fellowship with

---

[1] He (ἐκεῖνος) = Christ ; cf. 2[6] 3[3. 5. 7. 16]. *v. supra*, p. 89.

[2] The exactness of the parallelism between this verse and 3[18. 19] ought to be observed. Here, the purpose to be effected is " that we may have confidence in the Day of Judgment"; there, " that we may assure our hearts before Him." Here, the ground of confidence is that " as Christ is, so are we in this world "; there, that we are " of the truth." Here, the proof of this is that " Love is perfected in us "; there, that we love " not in word neither in tongue ; but in deed and in truth."

Christ. Here the same position is maintained from a complementary point of view: what is hostile to παρρησία is Fear, and what delivers from Fear is Love.[1] Fear towards God is the product of the self-accusing heart. But "there is no Fear[2] in Love." In loving one another there is no matter of self-accusation, there is nothing to give occasion to Fear.[3] Fear is the sentinel of life; the self-protective instinct that gives warning of danger, and calls to arms against it; and Fear towards God is the sign that not all is well in our relation to Him, and that we instinctively know it. But Love gives no such warning signal. When we are living in Love we are doing those things which are "well-pleasing in His sight" (3^{22}); we are "abiding in the Light" (2^{10}); we have "fellowship one with another, and the blood of Jesus, His Son, cleanseth us from all sin" (1^7).

Not only is there nothing in Love to produce Fear; it banishes Fear where it exists. "But perfect Love casteth out Fear." It says to Fear, "Begone!" and, so to say, flings it out of doors.[4] "Perfect Love" (ἡ τέλεια ἀγάπη) cannot signify anything else than the Love which has been spoken of in the foregoing verse as "perfected."[5] How love becomes "perfect" has been already declared (2^5 4^{12}); also how it casts out Fear. Even against a self-accusing heart, Love that is "in deed and in Truth"

---

[1] The verse thus carries on the parallelism to 3^{18-20}, expanding the thought contained in the words, "and shall assure our hearts before Him *whereinsoever our own heart condemn us.*"

[2] The order of words is the most emphatic possible: φόβος οὐκ ἔστιν ἐν τῇ ἀγάπῃ: "Fear there is none in love." φόβος is used of reverential fear (2 Cor. 7^1); but here (as in Rom. 8^{15}) of servile, self-regarding fear.

[3] φόβος οὐκ ἔστιν ἐν τῇ ἀγάπῃ=In love there is no occasion of Fear—nothing to make afraid. Cf. the analogous phrase, σκάνδαλον ἐν αὐτῷ οὐκ ἔστιν (2^{10}).

[4] "Casteth out" (ἔξω βάλλει). More vivid, and describing more vigorous action than ἐκβάλλει.

[5] Love is perfect which has its "perfect work." Cf. Jas. 1^4. Also *Shepherd of Hermas*, Vis. I. 2, 1. τῶν ἁμαρτιῶν τῶν τελείων=sins actually committed, as contrasted with sins only imagined or purposed. Westcott, on the contrary, has a characteristic note on the difference between "perfect" (τέλεια) and "perfected" (τετελειωμένη).

19

lifts up its testimony that we are " of the truth " (3¹⁸).
That we in this world are as Christ is (4¹⁷), forgiving them
that injure us, doing the most and the highest good we
can, loving men with the Love of Christ, " walking in Love
even as He loved us "—there is no attestation of our
fellowship with the Father and with His Son Jesus Christ,
and no ground of confidence like this. This casts out Fear
by Divine right.[1] And it does so, St. John adds, " because
Fear hath punishment." [2] The expression is peculiar and
obscure. The drift of the argument, however, is clear.
Fear itself is of the nature of punishment; it is, in fact,
the first reaction of sin upon the moral nature, the first
conscious penalty of wrong-doing. It is, moreover, the
consciousness of a relation to God of which punishment is
the proper and only issue; and, unless it be legitimately
overcome, drives the sinner to an ever-increasing distance
from God (Gen. 3⁸). And just because this is the nature
of Fear, Love prevails over it and casts it out. Conscious
of loving our fellow-men with a love that God has implanted
in our hearts, we are assured that God is our Father, that
Jesus Christ the Righteous is our Advocate—that our
relation to God is one which holds no place for the idea of
" punishment," in which nothing is possible except fatherly
forgiveness and discipline. If Fear is the natural reaction
of sin upon the soul, no less is confidence the natural
reaction of Love. Nothing can work in us such a loving
assurance of God's love to us as loving one another.
Nothing can make it so clear that God will forgive our
trespasses as our forgiving those that trespass against us.

---

[1] Here the Apostle only reproduces the most emphatic teaching of his Master
(Matt. 6¹⁴· ¹⁵ 18³⁵ 25⁴⁰, Luke 10²⁵⁻³⁷ 16⁹· ¹⁹⁻²⁶ etc.).

[2] " Hath punishment " (κόλασιν ἔχει). κόλασις has no meaning except
" punishment," whether retributive or disciplinary (cf. Matt. 25⁴⁶, 2 Pet. 2⁹)
and cannot be translated by " torment " (A.V.), or any word that expresses merely
a painful feeling. Here the meaning is not that Fear, " as rooted in unbelief, is
itself deserving of punishment " (Huther), but that Fear is itself a punishment or
chastisement.

It is by loving that we know God, Who is Love, and are assured that God dwelleth in us. Therefore "perfect" Love—Love that has done the work of Love—casts out the Fear which "hath punishment." The consequence necessarily follows that "He that feareth has not been made [1] perfect in Love." In the sphere of Love his life must be yet unfulfilled.[2] Inasmuch as he *fears*, his condition is more hopeful than that of him who "saith he is in the light, and hateth his brother" (2⁹); but inasmuch as he fails of genuine fruition in Love he lacks, and rightly lacks, the consciousness of union with God in Christ; or at least that consciousness is feeble as against the consciousness of sin. The Apostle evidently does not contemplate such a type of Christian as Bunyan's Mr. Fearing. Indoctrinated with the teaching of the Epistle, that loving and lovable saint might cease to be Mr. Fearing. Even he might recognise that he is "of the truth," and assure his "heart before God."

4¹⁹.

The paragraph is now exquisitely rounded by the return of thought to Him Who is the source of all Christian Life, all Christian Love, and ultimately, therefore, of all Christian Assurance.

Having just spoken of him "that feareth" because "he has not been made perfect in Love," the Apostle adds the earnest exhortation 'As for us, let us love,[3] because

---

[1] To be "perfected in Love" cannot mean anything substantially different from having "Love perfected" in one. That love has attained to its true issue in us as its sphere of action, and that we have reached our proper end or aim in Love as our sphere of action, are the same idea regarded from converse points of view.

[2] Cf. Rev. 3² "I have found no words of thine fulfilled (πεπληρωμένα) before my God."

[3] The strong position of ἡμεῖς, and, in fact, its presence at all, justifies the translation, "as for us."

By the general consent of textual authorities, αὐτόν is omitted after ἀγαπῶμεν. The whole term of the passage makes it clear that ἀγαπῶμεν is to be understood of brotherly love. As regards the rendering, "Let us love," *v*. Notes, *in loc*.

He first loved us." This brief sentence contains at once the ideal, the sovereign motive and the power of realisation for all Christian ethics. What God is, determines the mark at which the Christian must of necessity aim (Matt. 5[45]). What God is—" He first loved us "—summons and inspires heart, soul, strength, and mind to the effort. What God is —Love that wills to bestow nothing less than the Infinite Good, Eternal Life, upon sinful men—supplies the unfailing power to which all moral perfection is possible. Through the love of God in Christ Jesus our Lord, we may be holy as He is holy, righteous as He is righteous, and love as the children of Him who is Love.

In the exposition of these verses I have ventured upon a wide departure from the practically unanimous[1] exegetical tradition. I have taken the passage as closely parallel with 3[18-20], understanding " perfected " Love as Love fulfilled in " deed and in truth," and as casting out Fear, because it is objective evidence of union with Christ. But on the common interpretation, it is the *sentiment* of Love that is here spoken of as " perfected," and it casts out Fear, because the two are psychologically incompatible.[2] " Where Love to God exists in perfection it casts out all lingering dread of Him. Love and Fear are antagonistic principles. Love is a self-forgetting, Fear a self-regarding affection. Love is blessedness ; Fear, on the contrary, 'hath torment.' It contemplates the relation to its object as one of hostile opposition, and brings with it a feeling of distress. But Love has no thought of self, and, therefore, no Fear. Not every kind of Love, indeed, casts out Fear ; but only perfect Love, which is free from self-seeking. And if any man is yet subject to Fear, this only proves that he is not perfected in Love. But this is not true of us. We love God with this unselfish, happy, fearless Love, because He first loved us."

But this interpretation seems to me to be open to serious objection. According to it, the central thought of the passage is that the secret of confidence toward God lies in the psychological necessity by which the sentiment of Love to God excludes the opposite sentiment of Fear. But in the first place, this thought does not at all fit into the reasoning of 4[17], where the ground of confidence explicitly is, " Because as He (Christ) is, so are we in this world." Here it is, in my view, indisputable

---

[1] The only supporter I have found for the view I have advanced is J. M. Gibbon in his *Eternal Life*.

[2] By far the finest exposition of the passage on these lines is Rothe's, which I give here in condensed form.

that the "perfected Love" is brotherly love fulfilled in "deed and in truth," and that it gives confidence toward God because it is the sign and the test of our being spiritually identified with Christ. But if the central idea is that the sentiment of Love by its natural operation casts out Fear, the reference to Christ and to our union with Him is entirely irrelevant.[1]

With regard to 4^{18} I acknowledge that this interpretation satisfies the requirements excellently[2] and obviously—more obviously than that which I have advanced—if 4^{18} can be isolated from 4^{17}, and from the whole Epistle. It is evident that if this is the true interpretation of 4^{18}, the argument of the passage breaks in two. In 4^{17}, Love perfected in action casts out Fear, because it is evidence that "as Christ is, so are we"; in 4^{18}, Love perfected in sentiment casts out Fear by psychological necessity. It is not, of course, impossible that the writer should thus suddenly and insensibly change his point of view. But an interpretation that does not involve this supposition is, to that extent, preferable.

Besides, when thus interpreted, the passage stands solitary in the Epistle, without an assignable place in the organism of its thought. Here we should have the only idea in the Epistle that is not introduced again and again, and the only passage without a parallel. (*a*) On this interpretation, ἡ ἀγάπη is Love regarded exclusively as a sentiment, and exclusively in relation to God. But this is not according to the usage of the Epistle. ἡ ἀγάπη used absolutely, as here, means simply the disposition which is so called—the disposition which is revealed in God by His sending His Son as a propitiation for our sins (4^{10}), in Christ by His laying down His life for us (3^{16}), and which, according to the unvarying representation of the Epistle, is manifested and fulfilled in us by our loving one another. (*b*) But the strongest objection lies against the idea itself that confidence toward God is the effect of a

---

[1] This is recognised by Lücke, who in 4^{17} takes ἡ ἀγάπη as the brotherly love that attests our fellowship with Christ, but in 4^{18} as the love to God that casts out fear by its intrinsic power. Weiss includes brotherly love in the idea of ἡ ἀγάπη—inconsistently, as it seems to me, with the whole scope of his interpretation.

[2] I except from this statement the clause, "Perfect Love casteth out Fear, because Fear hath punishment" (κόλασιν ἔχει). *Ex hypothesi*, Love casts out Fear, because it is psychologically impossible that the two should coexist; and it is difficult to realise any force in the argument that Love casts out Fear, *because* Fear is the penalty of sin. By the majority of commentators, indeed, κόλασις is (unjustifiably) translated as "pain" or "distress." The argument might thus be taken as supplementary to the main one—"There is no fear in Love." Love and Fear are not only antagonistic in themselves: they produce opposite effects—blessedness and pain. Therefore, all the more, Love casts out Fear. Incompatible effects prove their causes incompatible. But to find this argument in the passage demands a good deal of ingenuity—in addition to the very doubtful translation of κόλασις.

sentiment or state of inward feeling. This seems incongruous with the whole tone and teaching of the Epistle. Everywhere else the writer drives us back upon the evidence of tangible facts. Everywhere else the Epistle strenuously insists upon the necessity of testing love to God by its realisation in action (2^5 3^{17} $4^{12.\ 20}$ 5^3). And if Love itself must submit to such tests, how is this compatible with making it, merely as a sentiment, the immediate source of assurance? It has just been said that if we love "not in word neither in tongue, but in deed and in truth, we shall recognise that we are of the truth, and shall assure our hearts before Him." How can we now be told that if any man feareth, it is because he is deficient in the feeling of love to God? The objective evidence is indispensable (3^{17}); how, then, is the subjective feeling sufficient? The objective evidence is sufficient (3^{19}), how, then, is the subjective feeling indispensable? Furthermore, this interpretation seems to involve a considerable departure from the normal lines of New Testament thought upon this subject. In the evangelical psychology it is confidence that makes perfect love possible, rather than perfect love that begets confidence. God is in Christ, reconciling the world unto Himself, taking away the causes of fear, in order that we may love Him with a free-hearted, unselfish, filial love, much rather than inspiring such a love in order that we may have confidence toward Him.[1] We may regard the Christian's assurance as resting immediately upon Christ, or we may regard it as resting upon the pledges he has given to Christ (2 Tim. 1^{12}),—the work of faith and labour of love that certify his union with Christ; but is there any other passage in the New Testament that represents this assurance as dependent upon the subjective perfection of our love to God?

Finally, one may ask to what purpose is the passage, thus interpreted? It states a psychological fact—that in proportion as we are possessed by self-forgetting love we are delivered from self-regarding fear. This is as true as that two and two are four; and if there are those on whose behalf it can be claimed that by the very perfection of their love to God, as a sentiment, they are delivered from all fear, this is, indeed, thankworthy. Yet even so they are apparently invited to regard the absence of fear as the proof of the genuineness and perfection of their love—a position which is absolutely inconsistent with the whole tenor of the Epistle, and which receives a direct contradiction in the very next verse (4^{20}). But it is admitted by those who maintain this interpretation, that in no actual instance is it fully applicable. "Though as certain

---

[1] Thus Rothe unconsciously glides into statements which are the exact converse of what his own exposition of the text requires. "Love to God, to be perfectly genuine, *demands* unconditional trust in Him." But what St. John says is that perfect love *produces* such trust. "So long as, in view of our sins and our reckoning for them, we have not full trust in God, our love to Him is not perfected." But what St. John says is that we cannot have this full trust until we have the perfect love. It is perfect love that casts out the Fear that has κόλασιν.

as any physical law, the principle that perfect love excludes all fear, is an ideal that has never been verified in fact; like the first law of motion, it is verified by the approximation made to it" (Plummer).[1] That is true; and it follows that all Christians are, in greater or less measure, included under ὁ φοβούμενος. Such a consequence is clearly against the whole purport of the passage,—a passage which is triumphant throughout, and could not conceivably have ended with the sternly sorrowful "he that feareth has not been made perfect in love," if these words contemplated any other than an abnormal experience. For these reasons, I have been compelled reluctantly to abandon this interpretation for 4^{17}, and, with more hesitation, for 4^{18} also, temptingly obvious as it is for the latter.

Having thus completed our exposition of the passages in which Assurance is specifically dealt with, we may now briefly consider the broader aspects of St. John's presentation of this subject. And, in the first place, let it be said once more that the whole tone and temper of the Epistle, in its treatment of this as of other subjects, must be appreciated in view of its polemical purpose. Its noble and enthusiastic delineation of the Christian Life is, at the same time, a manifesto against pseudo-Christianity; and if it is written to establish the genuine Christian in the certainty of his salvation (5^{13}), this is done only in such a way as to refute all spurious pretensions. Hence it comes that the Epistle has much more to say of the immediate *tests* than of the ultimate ground of Christian Assurance. The statement of the latter forms the entrance-hall, so to say, of the Epistle. And the statement is clear and strong: " The Blood of Jesus, His Son, cleanseth us from all sin " (1^7). " If any man sin, we have an Advocate with the Father, Jesus Christ the Righteous; and He is the Propitiation for our sins " ($2^{1, 2}$). The Christian's sole confidence is Christ.

> "Bold shall I stand on that great day;
> For who aught to my charge shall lay,
> While by Thy Blood absolved I am
> From sin's tremendous guilt and shame?"

---

[1] To the same effect, Rothe: " By this we may judge how elementary all our love to God is."

St. John, too, can sound this note.   Putting aside for a moment all intermediate thoughts, and beholding with open face the primal facts of God's Redemption, he breaks forth into joy :—" Beloved, what manner of love the Father hath bestowed upon us, that we should be called the children of God !   And such we are " (3^1).   It is the spontaneous utterance of the thoughts and emotions of a lifetime.   Yet it is only for a moment that the Apostle gets him up into the high mountain.   Presently he descends to the plain and the testing routine of daily life : " Every one that hath this hope in Him purifieth himself, even as He is pure " (3^3). The question indefatigably urged by St. John is as to our personal right to this " boldness "—as to the verifiable reality of our saving connection with Christ.

Further, we must observe that, so far as the teaching of the Epistle shows, this is solely inferential.   Salvation— Eternal Life—is not of the future only, it is a present reality ; and there is no assurance of it except what is a warrantable inference from its manifestations in character and conduct.

The characteristic word by which this inference is expressed is γινώσκειν [1] (to " recognise " or " perceive " a fact by its appropriate marks, $2^{3.\ 5.\ 29}\ 3^{19.\ 24}\ 4^{13}$).   At times, indeed, the Apostle seems to rise to an immediate consciousness of Divine sonship, as in " We know (οἴδαμεν) that we are of God " (5^{19}).   But this " We know " is only " We perceive " raised to a higher power by exultant emotion.   Even in its highest moments, Assurance does not change its ground : " We know (οἴδαμεν) that we have passed from death into life, *because* we love the brethren " (3^{14}).   The conception, whether right or wrong, of Assurance as a self-evidencing consciousness of acceptance with God, for which earnest souls have prayed in tears of agony and waited in many a darkened hour, is, to say the least, not

[1] See special note on γινώσκειν.

present in the Epistle. Equally remote from its teaching is that minute inquisition of the religious affections by which others have sought to eliminate misgiving. With St. John the grounds of assurance are ethical, not emotional; objective, not subjective; plain and tangible, not microscopic and elusive. They are three, or, rather, they are a trinity: Belief, Righteousness, Love. By his belief in Christ, his keeping God's commandments, and his love to the brethren, a Christian man is recognised and recognises himself as begotten of God.

The function assigned to Belief, in this regard, is specially characteristic, and demands consideration. According to the teaching of the Epistle, Christian Belief brings assurance of salvation, not by subjective psychological action as Trust, but because it affords objective testimony that the believer is "begotten of God"[1] (4^2 $5^{4, 5}$), and has God "abiding in him" (4^{15}). It is the same with the witness of the Spirit. To every believer the truth concerning the object of Christian faith—Christ the Incarnate Son of God—is directly certified by the teaching and testimony of the Spirit ($2^{20, 27}$ 4^2 5^7). But it is a misconception, though a common one, to regard the Epistle as teaching that the Spirit bears immediate and self-evidencing testimony to the Divine sonship of the believer. What the Spirit witnesses to is the Divine-human personality of Christ (4^2 5^7; cf. John 15^{26} 16^{14}). And it is only as an objective fact and by necessary inference that the reception of the Spirit's witness and the resultant confession of Christ give assurance that "we are of God" (4^4). Thus when it is said (3^{24}), "And hereby we recognise that He abideth in us by the Spirit which He gave us," it is not the intuition of a fact, but an inference from a fact, that is expressed,—not that the Spirit imparts the immediate consciousness that God abideth in us, but that the indwell-

---

[1] *v. supra*, pp. 262, 270-4.

ing of God is recognised by its appropriate sign, the gift of
the Spirit " that confesseth Jesus as the Christ come in the
flesh " (4^2).

It is thus evident that the Epistle's view of Assurance
stands somewhat apart from St. Paul's (Rom. $8^{15.\ 16}$).
While the same fundamental Christian experience as Paul
asserts, " Ye received not the spirit of bondage again to
fear ; but ye received the spirit of adoption, whereby we
cry, Abba Father," is no less asserted by " We know and
have believed the Love which God hath towards us," the
fact, nevertheless, is not to be slurred over, that in its
explicit treatment of the subject, which is uniquely
deliberate and systematic, the Epistle recognises no
assurance of fellowship with God which is not matter of
inevitable inference from the facts of life. And it is
precisely when it deals with the subject at closest quarters
that it most rigorously postulates Love, embodied and
" perfected " in actual deeds, as the crucial test by which
" we shall recognise that we are of the truth, and shall
assure our hearts before him . . ."   For this proof that
" as He is, so are we in this world," there is no substitute.

Prayer.

We turn now to the second branch of the subject,
Assurance in Prayer. This does not emerge in the first
Cycle of the Epistle, but in the second and the third it is
dealt with in passages which are closely parallel and
mutually explanatory ($3^{21.\ 22}$ and $5^{14.\ 15}$). In both places
assurance of our filial relation to God is seen to have as
its immediate result, confidence toward Him in prayer.
This assurance is differently expressed in the two contexts
(3^{19}—" we are of the truth " ; 5^{13}—" ye have eternal life "),
and is differently grounded (on Love " in deed and in
truth," 3^{18} ; on Belief " in the name of the Son of God," 5^{13}),

but is to the same effect and leads to the same practical issue—παῤῥησία toward God.

$3^{21.\ 22}$.

"Beloved, if our heart condemn us not, we have boldness[1] toward God; and whatsoever we ask, we receive of Him, because we keep His commandments, and do those things that are pleasing in His sight." παῤῥησία ("boldness") is to be understood as including both the right we enjoy—that of open and free speech—and the feeling of confidence with which this is exercised. The condition of this "boldness" is—"If our heart condemn us not." In the foregoing verse the Apostle has indicated how the true Christian, loving, "not in word neither in tongue," but "in deed and in truth," may recognise that he is "of the truth," and assure his heart, even his self-condemning heart, before God. And here "If our heart condemn us not" must be understood as assuming the whole result of 3^{18-20}. It includes not only the case in which the heart has found no matter of condemnation, but also the case in which the heart's condemnation has been silenced in the presence of Him "Who is greater than the heart." Upon this condition alone is confident approach to God possible. Unconfessed sin, or doubt as to our own integrity of heart, offers an insuperable obstacle. (Ps. 32^3 66^{18}, Matt. $5^{23.\ 24}$). But, unembarrassed by the accusation of conscience, conscious of walking in the Light as He is in the Light, we have the privilege, and the feeling which corresponds to the privilege, of open childlike speech with our Father. This is the glory and perfection of Christian prayer, and is the Christian's constant encouragement and invitation to pray.

---

[1] We have found the same word, παῤῥησία, used to express the faithful Christian's confidence towards Christ at His coming (2^{28}), and toward God at the Day of Judgment (4^{17}).

And this is no vain confidence we have toward God. " Whatsoever we ask of Him we receive, *because* we keep [1] His commandments, and do the things that are pleasing in His sight." [2]

What principle is expressed in this " because " is not immediately obvious. The idea of *merit* is to be absolutely excluded as irrelevant to the thought of the whole passage, and as opposed to the inmost truth of Christianity. Equally to be rejected, *a priori*, is the notion that by our obedience we acquire such favour with God and such influence in His counsels that He cannot refuse us what we ask (Candlish). Even if we are compelled to recognise such a thought in the primitive stages of revelation, it is intolerable in the New Testament. The key to the interpretation of the present passage is given in John 15⁷:—" If ye abide in Me, and My words abide in you, ask whatsoever ye will, and it shall be done unto you." It is no external and arbitrary but an intrinsically necessary condition of successful prayer that is here expressed. Our prayers are answered, because our will is in inward harmony with God's, the evidence of this being that we " keep His commandments and do those things that are pleasing in His sight." In our actions we prove that God's will is our will; and when we pray, our will does not change. Our life is a unity. Our deeds and our prayers are manifestations of the same God-begotten Life, are operations of the same will,—the will that God's will be

---

[1] The two expressions, "keep His commandments" and "do the things that are pleasing in His sight," are virtually synonymous, except in so far as they suggest a twofold motive for obedience—submission to moral authority, and the loving desire of the children of God to please the Father in all things (cf. 2 Cor. 5⁹). Catholic exegetes distinguish the two as obedience to what is enjoined (*præcepta*) and good works voluntarily undertaken (*consilia evangelica*), but this is entirely beside the mark.

[2] ἐνώπιον αὐτοῦ. Cf. ἔμπροσθεν αὐτοῦ (3¹⁹). ἐνώπιον is especially a Lucan word, used regularly to translate לִפְנֵי. ἔμπροσθεν conveys more particularly the idea of man's consciousness of God's Presence, ἐνώπιον more directly the reality of God's perception (cf. Luke 16¹⁵, Acts 4¹⁹ 10⁴·³¹, Rom. 3²⁰).

done.   Therefore, " whatsoever we ask of Him we receive."
" The effectual, fervent prayer of a righteous man availeth
much " (Jas. 5[16]), because, as the man is, so are his prayers
—righteous.   The desires of him who delights himself in
the Lord are desires that cannot, because they ought not,
to fail of accomplishment (Ps. 37[4]).   The prayers of those
who " keep God's commandments and do those things that
are pleasing in His sight," are nothing else than echoes of
God's own voice, impulses of the Divine Will Itself,
throbbing in the strivings of the human will and, in the
mystical circulation of the Eternal Life, returning to their
source.[1]

All this is more explicitly set forth in the parallel
passage—

5[14-16].

" And this[2] is the boldness which we have towards
Him, that, if we ask anything according to His Will,[3] He
heareth us " (5[14]).   Here the qualification, " according to His
Will," is explicit.   The marvellous and supernatural power
of prayer consists, not in bringing God's Will down to us,
but in lifting our will up to His.   And thus the words,

---

[1] This view is confirmed by the succeeding context.   3[23] and 3[24a] are both
explanatory of 3[22].   The first explains what the substance of God's commandments is : "This is His commandment, that we believe on the name of His
Son Jesus Christ, and love one another, as He gave us commandment."   The
second explains why, by keeping God's commandments, we are assured of obtaining what we pray for.   It is because this is both the condition and the evidence of
our fellowship with God : " And he that keepeth His commandments dwelleth
in Him, and He in him."   Since the keeping of His commandments is the
means by which we abide in God (John 15[10]) and the condition of God's abiding
in us (John 14[23]), it ensures that our prayers are such as it is meet that God
should answer.

[2] Here, it is to be observed, Prayer is related in the context to Eternal Life
(5[11-13]).   Prayer is a mode of action in which the Life God has bestowed upon us
in His Son characteristically manifests itself (John 14[13] 15[7. 16]).   And as Prayer
itself is an expression of the Eternal Life in us, so joyful confidence in prayer
comes from knowing that we have Eternal Life (5[13]).

[3] " According to His Will."   This defines not the manner of the asking, but
its object—" anything according to His Will."

"according to His Will," do not in reality, though verbally and in appearance they do, limit the exercise of true prayer. Rather do they display the breadth and sublimity of its scope as well as the certainty of its fulfilment. The Will of God is the final and perfect Redemption of men (John 6[39. 40], Eph. 1[9. 10. 11], Col. 1[9] etc.), and the providential appointment and control of events as contributory to this (Matt. 26[42], Acts 21[14], Rom. 15[32], 1 Pet. 4[19] etc.). And this Will of God has necessarily become the will of every one who is "begotten of God" and has Eternal Life abiding in him. With regard to particular events, he may have no certain knowledge of what that Will is; but, as the end of all his actions, so the end and sum of all his prayers is, "Thy Will be done."

5[15. 16].

"And if we know that He heareth us, whatsoever we ask,[1] we know that we have the petitions which we have asked of Him" (5[15]).

The emphasis of the verse falls upon the words, "We have." Since what we ask is according to God's Will, we know that we have it—"We have," not "We shall have." The statement is characteristically Johannine. Though the fulfilment may not yet be apparent, it exists in the sphere of Divine Thought and Will, which is the sphere of reality, and only awaits manifestation. The certainty of this ought to fill us with joyful expectation (John 16[24]). "A door is thus opened into all the treasures of heaven" (Haupt).

In the following verse (5[16])[2] illustrative examples are adduced both of assurance in prayer and of its limits. "If any man see his brother sinning a sin not unto death, he shall ask, and God will give him life (renewed spiritual life) for them that sin not unto death." Here there is

---

[1] *v.* Notes, *in loc.*   [2] *v. supra*, pp. 135–42.

absolute assurance.   It is the Will of God that the brother
who has sinned, yet not so as to sever himself from the
fellowship of Christ and His people, be restored; and in
answer to prayer it shall be done.   Again, " There is sin
unto death; I do not say "—he does not forbid, neither
does he encourage—" that he shall pray concerning this."
In the Apostle's view it is impossible, in such a case, to ask
with assurance of obtaining our request.

Prayer, then, according to the teaching of the Epistle, is
an expression of the Eternal Life—the Life of God—in
man.   For the desires and aims of that Life two channels
of effort are provided, Work—" to keep God's commandments and do the things that are pleasing in His sight "—
and Prayer.   Prayer is asking ($a\dot{i}\tau\epsilon\hat{i}\nu$); not devout meditation, but definite petition; not to wish only, but to will.
The peculiar characteristic of Christian prayer is confidence
($\pi a\dot{\rho}\rho\eta\sigma\dot{i}a$).   It is not the mere abject cry that pain,
helplessness, or blank despair sends up to an unknown God
on the chance that He may hear and help.   As little has
it the character of an endeavour to turn God from His
purpose or to convert Him to our way of thinking.
Christian prayer is essentially an active identification of
the human will with the Divine Will; and that confidence
which is its distinctive privilege consists in two things—
first, the persuasion that our will is in harmony with God's;
and, second, the certainty that God's Will shall be done.
The former is, in the nature of the case, contingent.   It is
ours, " If our heart condemn us not."   It is ours, " Because
we keep His commandments, and do the things that are
pleasing in His sight "; which things, the Apostle reminds
us, include pre-eminently believing on the name of His Son
Jesus Christ, and loving one another (3^{23}).   On the other
hand, the assurance that God's Will shall be done is
absolute.   " If we ask anything according to His Will,"
we have our petition.   When we look upon the wrongs

and confusions of our own hearts and lives, and upon those that seem to reign in the world around us, we have nowhere to cast anchor save in the Sovereign Will of the Eternal. God is Love. The Will of God is pure, unchangeable, holy Love working for the highest good of every creature. It is the Will of God that the Eternal Life of Truth, Righteousness, and Love shall everywhere grow and multiply; and when we will this together with Him, nothing shall prevent its accomplishment.

St. John's conception of prayer is removed by the whole diameter of thought from the secularist's taunting definition of it as " an appliance warranted by theologians to make God do what His clients want." Prayer is a mighty instrument, not for getting man's will done in Heaven, but for getting God's will done in Earth. But in that case it is said to be open to the alternative objection of superfluity. " If God is just, will He not do justice without being entreated of men? If God is allwise, and knows what is for man's good better than man can tell Him, is not prayer a futility and an impertinence?" [1] Those who urge this objection fail to see that what it involves is sheer fatalism—a scheme of the universe in which there is no place for the finite will. They fail to see that all that is urged against the need of prayer might be urged, with equal cogency, against the need of work or human action of any kind. If, because God is just, He will do justice without being entreated of men, it is equally true that he will do justice without any human effort on behalf of justice. If, because God knows what is best for us, prayer is a superfluity and an impertinence, then all thought about what is best for us and all effort to procure it must be equally superfluous.

And if every one sees that man's work is not an impertinent interference with the will of God, but is the fulfil-

[1] Blatchford, *God and my Neighbour*.

ment of His Will, it is equally rational to believe that God needs and uses man's prayers precisely as He needs and uses man's work. And for precisely the same reason—that the beings He has created in His own likeness and made partakers of His own spiritual Life may grow to "a perfect man, unto the measure of the stature of the fulness of Christ." By work and prayer alike our will-power may go forth to the accomplishment of His purposes. God needs the one from us no more and no less than He needs the other. And *we* need the one no more and no less than we need the other. All true work is one method, and all true prayer is another method, of putting our will in line with God's. We are conscious of this in our best prayers. It is this that gives power and assurance to prayer—the knowledge that we are desiring what He desires, seeking what He seeks, willing with the whole strength of our souls what He wills. This is the marvellous and immeasurable power God has entrusted us with, and which we employ so feebly and slothfully

CHAPTER XV

The Growth of Christian Experience.

2^{12-14}.

" I AM writing unto you, little children, because your sins are forgiven you for His Name's sake. I am writing unto you, fathers, because ye know Him Who is from the Beginning. I am writing unto you, young men, because ye have overcome the Wicked One. I wrote unto you, little ones, because ye know the Father. I wrote unto you, fathers, because ye know Him Who is from the Beginning. I wrote unto you, young men, because ye are strong, and the word of God is abiding in you, and ye have overcome the Wicked One."

This parenthetical address to the readers is, at first sight, difficult to account for. Not only is there a lack of obvious connection either with what precedes or with what follows ; it is thrust like a wedge into the middle of a paragraph, separating the positive exposition of the Law of Love (2^{7-11}) from the negative (2^{15-17}), and thus obscuring the continuity of thought. It seems, indeed, as if its introduction here might be cited as one of the strongest instances of that lack of logical coherence by which, in the view of many critics, the Epistle is characterised. On closer examination, however, these first impressions are dispelled.

The paragraph consists of a six-fold statement of the reason which justifies the writer in addressing to his readers such an Epistle as the present. And this six-fold statement is, in effect, one—that the impulse to write thus does not spring from doubt of their Christian standing or of their progress in Christian experience, but that, on the contrary, it is his confidence in their Christian character and attainments that inspires him to write as he does. The motive of the address is, in the first place, apologetic [1] and conciliatory—to obviate possible misunderstanding, or even possible offence. It might be felt that in the preceding paragraphs the tone was somewhat acrid and severe. The ill-omened " he that saith " has been much in evidence, while the sentence just completed [2] strikes a peculiarly sombre note. At this point, therefore, the writer might very naturally guard himself against the supposition that his words implied a gloomy view of his readers' spiritual state, or that they were barbed by any invidious personal application. But there is a deeper motive also. He secures a vantage-ground from which to press the yet more stringent demands that are to follow : " Love not the world, neither the things that are in the world " (2^{15-17}). It would be idle to make such a requirement of those in whom the foundations of the Christian life were not already firmly fixed ; and it is because he so gladly recognises that his readers have already " tasted of the heavenly gift," and that in good measure, that he is encouraged to incite them to fuller realisation of what is within their reach. That men " know the Father " is the strongest reason why they should not love the world, the love of which is so incompatible with the love of the Father (2^{15}); that men " know Him Who is from the Beginning " is the strongest reason why they should not set their affection upon things transient and evanescent (2^{17a}), but upon the abiding life (2^{17b}); that they

---

[1] The same quasi-apologetic strain appears in 2^{21} and 2^{27}.

[2] " But he that hateth his brother is in the darkness, and walketh in the darkness, and knoweth not whither he goeth, because the darkness hath blinded his eyes."

have overcome the Wicked One in the past, furnishes strong
reason why they should not allow themselves to be now
ensnared by "the lust of the eyes, the lust of the flesh, and
the vain-glory of life" (2^{16}).   It is because his readers are
what they are that he can spur them to fuller achievements;
and it is by reminding them of what they are that he can
best apply the spur.

The introduction of this parenthetical address to the
readers may be regarded as thus satisfactorily accounted
for.   The passage itself, however, as to both form and
contents, presents some peculiar features. Of the six clauses
it contains, the second three are an almost *verbatim* repetition of the first three; with, however, the singular variation
that, in the first triplet, the writer uses the present tense,
"I write" (γράφω); in the second, the aorist (ἔγραψα).
Now, a Greek letter-writer, when referring in the course of
his letter to the writing of it, may do so in either of these
ways. He may describe the process from his own immediate point of view, in which case he uses the present
indicative, γράφω; or, placing himself at his reader's point
of view, he may describe the action as completed and
already in the past, by using the "Epistolary Aorist," [1]
ἔγραψα. Why does St. John here change from the one
form to the other, and why does he repeat under the
second form what he has just said under the first?   There
is nothing in New Testament usage [2] to justify the view
(Huther, Ewald, De Wette) that γράφω refers to the
Epistle as a whole, ἔγραψα to the part already written.
The supposition that ἔγραψα is to be explained as an
allusion to some other writing, whether the Gospel (Ebrard,
Hofmann, Plummer) or an earlier Epistle (Rothe), has still
less to commend it.   And, while it may be argued (Haupt)
that in the first triplet (the γράφω clauses) the writer is

---

[1] Other verbs may be used in the same way, as ἔπεμψα, Eph. 6^{22}.

[2] *v.* Notes, *in loc.*

assuring his readers of his confidence in them, but in the second is preparing the way for the injunction that follows, "Love not the world," this, though it may explain the repetition, does nothing to account for the change of tense. I venture to suggest,[1] as the simple solution of the problem, that after writing the first ($\gamma\rho\acute{a}\phi\omega$) triplet the author was interrupted in his composition, and that, resuming his pen, he very naturally caught up his line of thought by repeating his last sentence, with "I wrote" instead of "I am writing." Every one does this mentally in the supposed circumstances, and the Apostle may easily be imagined to to have done so literally.

A more important question concerns the classification of the persons addressed. Of these, St. John distinguishes apparently three grades, the "children" ($\tau\epsilon\kappa\nu\acute{\iota}a$, 2[12]; $\pi a\iota\delta\acute{\iota}a$, 2[13b]), the "fathers," and the "young men." These terms have been understood as all indicating Christians in general.[2] But this is a gratuitous subtlety. By others, they have been taken in their literal sense (Calvin, with the majority of the older commentators). But the Epistle can scarcely be regarded as having been written for those who were actually "children"; and, besides, the order, "children," "fathers," "young men," is, on this view, unaccountable. The same objection applies to their designating *three* different stages of proficiency in the Christian life.

A closer consideration of the Apostle's *usus loquendi* reveals that he has in view, not three, but *two* classes of readers; whom he addresses in common as "little children," and, separately, as the older ($\pi a\tau\acute{\epsilon}\rho\epsilon s$) and the younger

---

[1] I leave this sentence as originally written. I find, however, that Plummer mentions this solution, and gives it the second place among the *seven* he enumerates. He regards it as "conceivable," but "a little fine drawn," preferring the view that $\gamma\rho\acute{a}\phi\omega$ refers to the Epistle, $\check{\epsilon}\gamma\rho a\psi a$ to the Gospel. I cannot share the preference.

[2] So Augustine, *Filii quia nascuntur; patres quia principium agnoscunt; juvenes quare? Quia vicistis malignum.*

(νεανίσκοι) members of the Christian community. "Little children" is the affectionate appellation which the writer habitually [1] applies to all to whom he stands in the relation of spiritual mentor. To them he writes because their sins are forgiven them for His Name's [2] sake. Fittingly does this stand in the first place. It is an impotent religion which cannot declare to men the forgiveness of sins, and make it the basis of fruitful aspiration and moral effort. The first and universal human need, the presupposition of all human fellowship with God, is the forgiveness of sins. Therefore it is the first and fundamental announcement of the Gospel (Luke 24[47]), the first element in the salvation which is given to men " for His Name's sake." Therefore, also, the first common characteristic of all who believe on that Name, at whatever stage of Christian advancement they be, is that their " sins are forgiven them."

The second is that they have known [3] the Father. This is the common privilege of the least and the most advanced, to " know the Father" as He is revealed in Christ (John 17[3]); not so as to comprehend all He is, but so as to be sure that there are in Him love, wisdom, and power beyond the measure of man's mind, and

---

[1] τεκνία, 2[1, 28] 3[18] 4[4] 5[21]. παιδία is found again in 2[18], with undoubtedly the same general sense. Westcott says that as τεκνία we are bound to one another by the bonds of natural kinsmanship and affection, as παιδία we all recognise our equal feebleness in the presence of the one Father. But there does not seem to be any definable difference in usage between the two words. Both are used merely as familiar and affectionate forms of address. It is as παιδία that our Lord hails the disciples (John 21[5], where it might be translated "lads").

[2] Here the "Name of Christ" is regarded, not as the object of human faith, but as the ground of Divine action. Thus the thought agrees with the specific function of Christ as "propitiation for our sins" (2[2]). *v.* Notes, *in loc.* As in the O.T. the "Name" of Jehovah, so in the N.T. the "Name" of Christ is scarcely to be distinguished from the Person. It is what conveys to men (cf. 1 Cor. 1[10], Rev. 2[3]), and is here conceived as conveying also to God, the thought of what Christ is ("the righteous," "the propitiation for our sins"). Our Lord forewarns the disciples that they will be hated of all men "for My Name's sake" (Matt. 10[22]). The same Name, the same connection with Christ, which is the ground of man's hatred, is the ground of God's forgiveness.

[3] ἐγνώκατε. See special note on γινώσκειν.

that our whole strength and blessedness lie in trusting Him. For human frailty and helplessness there is at last no other refuge, for the sinful and dying no other deliverance, for men beset before and behind by a darkness that neither sense nor intellect can penetrate, no other light, than to know Him of whom Jesus Christ said, " He that hath seen Me hath seen the Father." These two possessions of the " children," the forgiveness of sins and the knowledge of the Father, as they are both communicated in the " Name " of Christ, are necessarily coexistent in Christian experience.

The Apostle next addresses his readers according to their stages of growth; and, first, the " fathers," among whom would be included not only the Church-leaders or official elders, but all who, in contrast with the " young men," were more advanced in years and, presumably, of riper Christian attainment. That which peculiarly befits the mature Christian is to " know Him Who is from the Beginning." Obviously the title " He that is from the Beginning" is here given to Christ as the Eternal Word (John 1^1, 1 John $1^{1, 2}$); and obviously also, it is given with a special significance, as adding to the conception of the Divine already expressed by " the Father," the thought of eternal and changeless duration. In Christian experience the consciousness of the immediate personal relation to God, with its ethical and emotional elements—the certitude of God's fatherly character and forgiving grace, apprehended simply as a present and personal reality—may be, at first, everything. To " know the Father," to " know and believe the love which God hath toward us," is enough. It is by the rough pressure of the actual problems of existence that men are awakened to discover the fuller contents and issues of their faith. By the poignant experience Life brings of the evanescence of all creaturely good, fellowship with God is revealed as not only a present possession, but the one abiding reality.   The conflicts, in which the soul has to fight for its faith in a Divine fatherly purpose ceaselessly operating in our own and the world's history, first disclose the full significance of that faith.   Hence it is the "fathers" that "know Him Who is from the Beginning."   We look to mature experience for a largeness of view, a calm untroubled depth of conviction, a clear-eyed judgment upon life, which youth cannot have; for the pattern of the cloth is more clearly displayed in the web than in the patch.   In the course of a moderately long life a man may have witnessed great changes and commotions in society, violent oscillations of opinion, temporary eclipses of truth and triumphs of wrong; but he may have learned, at the same time, how through all these the undeviating purpose of God pursues its way, how the great principles of truth and right assert themselves, amid all changes, as things that God has settled, and that cannot be shaken.

It is no merely speculative knowledge that is here in view, but knowledge which has become part of a man's own being.   It has been learned in a costly school.   It is the prize of conflict.   "I write unto you, young men, because ye have overcome the Wicked One" (2^{13}).   "I wrote unto you, young men, because ye are strong, and the Word of God abideth in you, and ye have overcome the Wicked One" (2^{14}).   The "young men" thus addressed have already fought and conquered; and the victorious attitude has been maintained up to the present time.[1] That they have thus warred a good warfare is proof that they are strong, and that with a strength whose source and sustenance are Divine—strong, because the Word of God abideth in them.   .That the Word of God, the eternal principles of truth and right implanted in the soul and realised as being the Word of the living God, is the sole

---

[1] This is implied in the tense of the verb, νενικήκατε.

weapon by which *all* temptation is to be met and conquered, is one of the grand commonplaces of Scripture (Ps. 119[11], Luke 4[1-13]). The everlasting " No ! " of the Word to every sin (Gen. 39[9], Eph. 6[16]), and its everlasting " Yea ! " to every duty (Acts 4[20]), are nowhere more trenchantly expressed than in this Epistle (3[6-10] 5[17-19] etc.).

Thus, while the privilege of age is knowledge, the task of youth is conflict. Not that age also may not have its conflicts. But conflict is not characteristic of age, as it is of those years when the powers of the body and mind are coming to their full development, and when all the most critical decisions of life must inevitably be made. It is through such conflict faithfully waged, as the Apostle here so clearly implies, that the one path to true knowledge lies.

> " As it was better, youth
> Should strive, through acts uncouth,
> Toward making, than repose on aught found made :
> So, better, age, exempt
> From strife, should know, than tempt
> Further ! . . .
> Youth ended, I shall try
> My gain or loss thereby ;
> Leave the fire ashes, what survives is gold ;
> And I shall weigh the same
> Give life its praise or blame ;
> Young, all lay in dispute ; I shall know, being old."

There is a " knowing," that of the " children," which must precede the fight ; and there is a " knowing," that of the " fathers," which comes after it. The few great certainties which a man knows as he knows his own right hand, and in which he finds " the peace that passeth all understanding," are ever spoil captured from the field of conflict, the " hidden manna " given " to him that overcometh."

To take as starting-point the gift of God in Christ, the forgiveness of sins and the knowledge of the Father, then to advance, with this as our strength and the Word of God as our weapon, to faithful and victorious warfare; finally through this, to arrive at the sure perception of the Everlasting, in union with Whom our human life and its results become an eternal and blessed reality,— such is the curriculum which St. John here maps out for human experience. It is well to remember what is the alternative to this—the experience which teaches with equal intensity the illusiveness of all good; which writes " vanity of vanities " upon the life of man and all with which it is concerned; which proclaims, as the sum and end of all wisdom, that " The world passeth away and the lust thereof," because it has not " known Him that is from the Beginning," nor that " whosoever doeth His will abideth for ever."

CHAPTER XVI.

ESCHATOLOGY.

IN the vocabulary of the Epistle a word of notable significance, not yet adverted to, is the verb to "manifest" (φανεροῦν). This word may be said to contain the Johannine conception of history. History is manifestation; each of its successive events being merely the emergence into visibility of what already exists. Nor is this "manifestation" conceived exactly as an apocalypse. It is not the sudden snatching of a veil (ἀποκαλύπτειν) from what, though as yet unseen, exists in definite completed form (as from a finished picture or statue); it is the natural unfolding from within of what already exists though only in essence—the germination of the seed, the embodiment of potential in actual fact.[1]

Thus, for St. John, the Incarnation is not so much a new and supernatural event in human history as a natural event in Divine history. It has its roots in Eternity. It is the manifestation of "What was from the beginning"— the self-unfolding in humanity and to humanity of the Eternal Divine Life ($1^{1, 2}$).

In like manner, the sacrifice of Calvary brought no new thing into being. It did not reveal a new love of God toward men: it was the inevitable self-manifestation of all the Love latent in the depths of the Divine nature (4^9). So at His Second Advent, Christ will only be "manifested." He is here, though unperceived by the world (3^1); and all

---

[1] Cf. J. M. Gibbon, *Eternal Life*, chap. vii.

the glory that will then shine out from Him is already in Him. The splendour of the Parousia will simply be a manifestation of the reality (3^2). Then also the children of God will be "manifested" (3^2). "What they shall be" is what they essentially are; but as the bulb hidden in the earth unfolds itself in the perfect flower, so what they now are will then appear.

These are characteristic examples of the Johannine point of view; and it is evident that where it prevails the eschatological idea cannot hold more than a secondary place. The fashion of thought is not historical or scenic, but genetic and ideal. Events are contemplated only as the embodiment of eternal principles. For St. John there is but one Life—the Eternal; and there is but one world —the world of the ideal, which is also the only real (ἀλήθεια, ἀληθινός). The phenomenal is but the changing vesture of the essential; the temporal, of the everlasting.

Yet St. John is not an idealist pure and simple. For him, events are not merely symbols, history is not allegory. The Incarnation is a historical fact, not merely a parable of eternal truth, declaring the capacity of human nature for the divinest life. The Parousia is not the evolution of an idea, not the gradual dawning on the world of the true glory of the Spirit of Christ, but a definite future event. When St. John says that "The world passeth away," this signifies, not the inherent transitoriness of all that belongs to "the lust of the flesh, the lust of the eyes, and the vainglory of life," but the conviction that the present mundane order is near to dissolution. St. John has an eschatology;[1] and as is natural, it is more pronounced in the Epistle than in the Gospel.[2] It may be said, indeed, that the whole atmosphere of the Epistle is impregnated with the

[1] "All the ideas of the consummation of all things that belong to the Synoptic and primitive Apostolic teaching are present also in John, and by no preconceived critical notion can they be eliminated" (Beyschlag, ii. 478).

[2] See, further, Chapter XVII.

eschatological element. It is written in full and vivid view of the last things.

I. "The world is passing away" (2^{17}), and the time in which the Apostle and his readers are living is "the last hour" (2^{18} ἐσχάτη ὥρα ἐστίν). This is one of a family of phrases descended from the אַחֲרִית הַיָּמִים of the Old Testament, and the use of the derivatives in the New Testament is as elastic[1] as that of their original in the Old. Sometimes, from the Old Testament point of view, they denote the Messianic Age foretold by the prophets—the Gospel dispensation, in which all preceding stages of the world's history are consummated—without any suggestion of *its* end. (Thus, "In the last days," Acts 2^{17}; "At the end of the days," Heb. 1^1; "At the end of the times," 1 Pet. 1^{20}.) Sometimes, the Gospel age being itself regarded as preparatory to something beyond, there is a reference, more or less-definite, to its penultimate stages, which are to be marked by various woes, and especially by the uprising of many false teachers (*e.g.* 2 Tim. 3^1, 2 Pet. $3^{3. 4}$, Jude [18]). Sometimes, again, the reference is to the definite crisis which is to be the end of the present age and the beginning of that which is to come (1 Pet. 1^5 "in the last time"; "the last day," John $6^{39. 40. 44. 54}$ 7^{37} 11^{24} 12^{48}.

Obviously "the last hour" of our text falls under

---

[1] אַחֲרִית הַיָּמִים. This much debated phrase occurs chiefly in the prophets (Isa. 2^2, Jer. 23^{20} 30^{24} 48^{47} 49^{39}, Ezek. 38^{16}, Dan. 10^{14}, Hos. 3^5, Mic. 4^1), but also in the Pentateuch (Gen. 49^1, Num. 24^{14}, Deut. 4^{30} 31^{29}). Mostly it refers to the glorious Messianic period which should ensue upon the "Day of Jehovah." But a Messianic sense is excluded in Gen. 49^1, where the reference is to the settlement of the Tribes in Canaan, and in Deut. 4^{30} and 31^{29}, as also in Jer. 23^{20}, where it is used quite indefinitely of future time. Everywhere it is properly translated "in the after days," not "the last days." It does not signify a day or days after which there shall be no other, but describes "the farthest future which the eye of the seer reaches" (Davidson. Cf. Cheyne's note on Isa. 2^2). In post-Biblical times the אַחֲרִית הַיָּמִים came to be distinguished from "the age to come" (עוֹלָם הַבָּא = αἰὼν ὁ ἐρχόμενος, Mark 10^{30}, Luke 18^{30} etc., or αἰὼν ὁ μέλλων, Heb. 6^5), the former being understood as a season of conflict and suffering by which the latter should be ushered in. The general N.T. usage is that described in the text.

the second [1] class of these usages. Not only is it true that "the world is passing away and the lust thereof"; already the last hour of its day is running its course. At any moment we must be prepared to hear the clock strike and the great hammer of God's judgments ring out above a doomed world the announcement that all that has been the desire of its flesh, the desire of its eyes, and the boast of its life, is no more.

II. The Apostle next adduces from the existing state of things the proof that the age in which he and his readers are living is the "last hour." "Children, it is the last hour: and as ye heard that Antichrist cometh, even so now many antichrists have arisen; from which we perceive that it is the last hour" (2^{18}). In the New Testament the time immediately preceding the Second Advent is regarded as one of much and various tribulation, both for the Church and for the world; but the special symptom of the approaching end of the present era is, as has been said, the appearance of false Messiahs and false teachers.[2] These beliefs are equally developed in Jewish (in relation to the advent of the Messiah) and Jewish-

---

[1] "Ultimum tempus, in quo sic complentur omnia ut nihil supersit præter ultimam Christi revelationem" (Calvin). The interpretation has been much biassed by reluctance to admit a mistaken expectation of the immediate nearness of the Second Advent. Hence "the last hour" is identified by the majority of the older exegetes with the Christian dispensation. But ὅθεν γινώσκομεν ὅτι ἐσχάτη ὥρα ἐστίν renders this quite untenable. Equally groundless are Westcott's insistence upon the fact that ἐσχάτη ὥρα is anarthrous; his translation, "a last hour"; and his explanation, "It was a period of critical change, a last hour, but not definitely the last hour." A general instead of a definite meaning is no more necessitated by the want of the article than it is in Jas. 5^3, I Tim. 3^1, or I Pet. 1^5; in all of which it is impossible (cf. Sir. 1^{11} εὖ ἔσται ἐπ᾽ ἐσχάτων). If the phrase were as common in modern English as it was in primitive Christian parlance, we should come to speak of "last day," or "last hour," as readily as "the last day," or "the last hour." Besides, the idea of a succession of epochs, each of which may be regarded as "a last time," is one which, however it may commend itself, is nowhere expressed in the New Testament.

[2] Matt. $24^{5.\ 11.\ 23.\ 24}$ ψευδόχριστοι, ψευδοπροφῆται, Mark $13^{8.\ 9.\ 13.\ 19.\ 20}$, Luke 21^8, I Tim. 4^{1-3}, 2 Tim. $3^{1-5}\ 4^3$, 2 Pet. 3^3, Jude $^{18.\ 19}$. Cf. Acts $20^{29.\ 30}$; Didache 16^3 ἐν ταῖς ἐσχάταις ἡμέραις πληθυνθήσονται οἱ ψευδοπροφῆται.

Christian apocalyptic. But in the apocalyptic literature the manifold hostile forces are regarded as concentrated in one chief and head. As all that makes for the Kingdom of God and the salvation of God's people is personified in the Messiah, so all the powers of ungodliness are united in one ideal figure, Antichrist. The accounts of this anti-Messianic personage are by no means uniform;[1] but they are sufficient to establish the probability, if not the certainty, that the conception did not originate in the Christian Church, but that there was already in the popular Jewish eschatology a fully developed legend of Antichrist, which was accepted and amplified in current Christian belief. And, indeed, the expectation of the appearing of Antichrist, and of his appearing as a definite signal of the approaching Parousia, had formed a distinct element in the earliest Apostolic teaching of St. Paul (2 Thess. 2^5); while St. John's words, "Ye have heard that Antichrist cometh," seem to imply that the information had been obtained from some authoritative source, and, at all events, assume that his readers were well acquainted with, and probably concurred in, the belief as commonly held.

He now declares to them that this sign of the "last hour" is already visible, although not entirely in the anticipated form: "As ye have heard that Antichrist cometh, even so now many antichrists have arisen." And he explains that by these "many antichrists" he means the heretical teachers to whom, and to whose doctrine, he definitely refers (2^{22} 4^3, 2 John 7). The question thus arises, what relation he intends these "many antichrists" to be understood as holding to the Antichrist. Is Antichrist already come in the activity of these false teachers? Does this, in fact, constitute the fulfilment of all that the idea of Antichrist stood for? Or does he still sanction the popular belief in a personal Antichrist of whom these

[1] See note on Antichrist, appended to this chapter.

were only the forerunners, manifesting the same forces at work as should afterwards culminate in him? While the latter may be said to be the traditional view, it is certainly not established by any of the " antichrist " passages in the Epistle. On the contrary, the impression these convey is that of an implied correction, a tacit superseding of the popular belief. Thus in the present passage, when one gives due weight to the solemn and definite assertion, " It is the last hour," and when we observe the existence of the " many antichrists " adduced as a fact corresponding as closely as possible ($\kappa\alpha\theta\dot\omega\varsigma$ . . . $\kappa\alpha\iota$) to the accepted belief that " Antichrist cometh," and the unqualified fashion in which this is brought forward a second time as the unmistakable mark ($\ddot{o}\theta\epsilon\nu \gamma\iota\nu\dot\omega\sigma\kappa o\mu\epsilon\nu$) of " the last hour," the intended inference clearly seems to be that everything really signified by the current belief concerning Antichrist was already being realised.

The other passages point to the same conclusion. In 4[3] Antichrist is alluded to simply as a matter of common report ($\tau o\hat{v}\tau\dot{o}$ $\dot{\epsilon}\sigma\tau\iota\nu$ $\tau\dot{o}$ $\tau o\hat{v}$ $'A\nu\tau\iota\chi\rho\dot\iota\sigma\tau o\nu$: " This is that matter of Antichrist, regarding which ye have heard that it cometh; and now already is it in the world "). In 2 John [7] it is definitely said of those who deny that Jesus Christ is come in the flesh, " This is he that leadeth astray, and the Antichrist." Upon the whole, it seems evident that for the Apostle the present time is already the age of Antichrist, and that he alludes to the traditional belief only for the purpose of conveying more pointedly his own conviction, that the end of all things is at hand, and of dispelling the notion that some more sensational development is to be looked for before the " last hour " shall actually have arrived. This deeper spiritualising of the traditional conception and application of it to the tendencies already at work is thoroughly Johannine.

It is significant, moreover, that it is not in the World,

but in perversions of Christianity, that St. John finds the embodiment of the idea of Antichrist.[1] He has been writing of the Church's conflict with the world and its ideals (2^{15-17}); but now he points to a danger more subtle and more critical, originating within the Church itself. The great pagan world fought against Christ with its own weapons — pleasures seductive to the flesh, possessions and pursuits and splendours alluring to the eye, pomps and distinctions tempting to human vanity; but this enemy fights Christ in Christ's own name, using as its weapon, not the passion of pagan superstition or the sneering pride of pagan philosophy, but the corruption of Christian truth.

To such an antagonist the name Antichrist exactly corresponds; for this properly signifies one who opposes Christ by assuming the guise of Christ.[2] According to the popular conception, Antichrist would claim to be personally the Christ; his claims would imply the denial of the Messiahship of Jesus, and open war against Christianity as such. And though the false teachers whom the Apostle has in view did not ostensibly set up an "opposition" Christ, he asserts, nevertheless, that this is what they virtually did. It is another Christ they preach, and the supreme danger of the movement is that it assumes to be what it is not— Christian. Thus, in fact, it is the revelation of "The Man of Sin" who "as God sitteth in the Temple of God, showing himself that he is God" (2 Thess. $2^{3, 4}$). And not less strikingly apposite to the conception of Antichrist in the Epistle is the symbolical figure by which he is portrayed in the Apocalypse (Rev. 13^{11}). The "Beast" had two horns like a lamb (is evidently, therefore, a counterfeit of

---

[1] The "many antichrists" were Gnostic propagandists of the Cerinthian school. See Chapters II. and VI.

[2] In most words compounded with ἀντί (*e.g.* ἀντιβασιλεύς, ἀντιφιλόσοφος, ἀντιστράτηγος, *v.* Westcott's Note, *in loc.*) the prefix denotes not opposition simply, but opposition in the guise of similarity. Thus ἀντίχριστος is nearly equivalent to ψευδόχριστος.

the Lamb), but " He spake as a dragon." He is the
mouthpiece of the Father of lies; in him Satan has " transformed himself into an angel of light, to deceive, if it
might be, the very elect."

The whole subsequent history of the Church attests
the unerring insight with which St. John has interpreted
the essential significance of the legendary Antichrist. The
traditional identification of the Papacy with Antichrist was
based on a crudely literal conception of prophecy and its
fulfilment. It erred in being too specific and too exclusive;
but in so far as it expressed the truth that the Antichrist is
always found in the corruptions of the Church itself, it gave
a radically sound interpretation of the Johannine thought.

In the following verse the Apostle accounts for the
secession of the antichrists from the Church. " They went
out from us, but they were not of us; for if they had
been of us, they would have continued with us; but (they
went out from us) that it might be made manifest that
none of them were of us "[1] (2^{19}). " They were outwardly
of our number, but partakers of our life—of our fellowship
with the Father and His Son Jesus Christ—they never
were; therefore it was that they went out from us."

It would, of course, be out of the question to deduce
from these words the Cyprianic dogma, *extra ecclesiam
nulla salus*. That any Christian might be actuated by a
genuinely Christian motive in separating himself from the
external fellowship of the Church did not and could not
present itself as a possibility to the imagination of St. John
or of any of the Apostles. But it would be illegitimate to
infer from this what judgment they would have pronounced
upon the actual developments of history, had they been
able to anticipate these. They were not required to face
the specific question, what the Church is, in what variety
of forms its essential unity may subsist, or what, in every

[1] *v*. Notes, *in loc*.

case, is involved in outward separation from its communion. Here it is antichristianity, not schism, that is in
question. These separatists were not antichrists, because
they were outside of the Church; they were outside of
the Church because they were antichrists.

On the other hand, the Apostle expressly asserts that
their separation from the body of the faithful was nothing
more than a symptom. It brought no new moral element
into operation; it was only the hatching of the serpent
from the egg. These false teachers had not renounced
the truth; for the truth they had never possessed. They
had not fallen from the communion of the Church; for to
the communion of its inner life they had never belonged.
Otherwise, the Apostle argues, what had happened could
not have happened. Naturally, we ask what is the
ground of this reasoning? It seems unreasonable to say
that " The words do not admit of any theoretical deduction "
(Westcott).[1] One is tempted to ask, Why? " The test of
experience," it is said, " is laid down as final." But a test,
to be applicable in any instance, must be one which is
applicable in every similar instance. It must bring individual cases under some common law. Although here
the Apostle lays down no general thesis, but pronounces
judgment in a particular case, that judgment must
proceed upon some theoretical ground. And if his
argument is, that the visible decline and fall of these
heretical teachers from their Christian standing were
sufficient proof that they had never been in vital fellowship
with Christ and His Church, one fails to see what force
there is in the reasoning, except on the assumption of the
indefectibility of all who truly belong to the Divine
society. In point of fact, this assumption is strictly

---

[1] In like manner, Lutheran commentators (Weiss, *e.g.*) are careful to explain
(as against Augustine and Calvin) that no doctrine of a *gratia inamissibilis* is
implied in the passage.

involved in St. John's doctrine of the Divine Begetting. If
he asserts that the "begotten of God" cannot sin "because
His seed abideth in him" (3^9), equally would he assert that,
for the same reason, the begotten of God cannot become
an antichrist, denying the Father and the Son (2^{22}). The
whole verse has its motive in the feeling that the emergence
of these false teachers from the bosom of the Church
demanded explanation. Some of the Apostle's readers
might be tempted on that account to give a readier
credence to their doctrine, since those who break forth
from within are always more apt to secure a following
than those who assail the Church from without. To others,
again, the fact that men could thus apparently fall away
from Christian faith and fellowship might occasion serious
perplexity and misgiving. St. John's words meet either
case. They supply an impressive warning against giving
ear to schismatic teachers; and they afford the needed
explanation of their falling away. But their chief purpose
is the latter. "Do not grieve that they went out from
us; let not this shake your confidence that none shall
pluck the Good Shepherd's sheep out of His hand." Nay,
the Apostle has a further word of reassurance for the
disquieted. The secession of the antichrists was wholly a
benefit. It was but their unmasking ; and this, again, was
only the fulfilment of the Divine purpose (ἵνα φανερωθῶσιν),
which is ever the purity and edification of the Church.

The Parousia.

The distinguishing feature of St. John's mental individuality is, as has been said, that he so instinctively leans
to the ideal and spiritual in his contemplation of life,
grasping what is of universal significance rather than dwelling upon historical movements and embodiments. Yet, as
has also been said, he is no mere idealist. To regard him
as one whose thought moves in a world of abstractions,

for whom the facts of Christianity are only symbols of absolute spiritual Truth, is a complete mistake. His true distinction as a thinker lies in the success with which he unites the two strains of thought, the ideal and the historical. This has been exemplified in his conception of Antichrist. Tacitly waving aside the lurid figure of the popular imagination, he grasps the essential truth that is expressed by the name and the idea of Antichrist, and finds its fulfilment in the heretical teaching which substituted for the Christ of the Gospel the fantastic product of Docetic speculations. Yet he does not rarefy Antichrist into a mere symbol. This birth of antichristian falsehood is to him the real advent of the Antichrist; and in it he reads the manifest token that the World's day has well-nigh run its appointed course. And it is necessary to bear in mind the existence of this twofold strain of thought in the Apostle, when we consider his representation of the events with which "the last hour" is to be brought to an end—the coming of Christ and the Day of Judgment. On the one hand, these are conceived by St. John, in a quite peculiar degree, as present spiritual realities; on the other hand, they are still firmly held as objective future events; and the reconciliation of these diverse, but not inconsistent, points of view is found in his conception of history as the manifestation to actual experience of what, in essence and principle, already exists.

This is the key to the Johannine doctrine of the Parousia.[1] That doctrine is primarily spiritual, not eschato-

---

[1] ἡ παρουσία. There are three words which in the N.T. specifically designate the Final Coming of Christ :

ἀποκάλυψις is specially Petrine (1 Pet. 1⁷ 1¹³ 4¹³, but also in 1 Cor. 1⁷ and 2 Thess. 1⁷).

ἐπιφάνεια is characteristic of the Pastoral Epistles (1 Tim. 6¹⁴, 2 Tim. 1¹⁰ 4¹· ⁸, Tit. 2¹³).

παρουσία is common to St. Matthew, the Pauline Epistles, Second Peter and the Epistle of St. James. Here only (1 John 2²⁸) is it found in St. John. In classical Greek the word means primarily "a being present." Aesch

logical. The substitution in the Fourth Gospel of the Supper Discourse (John 14–16) for the apocalyptic chapters in the Synoptics is, however we may explain it, profoundly significant. It is not a Christ coming on the clouds of heaven that is presented, but a Christ who has come and is ever coming to dwell in closest fellowship with His people. He departed as to His bodily presence only to come nearer and be with them always in the power of His Spirit. His disciples were to hear no more the voice of their Teacher addressing to them words of Eternal Life; but this was only that He might come again as the very Spirit of Truth, a well-spring of Light from within, giving them "an understanding" to know Him that is true. The direct influence of His visible example was to be taken away only that He might dwell in them and they in Him, in a community of inward life like that of the vine and its branches. Formerly Christ had come to "tabernacle" with men, henceforward He would come to take up His abode with them for ever. Formerly He had been still external to them, now He was to be the life of their lives— an inward source of light, moral inspiration, and strength. The complete, vital, and permanent union of Christ and His people, which had been prevented by the limitations of

---

Persæ, 169, ὄμμα γὰρ δόμων νομίζω δεσπότου παρουσίαν. It has also the kindred meaning of "arrival." Eur. *Alc.* 207, ἀλλ᾽ εἶμι καὶ τὴν σὴν ἀγγελῶ παρουσίαν. Thuc. i. 128, Βυζάντιον γὰρ ἑλὼν τῇ προτέρᾳ παρουσίᾳ. (The quotations are from Liddell and Scott.) The word has the same double sense in the N.T. 2 Cor. 7⁷ ἡ δὲ παρουσία τοῦ σώματος ἀσθενής : "His bodily presence is weak"; Phil. 2¹² ὡς ἐν τῇ παρουσίᾳ μου : "As in my presence." On the other hand, 1 Cor. 16¹⁷ and 2 Cor. 7⁶ ἐπὶ τῇ παρουσίᾳ Στεφανᾶ, ἐν τῇ παρουσίᾳ Τίτου : "The arrival (and presence) of Stephanas and Titus. It is interesting to notice also that in the papyri παρουσία is often used as a kind of technical term with reference to the "visit" of a king or other official. Thus accounts are extant announcing preparations ἐπὶ τὴν παρουσίαν τοῦ Χρυσίππου (see Milligan's *Thessalonians*, pp. 145, 146). These usages show how appropriate the word was to the Coming of Christ, for which His people are to be in watchful preparation. Here also it combines the senses of "arrival" and "presence." The Final Coming of Christ introduces a new mode of His Presence, and one which will last for ever.

a local and corporeal state of existence, would be achieved when for these there was substituted the direct access of spirit to spirit. It was expedient that He should go away in order thus to come again.

Yet St. John by no means discards the primitive New Testament belief in the Parousia as a historical fact of the future. With him it scarcely predominates over the whole scene as with St. Paul; but still it is the great mountain-peak at the end of the valley. It is so in the Fourth Gospel, " Every one that seeth the Son and believeth in Him hath eternal life "—has already experienced a spiritual resurrection from death into life; but Christ will also " raise him up at the last day" (John 6⁴⁰). If Christ's abiding-place (μονή) is in those that love Him and keep His word (John 14²³), there is also a Father's House in which there are many abiding-places (μοναί), whither He goes to prepare a place for them, and whence He will come again to receive them unto Himself; that where He is, there they may be also (John 14². ³). Still more is this emphasised in the Epistle: here the atmosphere is more pervasively eschatological than in the Gospel. If, since the writing of St. Paul's earlier Epistles, there has been an abatement in the general expectation of the speedy coming of Christ, that expectation, in the mind of the author of this Epistle at least, has been vigorously revived. So far from its being true that " The Church is firmly established as an institution in the world, and looks forward to a period of continued existence," ¹ the times are very evil; Antichrist has come. The command, " Love not the world," is sharpened by the assurance that the world is on the verge, aye, in the process of dissolution (παράγεται, 2¹⁷). The dread of being put to shame in the presence of the Lord at His impending Advent enforces the exhortation to " abide in Him " (2²⁸); and the hope of their being made partakers of His manifested

¹ *DB* iii. 679.

glory is the consummation of all that is implied in our being now the children of God ($3^{2, 3}$).

But these two strains of thought unite in a third—that this future crisis will only be the inevitable manifestation of the existing reality. The Parousia will no more than the Incarnation be the advent of a strange Presence in the world.[1] Expectant souls will behold its dawning,

> "Like some watcher of the skies
> When a new planet swims into his ken."

It will be, as on the Mount of Transfiguration, the out-shining of a latent glory; not the arrival of One Who is absent, but the self-revealing of One Who is present.

Such a manifestation may be conceived as effected simply by a change in the mode or medium of perception. There will be that change which we dimly signify (not fully comprehending what the words denote) when we say that faith will become sight. Christ and the things of the spiritual universe will become the objects of a more direct consciousness. Now, Faith and Sense are at variance. The things that are seen and temporal appeal to one set of faculties; things unseen and eternal to another. We believe, but we believe against appearances. Then Faith and Sense will coincide. All false and misleading appearances will vanish for ever, all that we now take on trust will then be evident, when, every obstructing veil removed, we stand with open face in the presence of the eternal realities. But all this, while it is implied, does not exhaust the significance of the Parousia, neither, indeed, is it the chief factor in the conception of it. The Parousia takes place, not only through an increased power or a different mode of perception in men, but primarily through a different mode of self-revelation on the part of Christ. If there is a

---

[1] ἡ ζωὴ ἐφανερώθη (1^2; cf. John $1^{5, 10}$); ἐὰν φανερωθῇ (2^{28} 3^2).

withdrawing of a veil from the human eye, there is also an unveiling of the Divine Face. As to the manner of Christ's appearing, the Epistle is silent, except for the simple, sublime, and satisfying words (satisfying because they pass all understanding), "We shall see Him as He is." As to its significance we are not left in doubt. It is a historical event; occurring once for all; affecting simultaneously all mankind; the consummation of all Divine purpose that has governed human existence; the final crisis in the history of the Church, of the World, and of every man.

The Day of Judgment.

The Parousia is the coming of Christ to Judgment. In St. John's conception of judgment we must recognise the same dual tendency of thought that has already been remarked upon. In distinction from other New Testament writers, St. John regards judgment as essentially a present fact of life. He sees Christ always and of necessity judging men—or, rather, compelling men to judge themselves. For judgment He is come into the world (John 9³⁹) —it is the inevitable issue of His coming. By their attitude towards Christ men involuntarily but inevitably classify themselves, reveal what spirit they are of, automatically register themselves as being, or as not being, " of the Truth " (John 18³⁷). " He that believeth not is judged already, because he hath not believed in the name of the only-begotten Son of God" (John 3¹⁸). Judgment is not the assigning of a character to men from without; it is the revelation of character from within. Judgment is classification, a sifting of the wheat from the chaff.¹ And this

---

¹ This is the original meaning of κρίσις :

ὅτε τε ξανθὴ Δημήτηρ
Κρίνῃ ἐπειγομένων ἀνέμων καρπόν τε καὶ ἄχνας.

Iliad, v. 500–1.

is not future but present; for, in its essence, it is self-revelation, self-classification, self-separation. And nowhere is this thought of judgment so exhaustively developed and applied as in our Epistle. Though the word is not used, the writer from first to last does almost nothing else than declare and apply the three great tests,—Righteousness, Love, Belief,—in the presence of which men infallibly reveal themselves as being " of God " or " of the world," as " knowing God " or " knowing not God," as " of the truth " or as " liars." Yet, none the less, the Apostle indubitably looks forward to a future " Day of Judgment " (4^{17}). And I cannot agree with the criticism that this is simply an unconscious concession to orthodoxy, and that it is impossible to reconcile the idea of a future judgment, adopted from the current theology, with what we must regard as the distinctive Johannine view.[1] For here again the underlying thought is that judgment to come will be only the full manifestation of the judgment that now is, that is to say, of the principles by whose operation men are in reality approved or condemned already. Such manifestation is obviously necessary. It is true that men are immediately judged, sifted out, and classified by their relation to Christ, yet this, as spiritual fact, is hidden from the general sense of mankind; and though it will be progressively vindicated in the world by the work of the Spirit in convicting the world of sin " because they believe not on Me," yet plainly, as regards the unconvicted, the vindication must be consummated hereafter. It is true that on St. John's own presuppositions the vindication cannot even then be complete. Spiritual truth cannot be received by unspiritual men, here or hereafter; not even a Day of Judgment can effect in those who are unenlightened by the Spirit of Truth a recognition of the essential sin and shame of rejecting Christ. But I can find no shadow of

[1] Scott's *Fourth Gospel*, p. 216.

reason for asserting that St. John's view of Judgment, as in principle a present fact of life, is inherently irreconcilable with the common doctrine of the New Testament, that the consciousness of those who now reject Christ will hereafter contain a very awful testimony of God's reprobation.

The present judgment and classification of men by their relation to Christ is, moreover, a fact that is by no means fully realised even by the faith of Christians. Now are we the children of God; but it is not yet made manifest what we shall be. Only the intenser realisation of what Christ is can bring the fuller manifestation, even to ourselves, of what *we* are. In this glad sense the Parousia must be a Day of Judgment to the children of God. The Christian's faith, when he sees Christ as He is, will then appear to himself a far grander thing than it does now. What looks mean and meagre in the semi-darkness of this life will shine forth like the sun at the rising of the Sun. And, further, it must be said that the whole Epistle looks forward, clearly and inevitably, to a Judgment to come. Its practical aim is preparation for Judgment by self-judgment. It is an Epistle of tests—an Epistle that wages war against self-deception of every kind. There must be a Day when all self-deception shall cease, and when all reality shall be manifested. Without this certainty the whole tenor and purpose of the Epistle would be stultified.

The Day of Salvation.

Lastly, Christ's coming is a coming to salvation. We close our study of the eschatology of the Epistle with the great passage on the consummation of the Christian life: "Behold, what manner of love the Father hath bestowed upon us, that we should be called children of God: and such we are. For this cause the world doth not recognise us, because it did not recognise Him. Beloved, now are we children of God, and it is not yet made manifest what we shall be. We know that if He shall be manifested, we shall be like Him; for we shall see Him as He is" ($3^{1.\ 2}$).[1] In the preceding verse (2^{29}) the Apostle begins the second chief division of the Epistle—that in which the Christian life is considered as the life of Divine sonship. And this life is characterised, first of all, by Righteousness (2^{29}–3^{10}). But the orderly development of this theme is immediately arrested by the contemplation of its grandeur. That such a title should be ours because the full Divine reality it signifies is ours—that we should be called, and that we verily are, the children[2] of God—what manner of love![3] But having asserted this amazing truth, the Apostle, with the quick imagination of sympathy, apprehends a possible perplexity in his readers' minds: "If we are children of God in title and in fact, why does no ray of glory shine upon us? Why is it that, instead of winning the recognition and homage of the world, we are the objects of its contempt?" The answer is that it is precisely because we are the children of God. The world loves its own (John 15^{19}); no glimpse of the essential glory of the spiritual visits its darkened mind. And the supreme proof of this is, that it was blind to the glory of the only-begotten Son Himself (cf. 1 Cor. 1^{23} 2^8, 2 Cor. 4^4; contrariwise, John 1^{14}). If He Who was the Light of the world was so little known by the world; if He Who was ineffable Love was so little loved; if He Who was the

---

[1] For discussion of the exegetical complexities of these verses and of the variety of proposed interpretations, see Notes, *in loc.* In the exposition here given I assume, for the most part without discussion, the exegesis that most commends itself to me.

[2] "Children of God" (τέκνα θεοῦ). *v. supra*, pp. 194–5, and Notes, *in loc.*

[3] "What manner of love," ποταπὴν ἀγάπην. ποταπός (classically, ποδαπός) means originally "from what country" (in Latin, *cujas*). Thus it comes to signify "mysterious," "amazing," "unaccountable." The N.T. parallels are few but singularly suggestive. Matt. 8^{27} "What manner of man is this?" Luke 1^{29} "What manner of salutation this might be"; 2 Pet. 3^{11} "What manner of persons we ought to be."

Prince of Life received so scanty homage; if the world could see no brightness of the Father's glory irradiating the humble exterior of the Son of Man—what wonder that it does not recognise, in us, the children of God? This leads on to the magnificent assurance of the following verse: "Beloved" (the Apostle's heart is moved with solicitude by the thought of the consolation needed, with triumph by the thought of that he is about to give), "now are we children of God, and it is not yet made manifest what we shall be. We know that if He shall be manifested, we shall be like Him; because we shall see Him as He is." Here, once more, the peculiarly Johannine idea of "manifestation" is strikingly employed. "What we shall be" will be essentially what we now are—children of God. No new element will be added to the regenerate nature. All is there that ever will be there. As every faculty and every feature of the full-grown man are possessed by the new-born child, so the Image of God's Son is already formed in every one that is "begotten of God"—is there in embryo, in organic completeness, awaiting its full development. But the epoch of full development is not now. It is, according to St. John, at the Parousia. When Christ—the Christ Who already is in the world—shall be manifested, then also the children of God, who are in the world, will be manifested as being what they are. They will not be invested with a glory from without so much as manifested from within. They also will have come to *their* Mount of Transfiguration; inward reality will break forth in a visible splendour that will, in some sense and degree, manifest even to the world the essential glory of their nature.

This is no vague hope or questionable hypothesis. It is triumphant certainty: "*We know* [1] that we shall

---

[1] "We know" (οἴδαμεν) (absolute knowledge). Granted the premise, "We shall see Him as He is," the consequence, "We shall be like Him," is self-evident. See special note on γινώσκειν and εἰδέναι.

be like Him; because we shall see Him as He is."
The principle implied is certain and universal.   Vision
becomes assimilation.   We transfer to and fix upon our
own souls the beauty and the goodness on which we
gaze.   Such is the psychological principle of the Christian's
sanctification in this life.   Beholding with unveiled face
the glory of the Lord, we are transformed into the same
image from glory to glory (2 Cor. 3[18], Ex. 34[29]).   And
when He is manifested, " we shall behold Him as He is."
The words suggest what is beyond full comprehension.
We know whom we shall behold—Him,[1]—not Deity in
its essence, not the Invisible Father, not another and
unfamiliar Christ, a new out-shining of the Father's glory
—but *Jesus* Christ.

But we shall see Him *as He is*.   Is not the Christ, then,
who " tabernacled among us," Christ " as He is " ?   And
when we behold His glory, " the glory as of the Only-
Begotten of the Father, full of grace and truth," do we not

---

[1] " We shall be like Him ; because we shall see Him as He is " (ὅμοιοι αὐτῷ
ἐσόμεθα, ὅτι ὀψόμεθα αὐτὸν καθώς ἐστιν).   The most obvious antecedent to αὐτῷ
and αὐτόν is θεοῦ in the previous sentence.   " Now are we the children of God,
(and then) we shall be like Him " (Bengel, Ebrard, Huther ; " God in Christ,"
Westcott).   Nevertheless, this is untenable.   " It may be doubted," says
Westcott, " whether it could be said of the Father that men shall see Him *as
He is*."   But, surely, this may not be doubted.   Such beholding of the Father
is not only never suggested in the N.T. ; it is assumed to be impossible.   Deity
in its essence becomes the object of Faith only through its manifestations
(Rom. 1[20], John 1[18]) ; to direct perception it is inaccessible (φῶς οἰκῶν ἀπρόσιτον,
1 Tim. 6[16]).   This is implied in the whole N.T. conception of Christ as the
Revealer of the Father, in the Johannine doctrine of the Logos, in the Pauline
doctrine of Christ as the εἰκὼν τοῦ θεοῦ τοῦ ἀοράτου (Col. 1[15]), in the ἀπαύγασμα
τῆς δόξης καὶ χαρακτὴρ τῆς ὑποστάσεως αὐτοῦ of Heb. 1[3], in the words, " He that
hath seen Me hath seen the Father " (John 14[9], cf. 17[24]), implying that no other
perfect vision of the Father is possible to men than that which is given in Christ.
Similarly with ὅμοιοι αὐτῷ ἐσόμεθα.   A veritable likeness to the Father is asserted
of all who have the Spirit of His Son.   They are made θείας κοινωνοὶ φύσεως
(2 Pet. 1[4]).   They are to be " imitators of God, as dear children " (Eph. 5[1]).
But this likeness is ethical only ; and here not only ethical, but visible manifested
likeness is contemplated.   Always in the N.T. it is the attainment of such
likeness to Christ, never to God, that stands as the splendid goal of Christian
hope (John 17[22], Rom. 8[29], 1 Cor. 15[47-49], Phil. 3[21], Col. 3[4]).

behold Him as He is? Assuredly. In the most essential
element of the case there can be no change in what is
beheld or in the kind of beholding. The glory of the
Divine is spiritual—the glory of goodness, of love beyond
measure, and of purity without stain. And spiritual things
can never be otherwise than spiritually discerned. Yet,
obviously, this is not the whole thought of the passage.
The vision of the future is, in some fashion, corporeal as
well as spiritual. In it Sense and Faith will co-operate.
It will then have ceased to be expedient that Christ should
go away in order that the Spirit of Truth may come. We
shall possess in the same experience His manifested
presence and the inward ministry of the Spirit. Perception,
now dim and wavering, will be intense and vivid. Vision
will be freed from all obscurations of sin. It will be as
when sunshine draws forth the glow of colour in a landscape
that has been lying under a pall of cloud.

"We shall truly behold the True." And, seeing Him
as He is, "we shall be like Him." There will be sudden
development. It will be like passing at a stride from sub-
arctic regions to the tropics. Under the direct rays of the
Sun of Righteousness "buds of earth" will become "flowers
of Heaven." All that is within the children of God will
answer to Christ's call; every half-developed lineament of
holy character will shine out in the light of His countenance; the whole Christ-likeness latent in them will come
forth, vivid and glorious. Vision will beget likeness, and
likeness, again, give clearness to vision, their endless inter-
action securing endless progress towards the inexhaustible
fulness of Christ.

And as the vision is in some sense corporeal as well as
spiritual, so also is the assimilation (Phil. 3²¹). Even of
this body of flesh and blood the soul is, in wonderful
measure, the sculptor. Faces are made pure by purity of
heart. Strength and nobility sit upon the countenance,

when high resolve and heroic endeavour fill the mind. There is a calmness of feature which is an index to peace in the soul; a dignity and beauty which patient suffering alone gives; and when some strong tide of the spirit is sweeping through a man's heart, it alters the fashion of his countenance, causes his very form and figure to dilate, and makes the weakest like an angel of God. These facts, so far as they go, are a prophecy, and, indeed, a beginning of that final transfiguration by which Christ " shall fashion the body of our humiliation into the likeness of the body of His glory." The very idea of the Spiritual Body is that it perfectly represents the character to which it belongs. As the material body is strong or weak, comely or uncomely, according to the animal vitality, so is the spiritual body according to the spiritual vitality that animates it. The outward man will take the mould of the inward man, and will share with it its perfected likeness to the glorified manhood of Jesus Christ.

Such is the furthest view opened to our hope by the eschatology of the Epistle, and it is that which, of all others, has proved most entrancing to the imagination and stimulating to the aspiration of the children of God. " We know that, if He shall be manifested, we shall be like Him; for we shall see Him as He is."

And though it may appear as being, just where it is introduced, a digression from the main line of thought,—a magnificent development of a side issue,—this is not really so. It is a certainty that is contained in the Christian's consciousness of indissoluble union with Christ. And from the contemplation of that union in its perfect future manifestation, the Apostle brings us back by an inevitable transition to the test of its present reality: " Every one that hath this hope in Him purifieth himself, even as He is pure."

NOTE ON ANTICHRIST.

It is unnecessary for the interpretation of the Epistle to enter upon all the complexities of the Antichrist problem. The leading points, however, may be briefly stated. The name Antichrist is not older than the N.T., but the idea is pre-Christian. Recent investigation (especially by Bousset) has all gone to show how composite and how gradually developed the legend of Antichrist was. Gunkel (*Schöpfung und Chaos*) finds its ultimate origin in the primitive and widely diffused dragon-myth, which, he maintains, reached and impregnated Hebrew soil, in the form of the Babylonian Epos of the monster Tiâmat, who was overcome by the Creator (Marduk), but who, it was believed, would again rise in revolt, only to be finally destroyed (for criticism of this theory, however, see Kautzsch's article, "Religion of Israel," in *DB*, Extra Vol. p. 670). But even if it be allowed that this myth is alluded to in sundry passages of O.T. poetry, and has supplied certain materials to the imagery of the Apocalypse, there is nothing to lead us to suppose that it had any important part in familiarising the Jewish mind with the idea of an arch-enemy of God, or in the actual development of the idea. There is similarity, if not historical connection, between the later conception of Antichrist and Ezekiel's prophecy of a tremendous onslaught, led by Gog the prince of the land of Magog, against the resettled land of Israel, that is to say, after the dawn of the Messianic Age (cf. Ezek. 38–39 and Rev. 20[7] sqq.). But it is in the apocalyptic parts of the Book of Daniel that the lineaments of the future Antichrist are clearly discernible, and especially in the idealised representations of Antiochus Epiphanes (Dan. 7–9; 11; 12). It is probable that these predictions, while inspired by fear and hatred of Antiochus, and in part applicable to him, point also to some ideal impersonation of evil. It is at least clear that they furnish material which was worked up in the subsequent development of the Eschatological Antichrist. In later Jewish Apocalyptic this development is carried forward (Sibylline Oracles, Fourth Ezra, Apocalypse of Baruch, Ascension of Isaiah, Book of Jubilees. For references, *v. DB* iii. 227). But in the interval between the Old and the New Testament, the Jewish belief in Antichrist has been strangely influenced by the Beliar myths (Bousset, *Der Antichrist*, pp. 99 sqq.). The Antichrist is no longer of human origin, but becomes dæmonic. Beliar is a wicked angel, ruler of the empire of the air, who has become prince of this world ("Berial angelus magnus, rex huius mundi . . . descendet e firmamento suo . . . et venient cum eo omnes potestates huius mundi," Asc. Isa. 4[2]. For other references, *v.* Bousset, and Milligan's *Thessalonians*, pp. 161, 162). Bousset identifies the Beliar of 2 Cor. 6[15] with Antichrist. But if this identification is right, Beliar cannot have been to St. Paul angel or demon; for with him Antichrist is distinctly ὁ ἄνθρωπος τῆς ἀνομίας. The belief, as current in the first century A.D., is that Antichrist would not appear before the Fall of Rome; that he would then appear among the Jews, proclaim himself as God, and claim to be worshipped in the Temple at Jerusalem ; that Elijah would appear, and be slain by him ; that he would be born of the tribe of Dan (cf. Gen. 49^{17}, Deut. 33^{22}, Jer. 8^{16}. The Apocalypse omits Dan from the list of the Tribes) ; that his reign would last three and a half years ; that the faithful Jews, or all the Church, would flee into the wilderness, whither Antichrist would pursue them ; that he would then be slain by the Lord with the Breath of His mouth (Isa. 11^4).[1]

[1] See Brooke's very full additional note on Antichrist, pp. 69-79.

CHAPTER XVII.

ITS RELATION TO THE FOURTH GOSPEL.

THE virtually unanimous verdict of tradition assigns the authorship both of this Epistle and of the Fourth Gospel to the Apostle John; and, until the end of the sixteenth century, this opinion was held as unquestionable.[1] Of modern scholars, the first to challenge it was Joseph Scaliger (1540–1609), who rejected the entire trio of Johannine Epistles as unapostolic; and, in later times, a dual authorship of the Gospel and the First Epistle has been asserted by Baur, Hilgenfeld, H. J. Holtzmann, Pfleiderer, von Soden, and others;[2] although, on this particular point, other adherents of the critical school, like Jülicher, Wrede, and Wernle, accept the traditional view. Some of the reasons advanced for a different authorship are sufficiently arbitrary, and, indeed, mutually contradictory. Baur pronounces the Epistle a weak imitation of the Gospel, because of its poverty of thought, its tautology, and its lack of logical energy; by Hilgenfeld, on the contrary, it is esteemed as one of the most beautiful of New Testament writings, and, because of its rich and original spontaneity, is regarded as prior in time to the Gospel; and while Baur rejects its apostolic authorship because he finds the trail of Montanism over it, Hilgenfeld, on the other hand, finds it tainted with Gnosticism. Yet the arguments for

---

[1] *v. supra*, pp. 39, 40.

[2] Among English writers, Mr. Ernest Scott ranges himself on the same side (*Fourth Gospel*, p. 94). Hilgenfeld, in his *Einleitung* (1875), withdrew from it.

the dual authorship, as set forth briefly by Pfleiderer and, with exhaustive care and temperate candour, by H. J. Holtzmann, are by no means negligible.

Prima facie, the case for identity of authorship is over-whelmingly strong. On internal grounds, it would appear much more feasible to assign any two of Shakespeare's plays to different authors, than the Gospel and the First Epistle of " St. John." They are equally saturated with that spiritual and theological atmosphere, they are equally characterised by that type of thought, which we call Johannine, and which presents an interpretation of Christianity not less original and distinctive than Paulinism. In both we find the same fundamental positions regarding the Divine Nature; Eternal Life; the Person of Christ; the antecedents and consequents, metaphysical and ethical, of the Incarnation; the affinity and non-affinity of men with the Divine; Regeneration and the children of God; the mutual indwelling of God and man; the work of the Holy Spirit; the Christian Life as tested by Belief, Obedience, and the supreme duty of Love. In both, the writer views almost every subject with an eye that steadfastly beholds radical antagonisms, but is blind to approximations. Each conception has its fundamental antithesis:—Light, Darkness; Life, Death; Love, Hate; Truth, Falsehood; the Father, the World; God, the Devil. There is no shading, no gradation, in the picture. Affinities in manner and in substance of thought are not more remarkable than those in diction and style. The vocabulary in each is of the same simplicity and restricted [1] range, and is, to a surprising extent, identical in material. There is in both the same strongly Hebraistic style of composition, the same development of ideas by parallelism or antithesis;

---

[1] The paucity of ἅπαξ λεγόμενα in the Epistle is noticeable. While First Peter and James furnish about sixty, our Epistle has but four, ἀγγελία, ἱλασμός, νίκη, χρῖσμα (Holtzmann, *J. P. T.*, 1882, p. 131).

the same emphatic repetition of key-words like "begotten of God," "abiding," "keeping His commandments"; the same monotonous simplicity of syntax, with avoidance of relative clauses and a singular parsimony in the use of connecting particles; the same lack of dialectical resource; the same method of implying causal relation by mere juxtaposition of ideas; the same apparently tautological habit of resuming consideration of a subject from a slightly different point of view. In short, it seems impossible to conceive of two independent literary productions having a more intimate affinity. The relation between them is, in every way, closer than that between the Third Gospel and the Acts of the Apostles, where the identity of authorship is now generally admitted, the only case of approximation to it being that of the Epistles to the Ephesians and the Colossians.[1]

For these statements some evidence must be furnished in detail.[2] And I shall cite, in the first place, the coincidences of verbal expression; and, to begin with, those that are *peculiar* to the Gospel and the Epistle.

EPISTLE	GOSPEL.
ὁ λόγος, 1^1.	$1^{1.\ 14}$.
χαρὰ πεπληρωμένη, 1^4.	3^{29} 15^{11} 16^{24} 17^{13}.
ἑωράκαμεν καὶ μαρτυροῦμεν, 1^2.	1^{34} $3^{11.\ 32}$ 19^{35}.
τεθεάμεθα καὶ μαρτυροῦμεν, 4^{14}.	1^{32}.
σκοτία (metaphorically), 1^5 etc. (five times).	1^5 etc. (six times).
ποιεῖν τὴν ἀλήθειαν, 1^6.	3^{21}.
ἁμαρτίαν ἔχειν, 1^8.	9^{41} $15^{22.\ 24}$ 19^{11}.
ἀλήθειαν εἶναι ἐν, 1^8 2^4.	8^{44}.
λόγον εἶναι (μένειν) ἐν, 1^{10} 2^{14}.	5^{38}.
παράκλητος, 2^1.	14^{16} etc.
τηρεῖν τὸν λόγον, 2^5.	$8^{51.\ 52.\ 55}$ 14^{23} 15^{20} 17^{16}.

---

[1] Holtzmann, *J. P. T.*, 1882, pp. 1, 134.

[2] In the preparation of this and the following lists I have, of course, made use of the results brought out by Holtzmann in the series of articles referred to. But I have investigated the whole matter independently, and the lists of coincidences and divergences here given are by no means a reproduction of his.

EPISTLE.	GOSPEL.
μένειν ἐν θεῷ, Χριστῷ, τῷ λόγῳ, τῇ ἀγάπῃ, τῷ φωτί, τῇ σκοτίᾳ, τῷ θανάτῳ, 2⁶.¹⁰.²⁷.²⁸ 3⁶.¹⁴.²⁴ 4¹³.¹⁶.	6⁵⁶ 8³¹ 12⁴⁶ 15⁴.⁵.⁶.⁷.⁹.¹⁰.
ἐντολὴ καινή, 2⁷.⁸.	13³⁴.
τὸ φῶς τὸ ἀληθινόν, 2⁸.	1⁹.
ποῦ ὑπάγει, 2¹¹.	8¹⁴.²¹ (ὅπου) 12³⁵ 13³³.³⁶ 14⁴.⁵ 16⁵.
τυφλοῦν τοὺς ὀφθαλμούς, 2¹¹.	12⁴⁰.
τεκνία, 2¹ etc.	13³³.
μένειν εἰς τὸν αἰῶνα, 2¹⁷.	8³⁵ 12³⁴.
παιδία, 2¹⁴.¹⁸.	21⁵.
ἵνα (=ὥστε or ὅτι), *passim*.	*passim*.
ἀλλ' ἵνα (elliptical), 2¹⁹.	1⁸ 9³ 13¹⁸ 15²⁵.
χρείαν ἔχειν ἵνα, 2²⁷.	2²⁵ 16³⁰.
γεγεννῆσθαι ἐκ τοῦ θεοῦ, 2²⁹ etc.	1¹³ etc.
ὁ κόσμος οὐκ ἔγνω αὐτόν, 3¹.	1¹⁰ 17²⁵.
ὅμοιος εἶναί τινι, 3².	8⁵⁵ 9⁹.
ἁγνίζει ἑαυτόν, 3³.	11⁵⁵.
ποιεῖν τὴν ἁμαρτίαν, 3⁴ etc.	8³⁴.
αἴρειν τὰς ἁμαρτίας, 3⁵.	1²⁹.
ἐκ τοῦ πονηροῦ (διαβόλου) εἶναι, 3⁸.¹².	8⁴⁴.
ἔργα τοῦ διαβόλου, 3⁸.	8⁴¹.
τέκνα τοῦ διαβόλου, 3¹⁰.	8⁴⁴ (ἐκ τοῦ διαβόλου . . . τοῦ πατρὸς ὑμῶν).
μισεῖ ὑμᾶς ὁ κόσμος, 3¹³.	15¹⁸.¹⁹.
μεταβαίνειν ἐκ τοῦ θανάτου εἰς τὴν ζωήν, 3¹⁴.	5²⁴.
ἀνθρωποκτόνος, 3¹⁵.	8⁴⁴.
ἐκεῖνος (=Christ), 3¹⁶ etc.	19³⁵. ?
τὴν ψυχὴν τιθέναι, 3¹⁶.	10¹¹.¹⁵.¹⁷ 13³⁷.³⁸ 15¹³.
ἡ ἀγάπη, ζωὴ αἰώνιος, μένει ἐν, 3¹⁵.¹⁷.	5⁴² ; cf. 15¹¹.
ἐκ τῆς ἀληθείας εἶναι, 3¹⁹.	18³⁷.
μείζων (of God), 3²⁰ 4⁴.	10²⁹ 14²⁸.
τὰ ἀρεστά, 3²².	8²⁹.
ἐντολὴν διδόναι, 3²³.	11⁵⁷ 12⁴⁹ 13³⁴.
ἀκούειν (to hear believingly), 4⁵.⁶.	5²⁴ 6⁶⁰ 18³⁷.
ἀγάπην ἔχειν ἐν, 4⁹.¹⁶.	13³⁵ (but cf. 2 Cor. 8⁷).
ζῆν διά (c. gen.), 4⁹.	6⁵⁷ (c. acc.).
θεὸν οὐδεὶς πώποτε τεθέαται, 4¹².	1¹⁸ (ἑώρακεν).
ἐγνώκαμεν καὶ πεπιστεύκαμεν, 4¹⁶.	6⁶⁹ (in reverse order).
σωτὴρ τοῦ κόσμου, 4¹⁴.	4⁴².
δι' ὕδατος καὶ αἵματος, 5⁶.	19³⁴.
τὸ πνεῦμά ἐστιν τὸ μαρτυροῦν, 5⁶.	15²⁶.
νικᾶν τὸν κόσμον, 5⁵.	16³³.
εἰς τὸ ἕν, 5⁸.	11⁵² 17²³ (εἰς ἕν).
μαρτυρίαν λαμβάνειν, 5⁹.	3¹¹.³².³³ 5³⁴.

EPISTLE.	GOSPEL.
ζωὴν διδόναι, 5¹¹.	6³³ 17².
ἔχειν τὴν ζωήν (in present sense), 5¹².¹⁸.	3³⁶ etc.
πιστεύειν εἰς τὸ ὄνομα, 5¹³.	1¹² etc.
πρὸς θάνατον, 5¹⁶.	11⁴.
ἐρωτᾶν (of prayer to God), 5¹⁶.	14¹⁶ 17⁹.
ἥκειν (of Christ's Advent), 5²⁰.	8⁴².
πᾶς ὁ or πᾶν τό, c. part., 2²⁹ etc. (fifteen times).	3⁸ etc. (thirteen times).
ἐν τούτῳ γινώσκειν, 2³ etc. (eight times).	13³⁵.

A scrutiny of the foregoing table will show that none of the coincidences noted can be reckoned accidental.

I give next a list of verbal coincidences *not peculiar* to the Gospel and Epistle, yet characteristic.

EPISTLE.	GOSPEL.
ἀρχή (=past eternity), 1¹ 2¹³.¹⁴.	1¹·² (elsewhere only, 2 Thess. 2¹³).
ζωή (the Divine Eternal Life), 1¹ etc.	1⁴ etc.
φανεροῦσθαι, 1² etc. (nine times).	1³¹ etc. (nine times).
μαρτυρεῖν, 1² etc. (six times).	1⁷ etc. (thirty-three times. Once only in Matt., once in Luke, not at all in Mark).
ἀπαγγέλλειν, 1²·³.	4⁵¹ 16²⁵ 20¹⁸.
ἀναγγέλλειν, 1⁵.	4²⁵ etc. (six times).
φῶς (metaph.), 1⁵ etc. (six times).	1⁴ etc. (twenty times).
περιπατεῖν (metaph.) 1⁶ etc. (five times).	8¹² 12³⁵.
αἷμα Ἰησοῦ, 1⁷.	6⁵³·⁵⁴·⁵⁵·⁵⁶.
πλανᾶν, 1⁸ 2²⁶ 3⁷.	7¹² (rare, except in Apoc.).
δίκαιος (of God), 1⁹ 2²⁹.	17²⁵.
ἀφιέναι ἁμαρτίας, 1⁹ 2¹².	20²³.
ἀδικία, 1⁹ 5¹⁷.	7¹⁸.
ψεύστης, 1¹⁰ etc. (five times).	8⁴⁴·⁴⁵ (3 times elsewhere in N.T.).
ψεῦδος, 2²¹.	8⁴⁴.
γινώσκειν (God, Christ, or Spirit), 2⁴ etc. (eight times).	1¹⁰ etc. (ten times).
τηρεῖν τὰς ἐντολάς, 2³ 3²⁴ 5².³.	14¹⁵ 15¹⁰.
ἀληθῶς, 2⁵.	1⁴⁸ etc. (nine times ; only nine times elsewhere in N.T.).
ἀληθινός, 2⁸ 5²⁰.	1⁹ etc. (nine times ; Apoc. ten times ; elsewhere, five times).

EPISTLE.	GOSPEL.
ὀφείλειν, 2⁶ 3¹⁶ 4¹¹.	13¹⁴ 19⁷.
φαίνειν, 2⁸.	1⁵ 5³⁵ (three times in Apoc., elsewhere once only).
ἕως ἄρτι, 2⁹.	2¹⁰ 5¹⁷ 16²⁴.
ὁ πονηρός, 2¹³.	17¹⁵.
κόσμος, 2¹⁵ etc.	*passim.*
εἶναι ἐκ, 2¹⁶ etc.	1¹³ etc.
ἐπιθυμία, 2¹⁶·¹⁷.	8⁴⁴.
σάρξ (in evil sense), 2¹⁶.	8¹⁵.
σάρξ (without evil sense), 4².	1¹⁴.
ποιεῖν τὸ θέλημα, 2¹⁷.	4³⁴ 6³⁸ 7¹⁷ 9³¹.
ὁ ἅγιος, 2²⁰.	6⁶⁹.
ὁμολογεῖν Ἰησοῦν, 4²·³.	9²² (elsewhere, Rom. 10⁹).
τέκνα θεοῦ, 3¹·²·¹⁰ 5².	1¹² 11⁵².
πᾶς (πᾶν) ... οὐ (μή), 2¹⁷·²¹ 3¹⁵.	3¹⁵·¹⁶ 6³⁹ 12⁴⁶.
λύειν (=destroy), 3⁸.	2¹⁹ (elsewhere only, 2 Pet. 3¹⁰·¹¹·¹²).
οὐ δύναται (of moral impossibility), 3⁹.	7⁷ 8⁴³ 12³⁹ 14¹⁷.
ἀδελφός (=Christian brother), 3¹⁰ etc.	21²³.
ἀγαπᾶν ἀλλήλους, 3¹¹ etc.	13³⁴ etc.
ὃ ἐὰν αἰτεῖσθαι, 3²².	15⁷ (ὃ ἐὰν θέλητε, αἰτήσεσθε).
πνεῦμα διδόναι, 3²⁴ 4¹³.	3³⁴.
πνεῦμα τῆς ἀληθείας, 4⁶.	14¹⁷ etc.
μονογενὴς υἱός, 4⁹.	3¹⁶ etc.
ἀποστέλλειν (of mission of Christ), 4⁹·¹⁰·¹⁴.	3¹⁷·³⁴ 5³⁶ etc
ἔξω βάλλειν, 4¹⁸.	15⁶.
ἐντολὴν ἵνα, 4²¹.	11⁵⁷ 13³⁴ 15¹².
ἔρχεσθαι (of Messiah), 5⁶.	3³¹ 6¹⁴ 11²⁷.
ἔχειν τὴν μαρτυρίαν, 5¹⁰.	5³⁶ (elsewhere only in Apoc.).
αἰτεῖν, 3²² 5¹⁵·¹⁶.	15¹⁶ etc.
αἰτεῖσθαι, 5¹⁵.	15⁷ 16²⁶.
ἀκούειν (of answer to prayer), 5¹⁵.	9³¹.
ἅπτεσθαι, 5²¹.	12²⁵ 17¹².

Again, it may be asserted of these coincidences that none is insignificant.

Next, I subjoin a list of passages in which there is coincidence in thought, though not in words. Since to quote the passages in full would occupy too much space, only the references are given.

EPISTLE.	GOSPEL.	EPISTLE.	GOSPEL.
1^1.	1^1.	3^{23a}.	6^{29}.
1^{1-3}.	1^{14}.	4^6.	8^{47}.
2^2.	$11^{51.\,52}$	4^9.	3^{16}.
$2^5\ 3^{24}\ 5^3$.	$14^{15}\ 14^{21-24}$	4^{11}.	15^{12}.
	15^{10}.	4^{12}.	$1^{18}\ 5^{37}\ 6^{46}$.
2^6.	13^{15}.	4^{14}.	$3^{17}\ 4^{42}$.
2^{10}.	$11^{9.\,10}$.	5^1.	$1^{12.\,13}$.
2^{11}.	12^{35}.	5^4.	16^{33}.
2^{23}.	15^{23}.	5^9.	$5^{32}\ 8^{17.\,18}$.
2^{27}.	14^{26}.	5^{12a}.	$3^{15.\,36}$.
3^2.	17^{24}.	5^{12b}.	3^{36}.
3^5.	8^{46}.	5^{13}.	20^{31}.
3^{11}.	15^{12}.	5^{14}.	$14^{13.\,14}\ 16^{23}$.
3^{16}.	$15^{12.\,13}$.	5^{20}.	$17^{3.\,6}$.
3^{22}.	$15^{7.\,16}\ 16^{23}$.		

From the facts so far adduced, either of two conclusions is inevitable—that the Gospel and the Epistle are from the same pen, or that the one or the other of them is the composition of a writer whose mind was so saturated with the work of his predecessor that he unconsciously reproduces its thoughts and its phraseology, even to the minutest mannerisms. The former is the natural hypothesis. Strong evidence will be required to set it aside in favour of the latter. We shall now consider to what extent this is forthcoming; and first in respect of style and vocabulary.

The identity of vocabulary being so remarkable as we have seen it to be, it is surprising to discover how numerous and not unimportant the divergences are.

There is an observable difference in the choice and use of particles. δέ is found 212 times in the Gospel, only 9 times in the Epistle; μέν is found 8 times, οὖν nearly 200 times, τε thrice, in the Gospel, while there is no occurrence of any of them in the Epistle. γάρ is very frequent in the Gospel, but occurs only thrice in the Epistle, ὅτι being often used where γάρ might have been expected. Yet these discrepancies are not so hostile to unity of authorship as they seem. In the case of οὖν, the discrepancy is only apparent, is rather, indeed, a point of real similarity; for, in the Gospel, it is used only in narrative, no occurrence of it being found, *e.g.*, in chapters 14–16. The facts brought out regarding μέν, δέ, and γάρ, in so far as they are not accounted for by the absence of dialogue and narrative in the Epistle, point to the larger fact, that its style is more didactic and aphoristic than that of the Gospel.

The construction of the verbs ἀκούειν, αἰτεῖν, λαμβάνειν, with ἀπό instead of παρά (ἀκούειν παρά, John 1⁴¹; αἰτεῖν παρά, 4⁹; λαμβάνειν παρά, 5³⁴ etc.), is rather inexplicable, although in the Gospel itself there is a similar vacillation between παρά and ἀπό (ἀπὸ θεοῦ ἔρχεσθαι, 3² 13³ 16³⁰; παρὰ τοῦ θεοῦ ἔρχεσθαι, ἐκπορεύεσθαι, 16²⁷ 15²⁶ 17⁸). And, in a cumulative argument, a certain weight must be attached to these lexical differences, minute as they are.

The following words and phrases [1] in the Epistle are foreign to the Gospel: λόγος τῆς ζωῆς (1¹); κοινωνία (1³·⁶·⁷); * ἀγγελία (1⁵ 3¹¹); ἀκούειν ἀπό (1⁵; ἀκούειν παρά, John 1⁴¹ 6⁴⁵ etc.); * ψεύδεσθαι (1⁶); καθαρίζειν (1⁷·⁹; but καθαρισμός, John 2²⁶ 3²⁵); ὁμολογεῖν τὰς ἁμαρτίας (1⁹, nowhere else in N.T.); πιστός (of God, 1⁹); δίκαιος (of Christ, 2¹); ἱλασμός (2² 4¹⁰, nowhere else in N.T.); ἀγάπη τετελειωμένη (2⁵ 4¹²·¹⁷·¹⁸), * ἀγαπητοί (2⁷ etc.), * παλαιός (2⁷); παράγεσθαι (2⁸·¹⁷); * μισεῖν τὸν ἀδελφόν, * ἀγαπᾶν τὸν ἀδελφόν; * σκάνδαλον (2¹⁰; but cf. προσκόπτειν, John 11⁹·¹⁰); * πατέρες (2¹³); * νεανίσκοι (2¹³·¹⁴); * ἰσχυροί (2¹⁴); * ἀλαζονεία (2¹⁶); ἐσχάτη ὥρα (2¹⁸); * ἀντίχριστος (2¹⁸ etc.); χρῖσμα (2²⁰); * ἀρνεῖσθαι ὅτι (2²²); * ἀρνεῖσθαι πατέρα, υἱόν (2²²·²³; but cf. John 13³⁸); ἔχειν πατέρα, υἱόν (2²³ 5¹²); ὁμολογεῖν τὸν υἱόν (2²³; but cf. John 9²²); ἐπαγγέλλεσθαι (2²⁵); λαμβάνειν ἀπό (2²⁷ 3²²); παρρησία (Godwards, 2²⁸ etc.); * αἰσχύνεσθαι (2²⁸); ἡ παρουσία (2²⁸); * ποιεῖν τὴν δικαιοσύνην (2²⁹); * ποταπός (3¹); * ἐλπίδα ἔχειν ἐπί (3³); ἀνομία (3⁴);

---

[1] The asterisk marks those which are *not* important. *v. infra.*

σπέρμα αὐτοῦ (3⁹); * φανερός (3¹⁰); * σφάττειν (3¹²); * χάριν τίνος (3¹²); * βίος τοῦ κόσμου τούτου (3¹⁷); * κλείειν τὰ σπλάγχνα (3¹⁷); * λόγῳ . . . γλώσσῃ, ἔργῳ . . . ἀληθείᾳ (3¹⁸); * πείθειν τὰς καρδίας (3¹⁹); * καταγινώσκειν (3²⁰); ἐνώπιον αὐτοῦ (3²²); πιστεύειν τῷ ὀνόματι (3²³); ἐν θεῷ μένει καὶ θεὸς ἐν αὐτῷ (3²⁴ etc.); * δοκιμάζειν (4¹); * ψευδοπροφῆται (4¹); ἐληλυθέναι ἐν σαρκί (4²); * πνεῦμα τῆς πλάνης (4⁶); ἡ ἀγάπη (absolutely, 4⁷ etc.); θεὸς ἀγάπη ἐστίν (4⁸); * θεὸν θεᾶσθαι (4¹²); ἐκ τοῦ πνεύματος (4¹³; but cf. John 3³⁴); ἡ ἡμέρα τῆς κρίσεως (4¹⁷); * φόβος, φοβεῖσθαι (Godwards, 4¹⁸); * κόλασις (4¹⁸); * ἐντολὰς ποιεῖν (5²); * βαρεῖαι (5³); * τὸ γεγεννημένον ἐκ τοῦ θεοῦ (5⁴); πίστις (5⁴); * μαρτυρίαν μαρτυρεῖν (5¹⁰); θεὸν ψεύστην ποιεῖν (1¹⁰ 5¹⁰); * αἰτεῖν αἰτήματα (5¹⁵); * ἔχειν αἰτήματα (5¹⁵); κατὰ τὸ θέλημα αὐτοῦ (5¹⁴); * ἁμαρτάνειν ἁμαρτίαν (5¹⁶); * ὁ κόσμος ὅλος (5¹⁹); * ἐν τῷ πονηρῷ κεῖσθαι (5¹⁹); διάνοια (5²⁰); * εἴδωλον (5²¹).

The words which I have marked with an asterisk may be set aside as unimportant. They are merely accidental terms of expression, like ψεύδεσθαι, χάριν τίνος, ἐντολὰς ποιεῖν, and the three successive cognate accusatives μαρτυρίαν μαρτυρεῖν, αἰτήματα αἰτεῖν, ἁμαρτίαν ἁμαρτάνειν; or they express ideas that naturally do not occur in the Gospel, such as ἀγγελία, ἀγαπητοί, πατέρες, νεανίσκοι, ἰσχυροί, ἀλαζονεία, εἴδωλον, etc.; or they have a definite reference to the polemical object of the Epistle, as ἀντίχριστος, ψευδοπροφῆται, δοκιμάζειν, ἀρνεῖσθαι πατέρα, υἱόν (to the same cause are to be referred the unique ὁ λέγων and ἐὰν εἴπωμεν). In other cases, variation of expression is accounted for on exegetical grounds. Thus ἔχειν ἐλπίδα ἐπί conveys a stronger idea than ἐλπίζειν εἰς (John 5⁴⁵); and when Holtzmann asks why the Epistle uses ποιεῖν τὴν δικαιοσύνην (2²⁹ 3⁷·¹⁰) instead of ποιεῖν τὴν ἀλήθειαν (John 3²¹), it is evident that he has been absorbed in the Concordance to the neglect of the context (ἐὰν εἰδῆτε ὅτι δίκαιός ἐστιν, 2²⁹); and, again, when he asks why we read in the Epistle ὁ θεὸς ἀγάπη ἐστίν instead of πνεῦμα ὁ θεός (John 4²⁴), one asks in reply whether the statement, "God is Love," would have been relevant in our Lord's conversation with the woman of Samaria, or where the development of thought in the Epistle is weakened by the absence of the statement that "God is Spirit." παῤῥησία, αἰσχύνεσθαι, ἐνώπιον αὐτοῦ, πείθειν τὰς καρδίας, καταγινώσκειν, φόβος, φοβεῖσθαι, κόλασις, are all accounted for by the fact, that the topic of assurance is not explicitly treated in the Gospel. Others, again, of the terms peculiar to the Epistle are simply conveniences of language, signifying briefly and abstractly thoughts that are more concretely expressed in the Gospel. Thus κοινωνία expresses the contents of John 17²³; ἀγάπη τετελειωμένη, that of John 14²¹⁻²⁴; while διάνοιαν διδόναι ἵνα γινώσκομεν τὸν ἀληθινόν condenses the meaning of John 1¹⁸ 8¹² 17⁸ and 18³⁷. There remain, as suggestive of the question whether the Epistle does not contain theological and ethical conceptions alien to the Gospel, such words and phrases as λόγος τῆς ζωῆς, καθαρίζειν ἀπὸ πάσης ἁμαρτίας, ὁμολογεῖν τὰς ἁμαρτίας, πιστός (of God), δίκαιος (of Christ), ἱλασμός, ἐσχάτη ὥρα, ἡ παρουσία, ἀνομία, σπέρμα θεοῦ, ἐν θεῷ μένειν, ἐκ τοῦ πνεύματος διδόναι, ἡ ἡμέρα. τῆς κρίσεως. And it is upon these that the weight of argument for a dual authorship is chiefly laid.

Before proceeding, however, to the detailed consideration of these points, I desire to make an observation on the general question. It is the constant assumption of writers like Pfleiderer that the Gospel and the Epistle cannot have proceeded from the same author; for, otherwise, he would certainly have ascribed to Jesus in the Gospel the views (regarding, *e.g.*, propitiation and the Parousia) which he himself states in the Epistle, and that regardless of historical propriety. A naïve example of this point of view may be quoted from Dr. Scott's *Fourth Gospel*, in which he argues that the writer had a certain sympathy with Gnosticism—the evidence for this being that "He finds room within the historical limitations of his narrative to wage a sharp polemic with his Jewish adversaries; and he might just as easily have assailed the Gnostics in terms that could not be mistaken" (p. 95). Here the assumption is, not only that the Evangelist employed his " Gospel " as little else than a literary vehicle for his own conception of Christianity, but that in doing so he would naturally show himself destitute of all regard to historical probability. It was not any sense of the fitness of things, but a leaning towards Gnosticism, that prevented him from making Jesus the mouthpiece of an attack upon it in "terms that could not be mistaken." He must not be supposed even to have possessed enough of artistic faculty to invest his theological romance with an air of verisimilitude.

Now, if this be accepted as a canon of criticism, the question of a single or dual authorship for the Gospel and the Epistle becomes simple indeed. Any noticeable development in the latter of truths contained in the former, any difference of perspective or in the grouping of ideas is decisive for a different authorship. But I submit that this assumption is altogether unwarrantable. Without discussing the historicity of the Fourth Gospel, I claim, as a basis for our consideration of the real or alleged divergences between the Gospel and the Epistle, the fact that the one purports, at least, to be a Gospel, the other an utterance of the writer *in propria persona*.

1. It is objected[1] that the idea of Forgiveness, emphasised in the Epistle, is foreign to the Evangelist's conception of the relation between God and man. But it

---

[1] Cf. Drummond's *Character and Authorship of the Fourth Gospel*, chap. iii., from which I have derived not a few suggestions.

is not the fact that the idea of forgiveness is absent from the Gospel. It is implied in such utterances as "The wrath of God abideth on him" (3^{36}), and "hath eternal life, and cometh not into judgment" (5^{24}), and is explicitly enunciated in the promise, "Whosoever sins ye forgive, they are forgiven" (20^{36}). But the strength of the reply does not rest upon a few proof-texts. The word "sin" ($\dot{a}\mu a\rho\tau\iota a$) occurs sixteen times in the Gospel (with the idea of guilt definitely attached to it in six passages, 9^{41} $15^{22. 24}$ $16^{8. 9}$ 19^{11}); and to assert that, where the idea of sin enters into the conception of the relation between God and man, the idea of forgiveness is foreign to that conception, would be to assert a mere contradiction. What sin *means* is conduct that needs forgiveness.

It is true, indeed, that in the Epistle a clearer prominence is given to the confession and the forgiveness of sin than in the Gospel; but, in estimating the significance of this, due consideration must be given to the polemical factor in the Epistle. It was a characteristic tenet of Gnosticism that "Upon believing one receives the forgiveness of sins from the Lord; but he who has attained to Gnosis, having become as one who no longer sins, procures forgiveness thereafter from himself" (*Clem. Alex.*, quoted by Westcott, p. 22). The germs, at least, of this doctrine were in the atmosphere of the Johannine period.[1] And if in the Epistle the polemic is more directly pointed against contemporary error than in the Gospel, if, moreover, such a statement as "He is faithful and righteous to forgive us our sins" (1^{9}) has a more Pauline ring than any utterance of the Fourth Gospel, the question is relevant, here and elsewhere—Why not? The Gospel assumes, at least, to be a record of the teaching, not of the Evangelist, but of Jesus.

2. It is said also that the ideas of "cleansing" ($\kappa a\theta a\rho\iota\zeta\epsilon\iota\nu$) from sin by the "Blood of Jesus" (1^{7}), and of

---

[1] *v. supra*, pp. 32–35.

Christ as a "propitiation" (2^2 4^{10}), are alien to the Gospel (Martineau, von Soden). But this cannot be conceded in view of such utterances as "The Lamb of God that taketh away the sin of the world" (John 1^{29}), "And for their sakes I sanctify[1] Myself" (17^{19}); and of the interpretation of Christ's Death as effective "for the nation; and not for the nation only, but that He might also gather into one the children of God that are scattered abroad" ($11^{51, 52}$; cf. 1 John 2^2). The conceptions in the Epistle of propitiation, intercession, and cleansing belong to the same circle of religious ideas and spring from the same root in Old Testament ritual as those that are implied in the passages quoted from the Gospel. And if the Epistle presents these in a much more explicit and technical form, again we ask —Why not? In not ascribing to Jesus a fully developed doctrine of propitiation, the author of the Fourth Gospel only places himself in line with the Synoptics.

3. The objection, that a different view of the Christian relation to the Law is held by the writer of the Epistle and by the Evangelist, who sets the Law which "came by Moses" in absolute contrast to the "grace and truth" which came by Jesus Christ (John 1^{16}), is founded on a misapprehension of the statement that "Sin is lawlessness" ($\dot{a}\nu o\mu\dot{\iota}a$, 3^4), in which there is no special reference to the Jewish Law.[2] On the other hand, the insistence upon the keeping of the "commandments," especially the old-new commandment of Love, is one of the most obvious affinities between the Gospel and the Epistle.

4. It is asserted that the doctrine of the Spirit in the Epistle involves a departure from that of the Gospel. In the Gospel the Spirit, in the Epistle Christ, is the Paraclete. In the Gospel the Spirit is regarded as distinctly personal, in the Epistle as an impersonal "anointing" (2^{20}), and even (4^{13} ὅτι ἐκ τοῦ πνεύματος αὐτοῦ δέδωκεν ἡμῖν) as a

---

[1] *v. supra*, p. 173.   [2] *v. supra*, p. 133.

divisible entity (Pfleiderer, ii. 447). In answer, it is to be said, in the first place, that the Gospel expressly speaks of the Spirit as "another" Paraclete (14^{16}), implying that Jesus Himself is the first Paraclete; in the second place, that χρῖσμα denotes the Spirit, not in His essence or agency, but as the gift of the Holy One, with which He "anoints" believers; and that, in any case, the expression is not more impersonal than that of John 7$^{38, 39}$:—"He that believeth on Me, out of his belly shall flow rivers of living water. But this spake He of the Spirit"; in the third place, that the expression ἐκ τοῦ πνεύματος αὐτοῦ δέδωκεν ἡμῖν is no more inconsistent with the personality of the Spirit, than is the saying of John 3^{34}, that "To Him whom He hath sent" God "giveth not the Spirit by measure," or than *our* speaking of Christians as having much or little of the Spirit (*v. supra*, p. 268).

5. It is alleged that in the matter of the Last Things [1] the Epistle recedes from the idealism of the Gospel, placing itself more nearly in line with the apocalyptic conceptions of the traditional Eschatology. Whereas the Gospel speaks of Christ's departure in bodily presence as "expedient," because it is the necessary condition of His coming again in the Spirit to make His permanent abode with His disciples (John 16^7 14$^{18, 23}$ 15^{16}), the writer of the Epistle thinks of a visible Parousia as nigh at hand (2^{28}); and whereas the Gospel conceives of Judgment as a present spiritual fact (John 3$^{18, 19}$ etc.), the Epistle clings to the "popular" idea of a Judgment Day (4^{17}). In reply, it ought to be noted that in the Epistle, as compared with the Gospel, the eschatological point of view is necessarily different. The perspective is shortened. The author writes under the conviction that "the world is passing away," that "the last hour" of its day has come (2$^{17, 18}$). And even if the Fourth Gospel be regarded as containing nothing else than

[1] On the whole subject of this paragraph, see Chapter XVI.

the Evangelist's own conception of Christian truth, we need not, surely, deny him such a sense of historical propriety as would prevent the manifest anachronism of importing this conviction into it. Apart from this, the fundamental similarities between the eschatology of the Epistle and that of the Gospel are vastly more obvious than the differences. If the Gospel conceives of Eternal Life as a present rather than a future possession, this is the invariable conception in the Epistle also. If, in the Gospel, Christ's spiritual presence is an abiding reality, this truth, though naturally not presented in the Epistle with the exquisite pathos and glowing emphasis of the Farewell Discourse, is everywhere fundamental. "Our fellowship is with the Father, and with His Son Jesus Christ" (1^3). We are to "abide in Him," that we may not be "ashamed before Him at His coming" (2^{28}). We "have" the Son (5^{12}); and His coming again will be only the manifestation of what is now hidden reality (3^2). If the Gospel speaks of the revelation of Christ to men as bringing a present and inevitable κρίσις into the world, the Epistle is saturated with the same thought, and, indeed, has as its aim nothing else than to awaken, strengthen, and educate the consciousness of this. If, on the other hand, the Epistle speaks of a future and visible Parousia, this is quite obviously implied also in John $5^{28.\ 29}$. And if the Epistle makes a single reference to the "Day of Judgment" (4^{17}), the Gospel has no fewer than six passages which speak of the "Last Day," and in these the "Last Day" is explicitly the Day of Resurrection ($6^{39.\ 40.\ 44.\ 54}$ 11^{24}) and of Judgment (12^{48}). Except for the singular fact of its silence as to the Resurrection, the Epistle, in its eschatology, covers exactly the same canvas as the Gospel; and if, in the two writings, different features of the picture are made more or less conspicuous, there is no such diversity as to warrant the hypothesis of their separate authorship.

23

6. It is alleged that in the Epistle the unique conception of the Logos found in the Gospel is modified in the direction of conformity to traditional doctrine. The distinctly personal Logos, Who " in the beginning was, and was with God, and was God " (John I[1]), and Who " became flesh and dwelt among us " (John I[14]), becomes in the Epistle the less indubitably personal " Word of Life " (I[1]). The difference of expression, *quantum valeat*, being admitted, to have built upon this tiny basis such a superstructure of inference as Pfleiderer (following Holtzmann) has done is a marvel of ingenuity. The conception of the personal, preexistent Logos was new, we are told, and, because of its Gnostic tinge, suspect, and was therefore avoided and generalised into the " Word of Life." " The reason why the writer of the Epistle gives up the self-subsistence of the Logos (and of the Spirit) is, without doubt, his anxiety to keep at a safe distance from the æons and ' idols ' (5[21]) of Gnosticism, and to maintain his stand upon the solid ground of Biblical Monotheism " (Pfleiderer, ii. 446, 447). " The primitive Church had not yet, like the Fourth Evangelist, seen in Jesus the Incarnate Logos ; to it He was the Man filled with the Divine Spirit of Life, and it was because he was conscious of this difference in point of view and was desirous of obliterating it, that our author has avoided speaking of the personal Logos " (*ibid.* p. 392). And here, as elsewhere in the Epistle, one is to discern traces of the " universal Monarchianism [1] of the second century " (Holtzmann, *J. P. T.*, 1882, p. 141). This, it seems to me, is to make bricks not only without straw, but without clay ; to speak bluntly, it is mere moonshine. What ground is there for the assertion that ὁ λόγος τῆς ζωῆς necessarily signifies anything less personal than does the phraseology of the Gospel ? The phraseology in both cases is exactly adapted to its purpose. In the Gospel, ἐν ἀρχῇ ἦν ὁ λόγος . . . καὶ ὁ λόγος σὰρξ

---

[1] *v. supra*, p. 197.

ἐγένετο is right, because it sums up the contents of the Gospel—announces its subject, the history of the Incarnate Logos. In the Epistle, ὁ λόγος τῆς ζωῆς (with the emphasis on τῆς ζωῆς. See Note, *in loc.*) is right, because the theme of the Epistle is to be the Life, not as to its historical manifestation in the Incarnate Logos, but as to its essential qualities, in whomsoever it exists.

7. But while this microscopic detection of tendency in the phrase "Word of Life" borders upon the ridiculous, there is a real difference in point of view between the Gospel and the Epistle which has been already[1] alluded to, and is worthy of fuller consideration. The Gospel is, to speak broadly, Christocentric, the Epistle Theocentric. In the former, Life consists in our relation to Christ—He is the Vine and we are the branches; in the latter, Life consists in our relation to God—He is the Father and we are His children. There are important exceptions on either side to this generalisation; but upon the whole view of the facts it is strikingly justified.

EPISTLE.	GOSPEL.
1. God is Light (1^5).	1. Christ is the Light (1^4 8^{12} 9^5 etc.).
2. This is the true God and eternal Life (5^{20}).	2. Christ is the Life (11^{25} 14^6).
3. Christians abide in God (2^6 3^{24} $4^{13.\ 16}$. But in Christ, $2^{24.\ 28}$ 3^6).	3. They abide in Christ (6^{56} $15^{4.\ 5.\ 6.\ 7}$).
4. God abides in them (3^{24} $4^{12.\ 13\ 15.\ 16}$).	4. Christ abides in them (6^{56} $15^{4.\ 5}$).
5. The Love of God abides in them (3^{17}; cf. John 5^{42}).	5. They abide in Christ's Love ($15^{9.\ 10}$).
6. The Word of God (1^{10} 2^{14}).	6. The Word of Christ (5^{24} $8^{31.\ 37.\ 43.\ 51.\ 52}$ $14^{23.\ 24}$ $15^{3.\ 20}$).
7. The commandments of God ($2^{3.\ 4}$ $3^{22.\ 23.\ 24}$ 4^{21} $5^{2.\ 3}$).	7. The commandment of Christ (13^{34} $14^{15.\ 21}$ $15^{10.\ 12.\ 14.\ 17}$). The Commandment of God is given only to the Son (10^{18} $12^{49.\ 50}$ 14^{31} 15^{10}).

---

[1] *v. supra*, pp. 196, 197.

EPISTLE.	GOSPEL.
8. The pattern of Love is God's Love to us ($4^{11. 19}$. But also Christ's Love, 3^{16}).	8. The pattern of Love is Christ's Love to us (13^{34} 15^{12}).
9. The relation of believers to God is direct (1^6 2^6 2^{29} $3^{1. 9. 10}$ $4^{4. 6. 7}$ $5^{1. 4. 18. 19}$. But is mediated through Christ, 2^{23} $5^{11. 20}$).	9. The relation to God is mediated through Christ (1^{12} $14^{6. 20. 21. 23}$ $17^{21. 23. 25. 26}$ 12^{26}). On the other hand :—$\gamma\epsilon\nu\nu\eta\theta\hat{\eta}\nu\alpha\iota$ $\dot{\epsilon}\kappa$ $\theta\epsilon o\hat{v}$ (1^{13}) and $\epsilon\hat{\iota}\nu\alpha\iota$ $\dot{\epsilon}\kappa$ $\tau o\hat{v}$ $\theta\epsilon o\hat{v}$ (8^{47}).
10. No parallel.	10. The relation of the Father to Christ is a type of the relation of Christ to believers ($10^{14. 15}$ $15^{9. 10}$ $17^{8. 18. 22}$).
11. It is God in us that overcomes the world (5^4).	11. It is Christ in us that overcomes the world (16^{33}).
12. Prayer is successful, because we keep God's commandments (3^{22}), and when it is offered for things according to His will (5^{14}).	12. Prayer is successful, when we abide in Christ and His words abide in us (15^7), and when it is offered in His Name " ($14^{13. 44}$ $16^{23. 24}$).

Now, in the first place, this change of centre is exactly what we should expect to find, the Gospel being a narrative of the redemptive ministry of Christ, and the Epistle an analytical study of the Divine Life as it exists in God and in the children of God. And, in the second place, the exceptions on both sides are so numerous and important as to show that the change of centre is amply accounted for on this ground alone, and that, consequently, the supposition of Monarchian bias in the Epistle is quite unfounded.

In the Gospel we find passages as strongly Theocentric as any in the Epistle. In John $3^{16. 17}$ the source of salvation is the Love of God, as clearly as in 1 John $4^{9. 10}$. In John 17^3, as clearly as in 1 John 5^{20}, Eternal Life is to know God. So also in the Gospel we read that God "abides in" men (5^{42}), that men are "begotten of God" (1^{13}), and are "of God" (8^{47}); that the end of all Christ's work is that the Father may be glorified (15^8), and that Belief in Christ is the gift of God (1^{13} $6^{37. 39. 44. 45}$ 18^{37}).

On the other hand, the Epistle contains passages which are as strongly Christocentric as any in the Gospel. "He that hath the Son hath life, and he that hath not the Son of God hath not life" (5^{12}). From Christ believers receive the "anointing" of the Spirit (2^{20}). At His Parousia Christ is the Judge (2^{28}). To abide in the Son is tantamount to abiding in the Father (2^{24}). To be in Him that is True is to be in His Son Jesus Christ (5^{20}). Not only so; the offices of Christ as Intercessor and as Propitiation are more clearly displayed in the Epistle than in the Gospel ($2^{1.\ 2}$); and when Holtzmann asserts (*J. P. T.*, 1882, p. 145) that "the author is here, for a moment, in conflict with the tendencies of his own Christology," and "consciously and deliberately veers round to the popular conception according to which Christ is still active in Heaven as our Intercessor (contrary to the representation of John 16^{26})," the assertion is one which much more evidently fits his theory than it does the facts of the case. In full view of these facts, I submit that the allegation of Monarchian tendency in the Epistle is without foundation. If in the Gospel itself, we find that the point of view changes so rapidly that in one chapter Christ is the source of commandment (14^{15}), and in the next the pattern of obedience (15^{10}); that in one verse He is the Answerer of prayer ($14^{13.\ 14}$), and almost in the next that He is the Intercessor, while the Father is the Answerer (14^{16}); and if in the Epistle we find that in one chapter Christ is the Giver of the Spirit (2^{20}), and in the next that God is the Giver (3^{24} 4^{13}), the fact that the one point of view is, upon the whole, more distinctive of the one writing, the other of the other, cannot be held as disproof that both have emanated from the same mind, especially when the one is a biography of the Incarnate Word, the other, we may say, a biological study of the Divine Life itself.

It is to be observed that the inquiry we have undertaken is widely different from such a question as, for example, the Pauline authorship of *Hebrews*. In such a case, where the most pronounced characteristics of the reputed author are absent in the writing ascribed to him, the argument from the positive dissimilarities between it and his acknowledged writings tells with fatal effect. Here, on the contrary, the identity of the two writings in matter and manner of thought, in vocabulary and style, creates a presumption in favour of identity of authorship that can be resisted only by the discovery of differences very radical and profound, proving the existence of two systems of thought or lines of tendency that do not readily coalesce, and cannot be supposed to have been held, simultaneously or successively, by the same person. But, while there are, between the Fourth Gospel and our Epistle, differences of emphasis, of perspective and point of view, it is no insecure verdict to say that these differences do not yield even an approximation to the proof required.

But, further, the diversities as well as the similarities tell in favour of identity of authorship. The writer of the Epistle was either the author of the Gospel or one whose mind was so saturated and obsessed by it (or the oral teaching it embodies) that, for the most part, he could not move except in its circle of ideas, nor express them except in its diction. But, in the latter case, how are we to account for the diversities? Would such a mere copyist have ventured to introduce, or have been capable of introducing, so many and important elements of independence both in thought and language? " It is easy enough to imitate tricks of style, or to borrow some peculiarities of phrase; but to write in a required style without betraying any signs of imitation; to introduce variations into sentences which are, nevertheless, characteristic; to have shades of thought and suggestion which remind one of what has been said elsewhere, and, nevertheless, are delicately modified and pass easily into another subject; in a word, to preserve the whole flavour of a writer's composition in a treatise which has a theme of its own, and follows its own independent development, may well seem beyond the reach of the imitator, and must be held to guarantee the authorship of a work, unless very weighty arguments can be advanced on the other side." [1] I cannot but think that, in this case, the arguments so advanced have far too little substance to counterbalance the affinity, unique in kind and degree, between the two writings,[2] together with the testimony of a tradition which is ancient, unanimous, and unbroken.

The question of priority, as between the two writings, is not so easy of determination as at a first glance it might seem to be. For while it is true that to the modern reader the Epistle would be unintelligible without the Gospel,—such expressions as the "Word of Life" or the "new commandment" would be merely enigmatic,— it does not follow that its original readers would have been in the same case. That they were familiar, through oral communication, with the leading ideas and main contents of its author's Gospel is assumed in the Epistle itself (1^{1-3} 2^{24} 4^6). The relation of the two writings would be at once fixed, if we could adopt that tempting interpretation of the Prologue to the Epistle which refers 1^{1-3} to the habitual oral teaching of the author and 1^4 to his written Gospel. The Epistle would thus have been written simultaneously with the Gospel, and despatched along with it to its original readers. But the characteristics of the Epistle do not lend themselves to this supposition. It is an independent composition, concerned with other objects than the Gospel, and so persistently and exclusively devoted to these that it is difficult to think of it as a simultaneous production. The question then is—Are

---

[1] Quoted from Drummond's *Philo Judæus* by Sanday, *Criticism of the Fourth Gospel*, p. 56.

[2] One is tempted to quote the epigram on the *Phædo*: Εἰ με Πλάτων οὐ γράψε, δύω ἐγένοντο Πλάτωνες.

there distinguishable references in the Epistle to the documentary Fourth Gospel? It seems to me that there are. The Prologue to the Epistle is reminiscent of that to the Gospel.[1] In 2^{9-11} there are distinct traces of John $11^{9.\ 10}$ 12^{35}; and the coincidence is the more striking because it is chiefly verbal, the connection in thought between the passages being but slight.[2] Again, it seems as if in writing 3^{8-15} the echoes of John 8^{40-44} must still have lingered in the author's ear;[3] and when we compare the passages there can be little doubt which of the two is the original. Again, in 3^{13}, εἰ μισεῖ ὑμᾶς ὁ κόσμος is a verbal reproduction of John $15^{18}_{.}$, and θεὸν οὐδεὶς πώποτε τεθέαται (4^{13}) very nearly so of John 1^{18}; and in both cases the probability is that the occurrence in the Gospel is the original. Again, it seems more probable that $4^{9.\ 10}$ is an expansion of John 3^{16}, than that the latter is a condensation of the former.[4]

Upon a whole view of the case, the verdict must be, first and certainly, that the Epistle presupposes its reader's acquaintance with the substance of the Johannine Gospel; secondly, and with much probability, that it shows signs of being posterior to the composition of that Gospel in literary form.

How much posterior, we have not the means of determining. Writers of the critical school, whether admitting or denying identity of authorship, agree in

---

[1] ὃ ἦν ἀπ' ἀρχῆς; cf. ἐν ἀρχῇ ἦν ὁ λόγος. ἥτις ἦν πρὸς τὸν πατέρα; cf. οὗτος ἦν ἐν ἀρχῇ πρὸς τὸν θεόν.

[2] ἐν τῇ σκοτίᾳ περιπατεῖ, καὶ οὐκ οἶδεν ποῦ ὑπάγει (2^{11})=καὶ ὁ περιπατῶν ἐν τῇ σκοτίᾳ οὐκ οἶδεν ποῦ ὑπάγει (John 12^{35}). σκάνδαλον οὐκ ἔστιν ἐν αὐτῷ (2^{10})=οὐ προσκόπτει (11^{9}).

[3] τὰ ἔργα τοῦ διαβόλου (3^{8})=τὰ ἔργα τοῦ πατρὸς ὑμῶν (John 8^{41}). ἀπ' ἀρχῆς ὁ διάβολος ἁμαρτάνει (3^{8})=ἀνθρωποκτόνος ἦν ἀπ' ἀρχῆς (John 8^{44}). ὁ ποιῶν τὴν ἁμαρτίαν ἐκ τοῦ διαβόλου ἐστίν (3^{8})=ὑμεῖς ἐκ τοῦ διαβόλου ἐστὲ καὶ τὰς ἐπιθυμίας τοῦ πατρὸς ὑμῶν θέλετε ποιεῖν (8^{44}). The word ἀνθρωποκτόνος, found nowhere else in the NT, occurs in both passages.

[4] Other instances of dependence upon the Gospel are cited by Holtzmann, as that of $5^{9.\ 10}$ upon John 5^{32} 8^{18} and 10^{25}.

requiring a considerable interval between the two writings, in order to make room for their theory of the aim and tendency of the Epistle. This, it is said, was to "popularise" the ideas of the Gospel (Weizsäcker),[1] or to correct and tone down what in it was obnoxious to the feeling of the Church, and, at the same time, to add certain links of connection (ἱλασμός, παρουσία, παράκλητος, etc.) with the traditional type of doctrine, or to emphasise these where they existed (Holtzmann).[2] Pfleiderer compares it with the "mediating" successors of Schleiermacher. "In his earnest endeavour to make the great thoughts of the master useful and edifying for the whole Church, he became more conservative than the master himself had been. He wrote with more decisive repudiation of the heretical Gnosis, and gave to the Johannine Gnosis, wherever it appeared to come into dangerous approximation to the former, an application and a significance which were unexceptionable and in full accord with the common religious consciousness of the Church" (ii. 448). This account of the purpose of the Epistle, in so far as it is based upon an alleged retreat from the well-defined personality of the Logos and the Spirit taught in the Gospel, has been already shown to be groundless. And while it is admitted that the more definite statement of Christ's office as Propitiation and Intercessor, and of the near approach of a visible Parousia, does emphasise points of contact with traditional doctrine which are less discernible in the Gospel, this furnishes an extremely slender basis for the conclusion, that the Epistle as a whole is of a "mediating" tendency, and that in this lies the very motive of its composition.

A slightly different view is, that the Evangelist (or

---

[1] "Popularised and, at the same time, in part rendered superficial" (*Apostolic Age*, ii. 238).

[2] Its relation to the Gospel is "verwischende und corrigirende," *J. P. T.*, 1882, p. 152.

another) produced the Epistle after the earlier and greater work, " because his Gospel and his conception of Christianity were now being seriously threatened by the Gnostics, who actually employed some of his formulæ in order to commend themselves to the ignorant, and who in effect found many points of agreement between his views and their own " (Jülicher).[1] Jülicher offers no shred of evidence for this confident statement; and one is left to learn from other sources what formulæ or features of the Fourth Gospel there are which the Gnostics were able to appropriate, and which are retraced or modified in the Epistle. It is said [2] that " the Gospel itself bears a semi-docetic character," and yet the Epistle contains no utterance more strongly anti-docetic than several which are contained in the Gospel (*e.g.* 1^{14} 4^6 $19^{17, 34}$ 20^{27}). If "the Gnostic view that the Resurrection takes place here and now when a man attains to the true 'knowledge' has a striking parallel in Johannine doctrine," [3] it is to be noted that, while the Gospel is by no means silent regarding a future resurrection, the Epistle is. If, in the Gospel, the influence of Gnosticism appears in St. John's "favourite opposition of light and darkness," [4] and in the assumption that "certain elect natures have an inborn affinity to the light," [5] all this is equally characteristic of the Epistle. If, finally, it is true that, in the Gospel, St. John describes the supreme energy of the religious life as an act of "knowing," [6] this is equally true in the Epistle (2^3 4^7 5^{20}). Evidence for the theory, that the Epistle was written as an antidote to Gnostic appropriation of the Johannine Gospel, is very much to seek.

The sum of the matter is, that our knowledge of the historical situation is insufficient for an exact determination of the relative dates of the two writings.

---

[1] *Introduction to N.T.* pp. 249, 250.
[2] Scott's *Fourth Gospel*, p. 95.
[3] *Ibid.* p. 96.

[4] *Ibid.* p. 96.
[5] *Ibid.* p. 97.
[6] *Ibid.* p. 97.

That there was an appreciable interval of time seems probable. Gnostic tendencies have hardened into more definite form. Many false prophets have gone forth into the world. The "antichrists" have declared themselves. It is high time for the Evangelist to focus the rays of his Gospel upon the malignant growth which is acutely endangering the life of the Church. And there are other features in the case that are more easily explicable on the supposition of some appreciable difference of date. There are the diversities of diction, minute, but, as bearing on this point, not unimportant. And there is the fact that, while the leading thoughts in the Epistle are almost identical with those in the Gospel, they are placed in relation to a different centre: not the Incarnate Logos, but the Eternal Life, not the channel, but the living water it conveys is now the cardinal theme.[1] In this respect the Epistle may be said to represent a further stage of theological reflection. Its doctrine of the Divine nature, self-existing and self-imparting as Life, Light, Righteousness, and Love, is, it appears to me, the largest and loftiest conception in the New Testament.

[1] *v. supra*, pp. 196, 197.

NOTE TO THE THIRD EDITION.

Brooke, in his full and able discussion of the subject of this chapter, reaches the same conclusions. "It is practically impossible to *prove* common authorship, as against imitation, or similarity produced by common education in the same school of thought. . . . But there are no adequate reasons for setting aside the traditional view which attributes the Epistle and the Gospel to the same authorship. It remains the most probable explanation of the facts known to us" (p. xviii). He also finds the relevant facts decisive for the priority of the Gospel to the Epistle, so far as the substantial content of the two documents is concerned. "They do not, perhaps, preclude the possibility of a later date for the actual composition, or publication, of the Gospel. But in view of them such hypotheses are extremely unlikely" (p. lxvii).

NOTE

ON γινώσκειν AND εἰδέναι.

A DISTINCTIVE feature of Johannine thought and vocabulary is the prominence given to knowledge. The noun γνῶσις, indeed, is conspicuously absent, the reason possibly being that, like πίστις, which also is eschewed, it had become a watchword of Gnosticism. But there are, in the First Epistle alone, fifteen occurrences of εἰδέναι and no fewer than twenty-five of γινώσκειν. And, while there is nothing peculiar in the Johannine usage except a singular accuracy, yet to distinguish the shades of meaning conveyed by these verbs and their various parts is so necessary for the exegesis of the Epistle that I venture a special note on the subject.

γινώσκειν.

The root γνο- ((g)nosco, know, kennen) conveys the idea, not so much of knowledge in itself, as of the act of perception by which knowledge is acquired. It means to perceive or become aware of a fact, to distinguish an object, to recognise a person, as being what they are, from their proper marks or characteristics. Thus, to give but a single example from the classics, when Æacus is unable to distinguish between the god Dionysus and his attendant Xanthias, he conducts them to his master, Pluto. ὁ δεσπότης γὰρ αὐτὸς ὑμᾶς γνώσεται: "For the master himself will know you," i.e. "will discern what you really are" (Ar. Ran. 670).

In the different tenses of the verb, this root-idea assumes corresponding shades of meaning. The reduplicate form of the present γι(γ)νώσκειν signifies durative action,—to have continuous perception of the object, to be acquiring knowledge of it; the aorist γνῶναι, the act of perception and its immediate result,—to become aware of, ascertain, realise; the perfect ἐγνωκέναι, the act with its result down to the present time,—to have learned, to

364

have become acquainted with, and, therefore, to know. The knowledge acquired has become a permanent possession.

A few illustrative examples may be taken from the Fourth Gospel:

(*a*) *Present and imperfect.*—πόθεν με γινώσκεις (1⁴⁹) = By what means do you know me, *i.e.* read my character (as an Israelite indeed)? διὰ τὸ αὐτὸν γινώσκειν πάντας . . . αὐτὸς γὰρ ἐγίνωσκε τί ἦν ἐν τῷ ἀνθρώπῳ (2²⁴. ²⁵) = By reason of His discerning the real character of all men . . . for He always perceived what was in man. γινώσκω τὰ ἐμά, καὶ γινώσκουσί με τὰ ἐμά (10¹⁴). The Good Shepherd recognises His own sheep, and they recognise Him.

(*b*) *Aorist.*—ὡς οὖν ἔγνω ὁ κύριος ὅτι (4¹; cf. 4⁵³) = When, therefore, the Lord became aware that. γνοὺς ὅτι πολὺν ἤδη χρόνον (5⁶) = Noticing (from the man's appearance) that he had been a long time.

(*c*) *Perfect.*—καὶ οὐκ ἔγνωκάς με; (14⁹) = Hast thou not recognised (and so, dost thou not yet know) who and what I am?

In the Epistle the following uses are to be distinguished:—

Present.—1. γινώσκειν signifies the perception or recognition of a person. ὁ κόσμος οὐ γινώσκει ἡμᾶς (3¹). (We are the children of God, but) the world does not recognise us as being what we are. ὁ γινώσκων τὸν θεόν (4⁶) = He that recognises the Divine when it is presented to him. γινώσκει τὸν θεόν (4⁷) = (Only he that loves) has a true perception of the character of God. γινώσκομεν τὸν ἀληθινόν (5²⁰) = (By the understanding given us) we recognise the True One (in contradistinction to "idols," 5²¹).

2. The perception or recognition of a thing. ἐν τούτῳ γινώσκετε τὸ πνεῦμα τοῦ θεοῦ (4²) = By this recognise the Spirit of God (in distinction from other spirits). ἐκ τούτου γινώσκομεν τὸ πνεῦμα τῆς ἀληθείας καὶ τὸ πνεῦμα τῆς πλάνης (4⁶) = By this token we recognise the Spirit of Truth and the spirit of error. ὁ θεός . . . γινώσκει πάντα (3²⁰) = God observes all things—is aware of them and discerns their true character.

3. The inferential perception of a fact from the proofs of its existence. ἐν τούτῳ γινώσκομεν ὅτι (2³. ⁵ 3¹⁹. ²⁴ 4¹³ 5²) = By this we recognise that the fact is so and so. Similarly ὅθεν γινώσκομεν ὅτι (2¹⁸). γινώσκετε ὅτι (2²⁹) = (If ye know, as ye do, that God is righteous) recognise the consequence that every one also that doeth righteousness, etc.

Aorist.—ὅτι οὐκ ἔγνω αὐτόν (3¹) = (The world does not recognise us because) it did not recognise Him (pointing to the definite time when it failed to do so, namely, when He was manifested on earth. Or, the force of the aorist here may be the same as in the following example). ὁ μὴ ἀγαπῶν οὐκ ἔγνω τὸν θεόν (4⁸). Here the aorist gathers to one point the whole extent of the failure to perceive what God is (cf. John 17²⁵), and οὐκ ἔγνω may be translated "has never known." (This perfective sense of the aorist is shared by the past tense in English. "I never knew such a rascal" = I have never known until now such a rascal.)

Perfect.—1. Is used of *persons*, signifying perception of and acquaintance with their character. ἐγνώκαμεν αὐτόν (2³·⁴). ἐγνώκατε τὸν ἀπ᾽ ἀρχῆς . . . τὸν πατέρα (2¹³·¹⁴). The tense connotes that the spiritual perception of the object, which is always God or Christ, has become a permanent experience. An instructive case is ὁ ἁμαρτάνων οὐχ ἑώρακεν αὐτὸν οὐδὲ ἔγνωκεν αὐτόν (3⁶) = He that sinneth hath not seen Christ, nor had any true perception of Him at all.

2. It is used of *things* in the same sense as of persons. ἐν τούτῳ ἐγνώκαμεν τὴν ἀγάπην, ὅτι . . . (3¹⁶). We have learned to know what love is by this that . . . καὶ ἡμεῖς ἐγνώκαμεν καὶ πεπιστεύκαμεν τὴν ἀγάπην (4¹⁶) = We have perceived (come to know) the Love, and are persuaded of its reality.

It is thus clear that the word γινώσκειν everywhere contains the idea, not of purely intellectual cognition, but of a spiritual perception which, when God or Christ is its object, corresponds closely to the general N.T. conception of Faith as spiritual vision.

εἰδέναι.

While γινώσκειν always suggests, more or less distinctly, the perception through which knowledge is acquired, εἰδέναι, on the other hand, expresses the fact of knowledge absolutely. It frequently happens, however, that the same experience may be stated from either point of view; and thus it is not possible, in actual usage, to draw any rigid line of distinction between the two.

It may be noted that εἰδέναι expresses—

1. Knowledge of a fact, apart from consideration of how it is known. οἴδατε πάντα (2²⁰), οἴδατε τὴν ἀλήθειαν (2²¹).

2. Knowledge of self-evident or necessary truth. ἐὰν εἰδῆτε ὅτι δίκαιός ἐστιν γινώσκετε . . . 2^{29}. That God is righteous is self-evident—a matter of intuitive knowledge; that every one that doeth righteousness is begotten of Him is recognised only as a necessary consequence from this. The same self-evident certainty is expressed by οἴδαμεν in 3^2. ("We know," beyond question, "that if He shall be manifested, we shall be like Him"), in 3^5 ("Ye know," it is axiomatic, "that He was manifested to take away sins"), in 3^{15} ("Ye know that no murderer hath eternal life abiding in him"), in 5^{15} ("We know that He heareth" . . . "We know that we have"). Cf. Rom. 6^{16} 8^{28}, 1 Cor. 3^{16} $6^{9.\ 15.\ 19}$, Eph. $6^{8.\ 9}$, Col. 4^1, 1 Pet. 1^{18}.

3. It is equivalent to γινώσκειν heightened by exultant emotion (3^{14} $5^{13.\ 18.\ 19.\ 20}$).

4. It seems to be simply equivalent to γινώσκειν (2^{11}).

NOTES.

1^1–2^2.

1^{1-3a} Ὃ ἦν ἀπ' ἀρχῆς, ὃ ἀκηκόαμεν, ὃ ἑωράκαμεν τοῖς ὀφθαλμοῖς ἡμῶν, ὃ ἐθεασάμεθα καὶ αἱ χεῖρες ἡμῶν ἐψηλάφησαν, περὶ τοῦ λόγου τῆς ζωῆς (καὶ ἡ ζωὴ ἐφανερώθη, καὶ ἑωράκαμεν καὶ μαρτυροῦμεν καὶ ἀπαγγέλλομεν ὑμῖν τὴν ζωὴν τὴν αἰώνιον, ἥτις ἦν πρὸς τὸν πατέρα καὶ ἐφανερώθη ἡμῖν), ὃ ἑωράκαμεν καὶ ἀκηκόαμεν, ἀπαγγέλλομεν καὶ ὑμῖν.

These verses consist of a sentence begun (1^1), interrupted by a parenthesis (1^2), resumed, partly repeated, and completed in 1^3. The principal verb is ἀπαγγέλλομεν in 1^3; the series of appositional clauses, ὃ ἦν ἀπ' ἀρχῆς, ὃ ἀκηκόαμεν, ὃ ἑωράκαμεν, κ.τ.λ., declare the *substance*, and the adverbial clause, περὶ τοῦ λόγου τῆς ζωῆς, the *subject* of the announcement made.

1^1. The first verse, as construed by the majority of commentators, presents no small difficulty. The series of clauses, ὃ ἦν ἀπ' ἀρχῆς, ὃ ἀκηκόαμεν, ὃ ἑωράκαμεν . . . , are taken as denoting, not what the Apostle has to announce *concerning* the Word of Life, but the Word of Life Himself. The personal Christ is "what was from the beginning . . . what our hands handled." And the design of the collocation of these clauses is to identify the Eternal Word with the Christ of human experience. It is, however, confessedly difficult to account for the peculiarly abstract form in which the thought is clothed by the use throughout of the neuter relative ὅ, instead of the masculine, "Him who was from the beginning, whom we have heard," etc. The difficulty is not lessened by such explanations as Haupt's, that ὅ indicates that "the subject of announcement is not the personal Christ in Himself, and as such, but that quality in Him which is Life"; or Plummer's, that it indicates "that collective whole of human and divine attributes which is the Incarnate Word of Life"; or Weiss's, that the subject of consideration is "not Christ's Person or the facts of His Life, but His Being as it comes to manifestation in these facts."

Again, περὶ τοῦ λογοῦ τῆς ζωῆς is taken, not as depending on the clauses preceding it, but as an independent co-ordinate clause, supplying an additional definition of the object of the Apostle's announcement. (I venture to observe that in ordinary Greek this would be expressed by τὰ περὶ τοῦ λόγου; and, in the second place, that the more natural phrase would have been simply τὸν λόγον τῆς ζωῆς, "that is to say, the Word of Life.")

Another and in every way simpler construction is obvious. The predicate to be supplied in 1¹ is, of course, the ἀπαγγέλλομεν of 1³. But for the interrupting parenthesis (1²), ἀπαγγέλλομεν would come immediately after περὶ τοῦ λόγου τῆς ζωῆς. The sentence as originally conceived would run as follows: "What was from the beginning, what we have heard . . . concerning the Word of Life, we announce unto you." περὶ τοῦ λόγου τῆς ζωῆς defines in ordinary adverbial fashion either ἀπαγγέλλομεν or the series of clauses, ὃ ἦν ἀπ᾽ ἀρχῆς, ὃ ἀκηκόαμεν, κ.τ.λ. (so Westcott). This construction gives to the neuter ὅ its natural sense; and it is rendered almost necessary by the form in which the sentence is resumed in 1³, where it seems very unnatural to take ὃ ἑωράκαμεν καὶ ἀκηκόαμεν in any other than a strictly neuter sense. It may be said, indeed, that but for the opening clause, ὃ ἦν ἀπ᾽ ἀρχῆς, no other sense would have been suspected. But there need be no difficulty in supposing that the Apostle professes to announce "what was from the beginning" concerning the Word of Life. In point of fact, this is what he does announce (John 1¹⁻³). The only possible way, moreover, of announcing the personal Word of Life is to announce what is known concerning Him.

ὃ ἦν ἀπ᾽ ἀρχῆς is invariably understood of the "unbeginning beginning"; and the parallelism of John 1¹ and 1 John 2¹³·¹⁴ is in favour of this. Might not something, however, be said for taking ἀπ᾽ ἀρχῆς in the sense of "from the beginning of Christ's earthly ministry"? The purpose of the passage is to describe the content of the Apostolic testimony. And in John 15²⁶·²⁷ it is expressly said: "The Spirit shall bear witness of Me; and ye also bear witness, because ye have been with Me *from the beginning*" (cf. John 16⁴, Luke 1²).

Whichever view of the whole construction is preferred, the effect is to describe accurately the contents of the Apostolic Gospel. "What was from the beginning, what we have heard, what we have seen with our eyes, what we beheld and our hands handled concerning the Word of Life, we announce unto you."

ἐθεασάμεθα . . . ἐψηλάφησαν. On the significance of these aorists, *v. supra*, p. 47.

24

τοῦ λόγου τῆς ζωῆς. It has been assumed in the foregoing discussion that the reference is to Christ, the Personal Word. *v. supra*, p. 44 (n.).

The precise significance of the genitive τῆς ζωῆς is doubtful. From what follows—καὶ ἡ ζωὴ ἐφανερώθη, κ.τ.λ.—it is evident that the emphasis is not so much on λόγου as on ζωῆς; not so much on the Word as revealing the Life, as on the Life pertaining to the Word. Thus the phrase may be understood, after the analogy of the "Bread of Life," as meaning the "Word who communicates Life" (so Calvin: "Non dubito quin de effectu loquatur . . . beneficio Christi partam nobis esse vitam"); or better, perhaps, as "the Word who is the Life," "in whom the Life inheres" (ζωῆς, genitive of definition. Cf. John 2²¹ 11¹³ 13¹¹).

1² καί, with the force of γάρ. The purpose of the verse is to explain how the announcement summarised in the preceding verse is possible,—"for the life was manifested, and we have seen," etc.

ἀπαγγέλλομεν. The shade of difference between the ἀπαγγέλλομεν of this and the following verse and the ἀναγγέλλομεν of 1⁵ ought to be observed.

ἀπαγγέλλειν (to report with reference to the source from which the message comes) is appropriate to the historical Gospel, as ἀναγγέλλειν (to report with reference to the persons addressed) is appropriate to the Epistle, as carrying home to the readers the practical implications of the former.

ἥτις ἦν πρὸς τὸν πατέρα. In late Greek the distinction between ὅς and ὅστις is quite lost; but in the N.T. ὅστις, as a rule, retains something of its proper generic force (Moulton, p. 95), and may here be understood as "which by its very nature."

1³ ἵνα καὶ ὑμεῖς κοινωνίαν ἔχητε μεθ᾽ ἡμῶν· καὶ ἡ κοινωνία δὲ ἡ ἡμετέρα μετὰ τοῦ πατρὸς καὶ μετὰ τοῦ υἱοῦ αὐτοῦ Ἰησοῦ Χριστοῦ.

Exegetes are much divided as to the grammatical relation and the precise meaning of these two clauses. The Vulgate (followed by Augustine, Luther, Calvin, and others) places both clauses under the government of ἵνα ("ut et vos societatem habeatis nobiscum, et nostra societas sit"), "that ye may have fellowship with us, and that our (common) fellowship may be . . ." This may be at once set aside on the ground both of grammar (ἵνα . . . καί . . . δέ is an impossible sequence, *v.* Westcott, p. 12. And to supply the conjunctive ᾖ after κοινωνία δὲ ἡμῶν is difficult, and is not justified by cases like 2 Cor. 8¹¹. ¹³, where it is the inevitable supplement). and of sense (ἡμετέρα must refer to the preceding ἡμῶν, and does not readily suggest the idea of "ours and yours together").

On the other hand, some regard the second clause as implicitly contained in the first—"That ye also may have fellowship (with God) along with us; and, truly, our fellowship is with the Father." But there is no warrant for taking κοινωνία as meaning by itself "fellowship with God"; and, even if it could be so taken, the interpretation of κοινωνία μεθ' ἡμῶν as "fellowship with God in common with us" is very strained. The real difficulty is to determine the meaning of κοινωνία in the two clauses respectively. The abstract idea of fellowship is differently modified by the different objects to which it is related. In the first clause, it points to community of privilege between the Apostle and his readers in the possession of the historic Gospel, to bring about this being the purpose of his announcement. In the second, it is participation in the Life and the Light of God. And the logical link of connection is that the common basis of both "fellowships," the human and the divine, is found in the knowledge of God in Christ (John 17³) which is given to men in the facts of the Incarnate Life. By their participation with the Apostle in the possession of that knowledge, his readers also will enter, or enter more fully, into the "fellowship" which he possesses with the Father and the Son.

καὶ ἡ κοινωνία δὲ ἡ ἡμετέρα. καί . . . δέ; cf. Matt. 10¹⁸, Acts 3²⁴, 1 Tim. 3¹⁰, 2 Pet. 1⁵, John 6⁵¹ 8¹⁶. ¹⁷ 15²⁷, 2 John ¹². In this combination the conjunctive function belongs to δέ, καί being intensive. The double particles, καί . . . δέ, together with the reduplicated article in ἡ κοινωνία ἡ ἡμετέρα, give peculiar emphasis to the statement made. "And this fellowship of which I speak, our fellowship, is with . . ."

I⁴ καὶ ταῦτα γράφομεν ἡμεῖς ἵνα ἡ χαρὰ ἡμῶν ᾖ πεπληρωμένη.

καὶ ταῦτα γράφομεν. The preceding verses have reference to the writer's habitual oral proclamation of the Gospel, or to its literary embodiment. These words now introduce the Epistle itself.

ἵνα ἡ χαρὰ ἡμῶν ᾖ πεπληρωμένη. *v. supra*, p. 42 (n.).

The words are an almost verbal reproduction of John 16²⁴.

I⁵ σκοτία ἐν αὐτῷ οὐκ ἔστιν οὐδεμία. Cf. 1⁶ ἐν τῷ σκότει περιπατῶμεν.

σκότος is the concrete thing called "darkness" ("the dark"), σκοτία, its abstract quality. Here σκοτία is appropriately used: "Nothing of the nature of darkness is in Him at all." Elsewhere, however, St. John uses the two forms indifferently (cf. ἐν τῷ σκότει περιπατεῖν, 1⁶; ἐν τῇ σκοτίᾳ περιπατεῖν, 2¹¹).

I⁶ ἐὰν εἴπωμεν ὅτι κοινωνίαν ἔχομεν μετ' αὐτοῦ, καὶ ἐν τῷ σκότει περιπατῶμεν, ψευδόμεθα καὶ οὐ ποιοῦμεν τὴν ἀλήθειαν.

περιπατῶμεν. περιπατεῖν, as describing the whole course of life, outward and inward (the equivalent of הָלַךְ, *e.g.* Pss. 1¹ 15²), is characteristic of St. Paul and of the Johannine Epistles (1⁶· ⁷ 2⁶· ¹¹, 2 John ⁴· ⁶, 3 John ³· ⁴). In the Fourth Gospel only in explicit metaphor (8¹² 12³⁵).

ψευδόμεθα καὶ οὐ ποιοῦμεν τὴν ἀλήθειαν. By some (Huther, *e.g.*) ψευδόμεθα is taken as correlative to ἐὰν εἴπωμεν, as denoting the verbal falsehood, and "we do not the truth" as correlative to "walk in darkness."

But the natural sense is that "we lie" and "do not the truth"; both refer to the whole supposed situation. Nor can I agree with Westcott in his exposition of ψευδόμεθα: "The assertion is not only false, but known to be false." There are no lexical grounds for assigning this meaning to ψεύδεσθαι, which merely signifies to "say what is untrue"; nor is there any reason in the context for narrowing the meaning here to that of conscious falsehood. On the contrary, we have here the widest statement of the case, covering culpable self-deception as well as conscious hypocrisy.

οὐ ποιοῦμεν τὴν ἀλήθειαν. In St. John ἡ ἀλήθεια, objective Divine Truth, is to be distinguished from ἀλήθεια, subjective, moral truth (sincerity). ἡ ἀλήθεια denotes the reality of things *sub specie æternitatis*—the realities of the spiritual and eternal world, the revelation of which is the Light; *v. supra*, p. 62. So here "we do not the Truth" is more specific than "we lie." We do not act out what the Light of God reveals as the Truth. We say that we have fellowship with God, yet ignore or shun His Light as the guide of Life.

1⁷ ἐὰν δὲ ἐν τῷ φωτὶ περιπατῶμεν ὡς αὐτός ἐστιν ἐν τῷ φωτί, κοινωνίαν ἔχομεν μετ᾽ ἀλλήλων καὶ τὸ αἷμα Ἰησοῦ τοῦ υἱοῦ αὐτοῦ καθαρίζει ἡμᾶς ἀπὸ πάσης ἁμαρτίας.

κοινωνίαν ἔχομεν μετ᾽ ἀλλήλων. Instead of the expected "we have fellowship with God"—a surprising but characteristic turn of thought. For to understand "the fellowship with one another" as our fellowship with God and God's with us (Augustine, Calvin, and others) is inadmissible. The proximate result of walking in the Light is that we have fellowship with those who also are walking in the Light. When men have the light of the same spirit of sincerity and goodness shining in them, there is fellowship of the noblest kind; soul meets soul with brotherly trust and love and joy. Probably, however, the thought here is more definitely religious. Walking in the Light we are spiritually one with the "children of God," we are of the "commonwealth of Israel," and the "household of faith"; and we partake in the cleansing efficacy of the sacrifice by which Christ consecrates the people of God.

ἀπὸ πάσης ἁμαρτίας. πᾶς ought to be taken in its distributive sense, not "from all sin," but "from every (kind of) sin."

I⁸ ἡ ἀλήθεια. See note on 1⁶, *supra*. On the whole verse, *v. supra*, p. 130.

I⁹ ἐὰν ὁμολογῶμεν τὰς ἁμαρτίας ἡμῶν, πιστός ἐστιν καὶ δίκαιος ἵνα ἀφῇ ἡμῖν τὰς ἁμαρτίας καὶ καθαρίσῃ ἡμᾶς ἀπὸ πάσης ἁμαρτίας.

The expected antithesis would have been: "If we confess our sins, we do not deceive ourselves," etc.; but the thought (as in 1⁷) leaps immediately to the Divine action which is immediately consequent upon our action.

ἐὰν ὁμολογῶμεν τὰς ἁμαρτίας. Only here in the N.T. is ὁμολογεῖν used with reference to sin. Its invariable usage in other connections certifies the sense here, as not recognition only, but open acknowledgment—this, as is evident, being made primarily to God, but confession to man, when it is due, not being excluded.

πιστός ἐστιν καὶ δίκαιος. *v. supra*, pp. 68, 167.

ἵνα ἀφῇ. Haupt, Westcott, and Abbott notwithstanding, it is not possible in this and many Johannine passages to give ἵνα its strictly telic force. "The whole fulness of His unfathomable essence is turned to nothing else but the salvation of His creatures, so that it is to Him only the means, yea, His very self is only the means, to effect His creatures' happiness and good" (Haupt). Most true it is that God, Who is Love, uses all His attributes for our salvation, and, being what He is, could not do otherwise. But it is to press this truth very far to say that God regards His attributes, and even Himself, as existing only for this end (it comes too near Heine's "Dieu me pardonnera, c'est son métier"). There is no need to import such a difficulty into the passage, when a simple and adequate meaning is so obvious. The use of ἵνα without the telic sense (sometimes equivalent to ὥστε, sometimes to ὅτι) is amply attested in St. John (John 2²⁵ 4³⁴ 6²⁹ 9² 11⁵⁰ 15⁸ 16⁷. ³⁰ 17³, not to mention the passages in which it is used after ἐντολή, to give the purport of the commandment, John 13³⁴ etc.). Here the meaning simply is, that, in forgiving our sins and cleansing us from all unrighteousness, God is faithful and righteous.

ἀπὸ πάσης ἀδικίας. "From every (kind of) unrighteousness." Cf. ἀπὸ πάσης ἁμαρτίας, 1⁷. Cf. *supra*, pp. 134–5.

I¹⁰ ψεύστην ποιοῦμεν αὐτόν. *v. supra*, p. 131. This use of ποιεῖν (to "make one out to be") is characteristic of St. John (John 5¹⁸ 8⁵³ 10³³ 19⁷. ¹²). In this culminates the series of falsehoods: "We lie" (1⁶); "We lead ourselves astray" (1⁸); "We make Him a liar" (1¹⁰).

ὁ λόγος αὐτοῦ οὐκ ἔστιν ἐν ἡμῖν. ὁ λόγος here corresponds closely to ἡ ἀλήθεια in 1⁸. It regards the truth not only as true in itself, but as the message which God has addressed to men in Christ. If we say that we have not sinned, we make God a liar ; because we contradict what He has expressly revealed and declared.

2¹ τεκνία μου, ταῦτα γράφω ὑμῖν ἵνα μὴ ἁμάρτητε. καὶ ἐάν τις ἁμάρτῃ, παράκλητον ἔχομεν πρὸς τὸν πατέρα, Ἰησοῦν Χριστὸν δίκαιον.

ἵνα μὴ ἁμάρτητε. Not "that ye may not continue in sin," but "that ye may commit no act of sin" (aorist). So also, ἐάν τις ἁμάρτῃ : "if any one commit a sin."

πρὸς τὸν πατέρα. πρός may here have the definite sense of "turning towards" (in the act of pleading). Or it may have the more general sense which it has in 1² and John 1¹—"in relation to."

δίκαιον. The absence of the article imports that δίκαιον is not added to Jesus Christ as an epithet, or as pointing to Him, in contradistinction to others, as *the* Righteous One. Its effect is to emphasise the abstract quality indicated by the adjective, and so to bring out the relation between the character "righteous" and the office "Paraclete," "Jesus Christ being, as He is, righteous." Similarly, in John 1¹⁴ δόξαν ὡς μονογενοῦς παρὰ πατρός = "glory as of an only-begotten of a father," the thought being of a son to whom the full undivided glory of the father is transmitted. Thus also in John 6⁶⁸, the force of ῥήματα ζωῆς αἰωνίου is, "words that are words of eternal life." *v.* Moulton, p. 82.

2² περὶ ὅλου τοῦ κόσμου. Cf. John 3¹⁶.

There is no need to supply "the sins of" before "the whole world." ἐξιλάζεσθαι περί is often used directly of the person or object on whose behalf propitiation is made.

2³⁻⁶.

2³ τούτῳ is correlative to ἐὰν τὰς ἐντολάς, κ.τ.λ.

ἐάν is used instead of the usual ὅτι in order to avoid the clumsiness of ἐν τούτῳ γινώσκομεν . . . ὅτι . . . ὅτι. Cf. 5², where ὅταν is used for the same reason.

γινώσκομεν . . . ἐγνώκαμεν. See special note on γινώσκειν.

2⁴ μὴ τηρῶν. μή, because the phrase has a conditional force. ἐν τούτῳ ἡ ἀλήθεια οὐκ ἔστιν. ἔστιν, emphatic. The truth is not in him, whatever he may think.

2⁵ τηρῇ αὐτοῦ τὸν λόγον. The change of order from τὰς ἐντολὰς αὐτοῦ μὴ τηρῶν in 2⁴ is significant. In the former case, the emphasis is on τὰς ἐντολάς, "He who says that I know Him, and does not so much as keep His commandments." Here it is on τηρῇ, "But he who does keep His word, verily in him," etc.

ἐν τούτῳ γινώσκομεν. With prospective reference to 2⁶.

2⁶ καθὼς ἐκεῖνος. καθώς is a favourite Johannine word. Cf. 2¹⁸·²⁷ 3²·³·⁷·¹²·²³ 4¹⁷.

ἐκεῖνος. v. supra, p. 89.

περιπατεῖν. v. supra on 1⁶.

2⁷⁻¹¹.

The next two verses bristle with disputed points and also with real difficulties.

2⁷. 1. By some (Lücke, e.g.) the "old commandment" is understood as looking back to the requirement "to walk, even as He walked" (2⁶), or (Ebrard and Candlish) to all that precedes (2³⁻⁶); the "new" as looking forward to the requirement of brotherly love (2⁹⁻¹¹). This is erroneous. The command "to walk, even as He walked," is in no sense older than the command "to love one another"; and the identity of the "old" and the "new" is rendered certain by 2 John ⁵. 2. This identity being granted, there is still a diversity of view as to the reason why the commandment is "old." Because it is already given in the O.T. or, additionally, in the human conscience, is one explanation (Maurice; Rothe, who says a number of profoundly true things about the Christian being only man as he ought to be, and Christianity only the ideal life of humanity). But, unmistakably, the reason is that the commandment had been familiar to the readers of the Epistle ever since they knew the Gospel. "The old commandment is the word which ye heard." 3. The aorist ἠκούσατε denotes the Gospel message as heard at a definite point of time. The imperfect εἴχετε seems decidedly anomalous (cf. εἴχομεν, 2 John ⁵). Westcott's explanation, that it denotes the commandment as a continuous influence, is, no doubt, right. But one would have expected the perfect tense instead of an imperfect, with its suggestion of uncertainty as to the continuance of this influence down to the present time.

2⁸. 1. πάλιν is to be taken here as an adversative particle. Huther and others deny that it can be so used, and take it in a strictly temporal sense, "a second time I write unto you." But the use of πάλιν in a mildly adversative sense, exactly corresponding to "again" or "on the other hand" in English, is not unknown in classical usage (I have noted it in Lucian, *Zeus Elenchomenos*, 16; *Parasitos*, 43), and seems to be vouched for in the N.T. by John 16²⁸, 1 Cor. 12²¹.

2. The principal clause may be construed in two ways. (*a*) ὅ ἐστιν ἀληθές may be taken as the direct object after γράφω, with ἐντολὴν καινήν as an accusative of nearer definition: "I write to you, as a new commandment, what is true in Him and in you." But the parallelism with οὐκ ἐντολὴν καινὴν γράφω in the preceding verse is against this; and, besides, this construction is extremely improbable in a simple prose-writer like St. John. It is much more natural to take ἐντολὴν καινήν as the direct object of γράφω, with ὅ ἐστιν ἀληθές, κ.τ.λ., as a parenthetic clause in apposition.

3. ὅτι ἡ σκοτία παράγεται· καὶ τὸ φῶς τὸ ἀληθινὸν ἤδη φαίνει. "παράγεται is middle rather than passive—of a cloud withdrawing, rather than of a veil being withdrawn" (Plummer). Regarding the construction of the clause as a whole, we may at once reject the view that it is *declarative* of the "thing that is true in Him and in you" (Bengel, Ebrard, Candlish). This yields no tolerable sense. Without doubt, ὅτι = because. But to what preceding word or words is it related? The possible connections are (*a*) with γράφω (Huther and others), "I write this to you because the darkness passeth away," etc.; (*b*) with ὅ ἐστιν ἀληθές ἐν αὐτῷ καὶ ἐν ὑμῖν, either by taking the passing away of the darkness and the shining of the true Light as the reason why this thing is true both "in Him and in you," or by limiting the reference to ὑμῖν (Haupt). This limitation seems necessary; for it is extremely difficult to comprehend how the words "the darkness passeth away" can apply to Christ. The meaning of the verse, so construed, will be: "Again, a new commandment I write unto you—a commandment which is realised as a new and living power in His Incarnation, but also in you, because the same Law of Love that was embodied in Him is revealed to you in the Light of His Gospel, by which the darkness of the world is being overcome and dispersed."

The former of these two interpretations seems to me the simpler and more forcible. *v. supra*, pp. 234–5.

2⁹ ἕως ἄρτι. Cf. John 2¹⁰ 5¹⁷ 16²⁴.

2¹¹ ποῦ, "where," is constantly used in the N.T. for ποῖ, "whither." ποῦ ὑπάγει; cf. John 3⁸ 8¹⁴ 12³⁵ 14⁵ 16⁵.

It is not necessary to understand ποῦ ὑπάγει of the *final goal* (Westcott, who quotes Cyprian, "It nescius in Gehennam, ignarus et cæcus præcipitatur in pœnam"). The man blinded by hate does not see the way he is taking—has no true perception of the character of his own actions.

ἐτύφλωσεν seems to be a "gnomic" aorist, denoting what habitually happens, like ἐβλήθη in John 15⁶; cf. Jas. 1¹¹.

2¹²⁻¹⁴.

Regarding the structure, *v. supra*, pp. 306 sqq. Each of its six clauses contains a ὅτι, which, without doubt, is used in its causal, not in its declarative (Bengel, Neander, etc.), sense. The Apostle is not writing to inform his readers that their "sins are forgiven them," but to declare that this is the presupposition of all he is writing.

γράφω . . . ἔγραψα. Regarding the epistolary aorist, *v. supra*, p. 308; and cf. Moulton, p. 135.

2¹² διὰ τὸ ὄνομα αὐτοῦ. αὐτοῦ = Christ. *v. supra*, p. 89.

The construction (διά, c. acc.) differs from that usually found in the N.T. (διά, c. gen.; cf. Acts 10⁴³ ἄφεσιν ἁμαρτιῶν λαβεῖν διὰ τοῦ ὀνόματος αὐτοῦ). In the latter case, the name of Christ connotes the means through which forgiveness is instrumentally effected; in the former, as here, the reason for which it is granted. In the latter case it is regarded as the object of man's faith; in the former, as the ground of Divine action.

2¹⁵⁻¹⁷.

This paragraph resumes the subject of 2⁷⁻¹¹. The commandment to love the "brethren" is supplemented by the commandment not to love the "world." But there is also a close connection with the immediately preceding address to the readers (2¹²⁻¹⁴); *v. supra*, p. 307.

2¹⁵ οὐκ ἔστιν ἡ ἀγάπη, κ.τ.λ. The order is peculiarly emphatic: "There is not in him, whatever he may suppose, the love of the Father."

2¹⁶ πᾶν τὸ ἐν τῷ κόσμῳ. The form of expression is stronger than that used in the preceding verse, τὰ ἐν τῷ κόσμῳ. There is nothing else in the world's life than what he is about to mention. This is the whole of it—"the lust of the flesh," etc.

ἐπιθυμία τῆς σαρκός . . . τῶν ὀφθαλμῶν. The genitives are subjective, as is usual with ἐπιθυμία: "That which the flesh and the eyes long for."

ἡ ἀλαζονεία. In the N.T. ἀλαζονεία occurs only here and in

Jas. 4¹⁶; the adjective ἀλαζών in Rom. 1³⁰ and 2 Tim. 3¹⁰; in both of which places it is coupled with ὑπερήφανος. The distinction seems to be that ἀλαζονεία signifies atheistical, ὑπερηφανία egotistical pride. *v. supra*, p. 152. In classical usage ἀλαζών means: 1, a vagrant; 2, an impostor or quack; 3 (as adjective), boastful or braggart.

τοῦ βίου. βίος is not to be taken in the restricted sense of "possessions" (Mark 12⁴⁴, Luke 15¹², 1 John 3¹⁷ etc.), but as the whole course of human life in relation to the seen and temporal (Luke 8⁴⁴ 2 Tim. 2⁴).

2¹⁷ καὶ ἡ ἐπιθυμία αὐτοῦ. Again the genitive is subjective, expressing not desire for the world, but the desire which characterises the world of unspiritual men.

2¹⁸⁻²⁸.

2¹⁸ παιδία; cf. 2¹⁸. *v. supra*, p. 310 (n.).

καθώς . . . καί = "as . . . even so"; cf. John 15⁹ 17¹⁸ 20²¹. καί is used thus, *in apodosi*, often in the LXX, sometimes in classical prose.

2¹⁹ ἐξ ἡμῶν ἐξῆλθαν, ἀλλ' οὐκ ἦσαν ἐξ ἡμῶν. The sense of the preposition ἐξ is determined by the verb upon which, in each clause, it is dependent. With εἶναι, it denotes connection of the most intimate kind, spiritual affinity, nay, spiritual unity (ἐκ τοῦ κόσμου 2¹⁶ 4⁵; ἐκ τοῦ θεοῦ (πατρός), 2¹⁶ 3¹⁰ 4¹· ²· ³ etc.; ἐκ τοῦ διαβόλου, 3⁸; ἐκ τοῦ πονηροῦ, 3¹²; ἐκ τῆς ἀληθείας, 2²¹ 3¹⁹).

With ἐξῆλθαν the meaning is merely that of local severance (cf. John 8⁵⁹), as is proved by the antithesis μεμενήκεισαν ἂν μεθ' ἡμῶν.

μεμενήκεισαν ἄν may be noted as the solitary instance in the N.T. of the pluperfect with ἄν in the apodosis of a conditional sentence. It expresses "the continuance of the contingent result to the time of speaking."

ἀλλ' ἵνα φανερωθῶσιν ὅτι οὐκ εἰσὶν πάντες ἐξ ἡμῶν.

ἀλλ' ἵνα φανερωθῶσιν. This elliptical construction, requiring that we supply, after "but," "they went forth from us," is peculiarly Johannine (cf. John 13¹⁸ 15²⁵; less exactly parallel, 1⁸ 9³ 14³¹).

ὅτι οὐκ εἰσὶν πάντες ἐξ ἡμῶν.

ὅτι is taken causally (Rothe); a construction that has nothing to commend it. By others πάντες is not referred to the antichrists, but is taken absolutely ("that all who seem to be of us are not of us"), the meaning assigned to the whole clause being that the visible separation of the antichrists was providentially designed to make it evident that outward fellowship with the Church was no sufficient credential of genuine Christian life. But to obtain this meaning it is necessary to supplement the Apostle's diction (already elliptical) to the extent of inserting καὶ ἵνα φανερωθῇ after φανερωθῶσιν (so De Wette, Huther, Haupt, and others). However excellent and edifying the sense thus obtained, the construction proposed is absolutely needless, and would have occurred to no one, but for a supposed difficulty in the phrase οὐκ εἰσὶν πάντες ἐξ ἡμῶν, which, if it is translated "not all of them are of us," and is applied to the antichrists, is said to imply that, though not all are, yet some of them may be "of us" (so Huther, who insists that οὐ πάντες = *nonnulli*, not *nulli*). The difficulty, however, does not really exist. οὐκ εἰσὶν πάντες ἐξ ἡμῶν means, not "*not all* of them are of us," but "all of them *are not* of us," or "not *any* of them are of us." According to the idiom of N.T. Greek, πᾶς with the negative particle (except when immediately preceded by it) is to be translated, not as "all," but as "any," or, otherwise, by attaching the negative to the verb. Cf. 2²¹ 3¹⁵, and list of parallels in Westcott. It seems questionable whether this is a Hebraism, as is usually said. The explanation of the idiom probably is, not that πᾶς was used in a consciously distributive sense, but that, in vernacular Greek, the negative was attached in sense to the verb, where we attach it to the nominative (all are not = none are). The attachment of οὐ to what seems to us the wrong word is not unusual in Greek (in the *Wasps*, *e.g.* 1091, πάντα μὴ δεδοικέναι = μηδὲν δεδοικέναι), and is invariable in the common οὔ φημι τοῦτο εἶναι = I say that this *is not* so.

2²⁰ καὶ ὑμεῖς χρῖσμα ἔχετε ἀπὸ τοῦ ἁγίου καὶ οἴδατε πάντα. By the first καί, the verse is related to the last clause of 2¹⁹, as adding a new fact to what is there stated. "By the separation of the antichrists from the Church, it has been made visible to all that they had never truly been of it; and, besides, ye have an anointing from the Holy One, and know all things (and so, in any case, would have been able to discern the falsity of their teaching)."

2²¹ πᾶν ψεῦδος . . . οὐκ ἔστιν. "Not any lie . . . is." See note on 2¹⁹.

2²² ὁ ἀρνούμενος ὅτι Ἰησοῦς οὐκ ἔστιν ὁ Χριστός. ἀρνεῖσθαι and similar verbs are used either with or without (cf. Heb 11²⁴) a pleonastic negative (οὐ, μή, μὴ οὐ). When it is present, as here, it seems to impart a tone of special aggressiveness to the negation, expressing it in the very terms in which it may be supposed to have been originally spoken—Ἰησοῦς οὐκ ἔστιν ὁ Χριστός.

οὗτός ἐστιν ὁ ἀντίχριστος, ὁ ἀρνούμενος τὸν πατέρα καὶ τὸν υἱόν.

This clause is translated in R.V. :—"This is the antichrist, even he that denieth the Father and the Son." It is better, however, to take ὁ ἀρνούμενος τὸν πατέρα καὶ τὸν υἱόν, not as a further definition of ὁ ἀντίχριστος, but as an additional predicate: "This is the antichrist, (this is) he that denieth the Father and the Son." This sense is to be preferred, because the writer immediately proceeds to justify the statement that he who denies that Jesus is the Christ in effect denies both the Father and the Son. For "Whosoever denieth the Son hath not even the Father" (2²³). τὸν πατέρα καὶ τὸν υἱόν. The order is significant. We should have expected the Son and the Father; but the unexpected emphasis thus laid on the denial of the Father, as involved in the denial of Jesus as the Christ, is immediately explained by the following sentence.

2²³ πᾶς ὁ ἀρνούμενος τὸν υἱὸν οὐδὲ τὸν πατέρα ἔχει. πᾶς . . . οὐδέ. See note on 2¹⁹. οὐδέ is intensive in force (cf. Gal. 2³). "No one that denieth the Son hath even the Father; he that confesseth the Son hath the Father also." *v. supra*, p. 101.

2²⁴ Having thus exhibited in the strongest light the substance and also the infinitely momentous consequences of the Christian ἀλήθεια and the antichristian ψεῦδος, the Apostle addresses to his readers the practical exhortation that leaps irresistibly into utterance.

ὑμεῖς ὃ ἠκούσατε ἀπ' ἀρχῆς ἐν ὑμῖν μενέτω.

ἀπ' ἀρχῆς = from your first acquaintance with the Christian evangel. In 2⁷ the word "heard from the beginning" is specifically the old-new commandment of Love. Here, "that which ye have heard from the beginning" is the whole unity of the Gospel teaching, with particular reference to the cardinal truth that Jesus is the Christ, the Son of God. Both are only diverse sides of the same matter (Haupt). Christian morality derives all its contents from Christ, and His Divinity is the presupposition of its authority. It is "the truth as it is in Jesus" translated into practice.

ὑμεῖς. The form of the sentence is peculiar. The abrupt ὑμεῖς with which it begins is not a vocative (Ebrard), nor yet the nominative to ἠκούσατε placed out of the usual order for the sake of emphasis, but is an example of anacoluthon of a common type (cf. 2²⁷, John 7³⁸, Luke 21⁶), and suggests that the sentence, as it first flashed upon the writer's mind, ended with μένετε ἐν αὐτῷ instead of ἐν ὑμῖν μενέτω. Both forms are used of the relation of the Christian disciple to the Word. He abides in it (John 8³¹), not withdrawing himself from its influence, but continuing stead-

fastly under it. It abides in him (John 15⁷, Col. 3¹⁶, 2 John ²)
as a vitalising, fertilising power (John 6⁶³). This reciprocal relation
is brought out in our Lord's parables of the Sower and of the
Fruitful Soil. "These are such as in an honest and good heart,
having heard the Word, hold it fast and bring forth fruit with
patience" (Luke 8¹⁵); and "The seed springs up and grows, he
knoweth not how" (Mark 4²⁷). Here the expression is conflate.
What is to be done, the only thing necessary or effectual, is to let
that "which ye heard from the beginning" abide in you and do its
proper work. On the other hand, the fact that this is expressed
imperatively, shows that what is implied is not a merely passive
attitude towards the Truth. We cannot command the results of
its efficiency, but we can furnish the conditions.

2²⁴ᵇ ἐὰν ἐν ὑμῖν μείνῃ ὃ ἀπ' ἀρχῆς ἠκούσατε, καὶ ὑμεῖς ἐν τῷ υἱῷ καὶ
ἐν τῷ πατρὶ μενεῖτε.

Protasis and apodosis are finely balanced. The abiding of the
Truth in you will result in a further abiding—your abiding in the
Son and in the Father. Here the order of 2²² is reversed. There,
πατέρα stands first, under the influence of the thought that the
denial of the Son finds its unexpected yet inevitable consequence
in the denial of the Father. The order here is the natural one. In
the facts of experience, the Father is revealed and apprehended
through the Son (cf. 2 Cor. 16¹³). It is by abiding in the Son that
we abide in the Father. *v. infra* on 5²⁰.

2²⁵. The Apostle now brings the matter to its final issue. Eternal
Life is at stake. καὶ αὕτη ἐστὶν ἡ ἐπαγγελία ἣν αὐτός ἐπηγγείλατο
ἡμῖν, τὴν ζωὴν τὴν αἰώνιον.

The verse presents several peculiarities. ἐπαγγέλλεσθαι and ἐπαγγελία are not found elsewhere in St. John. τὴν ζωὴν τὴν αἰώνιον is
in the accusative by attraction to the ἥν of the preceding relative
clause (cf. Phil. 3¹⁸). αὕτη may be referred either to what precedes or to what follows. In the former case, the meaning is—
"This that has been just now spoken of—that we shall abide in the
Son and in the Father—is the promise that He has promised. And
this is, in effect, the promise of Eternal Life." In the latter case,
the meaning is—"This, namely, Eternal Life, is the promise He
hath given," *i.e.* on condition of our abiding in the Son and in
the Father. The former construction forces a too pregnant sense
upon the words τὴν ζωὴν τὴν αἰώνιον (=and this—to abide in
the Son and in the Father—is Eternal Life). The latter involves a
more abrupt transition of thought, but is preferable in point both
of sense and of grammar (cf. John 1²⁷· ²⁸).

2²⁶ ταῦτα ἔγραψα ὑμῖν περὶ τῶν πλανώντων ὑμᾶς.

ταῦτα ἔγραψα. Epistolary aorist (cf. 2¹⁴· ²¹ 5¹³).

τῶν πλανώντων ὑμᾶς. Cf. 3⁷ 4⁶, Matt. 24⁴· ⁵· ¹¹· ²⁴, 2 Tim. 3¹³. It is not implied, of course, that the effort to lead astray is successful. The force of the present tense is distinctly conative.

2²⁷ καὶ ὑμεῖς τὸ χρῖσμα ὃ ἐλάβετε ἀπ᾽ αὐτοῦ μένει ἐν ὑμῖν, καὶ οὐ χρείαν ἔχετε ἵνα τις διδάσκῃ ὑμᾶς, ἀλλ᾽ ὡς τὸ αὐτοῦ χρῖσμα διδάσκει ὑμᾶς περὶ πάντων, καὶ ἀληθές ἐστιν καὶ οὐκ ἔστιν ψεῦδος, καὶ καθὼς ἐδίδαξεν ὑμᾶς, μένετε ἐν αὐτῷ.

καὶ ὑμεῖς = "and as for you" (in contrast with those who would lead you astray). The anacolouthon is exactly the same as in 2²⁴ ἀπ᾽ αὐτοῦ, from Christ (ἀπὸ τοῦ ἁγίου, 2²⁰). μένει. The gift once bestowed is never, from the Divine side, recalled (cf. Rom. 11²⁹). χρείαν ἔχετε ἵνα (cf. John 2²⁵ 16³⁰). The telic sense of ἵνα is, as so commonly in St. John, much enfeebled. τις refers, not to the false teachers, but to the Apostle himself, and to human teachers in general. They have resources within themselves that render them independent of human teaching. ἀλλ᾽ ὡς τὸ αὐτοῦ χρῖσμα, κ.τ.λ. The first question is as to the construction of this second part of the sentence. By the majority of commentators it is divided into two parts, with a protasis and an apodosis in each. "As His anointing teacheth you concerning all things, even so is it true and is no lie; and as it taught you, even so you abide in Him." But the sense thus obtained is very weak. The affirmation that the Divine teaching "is true, and is no lie," is not in any way dependent upon the fact that "it teacheth you concerning all things." It is better to construe the whole as one continuous sentence—καὶ ἀληθές ἐστιν καὶ οὐκ ἔστιν ψεῦδος being taken as a parenthesis, and καὶ καθὼς ἐδίδαξεν as a resumption of ὡς διδάσκει (Westcott). "As His anointing teacheth you concerning all things—and it is true, and is no lie—even as it taught you, ye abide in Him."

τὸ αὐτοῦ χρῖσμα. The very unusual position of αὐτοῦ throws strong emphasis upon the pronoun; cf. 1 Thess. 2¹⁹ ἐν τῇ αὐτοῦ παρουσίᾳ.

καθώς, stronger than ὡς, fixing this "teaching" as the criterion of all truth by means of which we abide in Christ. διδάσκει . . . ἐδίδαξεν. The change of tense is significant. The teaching is, on the one hand, continuous. In another sense, it was complete from the first. The aorist can refer only to the time when, taught by the Spirit, they first understood and accepted the Gospel. In germ, at least, all legitimate developments were contained in that first illumination.

μένετε, indicative, not imperative,—as is necessitated by the
preceding μένει ἐν ὑμῖν, and also by the imperative μένετε which
follows in the next verse. The Apostle first expresses his confidence
in his readers, and then, as is his wont, proceeds to exhort them to
"make their calling and election sure."

ἐν αὐτῷ. In Christ, not in the anointing. The anointing is not
an end in itself, but the means of abiding in Christ.

2²⁸ ἐὰν φανερωθῇ. The conditional form throws no doubt upon
the actual occurrence. It might be argued, indeed, that "if He
appears," signifies more emphatically than "when He appears"
(ὅταν φανερωθῇ, Col. 3⁴) an event which quite conceivably, or even
probably, may happen at any moment.

φανεροῦσθαι, not ἀποκαλύπτεσθαι, is the Johannine term for the
manifestations of Christ (His Incarnation and Life on earth, 1²;
His appearances after His Resurrection, John 21¹· ¹⁴; His Second
Coming, 2²⁸ 3²). For the implications of the word, *v. supra*, pp.
315–6.

σχῶμεν παῤῥησίαν. Not in the sense of 1 Thess. 2¹⁹ or Phil. 4¹.
For the significance of the strange sequence, μένετε . . . ἵνα σχῶμεν,
v. supra, p. 279 (n.).

παῤῥησίαν ἔχειν. The phrase, introduced here for the first time,
is destined to further service. *v. supra*, p. 280.

αἰσχυνθῶμεν ἀπ᾽ αὐτοῦ. *v. supra*, p. 280. The converse idea is
expressed in Luke 9²⁶.

ἐν τῇ παρουσίᾳ αὐτοῦ. See p. 325 (n.).

2²⁹–3⁹.

2²⁹. This verse, introducing for the first time the subject of the
Divine Begetting (ἐξ αὐτοῦ γεγέννηται), is to be regarded as the
beginning of a new section, rather than as a practical summing up
of what precedes (Haupt). It may be urged (Haupt, Rothe) that
it gives the necessary completion to the thought, "that we may
have boldness, and not be ashamed before Him at His coming" (2²⁸).
For this naturally raises the question, what quality or qualities we
must possess in order to ensure this result. It has been said that
to this end we must "abide in Him." But it might still be asked—
in respect of what are we to abide in Him? And the answer is
that, as He is righteous, we must abide in Him by doing righteousness.

But this connection of thought is not really present.

1. It is not the case that (as Haupt maintains) to be "begotten

of Him" is not a new idea, but merely a resumption of "abiding in Him." It is very distinctly a new idea.

2. The readers *have* already been told in respect of what they are to "abide in Him,"—"Let that which ye heard from the beginning abide in you: if that which ye heard from the beginning abide in you, ye also shall abide in the Son and in the Father" (2²⁴).

3. Haupt's idea that this verse is introduced as a *caveat* against fanatical licence in the interpretation of "Ye need not that any man teach you," is without support in the context. The "anointing" which renders the Christian community independent of extraneous teaching is viewed simply as its strongest bulwark against antichristian falsehood, and there is no hint of its being regarded as offering the slightest pretext for antinomian licence.

It is true that in the following verses the Apostle goes on to denounce and warn against antinomian indifference to conduct, but the objects of this attack are almost certainly the same false teachers who already have been denounced as "antichrists" (cf. "Let no man lead you astray," 3⁷; and "those who are for leading you astray," 2²⁶).

The sentence is merely predicative, pointing to practical righteousness as the universal mark of a Divine birth, and laying down the basis for the subsequent rigorous application of this as a test of Divine Sonship.

ἐὰν εἰδῆτε. This use of ἐάν does not, as in classical Greek, indicate any uncertainty. "If ye know, as ye absolutely do know."

εἰδῆτε . . . γινώσκετε. See special note. It is difficult to choose between an indicative and an imperative sense for γινώσκετε. The imperative brings out, perhaps, more sharply the proper sense of γινώσκειν: "take note," "recognise."

δίκαιός ἐστιν . . . ἐξ αὐτοῦ γεγέννηται. The question as to the subject of δίκαιός ἐστιν and the reference of αὐτοῦ is much debated. Connecting the verse with what precedes, we must refer δίκαιός ἐστιν to the αὐτοῦ of 2²⁸, namely, Christ; while universal usage requires "God" as the antecedent to the pronoun in ἐξ αὐτοῦ γεγέννηται. But one feels this to be intolerable grammatically and also weak in sense. The sense, indeed, would have been excellent, if the idea of Christ's Sonship had also been expressed—"Since Jesus the Son of God is righteous, every one who does righteousness must also be begotten of God." But so much cannot be legitimately read into the words. Both the unexpressed subject of δίκαιός ἐστιν and the unexpressed antecedent of αὐτοῦ must, therefore, be the same, namely, "God."

I cannot agree with Bengel, Rothe, and Westcott that there is nothing against the tenor of Scripture in saying that Christians are "begotten of Christ." They are the "children of God" (3^2, John 1^{12}). They are "begotten of God" (3^9 etc., 1 Pet. 1^3). Instrumentally, they are "begotten of the Spirit" (John $3^{6. 8}$) and of the Word (1 Pet. 1^{23}, Jas. 1^{18}). On the other hand, those who do the will of God are Christ's brothers and sisters (Matt. 12^{50}). Christ is formed in them (Gal. 4^{19}). They are heirs of God, joint-heirs with Christ (Rom. 8^{17}). They are conformed to His likeness as "the firstborn among many brethren" (Rom. 8^{29}, 1 John 3^2). Everywhere Christ is the medium and the exemplar of Life, not its source. It is, therefore, against the tenor of the N.T. to speak of Christians as "begotten of Christ." *v. supra*, p. 193 (n.). And, in view of what immediately follows, such an interpretation is quite impossible.

3^1 ποταπὴν ἀγάπην. *v. supra*, p. 332 (n.). ὁ πατήρ, *The* Father—the Author of our Divine sonship.

δέδωκεν ἡμῖν. The expression, as to both word and tense, is peculiarly strong—stronger than ἠγάπησεν ὁ θεὸς τὸν κόσμον of John 3^{16}. The Father has endowed us with this astonishing love, once for all, as our inalienable possession. Westcott, with such Catholic interpreters as à Lapide, understands δέδωκεν in the sense of "imparted." "The Divine love is, as it were, infused into us," and it is in virtue of our being thus "inspired with a love like the love of God, that we truly claim the title of children of God." This thought is coming in 4^7, but it is not present here. Had this been the Apostle's meaning, some kind of exhortation to "love one another" must have been given in the immediate context, which, however, contains nothing in that vein. The only test of our being the children of God is, meanwhile, ποιεῖν τὴν δικαιοσύνην.

δέδωκεν ἡμῖν ἵνα. What is the love bestowed upon us? Does it consist in calling us and making us His children? This would be entirely in accordance with the frequent Johannine use of ἵνα as practically equivalent to ὅτι. Or does the love bestowed upon us consist rather in the costly means by which our Divine sonship has been made possible—the mission of Christ—the ἀγάπη of 4^9 and of John 3^{16}? This is in the background, at least, of the Apostle's mind. Had it been possible to make us His children by a simple *fiat*, to have done so would still have indicated that God is love; but it would not have been that amazing love that evokes the rapturous ἴδετε ποταπὴν ἀγάπην.

The anarthrous τέκνα is noticeable. Not "the children of

25

God" in contrast to others, but absolutely "children ot God." Cf. ἱλασμός (2² 3¹⁰) and σπέρμα θεοῦ (3⁹). See note on Ἰησοῦν Χριστὸν δίκαιον (2¹).

ἵνα . . . κληθῶμεν. "That we should be called." By whom? Not, surely, by believers themselves (Haupt, Westcott—"outwardly recognised as God's children in their services and intercourse with others"), nor yet, perhaps, by the Father, though this is implied. The meaning seems to be quite general—"that such a name should be ours."

διὰ τοῦτο . . . ὅτι. The parallel passages (John 5¹⁶·¹⁸ 8⁴⁷ 10¹⁷ 12¹⁸·³⁹) show that διὰ τοῦτο always refers to a fact already stated, while the clause introduced by ὅτι supplements the inference founded upon this fact. Thus, in the present passage διὰ τοῦτο is not directly relative to the ὅτι following, but to the τέκνα θεοῦ preceding. "The reason why the World does not recognise us is, that we are children of God; and the *proof* that this is the reason is, that it did not recognise Christ Himself."

οὐ γινώσκει. Not "does not understand our principles, methods, and character" (Westcott), but simply "does not recognise us as being what we are—children of God."

ὅτι οὐκ ἔγνω αὐτόν. By αὐτόν, the majority of commentators understand "God." The World does not recognise the children, because it does not recognise the Father Whose they are and Whom they resemble. It seems clear to me, nevertheless, that the reference is to Christ, Who is not yet manifested to the world (ἐὰν φανερωθῇ, 2²⁸ 3²). For αὐτός used absolutely of Christ, cf. 2⁸·¹²·²⁷·²⁸ 3³. With οὐκ ἔγνω αὐτόν cf. John 1¹⁰, 1 John 3⁶.

3² νῦν τέκνα θεοῦ ἐσμέν strongly resumes the statement already made. The World does not recognise us, nevertheless it is true that we now are children of God.

νῦν, in strictly temporal sense, antithetic to οὔπω.

καὶ οὔπω ἐφανερώθη τί ἐσόμεθα. The meaning is not that "what we shall be" will be essentially other or more than what we now are (Haupt, Holtzmann, Weiss, the last of whom suggests that our present τεκνότης may become the full υἱότης), but that what we are now—children of God—will then only be fully manifested. Haupt's contention, that to express this the Apostle would have written τί ἐσμεν, not τί ἐσόμεθα, is not without point, but is rather hypercritical. The thought, fully expressed, is that what we are can be fully realised only in what we shall be; but this is not yet apparent, therefore the World does not recognise us.

ἐφανερώθη. To insist (as Westcott does) upon the definite

aoristic sense, and to read into it a reference to the manifestation of Christ after the Resurrection ("Even these revelations of a changed and glorified humanity do not make known to us what we shall be") is an extraordinary super-subtlety. Whether a Greek aorist refers to a definite or indefinite past must always be decided from the context (*v.* Moulton, 135–140). Here ἐφανερώθη plainly has a perfective sense (οὔπω ἐφανερώθη = "has never yet been manifested"; and this may be rendered in English also by the simple past tense—"was never yet manifested." Cf. Heb. 12⁴: οὔπω μέχρις αἵματος ἀντικατέστητε = "Ye have not yet resisted unto blood"; and Matt. 9³³: οὐδέποτε ἐφάνη οὕτως ἐν τῷ Ἰσραήλ = Nothing like this was ever yet seen in Israel = has yet been seen in Israel).

τί ἐσόμεθα. St. John rarely uses the indirect interrogative.

οἴδαμεν ὅτι ἐὰν φανερωθῇ ὅμοιοι αὐτῷ ἐσόμεθα, ὅτι ὀψόμεθα αὐτὸν καθώς ἐστιν.

οἴδαμεν ὅτι. The absence of any connective particle is striking. It may be thought to set the confident οἴδαμεν in bolder relief.

ἐὰν φανερωθῇ. The question here is as to the unexpressed subject of φανερωθῇ. It may be τί ἐσόμεθα (Huther, Haupt, Holtzmann, and the majority of commentators), or it may be supplied from the following αὐτῷ, that is, Christ (Westcott, Rothe, Calvin, etc.). The former is the more obviously grammatical, and yields an excellent sense: "We know that the manifestation, when it comes, will be a manifestation of likeness to Christ." Yet the second alternative seems preferable, because ἐὰν φανερωθῇ has just been used (2²⁸) with unmistakable reference to Christ, and because the central thought of the sentence is, that the manifestation of Christ is the means by which perfect likeness to Him will be attained. ἐὰν φανερωθῇ is the prerequisite of ὀψόμεθα αὐτὸν καθώς ἐστιν.

ὅμοιοι αὐτῷ . . . ὀψόμεθα αὐτόν. The most obvious antecedent to the pronouns is θεοῦ (νῦν τέκνα θεοῦ ἐσμέν). "Now are we the children of God, and then we shall be like Him" (Bengel, Ebrard, Huther, Weiss, etc.). But this is untenable. The whole tenor of N.T. teaching demands that the object of vision and assimilation be Christ (so Holtzmann). This whole verse has the closest affinity with Col. 3⁴, ὅταν ὁ Χριστὸς φανερωθῇ, ἡ ζωὴ ἡμῶν, τότε καὶ ὑμεῖς σὺν αὐτῷ φανερωθήσεσθε ἐν δόξῃ. One other point remains to be touched upon before we pass from this verse. A certain ambiguity is discovered in the relation of the clause, ὅτι ὀψόμεθα αὐτὸν καθώς ἐστιν, to the rest of the sentence. The debate is whether this · gives the cause of our *being* like Him, or of our

knowing that we shall be like Him ; whether the "seeing Him as
He is" is the effect and the proof of the "being like Him" instead
of *vice versa*.   Both thoughts are, of course, essentially true—
that our power to see depends on what we are (Matt. 5⁸), and
that we are changed into the likeness of what we behold (2 Cor.
3¹⁸).   The former is coming in the following verse, where the
Apostle reminds us that only he can have a real hope of attaining
to the vision of Christ as He is, who is now purifying himself
even as He is pure.   But, before proceeding to this, the Apostle
must first complete the task he has in hand—to show "what
we shall be," and how we are assured of its being brought to
pass.   We shall be like Christ, because, beholding His glory,
we shall be changed into the likeness of the glory we behold;
even as the planets, when they face the sun, are clothed with its
radiance.

3³ πᾶς ὁ ἔχων τὴν ἐλπίδα ταύτην ἐπ' αὐτῷ.

πᾶς ὁ ἔχων. *v. supra*, p. 215 (n.).

ἔχων . . . ἐλπίδα . . . ἐπ' αὐτῷ. This phrase, ἐλπίδα ἔχειν ἐπί,
is unique in the N.T., and may be distinguished from ἐλπίδα ἔχειν
εἰς (Acts 24¹⁵) or ἐλπίς εἰς (1 Pet. 1²¹) as giving the idea of hope
"resting upon" instead of "reaching unto."   Westcott is of opinion
that, as compared with the simple ἐλπίζειν, it gives the specific
idea of maintaining or enjoying the hope.   But this is scarcely
supported by the N.T. parallels (Rom. 15⁴, 2 Cor. 10¹⁵, Eph. 2¹²,
1 Thess. 4¹³).

ἁγνίζει ἑαυτόν. On ἁγνός and ἁγνίζειν, *v. supra*, p. 90.

ἐπ' αὐτῷ . . . ἐκεῖνος. This use, in the same sentence, of different
pronouns to represent the same antecedent is not without parallel
in St. John (cf. John 5³⁹ 19³⁵, unless, in the latter, ἐκεῖνος means
Christ).

3⁴ καὶ ἡ ἁμαρτία ἐστὶν ἡ ἀνομία. *v. supra*, p. 133 (n.).

3⁵ καὶ ἁμαρτία ἐν αὐτῷ οὐκ ἔστιν. Grammatically, the clause is
independent, not under οἴδατε ὅτι.   Nevertheless, one feels that the
influence of οἴδατε covers this clause also.   The sinlessness of
Christ, as well as the fact that He was manifested to take away
sins, is an intuition of the Christian mind.

3⁹ ἁμαρτίαν οὐ ποιεῖ. ἁμαρτίαν, in this negative construction,
is stronger than either τὴν ἁμαρτίαν or ἁμαρτίας would be.   It puts
the question as to the fact in the broadest way.

σπέρμα αὐτοῦ. The absence of the article brings out the
qualitative or causative force of σπέρμα.   "A seed of Divine

Life abideth in him, therefore he cannot sin"; cf. τέκνα θεοῦ, 3¹; and
ἱλασμος, 2² and 4¹⁰. This unique σπέρμα αὐτοῦ has been variously
explained. By some (Augustine, Luther, with most of the older
commentators) it is understood of the "word" (after the analogy
of Matt. 13²³, Jas. 1¹⁸, 1 Pet. 1²³, 2 Pet. 1⁴). But this is entirely
foreign to the context, if not to all specific Johannine teaching.
By others (Bengel, *e.g.*), σπέρμα has been taken as signifying
God's children collectively (cf. σπέρμα Ἀβραάμ, John 8³³· ³⁷). But,
so understood, the whole sentence becomes singularly lame.
"Every one that is begotten of God sinneth not, because they
who are God's seed abide in Him; and they cannot sin, because
they are begotten of God." It is evident that, on this interpretation, the last clause must have been "and they cannot sin, because
they *abide* in Him." Unquestionably the σπέρμα is here the new
life-principle implanted by the Divine Begetting.

3¹⁰⁻²⁴.

3¹⁰ πᾶς ὁ . . . οὐκ ἔστιν. See note on 2¹⁹.

ὁ μὴ ποιῶν . . . ὁ μὴ ἀγαπῶν. The particle μή is used because
the phrase is conditional in sense though not in form. The
assertion is not that there is such an one, but that, if there be, he
is not of God.

3¹¹ αὕτη ἐστὶν ἡ ἀγγελία . . . ἵνα ἀγαπῶμεν. "The words do not
simply give the contents of the message, but its aim, its purpose."
So says Westcott, resolved, on all occasions, to maintain the telic
force of ἵνα, but disregarding the fact that if the ἵνα clause gives the
purpose of the message, the message itself is not given at all. It is
perfectly clear that in such constructions as αὕτη . . . ἵνα, the
ἵνα clause gives the purport, not the purpose, of the announcement
or command (cf. John 2²⁵ 4³⁴ 6²⁹· ⁴⁰ 11⁵⁰ 15⁸ etc., 1 John 2²⁷ 3²³ 4²¹
5³· ¹⁶). The laboured explanation given in Abbott's *Johannine
Grammar* [2094–6] of such passages as John 4³⁴ 6²⁹ 13³⁴ 17³ etc.,
is extremely convincing *in contrarium*.

3¹² οὐ καθώς (except 2 Cor. 8⁵) is purely Johannine (John 6⁵⁸
14²⁷). The sentence here is elliptical, and irregular in a high degree.
If we punctuate with a comma between this and the *preceding* verse
(Tischendorf), we must translate ". . . that we love one another, not
as Cain (did, who) was of the Wicked One," etc. Or we may
regard οὐ καθώς, κ.τ.λ., as the first member of a new sentence, the
conclusion of which is unexpressed: "Not as Cain (who) was of the
Wicked One, and slew his brother (let us be or do)." To make the

sentence grammatical, it seems necessary, in either case, to supply ὅς or ὅσπερ before ἦν, and also to change οὐ into μή. In John 6⁵⁸ the construction with οὐ καθώς is equally loose. Here the anacoluthon (if the second construction be preferred) is probably due to the sudden rushing upon the writer's mind of the question, καὶ χάριν τίνος. Cf. a similar construction with οὐχ ὥσπερ (Plato, *Symp.* 179 E.).

χάριν, as a preposition (= ἕνεκα, and usually found after its case, *e.g.* τίνος χάριν), is not uncommon in the N.T., but is here only in St. John.

τὰ ἔργα αὐτοῦ πονηρὰ ἦν. πονηρά marks the source as well as the character of the works. They were inspired by ὁ πονηρός.

3¹³ μὴ θαυμάζετε. "Do not be wondering (as you are in danger of doing)." In the Gospel and Epistles of St. John the μή of prohibition is found only once with the aor. subj. (John 3⁷), everywhere else (19 times) with the present imperative.

εἰ μισεῖ. Used thus with the indicative after verbs denoting strong emotion, εἰ = ὅτι. Cf. Mark 15⁴⁴, Luke 12⁴⁹, Acts 26⁸·²³, 2 Cor. 11¹⁵.

ὑμᾶς ὁ κόσμος. Both words are emphatic by position. You are to the World what Abel was to Cain. According to the interpretation I have adopted in my exposition of the passage, μὴ θαυμάζετε is connected with the preceding verse by an unexpressed "therefore." On another view (Haupt, Westcott) it is connected with what follows by an unexpressed "because." "Do not be surprised that the *World* hates you; because we know that to love the brethren (whom the World hates) is proof of nothing less than a transition from death into life." The insertion of καί before μὴ θαυμάζετε (by ℵ, C*, Peshitto, retained by Tischendorf in his text) shows that the interpretation I have given is a very ancient one.

3¹⁴ οἴδαμεν. A case in which εἰδέναι can scarcely be differentiated from γινώσκειν. It probably expresses a stronger *feeling* of the certainty of the thing known; cf. 5¹⁹. See special note on γινώσκειν and εἰδέναι.

ὁ μὴ ἀγαπῶν. Although τὸν ἀδελφόν αὐτοῦ (T.R.) may not belong to the authentic text, it must be supplied in thought. Westcott, indeed, takes ὁ μὴ ἀγαπῶν as "expressing the feeling in its most absolute form." But· it is not to be supposed that, in this single clause, the conception of Love is widened beyond that which obtains everywhere else in the Epistle. *v. supra*, pp. 256–7.

3¹⁵ καὶ οἴδατε. Ye know it at once, without instruction, or even reflection.

ἀνθρωποκτόνος. In the N.T. only here and in John 8⁴⁴.

πᾶς ἀνθρωποκτόνος οὐκ ἔχει. See note on 2¹⁹.

ζωὴν αἰώνιον = τὴν ζωήν in 3¹⁴. The same equivalence of article and adjective is found in 5¹¹·¹².

3¹⁶ ὀφείλομεν. Stronger than δεῖ. See note on 2⁶.

3¹⁷ χρείαν ἔχοντα. For the use of the phrase absolutely, cf. Mark 2²⁵, Acts 2⁴⁵ 4³⁵, Eph. 4²⁸.

τὰ σπλάγχνα = רַחֲמִים. Is found also in classical Greek with this sense. A favourite Pauline word, only here in St. John.

κλείσῃ. Not found elsewhere with σπλάγχνα.

3¹⁸ ἀγαπῶμεν. For the use absolutely, cf. 3¹⁴ 4⁷·⁸·¹⁹. λόγῳ . . . γλώσσῃ . . . ἔργῳ . . . ἀληθείᾳ. Haupt and Weiss find here a double contrast—λόγῳ (sincere good wishes) with ἔργῳ (good deeds), and γλώσσῃ (hollow phrases) with ἀληθείᾳ (sincerity). Obviously, however, there is only a single contrast. γλώσσῃ is merely a contemptuous synonym of λόγῳ, expressing how cheap such love is; while ἀληθείᾳ does not introduce a second idea, co-ordinate with ἔργῳ, but declares that only love in "deed" is love in "truth" (cf. John 4²⁴, where πνεύματι and ἀληθείᾳ stand in exactly the same relation). λόγῳ and γλώσσῃ are datives of instrument.

ἐν τούτῳ. Here only, in the Epistle, used with retrospective reference.

πείσομεν τὰς καρδίας. Not dependent on γνωσόμεθα ὅτι, but co-ordinate with it.

ἔμπροσθεν αὐτοῦ. αὐτοῦ stands for God (cf. 2³·⁴·²⁹), as is evident from μείζων ἐστὶν ὁ θεός following.

καταγινώσκῃ. καταγινώσκειν is not found elsewhere in the N.T. (except in perf. part. κατεγνωσμένος, Gal. 2¹¹). It has three shades of meaning: to accuse (= κατηγορεῖν), to declare guilty, to give sentence against (= κατακρίνειν). Here it is to be taken in the second of these meanings. When conscience accuses, it *ipso facto* brings in a verdict of guilty; but while it may anticipate, it does not pronounce sentence. These verses (3¹⁹·²⁰) present an exegetical problem of no little complexity. I do not propose to offer an exhaustive account of the many different views that have been taken of the syntax and of the sense (this may be found concisely in Westcott; at greater length in Huther or Haupt); but it is necessary, in the first place, to indicate where the main difficulties of the passage lie. One source of difficulty is the verb πείσομεν. This may be taken in its ordinary sense, "persuade" or "convince," with τὰς καρδίας ἡμῶν as direct, and the clause ὅτι μείζων ἐστὶν ὁ θεός, κ.τ.λ., as secondary predicate. But it is usually understood here in the sense of "over-persuade," "pacify," "assure" (A.V., R.V.). The extra-biblical parallels cited (Hesiod, *ap.* Plat. *Rep.* 390 E; Josephus, *Arch.* vi. 5. 6) are valueless. In both cases the translation "pacify" is possible, but in neither is it necessary.[1] In the N.T. the only passage at all parallel is Matt. 28¹⁴—ἡμεῖς πείσομεν αὐτόν—which might be translated "we shall talk him over." The strongest example is 2 Macc. 4⁴⁵ (Westcott), where πρὸς τὸ πεῖσαι τὸν βασιλέα has as its equivalent in the next verse ὡς ἀναψύξοντα τὸν βασιλέα, and may very well be translated "in order to reassure the king." But, even if the literary parallels be thought too meagre to establish the use of πείθειν in this special sense, virtually the same meaning may be got by translating it "persuade." "Herein shall we recognise that we are of the truth, and shall persuade our hearts before Him." Persuade our hearts of what? Of this, naturally, "that we are of the truth" (Plummer).

A second source of difficulty is the ambiguity of the words ὅτι ἐὰν καταγινώσκῃ ἡμῶν ἡ καρδία. This is capable of three different meanings—"that, if our heart condemn us"; "because, if our heart condemn us"; "whereinsoever our heart condemn us" (R.V.). The last of these is fully tenable. The construction (acc. rei. c. gen. pers.) is the normal construction after καταγινώσκειν; and though the special form ὅτι ἐάν is not well authenticated elsewhere in the N.T., this is of little importance in view of the fact that such forms as ὃς ἐάν, ὅπου ἐάν, ὅσοι ἐάν, ὁσάκις ἐάν are more or less common, and that the substitution of ἐάν for ἄν in such compounds is a feature of later Greek (*v.* Moulton, pp. 42, 43).

Of the text as it stands, then, various renderings are possible. Taking πείσομεν as "persuade," we may translate the whole— "We shall persuade our hearts before Him that, even if our own heart condemn us, (that) God is greater than our heart" (so Weiss, Holtzmann); or, "We shall persuade our hearts, whereinsoever our own heart condemn us, that God is greater," etc.

The former translation regards the second ὅτι as a rhetorical resumption of the first ("that, if"—"that, I say, . . ."); and this, with so few words intervening, seems to me intolerable, whether in Greek or in English. On either rendering, however, the meaning is virtually the same. We persuade our heart that God is greater than our heart, and, because He knows all things, is

---

[1] See additional note, p. 415.

better able to judge whether we are "of the truth." The objection to this, and to me it seems decisive, is that ἐν τούτῳ is quite left out of the thought. How can it be said that "herein—namely, in our loving in deed and in truth—we shall persuade our hearts that God is greater than our hearts"?

We are compelled to adopt the alternative translation of πείσομεν as "pacify" or "assure," or "persuade our hearts that we are of the truth." Even so, a double rendering is possible. "Herein . . . we shall assure our hearts before Him, because—even if our own heart condemn us — because (I say) God is greater than our heart." But, again, this meaningless repetition of "because" is intolerable; and we are shut up to the translation of the R.V. as the only possible one of the accepted text—"We shall assure our hearts before Him, whereinsoever our own heart condemn us, because God is greater than our hearts, and knoweth all things." All these renderings have, however, one chief feature in common—the fact that God is greater than our own heart is a fact that tends to tranquillise the heart. And so I have interpreted the passage in my exposition.

But it must be admitted that the thought most naturally suggested by God's being greater than our hearts and knowing all things is, that if even our own heart condemn us, much more must we dread the judgment of the All-knowing. And this is the view maintained by Professor Findlay (*Expositor*, November 1905), who would translate 3²⁰ "Because, if our own heart condemn us (because), God is greater than our heart, and knoweth all things." He recognises that the stumbling-block is the second ὅτι, which, accordingly, he dismisses from the text as a "primitive error of the copyist" or an "inadvertence of the author."

But there is a still greater difficulty remaining, namely, that this interpretation leaves 3²⁰ without any obvious link of connection with 3¹⁹. How can it be said that "Herein—by loving in deed and in truth—we shall . . . assure our hearts before Him; *because*, if our own heart condemn us, God is greater than our heart, and will judge more strictly"?

"But," not "because," is needed to indicate such a line of reasoning. To justify such a "because" some connecting thought must be supplied between 3¹⁹ and 3²⁰. "We shall assure our hearts before Him; (and it is the more necessary that we be able to do this) because if our own heart condemn us, God is greater," etc. Granted the right to amend the text by the omission of the second ὅτι (which is omitted in A, and in the Vulgate, Memphitic and

Thebaic versions), and to supply such a connecting link in the thought, this interpretation would be most acceptable. It greatly simplifies the passage; gets rid of the cumbrous "whereinsoever our own heart condemn us," and it secures a clear antithesis between the ἐὰν καταγινώσκῃ of 3²⁰ and the ἐὰν μὴ . . . καταγινώσκῃ of 3²¹. The last point is a strong one in its favour.

3²² ὃ ἐάν. See note on ὅτι ἐάν, 3²⁰.

ἐντολὰς τηροῦμεν. *v. supra*, p. 211.

τὰ ἀρεστά. Only here and in John 8²⁹ τὰ ἀρεστὰ αὐτῷ ποιῶ. εὐάρεστος is the Pauline term, Phil. 4⁸, Eph. 5¹⁰, Col. 3²⁰, also Heb. 13²¹.

3²³ καὶ αὕτη ἐστὶν ἡ ἐντολὴ αὐτοῦ ἵνα.

ἵνα indicates the purport, not the purpose of the command. Cf. John 13³⁴ 15¹². ¹⁷, 1 John 4²¹. See note on 3¹¹.

ἵνα πιστεύωμεν. The reading is doubtful, Tischendorf preferring πιστεύωμεν, W. and H. πιστεύσωμεν. Here the present tense gives a better sense than the aorist. It is more natural that the commandment should be that we maintain faith, than that it should refer to the initial act of faith. In the parallel passage, John 6²⁹, the tense is the present.

πιστεύωμεν τῷ ὀνόματι. The construction is unique. Elsewhere it is εἰς τὸ ὄνομα, (John 1¹² 2²³ 3¹⁸, 1 John 5¹³). The meaning, however, must be the same with both constructions. See note on πιστεύειν appended to Chapter XIII.

τῷ ὀνόματι. The ὄνομα of Christ is not distinguishable in effect from Christ Himself. It is the "self-revelation of Christ" (Westcott), or rather the true conception of Christ, by which He is present to the minds of believers, and is proclaimed to men in the Gospel. (Cf. Acts 9¹⁵.) It may be that the phrase πιστεύειν εἰς τὸ ὄνομα was a reminiscence of the baptismal formula (Acts 8¹⁶ 19⁵). But the present passage suffices to show how groundless is the supposition that "to believe in the name" of Christ signified a lower kind of faith than is implied in "believing in Christ"—a profession of faith such as might warrant baptism (Origen; adopted by Abbott, *Johannine Vocabulary*, p. 37, and by Westcott on John 2²³). Here the "Name" of Christ is nothing else than Christ Himself as He is presented in the Gospel, and is the object of human speech and thought.

καὶ ἀγαπῶμεν ἀλλήλους καθὼς ἔδωκεν ἐντολὴν ἡμῖν. The subject to ἔδωκεν is "His Son, Jesus Christ," not God. In 3¹⁴ the command was ὅτι ἀγαπῶμεν τοὺς ἀδελφούς: here it is ἀλλήλους, quoting the exact word of John 13³⁴.

3²⁴ᵃ καὶ ὁ τηρῶν τὰς ἐντολὰς αὐτοῦ. τὰς ἐντολάς may refer to the two great branches of the ἐντολή in 3²³; but preferably ὁ τηρῶν τὰς ἐντολάς is to be taken as a resumption of the similar phrase in 3²².

3²⁴ᵇ–4⁶.

3²⁴ᵇ καὶ ἐν τούτῳ γινώσκομεν ὅτι μένει ἐν ἡμῖν, ἐκ τοῦ πνεύματος οὗ ἡμῖν ἔδωκεν. With this begins the new paragraph extending to 4⁶. The matter to be tested is that God "abideth in us"; the test is the Spirit He has given us, that is to say, the Spirit that confesses Jesus as the Christ come in the flesh (4²).

ἐν τούτῳ γινώσκομεν . . . ἐκ τοῦ πνεύματος. This collocation of ἐν and ἐκ is certainly peculiar and, in fact, ungrammatical; but it is unwarrantable to say (Ebrard, Westcott) that it is impossible. It is probably accounted for by the fact that ἐν τούτῳ γινώσκειν is so much of a formula with the Writer that the proper prepositional force of ἐν is not fully felt. γινώσκειν ἐκ occurs in 4⁶. Cf. ὅθεν γινώσκομεν, 2¹⁸.

I must admit that the exposition I have given of this verse (*v. supra*, p. 263 sqq.) is not sustained by the commentators (except, in part, by Holtzmann and Plummer), who in one way or other all refer ἐν τούτῳ to the keeping of the "commandments" in the first half of the verse. Some (Lücke, Ebrard, Rothe, Westcott) do so directly; in which case not only does this clause become purely tautological, but ἐκ τοῦ πνεύματος, κ.τ.λ., is altogether left out of the construction. To obviate this difficulty, Westcott (following Ebrard) supplies a second γινώσκομεν before ἐκ τοῦ πνεύματος, and extracts from this the meaning (if I understand him rightly):—" We know that God abides in us by the love that prompts us to obey His commandments—in other words, we know it by the Spirit He hath given us." But, besides the arbitrariness of supplying this second γινώσκομεν, to identify the possession of the Spirit with the Love that prompts obedience is quite foreign to the doctrine of the Epistle, in which the function of the Spirit is solely to testify of Christ. Others (Huther, Haupt, etc.) correctly relate ἐν τούτῳ to ἐκ τοῦ πνεύματος, but in the sense that the Spirit is the source of the knowledge that God abideth in us, if we keep His commandments. The "keeping of the commandments," that is to say, is valid proof of God's abiding in us only when we are conscious of it, by the witness of the Spirit, as the fruit of a renewed nature. But this is to reason in a way exactly the reverse of St. John's, who tests spirit by deeds, not deeds by spirit—the tree by its fruits, not the fruits by the tree. Undoubtedly, the meaning is, not that the Spirit is the source of a subjective assurance that God dwelleth in us, but that the Spirit gives objective evidence of this by prompting the confession that Jesus is the Christ.　*v. infra*, 4^2 and ^{13}.

οὗ ἡμῖν ἔδωκεν. The relative is attracted into the case of its antecedent; cf. among numerous examples, John 4^{14} 15^{20}. But might not οὗ be a partitive genitive? cf. ἐκ τοῦ πνεύματος (4^{13}).

ἔδωκεν. We find δέδωκεν in 4^{13}. The aorist points to the time when the gift was bestowed; the perfect denotes its permanence.

4^1 μὴ παντὶ πνεύματι πιστεύετε.　See note on πιστεύειν, appended to Chapter XIII.

ἐξεληλύθασιν εἰς τὸν κόσμον. They have gone forth as ambassadors from their native sphere, the dæmonic world, on their errand of deceit (cf. 1 Kings 22^{22}, 1 Pet. 5^8, Rev. 20^8).　Probably these "false prophets" were identical with the "antichrists" who had gone out from the Church (2^{19}).

4^2 ἐν τούτῳ = by the test which is about to be laid down. γινώσκετε, following μὴ πιστεύετε and δοκιμάζετε, is better taken as imperative than as indicative. In all the three verbs, the present tense points to the duty enjoined, as one which must be performed as often as the occasion arises.

πᾶν πνεῦμα ὃ ὁμολογεῖ Ἰησοῦν Χριστὸν ἐν σαρκὶ ἐληλυθότα; cf. 2 John ^{7}. *v. supra*, p. 94 (n.).

4^3 ὃ μὴ ὁμολογεῖ τὸν Ἰησοῦν. μή in a relative clause with the indicative is exceedingly rare in the N.T. (Tit. 1^{11}, 2 Pet. 1^9). Here it is used with classical correctness, as expressing the subjective conviction of the writer that there are no exceptions to the statement he is making. "Every spirit whatsoever that confesses not," etc. In Polycarp's quotation of the verse (Westcott, p. 142) it runs: πᾶς γὰρ ὃς ἂν μὴ ὁμολογῇ. τὸν Ἰησοῦν. The article defines Ἰησοῦν in the full sense of the formula in the preceding verse. The only valid confession of Jesus is that He is "Christ come in the flesh."

καὶ τοῦτό ἐστιν τὸ τοῦ ἀντιχρίστου. πνεῦμα may be supplied both with τοῦτο and with τό (Weiss, Haupt, R.V., and most commentators).　But the natural interpretation, it seems to me, is to take τοῦτο as denoting the whole matter that has just been under discussion, and τὸ τοῦ ἀντιχρίστου in a similar general sense (Westcott). "And this that we have been speaking of—all these undivine manifestations—are the fulfilment of the current expectation of Antichrist." "That affair of Antichrist," as we might colloquially say.

ὃ ἀκηκόατε. ὅ, not ὅν. Antichrist is regarded as a principle or an event, not as a person. In 2¹⁸ we find ἠκούσατε in precisely the same connection—a warning not to insist too pedantically upon tense-values.

καὶ νῦν ἐν τῷ κόσμῳ ἐστὶν ἤδη. Cf. καὶ νῦν ἀντίχριστοι πολλοὶ γεγόνασιν (2¹⁸). Here the addition of ἤδη at the end of the clause lends a certain grim emphasis to the statement. There is no doubt about it; Antichrist is here—already upon us.

4⁴ νενικήκατε. This is not to be understood only in the sense that ultimate victory is assured in principle (Calvin, Neander, Rothe). They have already conquered by their steadfast adherence to the truth, which has resulted in the separation of the false teachers from the Church (2¹⁹). The tense indicates that the results of the victory will continue.

4⁵ αὐτοὶ ἐκ τοῦ κόσμου εἰσίν. αὐτοί, in strong contrast to the preceding ὑμεῖς and to the succeeding ἡμεῖς.

ἐκ τοῦ κόσμου λαλοῦσιν. Cf. ἐκ τῆς γῆς λαλεῖ (John 3³¹), although γῆ and κόσμος are not quite equivalent.

4⁶ ἡμεῖς ἐκ τοῦ θεοῦ ἐσμέν. ἐκ τοῦ κόσμου . . . ἐκ τοῦ θεοῦ. The two phrases, though parallel, do not express exactly the same relation. In the latter case, the source of the spiritual life is indicated; in the former, its affinities. Cf. *supra*, pp. 142–3.

ἡμεῖς . . . ἀκούει ἡμῶν. ἡμεῖς must refer, not to Christians generally (Calvin, Lücke, Haupt), but to the Writer himself and those whom he associates with himself as teachers of the Truth.

ἐκ τούτου. Here only in St. John is ἐκ τούτου found in an inferential sense (John 6⁶⁶ 19¹² in a temporal sense). Cf. ἐν τούτῳ γινώσκομεν . . . ἐκ τοῦ πνεύματος (3²⁴). Westcott suggests that ἐν τούτῳ indicates a more direct, ἐκ τούτου a less direct, inference. But a single instance supplies meagre data for any such conclusion.

γινώσκομεν. The subject is not the ἡμεῖς of the preceding clause. Such discerning of spirits by such means is the privilege of all who have the χρῖσμα (2²⁰).

4⁷⁻¹².

4⁷ πᾶς ὁ ἀγαπῶν ἐκ τοῦ θεοῦ γεγέννηται καὶ γινώσκει τὸν θεόν. The inter-relation of the three ideas—"loving," "begotten of God," "knowing God"—has been construed in a bewildering variety of ways. Let us call these, for the sake of brevity, *a*, *b*, and *c*. *b* and *c* are taken as both consequences of *a* (De Wette), which inverts the relation between *a* and *b*; *a* is taken as the consequence of *b*, and *b* again of *c* (Weiss), which inverts the relation between *b* and *c*; *a* and *c* are taken as both consequences of *b* (Haupt, Rothe, Westcott), which is true, but, as regards the relation between *b* and *c*, irrelevant, the relation of the knowledge of God to the Divine Begetting not being here in question. The true anatomy of the sentence is that *a* is the consequence, therefore, the test of *b*; and that *a* is either the consequence (Huther) or the condition, and, in either case, the test of *c*. The important point is that "loving" is the test and criterion both of being "begotten of God" and of "knowing" God. Beyond question, it seems to me, this is the purport of the verse.

4^8 ὁ μὴ ἀγαπῶν. μή is used because the phrase is conditional in effect, though not in form. In St. John οὐ with the participle occurs only once, John 10^{12}.

4^9. The order of the words is finely significant. Observe the emphatic position of τὸν υἱὸν αὐτοῦ τὸν μονογενῆ, also of ὁ θεός, following its predicate ἀπέσταλκεν.

ἐφανερώθη. Cf. 1^2. The Love is everlasting; the aorist points to the definite occasion of its manifestation.

ἐν ἡμῖν may be taken as dependent on ἐφανερώθη—"in us" as its objects (cf. John 9^3); or on ἡ ἀγάπη τοῦ θεοῦ. The latter, indeed, would seem to require ἡ ἀγάπη τ. θ. ἡ ἐν ἡμῖν. But see note on 4^{16}. For the sense of ἐν ἡμῖν, see the same note.

4^{10} ἐν τούτῳ ἐστὶν ἡ ἀγάπη. Herein *is* Love. Neither τοῦ θεοῦ nor anything else is to be supplied after ἡ ἀγάπη. This is Love in its purest essence.

οὐχ ὅτι ἡμεῖς . . . ἀλλ' ὅτι αὐτός. This is not an example of the frequent elliptical οὐχ ὅτι . . . ἀλλά, "not that" . . . "but" (a genuine case of which is found in John 7^{22}). Here the ὅτι in each clause is in strict logical and grammatical dependence on ἐν τούτῳ ἐστίν. What is said is, not that we did not love God, but that the true nature of Love is revealed, not in our love to God, but in God's Love to us.

ἠγάπησεν . . . ἀπέστειλεν. The aorists concentrate attention upon the definite act in which this Love was so wondrously embodied.

ἱλασμὸν περὶ, κ.τ.λ. A secondary predicate, in the same manner as σωτῆρα in 4^{14}. The absence of the article with ἱλασμός brings out the qualitative or generic force of the word. The thought is not of the fact that Christ is *the* propitiation for our sins (to the exclusion of all others), but that God's Love was so great that He sent His Son as a *propitiation* for sin. The whole clause corresponds to ἵνα ζήσωμεν δι᾿ αὐτοῦ in 4⁹. It is because He is a propitiation for our sins that we live through Him.

4¹² θεὸν οὐδεὶς πώποτε τεθέαται. This is almost a quotation of John 1¹⁸ θεὸν οὐδεὶς ἑώρακεν πώποτε. In both places the sentence begins with the accusative θεόν (the absence of the article giving to the word its most absolute sense—"God as God") followed immediately by the negative οὐδείς—the statement thus being made with the strongest possible emphasis: "God in Himself no man hath ever seen."

τεθέαται. In St. John θεᾶσθαι signifies either bodily vision (John 1³⁸ 6⁵ 11⁴⁵) or spiritual contemplation (John 1¹⁴ 4³⁵). Here it must be taken in the former sense.

By the majority of commentators quite a different interpretation is put upon this verse from that which I have advanced (*supra*, p. 250). τεθέαται is taken in simple and immediate contrast to μένει ἐν ἡμῖν. "Though no man hath seen God at any time, yet God may be abiding in us as the Life of our lives; and the sign (or the reality) of this is present when we love one another" (Westcott, Weiss, Haupt, Huther). This gives a sense that would be unexceptionable but for two things: (*a*) that "No man hath seen God at any time" is introduced with exceeding abruptness—there is no link of thought that attaches it to the preceding verse; and (*b*) that the parallel passage (4²⁰) is decisively in favour of the interpretation I have given.

καὶ ἡ ἀγάπη αὐτοῦ. Not the Love of God to us nor the Love which God commands, but the love which is ἐξ αὐτοῦ (4⁷) and is His own nature (4⁸).

Our loving one another is the sign that He (whose nature is Love) is abiding in us, and it is also the means by which His Love has been "fulfilled in us."

4¹³⁻¹⁶.

A new paragraph, as is recognised by Huther, Haupt, Ebrard, Brooke (vigorously opposed by Weiss).

4¹³. See note on 3²⁴ᵇ, of which this verse is almost a verbal reproduction.

ἐν τούτῳ γινώσκομεν . . . ὅτι ἐκ τοῦ πνεύματος, κ.τ.λ. The second ὅτι is in strict apposition to ἐν τούτῳ. "In this, namely, that He hath given us of His Spirit, we perceive that we abide in Him and He in us." By most of the commentators the verse is related to what precedes, either the entire paragraph (7–12) or, specially, to the words, ἡ ἀγάπη αὐτοῦ τετελειωμένη ἐν ἡμῖν ἐστίν. "We know that *it is God* Who abides in us, and in Whom we abide; because the Spirit teaches us to recognise the Love which is revealed in the mission of Christ as the true nature of God and as the source of the Love that is fulfilled in us" (Weiss). But the true connection of the verse is with what follows (Huther), as a comparison with the parallel passage (3^{24b}–4^6) plainly shows. There the test of Belief immediately follows the test of Love; so here. There the presence and work of the Spirit are manifested in the confession of the True Belief; so here ($4^{14.\ 15}$).

4^{14}. The first-fruit of the gift of the Spirit is the Apostolic testimony itself. καὶ ἡμεῖς. The writer and his fellow-witnesses. It is true that "The vision and witness remain as an abiding endowment of the Church," but not that "The Apostle does not speak of himself personally, but as representing the Church" (Westcott). On the contrary, it is the importance of the personal element in the vision and witness that is brought out by the emphatic καὶ ἡμεῖς.

τεθεάμεθα. See note on 4^{12}.

τεθεάμεθα καὶ μαρτυροῦμεν. Cf. 1^2. It is not necessary to regard the two verbs as forming only one compound idea (Westcott). Its full and proper force may be given to each. The witness-bearing is based on the beholding, exactly as in 1^2. The meaning is, "We have personally beheld the historic Jesus, and, taught by the Spirit, have recognised the true significance of what we beheld, namely, that the Father hath sent the Son to be the Saviour of the world; and to this we bear witness." ἀπέσταλκεν, as in 4^9—expressing the present and permanent reality of the mission of Christ.

σωτῆρα τοῦ κόσμου. Secondary predicate; cf. ἱλασμόν (4^{10}).

4^{15}. The permanent result of the gift of the Spirit is the believing response of others to the Apostolic testimony, ὃς ἂν ὁμολογήσῃ, κ.τ.λ.

ὁ θεὸς ἐν αὐτῷ μένει καὶ αὐτὸς ἐν τῷ θεῷ. The order of statement is the reverse of that found in 4^{13}; but, since the evidence of the mutual indwelling is the same in both places, this only shows that the order has no special significance.

4^{16} καὶ ἡμεῖς. Not those who bear the original testimony (4^{14}), but the writer and his readers, or Christian believers generally.

ἐγνώκαμεν καὶ πεπιστεύκαμεν. See footnote, p. 269.

τὴν ἀγάπην ἔχειν is simply a stronger expression for ἀγαπᾶν. In Greek, as in English, to "have" love, joy, grief, desire, etc., means nothing else than to love, rejoice, grieve, desire, etc. (cf. John 13^{35} $16^{21.\ 22}$ 17^{13}, Rom. 10^2 15^{23} etc.). And here τὴν ἀγάπην ἣν ἔχει ὁ θεός expresses, perhaps a little more emphatically, τὴν ἀγάπην τοῦ θεοῦ (4⁹).

Thus the question whether ἐν ἡμῖν is dependent on ἔχειν or on ἀγάπην does not arise. The verb and the associated noun are only the compound expression of a single idea (cf. John 16²¹ λύπην ἔχει, ὅτι . . .; Rom. 15²³ ἐπιποθίαν ἔχων τοῦ ἐλθεῖν; Phil. 1²³ τὴν ἐπιθυμίαν ἔχων εἰς τὸ ἀναλῦσαι).

The grammatical point, however, is of minor importance. The real question here is as to the meaning of ἐν ἡμῖν. And this, notwithstanding the protest of Westcott and Huther and the rendering of R.V., is, I maintain, practically equivalent to εἰς ἡμᾶς—"toward us." We may conceive of Love as going forth *toward* and reaching its object (εἰς), or as resting on and abiding *in* its object (ἐν), without any real difference of meaning. Both usages are sufficiently illustrated in the N.T. St. Paul everywhere uses εἰς (Rom. 5⁸, Eph. 1¹⁵, Col. 1⁴, 1 Thess. 3¹², 2 Thess. 1³) except in 2 Cor. 8⁷, where, with exactly the same meaning, he uses ἐν (τῇ ἐξ ὑμῶν ἐν ἡμῖν ἀγάπῃ, "*Your love to us*," R.V.). This proves the interchangeableness of the two prepositions with ἀγάπη. In the three cases where St. John uses ἀγάπη with a preposition following (John 13³⁵, 1 John 4⁹·¹⁶), the preposition is ἐν. But if ἀγάπην ἔχητε ἐν ἀλλήλοις (John 13³⁵) is translated "have love one to another" (R.V.), why should τὴν ἀγάπην ἣν ἔχει ὁ θεὸς ἐν ἡμῖν be pedantically rendered "the love which God hath in us"? (R.V.). To "have love in a person" is not an English idiom; and ἐν ἡμῖν must be rendered either by some periphrasis, or simply and quite adequately by "toward us." I plead, therefore, for the restoration of simplicity and common sense in the exegesis of this verse and also of 4⁹—for the rejection of such far-fetched subtleties as Westcott's explanation of "Herein was manifested the love of God, ἐν ἡμῖν" (4⁹):—"The Christian shares the life of Christ, and so becomes himself a secondary sign of God's love"; and of "the love which God hath ἐν ἡμῖν," here in 4¹⁶:—"The love of God becomes a power in the Christian body. Believers are the sphere in which it operates and makes itself felt in the world." The progress of thought in this section is simple as it is beautiful: "Herein was the love of God toward us manifested (4⁹). Herein is the reality that was manifested (4¹⁰). Herein is our response to the reality of Divine love thus manifested—we have recognised it and believed it" (4¹⁶).

4^{17}–5^{21}.

4^{17} μεθ' ἡμῶν. Instead of ἐν ἡμῖν (2^5 4^{12}). In grammar and sense it belongs to τετελείωται, not to ἀγάπη. By some commentators it is understood as signifying the mutual love between God and us (but St. John never includes God and man in ἡμεῖς); by Westcott, as implying that in the perfecting of Love "God works along with man" (an excessive weight of meaning to lay upon the preposition, and a thought foreign to the passage); better, as by the majority of commentators, of the mutual love which is realised in the Christian community. Or, might it simply mean what "with us" so often means in English—"in our case"?

παῤῥησία. *v. supra*, p. 280.

ἔχωμεν. The παῤῥησία is a present possession. The tense, however, does not exclude a reference to the future. Although in 2^{28} we find the aorist conj., the regular construction with ἵνα to express a purpose the fulfilment of which lies in the future, St. John uses the present conj. also in the same sense (John 16^4 17^{24}).

καθὼς ἐκεῖνος. Cf. 2^6 $3^{3.\ 7}$, John 17^{16}.

4^{19} ἀγαπῶμεν. May be construed as indicative (A.V., R.V., Huther, Weiss, Westcott, Holtzmann), or as imperative (Vulgate, Luther, Lücke, Rothe, Haupt). With the former construction the verse would appear to be an explanation or thanksgiving: "Why is it that we are not of those who, when they remember God, are troubled—that we are made perfect in love? It is owing to nothing in ourselves. We love, only because He first loved us." The sense given by the alternative construction seems to me more pointed as well as more obvious. "As for us, let us love," etc. It is quite in the Apostle's manner first to express confidence in the Christian attainments of His readers ("Herein is love perfected with us"), and then to exhort to further effort (cf. $2^{27.\ 28}$ $4^{1.\ 4}$). The exhortation "Let us love" is specially characteristic ($4^{7.\ 11}$).

αὐτός = God. Cf. $4^{7.\ 11}$.

πρῶτος for πρότερος. In John 1^{15} we find even πρῶτός μου ἦν.

ἠγάπησεν. The aorist points to the historical act in which the Love was realised ($4^{9.\ 10}$).

4^{20}. The order of words is very expressive. ἀγαπῶ τὸν θεόν, with the emphasis on ἀγαπῶ—there is profession of warm love to God; καὶ τὸν ἀδελφὸν αὐτοῦ μισῇ, with emphasis on τὸν ἀδελφὸν αὐτοῦ— and yet his own brother is to him an object of hate.

ἀγαπῶ τὸν θεόν. ἀγαπᾶν is not used in the Fourth Gospel of the feeling of man to God (although it is used of man's feeling to Christ, John 2φ$^{15. 16}$), and in the Epistle is so used only here and in 5^2; in the Synoptics, only in quotations from the LXX.; in other N.T. writings only in Rom. 8^{28}, 1 Cor. 8^3, Eph. 6^{14} (τὸν ?? κύριον), Jas. 1^{12} 2^5, 1 Pet. 1^8 (Ἰησοῦν Χριστόν).

ψεύστης ἐστίν. Cf. 1^6 2$^{4. 22}$.

4^{21} ἀπ' αὐτοῦ, *i.e.*, from God, not expressly from Christ. The reference, however, is to Christ's "new commandment." Cf. 3^{23}.

ἵνα, indicating the purport, not the purpose, of the commandment. See notes on 3^{23} and 3^{11}.

5^1 πᾶς ὁ πιστεύων anticipates, according to the Writer's wont, the subject which is to be treated in the next section (5^{3b-12}); but there is no reason for regarding it as the beginning of that section (Westcott, Weiss). Here it is introduced to define those who are the objects of the Christian's brotherly love.

ὅτι Ἰησοῦς ἐστιν ὁ Χριστός. In direct opposition to the doctrine of the antichrists (2^{22}). A full measure of brotherly love is claimed for all believers, but not for the antichrists and their adherents. *v. supra*, pp. 252–3.

5^2 ἐν τούτῳ. Correlative to ὅταν τὸν θεόν, κ.τ.λ.

τὰ τέκνα τοῦ θεοῦ = τὸν γεγεννημένον ἐξ αὐτοῦ (5^1) = τὸν ἀδελφόν (4$^{20. 21}$).

ὅταν. Cf. the ἐάν in 2^3. Both are used to avoid the clumsiness of ἐν τούτῳ γινώσκομεν ὅτι . . . ὅτι.

τὰς ἐντολὰς αὐτοῦ is not to be understood of the ἐντολή of 4^{21} nor as including it (Weiss). St. John always makes a distinction between αἱ ἐντολαί, the moral precepts in general, and ἡ ἐντολή, the commandment of Love. Thus in 2$^{3-6}$ the former exclusively are treated of, and then in 2$^{7-11}$ the latter. Obedience to the former constitutes δικαιοσύνη; obedience to the latter is conceived simply as Love, not also as Righteousness. Here, "to love God and keep His commandments" is equivalent to St. Paul's "soberly and righteously and godly."

ποιῶμεν. Whereas τηροῦμεν expresses heedful regard to the commandments (2^3 3^{22} 5^3), ποιῶμεν expresses the actual performance of them in opposition to Antinomian pseudo-spiritualism. Cf. 2^{29} 3^7 etc. *v. supra*, pp. 219–20.

5^3 αὕτη . . . ἵνα. See note on 3^{11}.

βαρεῖαι οὐκ εἰσίν. Cf. φορτία βαρέα, Matt. 23^4.

5^4. πᾶν τὸ γεγεννημένον. *v. supra*, p. 275 (n.).

ἡ νίκη νικήσασα. *v. supra*, p. 276 (n.).

ἡ πίστις. The solitary occurrence in St. John. *v. supra*, p. 258 (n.).

5⁵ ὁ υἱὸς τοῦ θεοῦ = ὁ Χριστός in 5¹. Cf. 2²², where the same interchange of Χριστός and υἱὸς τοῦ θεοῦ takes place.

5⁶ δι᾽ ὕδατος καὶ αἵματος . . . ἐν τῷ ὕδατι καὶ ἐν τῷ αἵματι. "διά marks the means by which Christ's office was revealed; ἐν the sphere in which He continues to exercise it" (Westcott). Even in point of grammar this is untenable, since ἐν as well as διά depends upon the aorist ἐλθών, which cannot refer to Christ's continuing to exercise His office. Here, ἐν does not differ materially from διά, c. gen., having that instrumental sense of which there are numerous examples in the N.T. (cf. Matt. 5¹³ 12²⁷ 26⁵², Acts 4⁷ 17³¹, Rom 5⁹· ¹⁰ 12²¹ etc.), and which is well established for popular Greek of the N.T. period (Moulton, pp. 12, 61, 104).

5⁷ ὅτι. *v. supra*, p. 119 (n.).

οἱ μαρτυροῦντες. The participle, as distinguished from the noun, οἱ μάρτυρες, sets the witnesses more vividly before us, as employed in the actual and present delivery of their testimony. The Water and the Blood, no less than the Spirit, are personified; hence the masculine μαρτυροῦντες qualifying the neuter nouns, πνεῦμα, ὕδωρ, αἷμα.

5⁹ εἰ. c. pres. indic., assuming the truth of the supposition (cf. *e.g.* John 13¹⁷).

The sentence is extremely awkward. *v. supra*, p. 124. The second part of it may be construed in three different ways, according as the second ὅτι is translated "that," "because," or "whatsoever." "Because the witness of God is this (pre-eminently consists in this), that He has borne witness concerning His Son" (Westcott, Huther, Holtzmann, R.V.); or, "Because the witness of God is this, (namely), whatsoever He has witnessed concerning His Son" (Rothe); "Because this (namely, the triple witness cited in the preceding verse) is the witness of God, because God *hath* borne witness concerning His Son" (Haupt, Weiss). Of these, the third seems to yield the most natural sense. The first and second seem to strain unduly the sense of αὕτη ἐστὶν ἡ μαρτυρία (= this is *par excellence* the witness of God).

5¹⁰ πιστεύων εἰς τὸν υἱόν . . . ὁ μὴ πιστεύων τῷ θεῷ . . . πεπίστευκεν εἰς τὴν μαρτυρίαν. The distinction between πιστεύειν εἰς (= to "believe in," to commit oneself unto), and πιστεύειν, c. dat. (= to "believe" or credit), is very clear in the first two phrases; but to draw the same clear distinction between the second and third is difficult. εἰς τὴν μαρτυρίαν is explained by Westcott as carrying on belief of the testimony to belief in its object, the Son of God. It is better to regard it as looking beyond the testimony to its source. It is not only disbelief of the testimony, but distrust of the person who bears it, that is signified; as, in English, "I do not trust your word," has a different implication from, "I do not believe what you say."

μὴ πιστεύων . . . οὐ πεπίστευκεν. μή and οὐ are here used with grammatical nicety. μή with the participle (equivalent to ἐάν τις μή) stating the general case, οὐ with the indicative the definite fact.

5^{11} ἡ μαρτυρία. This may be taken as applying to the "witness of God," spoken of in 5^{10b}, or to the "witness in Himself," spoken of in 5^{10a}. Our assurance of possessing Eternal Life rests, in the one case, on Divine testimony (cf. 2^{25}, John 3^{16}); in the other, on a conscious experience confirming Divine testimony. The former interpretation is preferable, both because αὕτη ἐστὶν ἡ μαρτυρία is more naturally referred to the nearer than to the more remote antecedent, and because this is more agreeable to the succeeding context, in which ($5^{12.\ 13}$) Belief is emphasised as the condition and test of Life, not Life as the confirmation of Belief.

καὶ αὕτη ἡ ζωὴ, κ.τ.λ. The clause is under the government of ὅτι. The witness of God is not only that He gave us Eternal Life, but that the sole medium of its bestowal is His Son.

5^{12} ὁ μὴ ἔχων . . . οὐκ ἔχει. Cf. note on 5^{10}.

5^{13} ταῦτα ἔγραψα ὑμῖν ἵνα εἰδῆτε, κ.τ.λ. These words accurately define the governing aim of the whole Epistle. Contextually, however, they refer to the contents of 5^{6-12}, and most directly to $5^{11.\ 12}$. At the same time, they effect the transition to the new subject, confidence in Prayer—that being an immediate result of the knowledge that we have Eternal Life.

ἔγραψα. Epistolary aorist. *v. supra*, p. 308.

εἰδῆτε. In such a connection we might have expected the familiar γινώσκειν. But the more absolute εἰδέναι is justified by the added clause τοῖς πιστεύουσιν εἰς τὸ ὄνομα τοῦ υἱοῦ τοῦ θεοῦ. It is taken as self-evident truth, that they who believe on the name of the Son of God have Eternal Life.

ζωὴν ἔχετε αἰώνιον. The peculiar order gives a separate emphasis both to the noun and to the adjective: "Ye have Life, and that Eternal."

εἰς τὸ ὄνομα. See note on 3^{23}.

τοῦ υἱοῦ τοῦ θεοῦ. By the full title of the Saviour, the Apostle finally recalls the central truth of the whole preceding section. (In this brief section alone, "the Son of God," or "His Son," occurs seven times.) And here he brings to a completion his consideration of the subject of Belief. Except in a parting word (5²⁰) he does not recur to it.

5¹⁴⁻¹⁷. Subsection on Prayer.

5¹⁴ αὕτη correlative with ὅτι ἐάν τι αἰτώμεθα, κ.τ.λ.

παρρησία. *v. supra*, p. 280. This παρρησία springs directly, not from the ζωὴν ἔχετε αἰώνιον of the preceding verse, but from the εἰδῆτε.

κατὰ τὸ θέλημα αὐτοῦ. This defines, not the manner of the asking, but its object—τι. This qualification is not expressed in 3²², but is implied there in the character of the suppliants, who are such as "keep His commandments, and do those things that are well-pleasing in His sight," as it is also implied in John 15⁷ by the condition, "If ye abide in Me, and My words abide in you."

ἀκούει = hears and answers. Cf. John 9³¹ 11⁴¹.

This sense of ἀκούειν is peculiar to St. John.

5¹⁵ καὶ ἐὰν οἴδαμεν. ἐάν, c. indic. is, grammatically, an atrocity, and is without parallel in St. John, although it is found in I Thess. 3³. Elsewhere, however, ὅταν, ὅπου ἄν, and ὅσοι ἄν are found with the indicative, and examples for ἐάν are furnished by the papyri (Moulton, p. 168). Westcott's explanation, that the unusual construction "throws the uncertainty upon the fact of the presence of the knowledge, not upon the knowledge itself," is beyond my comprehension. The one thing clear about it is that it is wrong. Uncertainty is not always implied by ἐάν c. subj. (2²⁹), and still less need it be implied with the indicative.

αἰτώμεθα . . . ᾐτήκαμεν. The active and middle forms of αἰτεῖν are used by St. John without difference of meaning (*pace* Westcott). The only difference is that he prefers αἰτεῖν, c. acc. pers. The only exception to this is John 11²². .

Moulton's suggestion (p. 160), that αἰτεῖσθαι is the stronger word, does not seem to be borne out by Johannine usage.

ὅτι ἔχομεν. "We have," not "we shall have." The whole emphasis of the verse falls on this ἔχομεν.

ἀπ᾽ αὐτοῦ. Connects much more naturally with ᾐτήκαμεν than with the more remote ἔχομεν.

5¹⁶. It is no accident that the one kind of prayer to which St. John refers is intercession. It is in accordance with the conception of Eternal Life which the whole Epistle expounds. That Life in its essence is Love; for God is Love, and Love is fulfilled in us only by our loving one another (4¹²). But Prayer is one of the modes of action in which that Life puts forth its energies. All prayer, indeed, which is according to the Will of God is in effect intercessory. By the Will of God all who are "begotten of Him" are members one of another. The good of each is the good of all, and the good of all the good of each. Even in praying for his own forgiveness and sanctification, the Christian is praying, in a true sense, for the Body of Christ, is praying that he may contribute a stronger and more healthful influence to the Life of the Body.

ἐάν τις ἴδῃ. The supposed case is stated, not as one of suspicion or of hearsay, but of personal observation.

ἁμαρτάνοντα ἁμαρτίαν. The cognate accusative is not a frequent construction with St. John. But cf. αἰτήματα ᾐτήκαμεν, 5¹⁵, also 2²⁵, John 7²⁴ 17²⁶.

ἁμαρτάνοντα. The tense shows that a persistent course of action and not an isolated act is contemplated.

μὴ πρὸς θάνατον. The μή does not signify that in *his judgment* the sin is not unto death,—"that the decision can only be a subjective one" (Huther),—for it is found also in the next phrase, τοῖς ἁμαρτάνουσιν μὴ πρὸς θάνατον, where this meaning is not admissible. In both cases μή is due to the influence of the supposition, ἐάν τις ἴδῃ.

αἰτήσει. He shall ask = let him ask. A milder imperative sense is intended, as is clear from λέγω ἵνα in the next clause. The imperative form, however, is avoided. It is assumed that this is what he will naturally and spontaneously do.

καὶ δώσει αὐτῷ ζωὴν τοῖς ἁμαρτάνουσιν μὴ πρὸς θανάτον.
1. The subject to δώσει may be the intercessor, αὐτῷ may be the "brother," with τοῖς ἁμαρτάνουσιν in apposition : "He will give his brother Life (*i.e.* he will be the means of doing so through his intercession), even to them that sin not unto death." In favour of this is the continuity of the construction—αἰτήσει καὶ δώσει ; against it, the awkwardness of the immediate apposition of αὐτῷ and τοῖς ἁμαρτάνουσιν.

2. The subject to δώσει may be God, αὐτῷ may be the intercessor, and τοῖς ἁμαρτάνουσιν a dative of advantage : "God will grant to him life for them that sin not unto death." After the express reference in the preceding verse to God's answering prayer, there is no difficulty in supplying θεός before δώσει. And upon the whole this interpretation seems, both in grammar and in sense, the more natural (so Lücke, Westcott ; contrariwise, Weiss, Huther, Rothe).

ἔστιν ἁμαρτία πρὸς θάνατον. ἔστιν, emphatic. There is such a thing as a sin unto death.

οὐ περὶ ἐκείνης λέγω ἵνα ἐρωτήσῃ. The sentence is not a prohibition, in which case the negative must have been attached to ἐρωτήσῃ. The οὐ does not go directly even with λέγω, so as to constitute a strong dissuasion, but with περὶ ἐκείνης—"It is not concerning that sin that I say he shall ask."

λέγω ἵνα. Cf. Acts 19⁴, Matt. 4³, Mark 9¹³, Luke 10⁴⁰ etc. Even in such cases the original telic force of ἵνα is almost lost, as is shown by the fact that it is often replaced by the simple infinitive. Matt. 23³, Mark 5⁴³, Luke 9⁵⁴ etc.

ἐρωτήσῃ. The word properly means to ask interrogatively; and so it suggests prayer in which our requests are made known, as it were, with the inquiry whether they may be granted. But, in actual usage, it does not appear to have this meaning. It is noteworthy that ἐρωτᾶν, not αἰτεῖν, is the word by which our Lord always refers to His own prayers (John 14¹⁶ 16²⁶ 17⁹·¹⁵·²⁰).

5¹⁷. On the verse as a whole, *v. supra*, p. 134, and note there.

ἀδικία. *v. supra*, pp. 134–5.

καὶ ἔστιν ἁμαρτία οὐ πρὸς θάνατον. οὐ instead of the μή of 5¹⁶·¹⁷. Here there is an express statement of fact. The verse as a whole effects, in the Apostle's usual manner, the transition to the next section. The idea of intercession, though still lingering in οὐ πρὸς θάνατον, has become secondary; whereas the idea of sin, which is to be further dealt with, is primary. For similar transitions, cf. 3¹⁰ᵇ 3²³ 5³.

5¹⁸ οἴδαμεν. See special note on γινώσκειν and εἰδένας. Upon the whole, γινώσκειν has been the key-word in the earlier parts of the Epistle; but here, in the closing section, it is displaced by εἰδέναι. The process of testing and self-discernment having been accomplished, the Apostle assumes its results, and lifts up his soul in a three-fold "we know" of joyful certainty.

οὐχ ἁμαρτάνει. *v. supra*, p. 229. To supply πρὸς θανάτου after ἁμαρτάνει (Rothe, after the older expositors) is entirely to miss the point; which is, that though the Apostle has been speaking of "sin not unto death" as giving occasion for brotherly intercession, not even this "sinning not unto death" but not sinning at all, is the true characteristic of the Christian Life.

ἀλλ' ὁ γεννηθεὶς ἐκ τοῦ θεοῦ τηρεῖ ἑαυτόν. Certainty as to whether the true reading is αὐτόν or ἑαυτόν would at once decide the interpretation of γεννηθείς. But, although the majority of editors (Tisch., Trg., W. and H., Nestle, R.V.) favour αὐτόν, the ground for doing so is so narrow (A¹, B, 105, and Vulgate for αὐτόν; א, the Peshitta, and all other authorities for ἑαυτόν) that here exegesis may claim to have a voice in the question of text.

(a) If ἑαυτόν be read, then clearly ὁ γεννηθείς is simply a synonym for the preceding πᾶς ὁ γεγεννημένος ἐκ τοῦ θεοῦ. To this it is objected that elsewhere in St. John the Christian is not said to "keep himself," but is said to be kept by Divine power (John 17[11. 12. 15]; cf. Rev. 3[10], 1 Pet. 1[5]). But it is to be observed—(1) that the examples from the Gospel are only found in the Intercessory Prayer, where it is inevitable that this aspect of the truth should be presented; (2) that elsewhere in the N.T. the Christian is almost as often said to "keep himself" (1 Tim. 5[22], Jas. 1[27], Jude [21]) as to be kept by God; and (3) that precisely in the same sense in which the Christian is said to "purify himself" (3[8]) he may be said also to "keep himself" (the two ideas are virtually identical).

The question remains, why, if the subject be the Christian himself, ὁ γεννηθείς should be substituted for the ὁ γεγεννημένος of the preceding clause. Westcott calls the substitution "impossible"; Plummer, "arbitrary and confusing."

But there are other passages in the Epistle in which the perfect and the aorist points of view are changed quite as suddenly and apparently quite as arbitrarily as here (cf. *e.g.* 4[9. 10]). And here the literal translation—"Every one who has been begotten of God sinneth not; but he that was begotten of God keepeth himself"—does not strike me as "impossible" or even as "confusing." For a possible explanation of the change of tense, *v. supra*, pp. 229–30.

(*b*) If αὐτόν be read, ὁ γεννηθεὶς ἐκ τοῦ θεοῦ can only refer to Christ (for Weiss's proposed explanation with the reading αὐτόν, "He who was once begotten of God keeps that which is the result of the Divine Begetting," that is, ὁ γεγεννημένος (= himself), is frankly impossible). To this there is the objection that ὁ γεννηθείς, as applied to Christ, is without parallel. And to me it does seem very improbable that, having just described the Christian as ὁ γεγεννημένος, the Apostle should immediately expect us, without a hint of any kind, to understand by ὁ γεννηθείς the Only-Begotten Son of God. If this had been his meaning, it seems to me that he would certainly have written ὁ υἱὸς αὐτοῦ or some such phrase; for there is nothing in ὁ γεννηθείς, any more than in ὁ γεγεννημένος, by which it is intrinsically a fitting appellation for the Divine Son. It seems, indeed, less fitting. For these reasons, and against my prepossessions, I conclude that the more probable reading is ἑαυτόν (A.V. and R.V. marg.). The remarkable rendering of the Vulgate, "generatio Dei conservat eum," is evidently to be understood in the light of 3[9] ὅτι σπέρμα αὐτοῦ ἐν αὐτῷ μένει.

καὶ ὁ πονηρός. Cf. 2¹³. All the influences of temptation are regarded as proceeding from him in whose personal agency they are concentrated.

οὐχ ἅπτεται αὐτοῦ = layeth not hold of him; cf. Ps. 105¹⁵. *v. supra*, p. 230, and note there.

5¹⁹ οἴδαμεν. The relation to the preceding verse is not that of inference—"We know, inasmuch as we fulfil the aforesaid condition." The οἴδαμεν here is equally absolute with that of 5¹⁸ : the present verse reduces to concrete terms the general proposition there announced.

ὅτι ἐκ τοῦ θεοῦ ἐσμέν. The emphatic ἡμεῖς of 4⁶ is here noticeably absent. The chief point of the antithesis is not the difference between us *personally* and the world, but the difference of the principle embodied in us and in it respectively.

It is *from God* we derive what constitutes our essential being; the World as a whole lies in the Wicked One.

ὁ κόσμος ὅλος. This order is common in the N.T. instead of the more regular ὅλος ὁ κόσμος (Matt. 16²⁶ 26⁵⁹, Mark 1³³ 8³⁶, Luke 9²⁵ 11³⁶, John 4⁵³, Acts 21³⁰, 1 Cor. 14²³). It seems in the majority of these cases to denote unity of state or action rather than wholeness of extent. Thus ὅλον τὸν κόσμον (2²) = "all the World," "the whole of that which is called the World"; here, ὁ κόσμος ὅλος κεῖται = The World lieth as a whole (or wholly) in the Wicked One.

ἐν τῷ πονηρῷ. That τῷ πονηρῷ is masculine, not neuter (A.V.), is certain from the preceding verse.

κεῖται. The Wicked One does not "lay hold" of him who is "begotten of God" (5¹⁸); but he does not need even to "lay hold" upon the World. Already it lies wholly in his grasp. This metaphorical use of κεῖσθαι ἐν is not found elsewhere in the N.T. The sense seems to be that of helpless passivity—to be "in the power of." The Wicked One is the ἄρχων of the world, and it lies utterly under his dominion and at his disposal. So in Soph. *Oed. Col.* 248 : ἐν ὑμῖν ὡς θεῷ κείμεθα τλάμονες (Liddell and Scott, *sub voce*).

5²⁰ οἴδαμεν ὅτι. The third of the "triumphant certainties." In 5¹⁸ the Apostle has asserted as a matter of certainty that the outstanding characteristic of the Life that is begotten of God is Holiness—its victorious antagonism, not to some sin, but to all sin, and that upon those who possess this Life the Wicked One takes no hold. In 5¹⁹ this becomes the further assertion that we possess this Life, while the world lies entirely in bondage to the

Wicked One. But this assertion naturally raises two questions. First, it may be asked—on what grounds is it made? That we, the small handful of Christian believers, are right, and all the rest of the world wrong; that we alone are in possession of Divine truth and life, while the world as a whole is in bondage to falsehood and sin: this seems to be an enormously egotistical assumption. What gives us the right to make it; nay, compels us, on penalty of treason to the truth itself, to maintain it? And then the second question arises. If it be true that there does run between men this awful moral cleavage, and if we are standing on one side—the Godward side—of that gulf, while the mass of mankind are on the other, how comes this to pass? Is it due to any moral or intellectual superiority in ourselves; and, if not, to what is it due? The present verse may be taken as answering either of those questions (though not stating the point quite as I have done, Haupt and Weiss take it as answering the former; Huther and Rothe as answering the latter). But in fact it answers both; for, in indicating the means by which this has come to pass, it also indicates the ground of our certainty that it has come to pass.

οἴδαμεν δέ. The verse is in substance explanatory of the first half of 5¹⁹—"We know that we are of God"; but the explanation is occasioned by the statement of the second half—"and the whole world lieth in the Wicked One"; to which, therefore, it is connected adversatively by δέ.

ὅτι ὁ υἱὸς τοῦ θεοῦ ἥκει καὶ δέδωκεν. According to the point of view, the Apostle speaks of Christ either as ἐληλυθότα (4²) or as ἐλθών (5⁶); describes His mission by ἀπέσταλκεν (4⁹) or ἀπέστειλεν (4¹⁰); and His gift by δέδωκεν (4¹³) or ἔδωκεν (3²⁴). Here the perfect sense is to be clearly marked. Both His coming and His gift are present and permanent facts.

ἵνα γινώσκομεν. Westcott's suggestion, that the quite abnormal γινώσκομεν is simply a "corrupt pronunciation" of γινώσκωμεν, is amply confirmed by the more recent additions to our knowledge of vernacular Greek. By the time that the oldest extant MSS of the N.T. were written, ο and ω were no longer distinguished in pronunciation (cf. Moulton, p. 35).

γινώσκειν. As throughout the Epistle, to recognise or discern, not to know with full experiential acquaintance (ἐγνωκέναι).

τὸν ἀληθινόν. ἀληθινός, found only once in the Synoptists, once in St. Paul, four times in Hebrews, has nine occurrences in the Gospel, four in this Epistle of St. John, and ten in the Apocalypse. Everywhere in the Gospel and Epistle it has its proper meaning of "genuine" or "real"—that which perfectly corresponds in fact to the idea which its name expresses (cf. John 1⁹ 4²³ 6³² 15¹ 17³, 1 John 2⁸, Heb. 8² 9²⁴).

The full knowledge of the True One is first made possible through His Son. While the God of the O.T. was ὁ ἀληθινός as opposed to the idols of heathenism, the God revealed in Christ is ὁ ἀληθινός in comparison with the limited and symbolical conceptions of the O.T. itself. In Him we find completely realised that idea of Godhead which, when it reveals itself to us, we intuitively know to be the highest, transcending all other conceptions of the Divine, or rendering them intolerable. Christianity is not *a* revelation, but *the* revelation of God. In it we reach the absolutely and only Divine.

καί ἐσμεν ἐν τῷ ἀληθινῷ. Not under the government of ἵνα, but a thought hurriedly added to the foregoing, as if the Writer felt that he had understated the case in saying only that "We know Him that is true" (cf. καὶ ἐσμέν, 3¹). And yet another clause has to be added to express the fulness of the thought.

ἐν τῷ υἱῷ αὐτοῦ Ἰησοῦ Χριστῷ. This explains how "We are in Him that is true." "No man cometh unto the Father but by Me," our Lord had said; so here the Apostle implies that no man can be "in" the Father but by being "in" the Son. For the thought, cf. 2²³; for the epexegetic construction, 5¹³. In both A.V. and R.V. the word "even" is inserted before this clause, presumably to make it clear that "in Him that is true" and "in His Son Jesus Christ" are to be taken as in apposition—that is to say, that the words "Him that is true," at their second occurrence, denote Christ. This interpretation, favoured by the older exegetes, is stoutly contended for by Weiss. It gives, however, an unnatural turn to the sentence. For it is most unnatural to suppose that τὸν ἀληθινόν first signifies Him Whom the Son of God has come to reveal, and then, without a hint of change of subject, the Son Who has come to reveal Him; and it is almost equally unnatural to suppose that the αὐτοῦ in ἐν τῷ υἱῷ αὐτοῦ, κ.τ.λ., has not as its antecedent the τῷ ἀληθινῷ immediately preceding. The objection taken by Weiss, that to understand ἐν τῷ υἱῷ αὐτοῦ as explaining the possibility of our being ἐν τῷ ἀληθινῷ (if this means God) involves a Pauline, not a Johannine conception, is groundless. Cf. John 17²³ where, though conversely stated, the relation of Father, Son, and believers is conceived precisely as here.

οὗτός ἐστιν ὁ ἀληθινὸς θεὸς καὶ ζωὴ αἰώνιος. οὗτος. Not "His Son Jesus Christ," but He Who is the subject of the foregoing delineation, He Whom we recognise as the True God by means of the "understanding" which His Son has given us, and with Whom we are in fellowship through His Son. This clause was long a battle-ground between the champions of orthodoxy and those of heterodoxy. And, no doubt, if it could be made good that, when the Apostle says, "This is the true God," he means, "His Son Jesus Christ," we should have the most explicit statement in the N.T. of the Divinity of Christ. But the day is past when such a truth was thought to be substantiated or invalidated by proof-texts. Besides, for determining the doctrine of the Apostle himself, the materials are so abundant that little is to be gained or lost by the interpretation of a single clause. Apart, however, from dogmatic interests, it is still urged by some (Weiss, Rothe, Ebrard, *e.g.*) that οὗτος refers to Ἰησοῦ Χριστῷ, both because that is the nearest antecedent, and because, otherwise, the statement, "This is the True God," is a pure tautology. But to this it may be replied that οὗτος does not necessarily refer to the nearest antecedent, but may more naturally refer to the *main* subject of the whole preceding statement, namely, ὁ ἀληθινός; and that the repetition, "This is the true God," *with the addition*, "and Eternal Life," so far from being a mere tautology, is singularly impressive, especially when followed, as it is, by the warning, "Keep yourselves from idols."

καὶ ζωὴ αἰώνιος. *v. supra*, p. 54, and note there. Only He Who is eternally the Living One can be the essence of all Life. Thus the close of the Epistle bends round to meet the beginning (1²). There, the Apostle bore testimony to the historic manifestation of the Eternal Divine Life in Jesus Christ; here, He testifies that this historic manifestation becomes, in experience, an inward certainty. "We know," because the Son of God hath come, and "hath given us an understanding."

5²¹ τεκνία, φυλάξατε ἑαυτὰ ἀπὸ τῶν εἰδώλων. No writer is more urgently and severely practical than St. John. From the thought of our knowledge, he turns instinctively to our present duty (cf. John 13¹⁷); from the thought that "we know Him that is true" to the thought that we are in a world full of "lying vanities," against which that knowledge must be our shield and salvation.

τεκνία. The thought of that danger, actual and inevitable, calls forth once more and finally the note of paternal solicitude, "Little children." *v. supra*, p. 41, and note there.

φυλάξατε ἑαυτά. The command is expressed in the most

urgent fashion. φυλάσσειν is, if anything, more vivid than τηρεῖν (5¹⁸). The more pungent and "instant" aorist is used instead of the quieter present imperative (v. Moulton, 173, 189); while the verb in the active voice with the reflexive pronoun conveys more strongly the necessity of personal action than the usual middle (cf. Luke 12¹⁵, 2 Pet. 3¹⁷ φυλάσσεσθε).

ἑαυτά. The use of the neuter, in direct agreement with τεκνία, appears to be unique. (Although cases nearly analogous may be found, e.g. Plato, *Theaetetus*, 146 A, τῶν μειρακίων τι κέλευέ σοι ἀποκρίνεσθαι, and *Euthydemus*, 277 D, γνοὺς βαπτιζόμενον τὸ μειράκιον, βουλόμενος ἀναπαῦσαι αὐτό). The use of ἑαυτός for the second person is common, especially in the plural, in N.T. and in Hellenistic Greek generally (Moulton, p. 87). But it is found also in Attic (e.g. in Xenophon's *Anabasis*, vii. 5. 5).

ἀπὸ τῶν εἰδώλων. The interpretations of τῶν εἰδώλων vary widely, from "idols" in the literal sense (Plummer, Rothe) to the false ideas substituted by antichristian teaching for the True God revealed in Christ (Haupt, Huther), and even to the inclusion of such self-deceptions as the profession of "knowing God" without keeping His commandments, and loving one's brother (Weiss). It is true, as Plummer urges, that elsewhere in the N.T. εἴδωλον is invariably used in the literal sense. That, however, is no reason why it should not here express a more comprehensive idea, provided that this would be intelligible by those to whom the Epistle was addressed. On the other hand, it is urged that everywhere in the Epistle the pressing peril is antichristian teaching, and that there is no reference to any temptation to idolatry. That, however, is rather a reason why the Apostle should now guard his readers against that danger, if it actually existed. Upon the whole, it seems very doubtful that the Apostle would describe the phantasms of Gnostic theology, not to say unreal professions of Christianity, as "idols," or that, if he had done so, the first readers of His Epistle would have understood him in that sense. Nevertheless, the Apostle's closing word is of far-reaching and deep-reaching application. And most impressively does the Epistle close with this abrupt and sternly affectionate call to all Christians, to beware of yielding to the vain shadows that are always seeking to usurp the shrine of the True God, the homage of the heart's desire and dependence.

ADDITIONAL NOTES.

---

² Cf. Eur. *Phœn.* 391, where to the question, What is the greatest hardship of an exile's lot ? the reply is ἓν μὲν μέγιστον, οὐκ ἔχει παρρησίαν ; and the rejoinder to this, δούλου τόδ᾽ εἶπας, μὴ λέγειν ἅ τις φρονεῖ.

¹ I am admonished, however, that what may seem intolerable is not impossible, by the discovery of a passage in Xenophon (*Anabasis*, vii. 4, 5) the construction in which is strikingly parallel to that in St. John . . . ὁ Σεύθης ἔλεγεν ὅτι, εἰ μὴ καταβήσονται καὶ πείσονται, ὅτι κατακάυσει καὶ τούτων τὰς κώμας καὶ τὸν σῖτον. . . . Here the number of words in the parenthetical clause is exactly the same as in the present passage. A similar repetition of ὅτι, though with a longer parenthesis, is found in the *Anabasis*, v. 6, 19. A comparison of the passages suggests that the second ὅτι may not be a mere inadvertence, but may have the effect of giving additional emphasis to the subsequent statement. Still, this does not seem natural to the style of St. John. Windisch regards the passage as corrupt, and proposes to read οὐ πείσομεν and to omit ὅτι ἐάν . . . καρδία, as an interpolation suggested by *v.* 21. The emendation does not seem a happy one ; and Windisch acknowledges that the wiser course is to abide by the statement that the text is corrupt. But a better extra-biblical parallel seems to have been overlooked in an epigram of Antipater (*Anth.* ix. 420)—

> Μὴ κλαίων τὸν Ἔρωτα δόκει, Τηλέμβροτε, πείσειν
> μηδ᾽ ὀλίγῳ παύσειν ὕδοτι πῦρ ἀτελές.

Here πείσειν is parallel to παύσειν, and its meaning can scarcely be other than " pacify," " persuade to be quiet."

INDEX I.

———◆———

THE MORE IMPORTANT EXPOSITIONS.

INDEX II.

———✦———

OTHER REFERENCES.

INDEX OF SUBJECTS.

I. ENGLISH.

II. Greek.